A Dignity Economy

Dignity Press
World Dignity University Press

Other Books by Evelin Lindner

Making Enemies: Humiliation and International Conflict (2006)
Westport, CT: Praeger Security International, Greenwood

—

*Emotion and Conflict: How Human Rights Can Dignify Emotion
and Help Us Wage Good Conflict* (2009)
Westport, CT: Praeger Security International, Greenwood

—

*Gender, Humiliation, and Global Security: Dignifying Relationships
from Love, Sex, and Parenthood to World Affairs* (2010)
Santa Barbara, CA: Praeger Security International, ABC-CLIO

—

More publications on
www.humiliationstudies.org/whoweare/evelin02.php

Evelin Lindner

A Dignity Economy

Creating an Economy that Serves Human Dignity and Preserves Our Planet

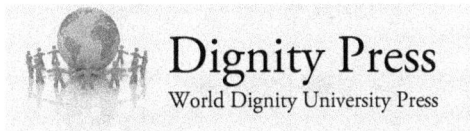

Dignity Press
World Dignity University Press

Published by World Dignity University Press, an imprint of Dignity Press
16 Northview Court
Lake Oswego, OR 97035
USA
www.dignitypress.org
Visit the book's website: www.dignitypress.org/dignity-economy

Art direction and cover design by Uli Spalthoff.
Cover photo (*Farmer land rights protest in Jakarta, Indonesia*) by Jonathan McIntosh (www.rebelliouspixels.com).
Back cover photo ©Evelin Frerk 2011 (www.evelinfrerk.de).

Printed on paper from environmentally managed forestry. See www.lightningsource.com/chainofcustody for certifications.

ISBN 978-1-937570-03-3

This book is also available as eBook: eISBN 978-1-937570-04-0

Dedicated to my father, who, through his example,
gave me the courage to stand *up* rather than stand *by*
in the face of indignity.

Contents

Foreword by the Directors of Dignity Press

Foreword by Linda Hartling

I have had the honor and privilege of collaborating with Evelin Lindner for more than a decade. We met through Donald C. Klein, a pioneer in the field of community psychology who was one of the first psychologists to launch an in depth discussion of the dynamics of humiliation. In 1995, I had just completed my dissertation developing the first scale to assess the internal experience of humiliation; while, in another part of the world, Evelin was formulating her research exploring the connection between humiliation and violent conflict. During those years, each of us knew we were virtually lone researchers in a new field of study. After Don's introduction in 1998, we celebrated that we were no longer alone.

From the beginning, I realized that Evelin Lindner was on her way to becoming the world's leading scholar on the experience of humiliation and human dignity. Her decision to live as a global social scientist has given her the broad-based knowledge, experience, and perspective that make this book possible. Transcending the limits of working in a conventional academic setting, Evelin sees the world as her university. She dedicates herself to synthesizing and integrating knowledge gained from engaging a richly diverse community of scholars, researchers, and practitioners. Her life as a *citizen of the world* has allowed her to question economic systems that deprive and deplete humankind of vital social and natural resources, threatening our existence on this planet.

One of the most remarkable aspects of Evelin Lindner's research over the years is its complete freedom from corporate and other profit-driven influences. In a world that worships the accumulation of wealth, Evelin is a living example of how "money should serve, not lead one's efforts." Practicing this principle has allowed her to sustain a level of independent thinking and writing that is essentially unheard of in science today. This book is a tribute to her stunning creative ability to walk the talk of her work, both intellectually and economically. Her whole life is a portal into what can be accomplished without giving in, giving up, or selling out.

Evelin Lindner demonstrates her commitment to intellectual integrity by choosing Dignity Press as the publisher of *A Dignity Economy*. Other publishers, influenced by today's profit-maximization motive, might undermine the fundamental message of her work. The author's incomparable commitment to integrity, combined with her spirit of humility, makes this publication a one-of-a-kind intellectual treasure. This book will enrich the lives of readers seeking new economic thinking that can lead us to a sustainable future that dignifies the lives of all people.

Linda Hartling
Director
Human Dignity and Humiliation Studies
November 7, 2011, Portland, Oregon, U.S.A

Foreword by Ulrich Spalthoff

Evelin Lindner and I first met in 2003 at the airport in Paris, queuing up for the security check before flying to Tel Aviv. She told me about her life and invited me into her life project, called Human Dignity and Humiliation Studies. I was impressed by her passion and zest for action. In addition to organizing a network and two annual conferences on Humiliation Studies, she has published extensively, including three books.

Her first book, *Making Enemies: Humiliation and International Conflict*, presented a ground-breaking analysis of international conflicts and how these often result from humiliating practices. This book received an award as "Outstanding Academic Title" by the journal *Choice* for 2007. In her second book *Emotion and Conflict: How Human Rights Can Dignify Emotion and Help Us Wage Good Conflict* she extended the discussion to personal emotions and conflicts. In her third book, *Gender, Humiliation, and Global Security: Dignifying Relationships from Love, Sex, and Parenthood to World Affairs,* she emphasized the important role of gender when analysing humiliating systems. That book again was highly recommended by the journal *Choice*.

With this new book she extends the analysis of humiliating systems to the realm of economics. I know from our conversations that she has observed for some time how Western-style capitalist economic systems contribute to humiliating practices that pervade personal lifestyles and political decision-making.

How timely it is that she is able to present her analysis just now, when the malfunction of our financial system becomes so obvious to people on all continents. But Evelin Lindner's personality does not allow her to simply present an analysis. She goes beyond traditional academic research. She is also an activist wanting to make an impact. Starting with a description of the disastrous and highly alarming situation, she then looks for solutions on a global scale. Hope springs eternal, as Alexander Pope said in his *Essay on Man*. Evelin Lindner's intellectual frame-work—identifying dynamics of humiliation and searching for solutions that bring dignifying systems to the fore—allows her to present a multitude of initiatives, proposals, and calls for action. She does this in a way that the reader can feel deeply motivated to contribute personally to the necessary changes we all have to make.

Necessary systemic change can only be achieved by many people making personal changes in their attitudes and their behavior. Therefore I find Evelin Lindner's highly personal presentation of the subject very appropriate. When reading this manifest, I not just learned about our economic system, I was also freshly motivated to be part of the necessary change. I wish many readers a similar experience.

Ulrich Spalthoff
Director of Projects and System Administration
Human Dignity and Humiliation Studies
October 25, 2011, Dörzbach, Germany

Preface

You never change things by fighting the existing reality. To change something, build a new model that makes the existing model obsolete.

—Buckminster Fuller

We, the human family, live in times of unparalleled opportunity. So far, we have created unparalleled crises. Together, we can change that. We can recognize our good fortune.

In the past, we adapted to changing conditions haphazardly. Today, we are much less the puppets of history. Never before have we had such a good understanding and such good tools to shape our fate in systematic and intentional ways. Today, we can sit together and reflect and plan intentionally.

This book advocates deep paradigm shift, not from one rigid paradigm to another, but away from rigidity altogether. Away from monolithic fixity toward co-created fluid processes. Away from inflexible edifices toward organic coming-into-being, growing like trees grow. Away from monolithic institutions toward a global movement that is co-created by people and their energy of passion and enthusiasm. Away from a combative dominator world, into which people are installed like little cog-wheels, toward global partnership that allows rich diversity to flourish.

This book exemplifies this approach. The first version of this manuscript was presented on August 20, 2009, at a conference we organized at the University of Hawai'i at Manoa.[1] Since then, it has been growing almost daily and has had many titles.[2] It is not a traditional manuscript planned at the drawing board, designed "to sell." It is rather a snapshot taken at one moment of an ongoing process, an ever unfinished book, a "walking" book, part of a journey.

This book is not just about a new *what*. The book is also about a new *how*. The new *how* is about fluid conversation, about *public deliberation*,[3] about *grappling* with issues.[4] And it is more personal in that I use "I," because I wish to model academic work as embedded into a context, rather than pretending to exist in a social and psychological vacuum. This book brings a very personal journey to the table, a journey that travels the circles of the *reflective equilibrium* (chapter 12). This book brings a very personal journey to the table, a journey that travels the circles of the reflective equilibrium (chapter 12), and a journey that is embedded into the confluence of a large global network of relationships, the Human Dignity and Humiliation Studies network. The book models its emphasis on the significance of social relationships by acknowledging the members of this network. The clarity of the flow of the argument may sometimes be interrupted by these acknowledgments, yet, in the spirit of Jean Baker Miller's *relational-cultural theory* (chapter 3), this practice brings more clarity into the social embeddedness of those arguments.

For a long time, I thought that this book could never be published. How could a book on dignity be published in an undignified context? It would be undermining itself. "Academic Publishers Make Murdoch Look Like a Socialist," is a particularly provocative heading that decries the practices of some academic publishers.[5] Then, Linda Hartling and Uli Spalthoff developed Dignity Press for our Human Dignity and Humiliation Studies network and our World Dignity University initiative, finally opening a path for this book to be published.[6] This book is among its first publications.

This book's publication has also been hastened by the Occupy Wall Street movement. This movement gave me the motivation to sit down and bring an unfinished manuscript from the drawer to the level of publication.

In 2010, I finished another manuscript about deep paradigm shift, a book about how we, as humankind, can dignify all relationships, at all levels, from micro to meso to macro, by focusing on what I call *big love*.[7] I worked on that book for years. It started with the following paragraph:

> The economic crisis that broke in 2008 has changed the path of this book. The crisis has many labels ranging from "subprime crisis" to "credit crunch," to "financial tsunami" or "economic Armageddon," preceded by an "Enron crisis," possibly leading up to a "credit default swap crisis."[8] But, around the world, people are coming to a single diagnosis: "Something is deeply unhealthy in our world." Even one year earlier, most people I met were much more accepting: "The world is as it is, and if we want to be competitive, we should work harder and not complain!"

> When I ask about the reasons for the crisis, people point to greed and lack of morality. However, let us ask: Is it greed? Is it immorality? The bank employees I know tell me that they are under extreme pressure to maximize profit and that this pressure has increased since the crisis began, to the point that some can no longer endure it. Managers report that they will lose their jobs if they do not place short-term shareholder value first. All seem to be victims to a mind-set that races toward crisis by default. If there is unethical behavior, it is nourished by the very design of our systems. It appears that the roots of our crises are more complex and systemic than one-dimensional and personal. Could lack of dignity be a systemic challenge?[9]

In 2011, when "the Arab Spring" unfolded, I added the following paragraph to this economy manuscript:

> We need a dignity revolution, and not just in Tunisia or Egypt. Now we need a global dignity revolution, a world dignity movement, a movement that creates inclusion, both locally and globally. We need a dignity movement that forges global public policies and institutions that help dignity to manifest in our realities. We need to transcend policies and institutions that cause the sellout of dignity, that "exclude people from access to dignified lives, both socially and economically,"[10] and that make

environmental damage invisible by treating it as mere "externality." If we do not succeed with such a dignity revolution (or refolution, the word that Timothy Garton Ash drew together from *revolution* and *reform*), we might engineer yet another collapse, as Jared Diamond describes it, this time a global collapse of human civilization.[11]

If the Arab Spring is the uprising of the "Arab street," then the Occupy Wall Street movement may be just the uprising of the *global street* that I called for, despite my despair that the world seemed to be asleep. It may be *people pressure* awakening as suggested by analysts like Paul Hawken.[12] It may be what economist Jeremy Rifkin calls a *pro-democracy revolution*, carrying us by *lateral power* toward an *empathic civilization*.[13] This may be the beginning of a *global refolution*, the start of a global *evolutionary reconstruction*, as another economist, Gar Alperovitz would call it,[14] or the beginning of Paul Raskin's *great transition*.[15]

As any movement that intends to shift paradigms, it risks being coopted into the old paradigm and derailed. If this happens, it will have to be reinvigorated, refreshed, and renewed.

We can take any liberation movement as an example. Take the liberation from narrow-mindedness and bigotry with respect to sexuality. What is the result, for all to see, at any kiosk that sells magazines? We see women's bodies dismembered into legs, breasts, or thighs, reinforcing the message that women are objects rather than whole human beings.[16] Mary Roach asks: When did sex research shift from prudish to freewheeling to corporate-controlled? How did this happen, and why?[17]

The Arab Spring and the Occupy Wall Street movement will face many attempts at control by ulterior interests. My Egyptian friends believe that the system is still a Nasserist regime and that the Arab Spring has yet to succeed. Hala Mustafa, one of Egypt's most prominent liberal intellectuals and the founder and editor of Egypt's journal on democracy, is distraught.[18]

Danger looms from outside and inside liberation movements. The true believers of change have to be the ones most on guard. In the past, those who refused being bribed or coerced into forsaking their principles were among the first victims to be "cleansed out" when power hijacked values.

The Occupy Wall Street movement has been criticized for its apparent lack of concrete calls for action. My recommendation: when big paradigms need to change, small-scale Band-Aids that fit into the old paradigm are insufficient. New large-scale visions that fit new paradigms are not easily created, not least because the language for them does not yet exist. From collecting ideas outside of the present grid, to forging innovative visions, to deciding on which visions to enact, to planning how to realize next steps—none of this can be done quickly and neatly. We no longer live in a top-down command-and-obey world. Calls for immediate solutions betray ignorance of the depth of change that is needed.

I felt very assured when I heard the representatives of the Occupy Wall Street movement on November 5, 2011, at the 31st Annual E. F. Schumacher Lectures in New York City.[19] They were very clear in standing up to the fact that deep reflection is now needed, rather than frantic "projectism" (chapter 2).

Politicians from all camps seem to have problems understanding this; they believe this movement is about frustrated voters or the middle class losing jobs. Yet, much more is at stake. Dignity is at stake. The dignity of people, their equality in dignity, the dignity of all living beings, the dignity of our planet. We humans need to dramatically change course to reverse the short-sighted human actions that threaten all life on this planet. So far, we have blown it. So far, we are going down a ravaging path. Those familiar with Jared Diamond's work will understand when I say we seem intent on following the Easter Island model, a recipe for depleting resources and destroying social and ecological systems in the process.[20]

Perhaps now it is time to briefly explain who I am?[21] May I start with a question: Do you believe people are inherently lazy? Would nobody do any serious work if not humiliated into compliance or rewarded with incentives? Do our best and brightest go where the money is? Or do our best and brightest go where dignity is, where the ethics are? Who are our best and brightest, in your opinion?

xviii   A Dignity Economy

I think the view that it is proof of excellence and brightness to "go where the money is" degrades the humanity of all involved. I presented my perspective in an earlier book as follows:

> I feel personally humiliated when I am expected to draw my motivation for what makes my life meaningful from status or monetary remuneration. I am motivated by *stature*—my pro-social contributions—rather than *status*, social rank, or class. I work very hard, day and night, seven days a week. I receive neither traditional status nor salary for my efforts. My motivation is entirely independent from such rewards, and if it were otherwise, I would find the degradation and humiliation unbearable. Therefore, my path is not altruistic or egoistic; it is both, because I would not survive the humiliation of having to define myself as a status- or salary-making machine that endangers the common good. I am not a Pavlovian dog who needs status or monetary remuneration as incentives to work. I would not survive such emptiness of meaning and such poverty of spirit.[22]

Have you seen the film *Pleasantville*?[23] I would feel like I were in Pleasantville, and I would get severely depressed, if I accepted to be nothing but the supplier or consumer of sales of products or services. I react with disgust when the first information I receive about a product or service is that it is "free" or "discounted" or "expensive, since you are worth it." I react with revulsion when I hear the ingenuous sweetness of the advertising voice, or see the strained smile of an actress who sells her soul to pretend that a certain product or service has changed her life. The effect on me of the fake world that advertisement has created around us is that I do not wish to buy anything anymore. And I staunchly refuse to reduce my creativity to serve "personal branding" so as to become a product myself.

> Allowing myself to feel deficient lest I buy or sell something, would humiliate my humanity at its core. Cleverness is repulsive to me—nothing of what I do is done because it is smart—and I draw no satisfaction from petty power games. I only engage in activities that are profoundly meaningful to me.[24] I respond to the

fact that I have to eat, clothe myself, and have a roof over my head in ways that do not require me to compromise what I regard as meaningful, on the contrary, they contribute. I do not wish to have a job, I want to have a life. I am profoundly selfish in this point because I could not live otherwise.[25]

I bring very rare experiences to the table, so rare that I often lack the language to describe them. I am the artist so to speak, not the art critic. I have created a global life design that could be described to be a social sculpture.

The insights offered in this book are the result of decades of living and working all over the world—in many countries within Africa, Asia, Europe and America. I lived for longer periods in Norway (regularly since 1977), Germany (intermittently since 1954), Switzerland (intermittently since 2000), France (intermittently since 2001), Belgium (intermittently during 1984–1991), the Middle East (intermittently since 1975), Egypt (1984–1991 and since), Somalia (1998), the Great Lakes in Africa (1999), Thailand, Indonesia, Malaysia, Burma (1981), China (intermittently since 1983), Japan (2004–2007), New Zealand (1983, 2011), Australia (2007, 2011) and the United States (intermittently since 1982).

My international life has given me the opportunity to observe global trends before most people do. It provides me with a bird's eye perspective and at the same time with an intimate closeness to the many cultures that make up our human culture. During the past 40 years, all around the globe, my intuition has grown that dignity and humiliation—or, more precisely, equality in dignity or *nondomination*,[26] with humiliation as its violation—are gaining significance as never before in human history.

I was born into a family deeply traumatized, like many others, by the forced displacements from Eastern Europe after World War II. That initial experience set me on a path to work for "never again," never again war and genocide. What followed were by now close to four decades of international life.

My aim was to become part of as many cultures as possible and learn as many languages as possible, to understand, deeply, what we humans are capable of, in love and hatred, in war and peace, in conflict and conflict resolution. My goal was to acquire a gut feeling for as many cultural perspectives as possible. I wanted to bring these perspectives into my body, under my skin, rather than do "field work," where I would have to look *at* people. I wanted to become a part of as many social webs and local cultural outlooks as possible. How does it feel to grow up in China, for example, where a child cannot avoid taking in an elaborate philosophy simply by learning how to read and write, something which takes a lifetime? In contrast, how does it feel to grow up with Arabic, a script so phonetic and easy to learn that it can be done in a single afternoon, while the language itself is so rich that a lifetime is insufficient for grasping all of its elegance? Or, how does it feel to be proud of a history that eclipses most peoples' history—as Chinese and Arab history does—while being humiliated by Western powers during recent centuries? The list of similar questions I have asked myself throughout the past 40 years of global life is endless.

My roots in displacement gave me a considerable degree of inner freedom. Displacement gave me distance from the cultural dictates of the world, and this distance has increased through moving between cultural realms. For instance, attaining higher status in one context may undermine one's status in another, and in this way the clamoring for status reveals itself as an altogether rather futile endeavor. I became ever more independent from local formalities and ever more at home in direct egalitarian human-to-human relationships, all around the globe, in all cultural realms.

Today, I resonate with 14th century Persian Sufi poet Hāfez-e Šīrāzī's saying: "I have learned so much from God that I can no longer call myself a Christian, a Hindu, a Muslim, a Buddhist, a Jew. The truth has shed so much of itself in me that I can no longer call myself a man, a woman."

If asked about my religion, I say: "My religion is love, humility, and awe for a universe too large for us to fathom."

Recently, I was queried: Why are you so "pure" and so "unbribable"? I replied that I am not able and willing to sell out meaning for illusionary "shortcuts." What do you mean? was the perplexed response. I posed a question in return: Is it possible for people who have money to buy a home? Yes, was the answer. No, was my reply. You can only buy a *house*. A house can also be a prison. A house is a home only if you nurture the relationships with the people who live in this house, including the relationship with yourself. You cannot buy relationships, not with yourself, not with your family, not with God, and you cannot buy happiness. Therefore, you can only buy a house, not a home. It is an illusionary hope to believe that it is possible to shortcut to happiness by way of money, and this illusionary hope is built into the usage of the phrase "buying a home." I am unable to be part of this, as culturally accepted as it may be.

Do you never feel greed? Do you never feel envy at those who have more than you? This was the next question. My reply: I am much more greedy and envious than anybody else I know. I am greedy for meaning, for being able to give love and be loved—I am too greedy to sell out quality for quantity. And I am envious of the birds, the clouds, and the stars, not of the trappings of luxury that keep their victims in golden cages (chapter 9).

I recently added the following paragraph to my biographical page on our website:

> It is important for me to make clear that my global life is not a homeless or restless life. I do not even use the term "travel," since I live in the global village and in a village one does not travel, one lives there, even if one moves around in it. When I look for cultural templates for my life, which treats our planet as one undivided locality, I think of migrating animist hunter-gatherers, a way of life that defined being human prior to 10,000 years ago. I resonate with what indigenous Native American leader Sitting Bull (1831–1890) said: "White men like to dig in the ground for their food. My people prefer to hunt the buffalo… White men like to stay in one place. My people want to move their tepees here and there to different hunting grounds. The life of white men is slavery. They are prisoners in their towns or farms. The life my people want is freedom." Clearly, I do not hunt buffalo and I do not have a teepee. Yet, I refrain from defining a small geographical locality as "my home." My home is the entire global village, or more precisely, the people I love in that village. I do not see my life as nomadic, and, as mentioned above, I do not resonate with the notion of travel. To my view, I "stay in love,"

rather than "travel in circles in a caged rat race." In other words, I see myself being much more "still" and true to "my place," namely love, than those who sell out their soul for a rat race that is defined by large-scale societal frames that have increasingly become toxic during the past decades. Many people travel extensively, yet, usually, they have a "caged rat race" frame within which they travel. I prefer to "stay still" in the realm of love. I am closer to a person who chooses to opt out of the rat race to live a simpler life nearer to nature, for example, than to a frequent business flyer who travels in circles in the isolated elite bubble of international hotels. I never search for a "place to stay." I move between different relational contexts of love and "a place to stay" is secondary to being embedded into relationships of mutual care.

I see my roots in displacement and the path that ensued from it as a responsibility. It is a path that is extremely difficult, and I pay a very high price, in many ways and at many levels. However, it is also an utterly enriching path, and, for me, it is without alternative. Manifesting humanity to the fullest represents the only way for me by which I can be in a world that otherwise sells out humanity for profit.

Along with Linda Hartling[27] and a valuable and dear team of like-minded people,[28] we have founded the Human Dignity and Humiliation Studies (HumanDHS) network,[29] and launched the World Dignity University (WDU) initiative.[30]

On the home page of our website you can read (as of November 2011):

We are a global transdisciplinary network and fellowship of concerned academics and practitioners. We wish to stimulate systemic change, globally and locally, to open space for dignity and mutual respect and esteem to take root and grow, thus ending humiliating practices and breaking cycles of humiliation throughout the world.

We suggest that a frame of cooperation and shared humility is necessary—not a mindset of humiliation—if we wish to build a better world, a world of equal dignity for all.

We are currently around 1,000 personally invited members, with more than 2,000 more people supporting our work, and our website is being accessed by ca. 40,000 people from more than 180 countries per year.

This economy book is different from my first three books. It is more open, more "unfinished" in that it follows a never ending journey as it is unfolding.

In my first book on dignity and humiliation, *Making Enemies: Humiliation and International Conflict* (2006), I describe my vision of a more dignified world.[31] First, this book lays out a theory of the mental and social dynamics of humiliation and proposes the need for "egalization" (the undoing of humiliation) for a healthy global society. It then presents chapters on the role of misunderstandings in fostering feelings of humiliation; the role of humiliation in international conflict; and the relationship of humiliation to terrorism and torture. It concludes with a discussion of how to defuse feelings of humiliation and create a dignified world. This book was characterized as a path-breaking book, honored as "Outstanding Academic Title" by the journal *Choice* for 2007 in the USA.

My second book, *Emotion and Conflict: How Human Rights Can Dignify Emotion and Help Us Wage Good Conflict* (2009) is an expansion of a chapter that I wrote for Morton Deutsch's *Handbook of Conflict Resolution*.[32] I describe how realizing the promise of equality in dignity can help improve the human condition at all levels—from micro to meso to macro.[33] This book uses a broad historical perspective that includes all of human history, from its hunter-gatherer origins to the promise of a globally united knowledge society in the future. It emphasizes the need to recognize and transcend malign cultural, social, and psychological effects of the past. The book calls upon the world community, academics and lay people alike, to own up to the opportunities offered by increasing global interdependence.

My third book, *Gender, Humiliation, and Global Security: Dignifying Relationships from Love, Sex, and Parenthood to World Affairs* (2010), examines the social and political ramifications of human violations and world crises related to humiliation.[34] Archbishop Desmond Tutu contributed with the Foreword. It is a book about *big love*, in the spirit of Gandhi's *satyāgraha* (nonviolent action), a term that is assembled from *agraha* (firmness/force) and *satya* (truth-love).[35] It analyzes why women were devalued during the past millennia, and why the work of nurturing relationships, including the work of love, became invisible. The book encourages constructive social, political, and cultural change through the force of *satyāgraha*. The book is being "highly recommended" by *Choice*.

In all of my work, I make the point that equality in dignity, with humiliation as its violation, becomes ever more salient when global interdependence increases. Never before did anything called a *global village* exist.[36] Until recently, the world was fragmented into many "villages," all afraid of their neighbors who could quickly turn into enemies. No history lesson helps us, because the notion of *one* global village turns the whole of humanity into *one* single in-group (with inner diversity) on *one* tiny planet, something that has never occurred before.[37]

Like my first three books, *A Dignity Economy* was written in dialogue with Linda Hartling and the other members of our network. It is part of a larger body of work that aims at creating new visions for the future, visions for systemic paradigm shifts, visions of *unity in diversity*, not just locally but globally.

Our aim is to nurture the next Rosa Parks and Nelson Mandelas to change the world. To serve this aim we strive to bridge existing gaps. We connect academic disciplines, we build bridges between academia and practice, and we bring together those who focus on creating a new consciousness *within* with those who have their attention on building new institutional frames *out* in the world.[38]

> *Entre le fort et le faible c'est la liberté qui opprime et la loi qui affranchit.*
> *(Between the weak and the strong, between the rich and the poor, between the lord and the slave, it is freedom which oppresses and the law which sets free.)*
> —Jean-Baptiste Henri-Dominique Lacordaire

Introduction

When all the trees have been cut down,
when all the animals have been hunted,
when all the waters are polluted,
when all the air is unsafe to breathe,
only then will you discover you cannot eat money.

—Cree prophecy[1]

We, the human family on planet Earth, live in historically unprecedented times of risk, but also in historically unprecedented times of opportunity.

Did our ancestors see pictures of our Blue Planet from the perspective of an astronaut? Were our forefathers able to *see*, as we do, how we humans are *one* species living on *one* little planet? Did our grandparents have access to as comprehensive a knowledge base about the universe and our place in it as we have?

We modern humans emerged roughly 200,000 years ago on planet Earth. Since then, we faced many challenges. Conditions of life changed dramatically. We survived as a species because we are so adaptable. So far, our adaptation efforts were rather haphazard. To a large extent we were puppets of history. Today, we have an understanding of our situation that is much more comprehensive, and we have the tools to shape our fate in intentional ways. Today, we can sit together and reflect, and act more intentionally and effectively than ever before in our history.[2]

Never before did anything called a *global village* exist.[3] In the past millennia, the world used to be compartmentalized into many "villages," all fearful of their neighbors. Neighbors could be friends, but also quickly turn into enemies. In a fragmented world of Hobbesian anarchy,[4] the fastest path to power and riches was to raid the resources others had nurtured and guarded. Colonizers, for instance, were in essence raiders, free riders on the resources of others.

Yet, raiding becomes ever more infeasible the more the world grows interdependent, while dignity and humiliation become salient on a scale that was hitherto unknown. Or, to be more precise, equality in dignity or *nondomination*,[5] becomes more salient, with humiliation as its violation. In the past, humiliation was something the broad masses were expected to accept subserviently. Only aristocratic elites had the right to respond to humiliation with anger and proceed to duels or duel-like attacks or wars. With the coming-together of the human family, and with an increasing acceptance of the human rights ideal that every human being is an equal member of the human family, the right to get angry when humiliated is "democratized." Millions of people who were used to quietly accept that they were "lesser beings," deserving to be exploited, no longer do so. I wrote in 2006:

> The desire for recognition unites us human beings and thereby provides us with a platform for contact and cooperation. Ethnic, religious, or cultural differences or conflicts of interests can lead to creative cooperation and problem solving, and diversity can be a source of mutual enrichment, but only within relationships characterized by respect. When respect and recognition fail, however, those who feel victimized are prone to highlight differences to "justify" rifts caused by humiliation. *Clashes of civilizations* are not the problem, but *clashes of humiliation* are.[6]

In the new context, many new concepts arise. *Human security*, rather than national security, means "freedom from fear" and "freedom from want" for human beings, rather than the security of states.[7] It means a "people-centered security" or "security with a human face." Article 1 of the Universal Declaration of Human Rights (UDHR) begins: "All human beings are born free and equal in dignity and rights." Human security is when this sentence is taken seriously.

How can human security be achieved? Should it be built on the existing global human rights legal framework, or is this framework part of the global insecurity problem? How are the root causes of insecurity, such as underlying sources of inequality in today's world, best addressed?[8]

Indignez vous! Cry Out! This is the voice of Stéphane Frédéric Hessel, a French wartime resistance hero, born in 1917. In the 1940s, he cried out against Nazism. Today, he calls on people to "cry out against the complicity between politicians and economic and financial powers" and to "defend our democratic rights."[9]

Many people today ask: What do they want, these people who cry out? What is their message?

My response (as in the preface): When windows of opportunity open up for large-scale paradigm shifts, they cannot be formulated as "small changes" within the old paradigm. Massive shifts require a concerted collection of ideas, collaborative "fantasizing," cooperative creation of innovative visions for a better future, and consensus-based planning for action, big scale. "Dreams come a size too big, so that you can grow into them." Our first duty is to refrain from crying "it can't be done." All visions for a better future need to be put on the table and protected from being aborted before birth through "it is impossible" interventions. At a minimum, the Chinese proverb must be heeded that advises, "The person who says 'it cannot be done' should not interrupt the person doing it."

Next, we need new words, new languages, new linguistic anchors. What about *inclusionism* (Linda Hartling's coinage), or *dignism* (Evelin Lindner's coinage), rather than *communism* or *capitalism*? What about "humanizing globalization with *egalization*"? What about *globegalization* (Evelin Lindner's coinage, see more in chapter 3)?

And we need new methods to fill new language with new meaning and manifest it in new realities. In an interdependent world, there is no "black hole" into which to safely dispose "trash," be it people or things. We have to stop producing *enemies*, and we have to stop producing *waste*. We must sit together and think up solutions that work for the entire human family and its habitat. The 99% and the 1% will all have children who will not find a decent planet to live on if we do not get beyond finger-pointing and humiliation entrepreneurship now. The Nobel Peace Prize 1993 was awarded jointly to Nelson Mandela, who helped end apartheid, and Frederik Willem de Klerk, a former enforcer of apartheid. (Gandhi, Mandela, Tutu, and all other peacemakers are treated in this book in a Weberian *ideal-type* fashion;[10] their names stand for the essence of their constructive strategies, which are not diminished by criticisms that some may want to level at them in other areas.)

We have all heard of how native people were given shiny worthless glass beads and mind-fogging liquor in exchange for their most priced possessions. It was a double raid. First their valuables were taken from them, then, their souls. They were manipulated into being complicit with a system that raided them. And the colonizers who profited, in the long run, had their reputation blackened; today, they are no longer seen as heroes, they are the villains. In the long run, nobody won.

Today we, the majority of the human family, are agreeing to being raided. Nowadays, we are the duped ones. We leave the world to a very small group of speculators who believe their gambling is good for all of us, not just for a chosen few, and not just in the short term. We even sell our politicians and legal systems to big money, so that new laws will create even bigger money.[11]

As a result, we live in times of meltdowns—from the financial meltdown that shocked the world in 2008, to the Fukushima meltdown in Japan in 2011—all avoidable catastrophes, at least partly, if it were not for the profit maximizing motive. These meltdowns are breathtaking and they show how dangerous this game is, for the 99 percent as well as for the 1 percent, when the entire globe becomes affected. Yet, there are other meltdowns—less overtly shocking, more hideously insidious—that should alarm us even more: we witness the long-term global meltdown of our ecological and social carrying capacities. Our ecological habitats are degraded along with our global social cohesion. And, lack of global social cohesion can translate into global terrorism, which, in turn, can combine all meltdowns in ways that dwarf September 11, 2001. If terrorists were to get hold of enough nuclear material to build and explode "dirty bombs," the mayhem would be unspeakable.

In the wake of the dignity revolution in the Arab World and Osama bin Laden's demise, many people in the West react with a triumphalism that is reminiscent of the end of the Cold War and sometimes appears to reach back to the imperialistic sentiments of superiority in colonial times. Is Western triumphalism warranted?

Perhaps the West would benefit from humility, warns journalist Matthias Matussek in May 2011: "If enlightenment is the way out of self-inflicted immaturity, we must admit: it has failed," he writes, and continues:

> The market has us in its grip more firmly than ever any church had. It has sewn price tags on us and removed the dignity of each of us. At the same time building this rational world is inextricably linked to a significant degree of irrationality. We breed the genetically improved turbo potato, but every day 30,000 people die of hunger. We drill into the seabed, we cut down the forests and exploit nature until ecosystems tip over, and species die out. Yes, what we do is that we subjugate nature to a degree that it breaks down panting under us. Or we deliver us to a technology that can destroy us, as we are seeing now in Fukushima. It is a mystery to me where the pride for this form of reason comes from."[12]

"The history of the world economy has proved that nothing is so reliable as the triumph of the free market—over reason." Unfortunately, this sentence by octogenarian thinker and speaker Dieter Hildebrandt in Germany seems to be a fitting motto for current times.[13] Nadine Gordimer, famous South African writer, describes how the same people who were brave in the struggle against apartheid, who were brave when in prison, fail to be brave in the face of economic greed and have become corrupt.[14]

Do we wish to live in such a world? In a world where even the psyches of babies are manipulated for money? *Adweek* reports that "desperate" marketers from Disney to Versace are "aggressively targeting babies up to three years old."[15] Studies show that American children can recognize an average of 100 brand logos by the age of three, and that some babies "request brands as soon as they can speak."[16] Eighty percent of children under the age of five surf the internet regularly, a new "market" that online advertisement campaigns heavily invest in.

Do we wish to live in a world where education is turned into a commodity that ruins its students? The total amount of outstanding student loans in America will exceed $1 trillion in 2011—Americans now owe more on student loans than on credit card debt.[17] Where is the respect for the *right to education*, which is part of the International Covenant on Economic, Social and Cultural Rights, signed 1966, in force from 1976?[18]

Is it not high time to draw serious lessons? Is it not time that we, as a human species, transcend our blind acceptance of self-destructive ideological dogmas? Is it really necessary, for example, to maximize profit at all cost, even at the cost of global meltdown? If the current use of "reason" is unsustainable for our collective future as a human species, shouldn't we envision deep change rather than symptomatic placation? A well functioning system requires "social rationality" as well as "economic rationality," says nonagenarian scholar Morton Deutsch "father" of the field of conflict resolution.[19]

In this book, we wish to approach the role of economics and monetary structures for *right relationships*—mutually beneficial and just relationships, economic and otherwise—with the necessary humility, but also with due candidness.

> *In times of change, the learners inherit the world, while the learned find themselves beautifully equipped to deal with a world that no longer exists.*
>
> —Eric Hoffer

Part I

Where Do We Stand?
Where Might We Go?

Chapter 1
While Critical Voices Get Louder, a Sense of Helplessness Prevails

We can't solve problems by using the same kind of thinking we used when we created them.

—Albert Einstein[1]

"Only the small secrets need to be protected. The big ones are kept secret by public incredulity."[2]

The biggest secret of our time is that we, the human family, face historically unprecedented opportunities. These opportunities are so vast that they appear to be almost too big to grasp. We shrink in front of them. We dig down in scrambling for solutions of the past that are insufficient for today.

Why not wake up. The solutions of the past were shaped by people who did *not* have the opportunity to see pictures of our Blue Planet from the perspective of an astronaut. The solutions of the past were crafted by people who were *not* able to *see*, as we do, that we humans are *one* species living on *one* little planet. The solutions of the past were forged by people who did *not* have access to our knowledge about the universe and our place in it. Our forbears deserve our fullest respect, but not blind respect.

None of our forbears had the privilege of facing such a window of opportunity as we do now. Therefore, we can not learn from history, we can only "harvest" from those historical and present cultural practices that help us in our profoundly novel situation; we must move beyond what does not help us.[3] Just to make one suggestion: Let us move beyond traditional raiding cultures and study indigenous wisdom to protect commons. "Living Well," for instance, is an indigenous social system that focuses on reciprocity between people and Earth.[4]

It is getting urgent. Critical voices keep getting louder. Suffering from the economic downturn increases in ever larger parts of the world. Some are still happily wasting our planet's resources—China is building ghost cities devoid of people, for instance,[5] and Germany's industry is proud of being of assistance—but fewer and fewer regions can continue the big bulimic party. More people doubt whether the big party ever was a good idea. Frustration finds a myriad of expressions in different world regions. "American Indignees Put their Money in Cooperative Credit Unions" is the title of a video clip that may stand here as one of a myriad of signs.[6]

At the same time, a sense of helplessness defines the situation—if only it were as easy as choosing between two kinds of soft drinks! If only it were as easy as choosing between two presidential candidates! But it is not.

We know we must avoid the oppressive *communism* of a North Korea. We also want to steer clear of the de-solidarization that flows from extreme Wall Street *capitalism*. What then do we really want?

In my doctoral research, I found that the analytical frame of *health* is useful.[7] What is being called *casino capitalism*, or *predatory capitalism*, could perhaps be called *bulimic capitalism*. A *throughput* economy, ruthlessly proceeding from resource to waste,[8] resembles *bulimia*, from binge eating to vomiting.[9]

Where might we go from here? How do we overcome bulimic capitalism?

Linda Hartling suggests *inclusionism*.[10] I suggest *dignism* (or *dignitism*, this is a term that starts with dignity, then becomes *dignity-ism*, then *dignitism*, and in its shortest form *dignism*).

Both terms, inclusionism, and dignism, could also be expressed as *ethical economy*, or *plural economy*,[11] or *solidarity economy*.[12]

Unity in diversity and the *subsidiarity* principle are central to inclusionism and dignism. We, as humankind, should not allow *unity* to degrade into *uniformity* as in oppressive communism, for example, and global consumerism. And we should not allow *diversity* to degrade into the *division* of everybody-against-everybody, as it happens in the extreme individualism we see in disintegrating capitalist contexts.

Subsidiarity is a promising principle for making unity in diversity operational. It means that local decision making and local identities are retained to the greatest extent possible. The European Union uses this principle.[13] *Holarchy*[14] or *regulatory pyramids*[15] are similar concepts. In legal thought notions such as *legal pluralism, complementarity*, and *qualified deference* are discussed.[16]

The concept of *pluralism* combines the *what* and the *how* (preface). It entails *content* perspectives (like unity in diversity) and *process* perspectives (like subsidiarity).[17] "Promoting pluralism does not mean prescribing any specific way of organising society or political system. It means opening spaces for dialogue and enhancing human dignity and equality... Pluralism promotes active engagement with diversity... Pluralism is not a 'universal' value, but a pluralistic notion itself" argues the Pluralism Project.[18] The *capabilities approach* as developed by economist Amartya Sen and philosopher Martha Nussbaum, states that people should be respected for what they have reason to value in their lives.[19]

It would be useful to find models or initiatives to serve as blueprints for a global system of inclusionism and dignism. Linda and I, and our network members, go around the globe to "harvest" from all cultural traditions, past and present, to harvest those beliefs and practices that help protect the dignity of unity in diversity.[20] As mentioned earlier, "Living Well" is an indigenous social system that focuses on reciprocity between people and Earth.[21] Bob Randall, a Uamlimutkatkar elder and traditional owner of Uluru (Ayers Rock) in Australia is a member in the global advisory board of our Human Dignity and Humiliation Studies network.[22] Carmen Hetaraka, a bearer of oral Maori tradition was one of the "pillars" of our 17th Annual Conference in Dunedin, New Zealand, in August 2011, brought to us by Michelle Brenner in the context of her Holistic Communication approach.[23] Alvin Cota, a Native American Yoeme from Arizona, has been generously sharing his historical knowledge with us in October 2011.[24]

The first draft of this book was written in the wake of the economic crisis that began to show in 2007 and broke in 2008.[25] Linda and I were concentrating on the Human Dignity and Humiliation Studies network, our transdisciplinary network of social scientists and practitioners in fields as diverse as anthropology, psychology and political science. Linda had written her doctoral dissertation about humiliation in 1995,[26] and I in 2001.[27]

When the economic crisis unfolded, we were busy formulating our thoughts about dignity, pride, honor, humiliation, humility, and shame, at all levels, from individual to national to international levels. This book would become much too long, were we to include a comprehensive overview over our work here. We hope that the reader will have acquired a sense of our approach after having read this book, and will feel moved to delve into more of our work later. The topic of humiliation is rather new; there is, however, an important body of work on dignity. Linda and I had the pleasure of conversing with conflict resolution expert Donna Hicks when she wrote her book on dignity, and this may stand for this field of inquiry here.[28]

Since we are not experts in the discipline of economy, we did not envision to ever write about it. But we became increasingly uneasy when ever more alarming messages came in from our network members from all around the world. The messages below may exemplify them. Harsh Agarwal, a member of the network from India, wrote to us: "Corporations have become the voice of the country on each and every issue while thinkers, philosophers and academicians have lost their voice and have been cornered."[29] Yves M. Musoni from Goma, Congo, wrote (from Nashville, Tennessee): "I believe our global future lies on our capacity to re-think our humanity. We need to find a new dress for our beautiful world which has already started the process of 'eclosion.' Like an adolescent, our world is not in the age of maturity. It is in 'turbulence.' From an atmospheric scientist's perspective, 'turbulence can shake any airplane, no matter how big and no matter the importance of the passengers.'"[30]

Members of our worldwide network observe how the fallout of the economic crisis unmasks the malignant aspects and effects of global economic systems that provide the frame for almost all people. What we hear from all corners of the world, confirms that we need the *great transition* that Paul Raskin calls for.[31] A great transition means more than simply reforming the status quo.

Linda and I increasingly felt that we could not afford hiding behind the excuse that we are not economists while we at the same time witness the increase in humiliating effects from existing economic practices and institutions. Since economic structures represent the largest frames within which human activities occur, they are of utmost importance and cannot be overlooked. If the largest frames were to introduce systemic humiliation, in the way apartheid did, this would be extremely significant. Under apartheid, since it was an all-encompassing system, all lives and relationships were tainted with humiliation. It was impossible to dignify apartheid by being kinder to each other or creating well-intentioned small-scale initiatives: the entire system had to be reshaped at the appropriate larger-scale level. What if today's apartheid is represented by the fact that (exponential) growth is incompatible with sustainability?[32]

Herman Cain, United States Republican presidential candidate, contends that we need to individualize systemic problems. He said on October 5, 2011: "Don't blame Wall Street. Don't blame the big banks. If you don't have a job and you're not rich, blame yourself."[33]

Should we follow Cain and try to make people fitter for a rat race that becomes ever more unfeasible and damaging for us and our environment?

Linda and I often feel as helpless as the Archbishop of Canterbury, who called for a "rehumanising of economics" and a "discussion on the relationship between wealth and well-being," in a debate at the British Library on October 1, 2010. "The Archbishop described himself as an 'economic illiterate.' He said the Church had been 'hypnotised by the assertion of expertise' on issues related to the economy."[34]

But Linda and I also try to live up to the words of Ole Danbolt Mjøs, past chair of the Nobel Peace Prize Committee of the Norwegian Parliament, who wrote the following for my book *Gender, Humiliation, and Global Security*[35]: "The future of humankind is at stake. In times of crisis, we need people of courage, people who step out of the beaten track of familiarity and look at the situation from a new perspective. Few people have the global experience and transdisciplinary background that Evelin Lindner brings to this task. This book is a wake-up call and a guideline for humanity to follow if it wishes to survive."

Linda and I were encouraged when we saw people in widely disparate parts of the world linking economics with themes such as dignity or peace. We recently organized our 17th annual conference in New Zealand[36] and, as mentioned above, had as a central part of the conference Carmen Hetaraka, a bearer of oral Maori History. Carmen shared his indigenous Maori wisdom, a wisdom that is crucial if we wish to create visions for a better future. We were also encouraged by many other initiatives in the South Pacific region, for example, by the work of the Institute for Economics and Peace (IEP) in Australia.[37] The IEP institute's research includes the Global Peace Index (GPI), which ranks 153 countries on their peacefulness.

People in all corners of the world increasingly draw very critical conclusions. *Redet Geld, schweigt die Welt: Was uns Werte wert sein müssen* is a 2011 book by renowned German author Ulrich Wickert. Translated the title means *When Money Speaks, the World Is Silent: How We Should Value Our Values.*[38] Philosopher David Richard Precht, also based in Germany, wonders, why "immer mehr ist immer weniger" or why it seems that we always have less, even though we supposedly have ever more. He asks, "Wer bestimmt eigentlich über den Fortschritt?" or "Who decides what progress is?"[39]

Michael Heilemann is an expert in anti-aggression training in Germany. He concludes from his work in prisons that present-day forms of casino capitalism have made it almost impossible for "normal people" to obtain an individual sense of worth. He writes:

> What can the individual do at all? What is expected is good behavior. To insert oneself into casting shows or categories of entitlement so that one appears as a role model for the conformity of the others—this is rewarded... Otherwise there is little opportunity: a few extreme-charismatics from the under classes may succeed in climbing to the top—but once at the top, they remain cannon fodder. In such a situation, diving into revolution (returning humanity to humans) then remains the reserve of suicide ideas, or highly organized terrorist machineries. Little room for the 'normal people'![40]

Linda and I initially had hopes that our intellectuals, particularly our economists have the answers; yet, we were disappointed. For more than three decades, I have been asking people all around the world the following question: "How do you think that we, as humankind, must change our world to make it worth living in?" Almost always, I reaped replies that shocked me: "This is too big a question. I am a specialist, not a generalist. Sorry."

This seems to be a defining characteristic of our time: Specialization blinds even our most highly knowledgeable experts. In former times, powerful elites hid behind thick and high walls, they built palaces and temples like the Forbidden City in Beijing. Today, we meet the same walls in the form of smokescreens of complicated "expert language" that fragment reality so that no coherent overall picture can be discerned. "Fog of war" is a phrase ascribed to Prussian military analyst Carl von Clausewitz. Today, we seem to be surrounded by a "fog of words" that erects walls as effective as the walls of the Forbidden City. One wonders whether there is a war of domination going on, even though it is not a clearly defined war in the classical sense.

When Linda and I despair at the complexity of the situation or feel discouraged because we have not trained as economists, we remind ourselves that when we look at the world from a bird's eye perspective, and when we let our empathy resonate with the daily experiences of people on the ground, we do not need to be experts in economics to hear the critical voices that are getting louder almost everywhere on the globe,[41] and we do not need to be experts in economics to understand that these voices have a point.

Critical voices were marginal prior to 2008. Now, they enter mainstream media. We read about "The Rise and Fall of the G.D.P."[42] and how "the economists messed everything up," as Alex Michalos, a former chancellor at the University of Northern British Columbia, warns. Renowned scholars, such as Thomas Homer-Dixon or Immanuel Wallerstein, caution that economies cannot keep growing and that the global economy will not recover, now or ever.[43] Mervyn King, head of the Bank of England, said in a speech in New York City in 2009 that, of all the systems one might use to organize banks, "the worst is the one we have today."[44] He pointed out that Britain's banks pose unusual risks because they have "assets" (bubble valuations?) 4.5 times the size of the British economy.[45]

Have bankers learned from the economic crisis they unleashed? An extensive survey of the quality of bank services carried out in 2009 in Germany indicates that they have not.[46] The results show that bank services are still catastrophically flawed despite the financial crisis. Worse, bank employees are pushed into unethical behavior more often than before. Only *one* of 25 bank advisors passed the test of gathering the necessary information about the financial background of a potential customer and advised that individual correctly.[47] German banks, in their urge to be competitive in the international market, sold so-called "structured products" that are forbidden even in the United States. Investment bankers marketed these products to the wider clientele while taking great care never to invest their private capital in such products.

It is illuminating to understand the extent to which the amount of pay may not reflect the true value of a job. Justifications for high pay may belong to the realm of myth. A study in the UK reveals:

- Elite City bankers (earning £1 million-plus bonuses) destroy £7 of value for every £1 they create.
- Hospital cleaners create over £10 in value for every £1 they receive in pay.
- Advertising executives destroy £11 of value for every £1 created.
- Child care workers generate between £7 and £9.50 for every £1 they are paid.
- Tax accountants destroy £47 for every £1 they create.
- Waste recycling workers generate £12 for every £1 spent on their wages.[48]

·

One does not need to be an expert in economics to observe that throughout history, new and improved tools and weapons (or methods of making them) gave superior leverage. At present, action from the global financial market seems to be the most innovative "weapon" of our time, more effective for achieving domination than any national military equipment. Legendary investor Warren Buffett famously describes derivatives that are bought speculatively as "financial weapons of mass destruction"[49] Buffet also lashed out against those who engineer this new kind of domination, calling them "overpaid, unaccountable finance-industry bigwigs."[50]

Why are those "bigwigs" still so influential? Bo Lundgren, Sweden's minister for fiscal and financial affairs who managed Sweden's financial crisis in the 1990s, believes that people influenced by Anglo-Saxon culture are prone to dangerous definitions of liberty and freedom.[51] It seems, says Lundgren—in the spirit of philosopher Isaiah Berlin (1909–1997)—that a culture that defines liberty as *unrestrained freedom*, including freedom for dominators to make *might* be *right*, tends to keep those dominators in power, dooming the broader masses to the role of exploited victims. Only a culture that defines liberty as a *level playing field protected by appropriate regulations* can protect the common good for all (chapter 8).[52]

As it seems, Lundgren has a point. Collective action in the European Union to regulate financial markets has been slowed down by vetoes from the United Kingdom in their effort to protect the special interests of the City of London.

As it seems, when a society gives primacy to profit maximization, politicians become vulnerable, per design, to being bribed to bend legislation. Tax analyst Larry Bartels explains that "our current tax system reflects a broader pattern of policy-making skewed toward the interests of affluent citizens."[53] In a distinctly unequal United States, "low-income people are likely to get their way only when their preferences happen to agree with the preferences of high-income people."[54] The present level of inequality in the United States is medieval.[55]

All political camps seem to be aware of this situation. We read in *Time Magazine*:

> When John McCain was still a raging reformer, he pointed to the tax code as the foundation for the corruption of American politics. Special interests pay politicians vast amounts of cash for their campaigns, and in return they get favorable exemptions or credits in the tax code. In other countries, this sort of bribery takes place underneath bridges and with cash in brown envelopes. In America it is institutionalized and legal, but it is the same—

cash for politicians in return for favorable treatment from the government. The U.S. tax system is not simply corrupt; it is corrupt in a deceptive manner that has degraded the entire system of American government. Congress is able to funnel vast sums of money to its favored funders through the tax code—without anyone realizing it. The simplest way to get the corruption out of Washington is to remove the prize that members of Congress give away; preferential tax treatment.[56]

One does not need to be an expert in economics to observe current power imbalances not just at national levels, but also between global financial markets and national politicians. The "Leaders' Statement of the G-20 Pittsburgh Summit, September 24–25, 2009"[57] started with the sentence: "We meet in the midst of a critical transition from crisis to recovery to turn the page on an era of irresponsibility and to adopt a set of policies, regulations and reforms to meet the needs of the 21st century global economy."

After promising rhetoric, usually the disappointing results are open for everyone to see. And the reasons for failure are evident, identifiable in many parts of the world. As a result, as Halldór Gudmundsson warns in his book *We Are All Icelanders*, the fate of Iceland will catch up with the rest of the world sooner or later.[58]

Why is political rhetoric so empty? Financial speculators work in informal collectives with a global outreach—*The Wall Street Journal*, for example, openly reports how "Hedge Funds Try 'Career Trade' Against Euro."[59] At the same time national politicians are divided. Collective action of nations depends on processes of consensus-seeking that are tedious at best. Evocative headings abound, such as "How Fear of Speculators Drives European Leaders"[60] or, "Revealed—the Capitalist Network that Runs the World."[61]

"Political will" is lacking, and we should not be surprised. Many leaders would even lose their positions if they seriously promoted the change that is needed in the world. Former president of the United States, Bill Clinton said: "What works in real life is people getting together with different perspectives and figuring out how to solve problems. Cooperation works. What works in politics is conflict."[62]

One does not need to be an expert economist to see that deep cultural transformation is the call of the day, locally, but particularly at global levels. It may be interesting to begin by inquiring how Anglo-Saxon culture, continental European, and Scandinavian culture differ.[63] Everybody agrees that Anglo-Saxon victory over Nazi Germany was extremely important for the world. The Nazi belief system was disastrous. However, confidence flowing from victory may be "happily" and dangerously misinvested later. It should not be misinvested in new disastrous beliefs, defining freedom as the absence of oversight, for instance. The City of London and Wall Street may still squander that earlier victory.

One does not need to be an expert economist to see that economic crises cannot be remedied by unfettered growth of high *throughput* economies (proceeding from resource to waste,[64] in contrast to *cradle-to-cradle* economies, for example, that would create circles from resource to resource,[65] or to *no growth economies*).

The Earth's continuing ecological losses may soon begin to stress national economies, warns a major UN report, the third Global Biodiversity Outlook (GBO-3[66]). It says that some ecosystems may soon reach "tipping points" at which they rapidly become less useful to humanity. "Many economies remain blind to the huge value of the diversity of animals, plants and other life-forms and their role in healthy and functioning ecosystems," said Achim Steiner, executive director of the UN Environment Programme (UNEP).[67] "Humanity has fabricated the illusion that somehow we can get by without biodiversity, or that it is somehow peripheral to our contemporary world. The truth is we need it more than ever on a planet of six billion heading to over nine billion people by 2050."[68]

The more degraded ecosystems become, the UN says, the greater is the risk that these systems will be pushed "over the edge." For example, freshwater systems polluted with excess agricultural fertiliser will suffocate with algae, killing off fish and making water unfit for human consumption.[69]

One does not need to be an expert economist to see that a nexus of corporations and governments that races to the bottom under the cover of a "free market" ideology, when freedom means might is right, will come at the price of ecological and social unsustainability.[70]

A sense of helplessness is the only real "realism" in times of crisis, in times when business as usual is utopian.[71] To create a future that does not even have a language yet is a task so grand that it ought to leave us in awe. Admitting to this sense of helplessness, in shared humility, instead of fighting about outdated beliefs and solutions, is the path to take. Joining hands in search of new and more inclusive futures is the path to walk, rather than defending ideologies and arrangements that will save neither the planet, nor the 99 percent, nor the children of the 1 percent.

Perhaps it is time for us to be humble and to be humble together. This is why I wrote my last book on love, *big love*.[72] Only in shared humility and loving mutuality can we embark on the grand tasks that lie before us.

We need a new generation of Rosa Parks and Nelson Mandelas who are able to lead in new ways. "Selfless leadership" is required, rather than autocratic "big-ego" styles. Social ecologist Peter Drucker calls for organizations to function like orchestras.[73]

In my conversations with Morton Deutsch in November 2011, I explained why we founded the World Dignity University initiative. It is precisely to manifest a new future by starting a new kind of institution that is far enough outside of existing paradigms conceptually to encourage change, while close enough for cooperation in practice.

> *You cannot put a rope around the neck of an idea; you cannot put an idea up against a barrack-square wall and riddle it with bullets.*
>
> —Sean O'Casey[74]

Chapter 2
Let Us Work Together to Dig Up the Facts!

*None are more hopelessly enslaved than those who falsely
believe they are free.*

—Johann Wolfgang von Goethe

In our work in the Human Dignity and Humiliation Studies
network, we attempt to acquire a sense of the contemporary *Zeitgeist* by
keeping our fingers on the pulse of change. We always make an effort to
understand all sides of an argument, including its extremes.

Linda and I always try to find experts who can explain the situation to
us in an easily accessible way. For example, what is *fractional reserve
lending*, we ask, and is this practice perhaps at the core of our worries? If
yes, what would be a better arrangement? What is a *haircut*? What is
quantitative easing?

As reported earlier, to our dismay, most people, even people within
the field of economics, have confessed to us that they do not fully
understand the workings of the overall economic and monetary systems.
A cloak of mystery and uncertainty surrounding economic dealings
keeps us in the dark.[1]

Neva Rockefeller Goodwin, a pioneer of contextual economics
education, was asked by a young student which business school she
would recommend to him. This was at the Thirtieth Annual E. F.
Schumacher Lectures on November 20, 2010, in New York City. He
wanted to learn about the real economic challenges she had discussed in

her talk. She recommended that he look outside of business schools or economics programs, at anthropology or sociology.

Linda and I began our journey into the field of economics by looking at classics. Henry George (1839–1897) was an American writer, politician and political economist and the most influential proponent of the land value tax.[2] Edwin Clarence (E. C.) Riegel (1879–1953) was praised for delivering "the best explanation of the free market." He promoted an alternative monetary theory and an early private enterprise currency alternative.[3] Paul Anthony Samuelson (1915–2009) was the first American to win the Nobel Prize in Economics. He was author of the best selling economics textbook of all time, *Economics: An Introductory Analysis*, first published in 1948 and now in its 19th edition.[4] James E. Meade, was a British Nobel Prize Laureate in Economics in 1977 (jointly with the Swedish economist Bertil Ohlin) for his contribution to the theory of international trade and international capital movements.[5]

For the history of interest or *usury*, we turned to John M. Houkes who, during his tenure as head of the Management and Economics Library at Purdue University, compiled an exhaustive bibliographic work on this topic.[6]

We studied the role of religion and heard Giles Anthony Fraser, a priest of the Church of England, former Canon Chancellor of St Paul's Cathedral in London, saying he thinks "Jesus would be more extreme than him on the shape of modern capitalism."[7] When the police prepared to act against Occupy protesters outside St Paul's, Fraser resigned, since he felt he could not sanction the use of force. He said, "I think there's an irony that we are having this conversation today, on the 25th anniversary of Big Bang,[8] the deregulation of the Stock Exchange, liberalisation of the rules and regulations regulating the City… it seems to me quite clear that markets were made for man and not man for market… I am not against capitalism. I am not one of these people who thinks that capitalism is inherently wicked."[9]

Linda and I attempted to understand how "greed is bad" could ever transmute into "greed is good."[10] We watched the conservative Americans for Prosperity Foundation's annual RightOnline Conference[11] as attentively as we read the blog of the recipient of the

Nobel Memorial Prize in Economics in 2008, Paul Krugman.[12] Chapter 11 presents a longer list of initiatives we looked at.

On July 25, 2009, we paid a visit to Canadian activist Paul Grignon on Gabriola Island, Canada. He is the author of the animated features *The Essence of Money*, and *Money As Debt I, II*, and *III*.[13] *Digital Coin* is a proposal developed by Grignon.[14]

We attended the Annual E. F. Schumacher Lectures in New York City in 2010 and 2011.[15] "Small is beautiful" is a collection of essays by economist Ernst Friedrich "Fritz" Schumacher (1911–1977).[16] "Voices of a New Economics" was the lectures' title on November 20, 2010, and "Voices of Today's Youth: Occupy Wall Street and Youth for a New Economy" were included on November 5, 2011.

Schumacher Lecture speakers in 2010 were Gus Speth, Neva Rockefeller Goodwin, and Stewart Wallis.[17] Gus Speth is a prominent environmentalist who has been at the forefront of rethinking the connection between the health of the environment and the nature of our economic system.[18] Neva Rockefeller Goodwin, as mentioned above, is a pioneer of contextual economics education at the Global Development and Environment Institute at Tufts University.[19] Stewart Wallis is the executive director of the New Economics Foundation (nef) of London.[20]

Speakers in 2011 were Juliet B. Schor and Gar Alperovitz. Juliet Schor is the co-founder of the Center for a New American Dream.[21] Schor spoke of the *captured state*, contending that it needs to be "re-captured." Gar Alperovitz is a member of the board of directors of the E. F. Schumacher Society,[22] which recently worked with the New Economics Foundation (nef) in London to form the New Economics Institute in North America.[23] Gar Alperovitz's verdict was that deeper change is needed now: "The time of regulations is over."

Included in the 2011 Schumacher Lectures was a Youth Panel, where Charlie Young, Kyle Gracey, Rina Kuusipalo, Karanja Gacuca, and Annie McShiras reflected on their generation's approach to economic justice, Occupy Wall Street, international government, sustainability, social movements, and global youth culture. As mentioned earlier, their presentations gave me great hope. All panelists understood that this is not the time for quick solutions; a long term process of change has to be shaped.

Over time, Linda and I meet ever more people who contend that every part of life is "contaminated" by the fallout of harmful large-scale frames and who insist that a radical overhaul is needed. Margrit Kennedy, an architect who works internationally, is one of those voices. Her work on ecological architecture, beginning in 1982, led her to the discovery that it is "virtually impossible to carry out sound ecological concepts on the scale required today, without fundamentally altering the present money system or creating new complementary currencies."[24] Kennedy recommends considering Bernard Lietaer's argument that complementary currencies can protect against the destructive effects of major currency crashes.[25].

Linda and I are encouraged by economist Rodrigue Tremblay and his 2010 book on global ethics.[26] He exposes the smokescreen of "expert terminology" and makes it less opaque for non-economists.[27] We have written to Paul Krugman and others with the idea of creating a *Dignity Bank*, a bank that puts money at the service of society and not at the service of profit maximization, a bank that operates without interest and nurtures inclusionism and dignism, instead of oppressive communism or bulimic capitalism.

Yet, so we learned, perhaps it is impossible to put money at the service of society? Perhaps even the most well-meaning initiative in an apartheid-like system is futile? Howard Richards, scholar of peace and global studies and philosophy,[28] contends that the entire system must be reshaped and that all attempts to bring people out of poverty by bringing them into the money market as it is defined today, are doomed.[29] The film *Caught in Micro Debt*, shown on Norwegian state television November 30, 2010, underpins Richards' message by shedding critical light on the practices of micro lending, once hailed as a way forward.[30] Howard Richards explains:

> The bottom line, which marks modern civilization as fundamentally defective, as distinct from incidentally troubled, is, as Daniel Quinn, author of *Ishmael*, tells us, whether people share food. Amartya Sen corroborates Quinn's point in his study of famines and entitlement. In the modern world people starve not because there is no food, but because there is no norm prescribing its sharing, while there are norms separating ownership from

need. This is a bottom line that illustrates a key point; it describes not so much what we think as what we presuppose; not so much our scientific conclusions as the mythic normative framework that constitutes the paradigm within which mainstream social scientists do normal social science.[31]

Social entrepreneur William Drayton once said about social entrepreneurship: "Our job is not to give people fish, it is not to teach them how to fish, it is to build a new and better fishing industry."[32] It seems that nowadays, we need more than a better fishing industry. Is it possible that the basic foundations of our economic structures and monetary systems (or their absence) are at fault?

Douglas Hurd, a former diplomat and conservative foreign secretary in the UK, explains in an interview,[33] as well as in his 2010 book,[34] how multilateral institutions (such as United Nations, Bretton Woods institutions, NATO) are failing. We missed our opportunity to reimagine the big institutions of the world back in 1989, he warns. The world community needs institutions that can deal with climate change and that can sort out when to intervene in other people's affairs and when to stay out. These are the "loose canons" that were not settled at the last great settlement in 1945. They must be settled now, Hurd urges.

"Financial Reform: Unfinished Business," is the title of an article by Paul Volcker, Chairman of the Federal Reserve.[35] As it seems, a *long unfinished revolution* cries out to be carried into the future.[36]

Paul Krugman and Robin Wells analyze the situation as follows:

By the late 1940s, most important economies had tightly regulated banking systems, preventing a recurrence of old-fashioned banking crises. At the same time, widespread limitations on the international movement of capital made it difficult for nations to run up the kinds of large international debts that had previously led to frequent defaults. (These restrictions took various forms, including limits on purchases of foreign securities and limits on the purchase of foreign currency for investment purposes; even advanced nations like France and Italy retained these restrictions into the 1980s.) Basically, it was a constrained world that may have limited initiative, but also left little room for large-scale irresponsibility.[37]

Krugman and Wells continue to explain that as memories of the 1930s faded, constraints began to be lifted. In the 1980s, after many constraints were gone, the Latin American debt crisis broke, followed by the Asian crisis of the 1990s. The authors describe how the weakening of bank regulation enabled the mid-1980s savings and loan debacle in the United States and the Swedish bank crisis of the early 1990s. By the early twenty-first century, "shadow banks" such as Lehman Brothers were growing rapidly. They did not accept deposits and were not covered by conventional banking regulations.

Krugman and Wells explain that the main advantage of laxer controls was easy access to credit, something that can spur growth, however, only when used conscientiously. The problem was that there were some who were not conscientious and who used the lack of controls "to pull down fast money," fueling the old and dangerous cycle of debt, crisis, and default.

Why didn't more people see this coming? Krugman and Wells point out that seemingly more sophisticated financial instruments, and the (illusionary) wider spreading of risks made people believe that the old rules of prudence that our grandparents heeded were no longer needed. Others had a vested interest in keeping debt exploding and the financial industry ballooning: they were making a lot of money from it. Krugman and Wells conclude:

> The world's two great financial centers, in New York and London, wielded vast influence over their respective governments, regardless of party. The Clinton administration in the US and the Labour government in Britain succumbed alike to the siren song of financial innovation—and were spurred in part by the competition between the two great centers, because politicians were all too easily convinced that having a large financial industry was a wonderful thing. Only when the crisis struck did it become clear that the growth of Wall Street and the City actually exposed their home nations to special risks, and that nations that missed

out on the glamour of high finance, like Canada, also missed out on the worst of the crisis.[38]

Another very cogent summary of the dilemma of money is given by community economist Thomas Henry Greco, Jr.:

Money is said to serve several functions: it is (1) a generally accepted "medium of exchange," (2) "a store of value," (3) a "standard of deferred payment" and, most fundamentally, (4) "a unit of account" or "measure of value" (Dunkman, 1970.) We think we know what we are talking about when we use the word "money," but in fact we do not. All of the orthodox definitions of money describe its supposed functions and not its essence. Further, because the term "money" is commonly applied to a diverse array of financial instruments which are created in a variety of ways, the whole subject has degenerated into a sea of confusion. It is a curious fact that the problems arising from these contradictory functions, while they have not gone completely unrecognized, have been so completely swept under the rug.[39]

Michael Hartmann, sociologist at the University of Darmstadt, examined the sociology of elites and came to the conclusion that it is not the individual psychology (greed), nor the system (lack of regulations), but the interest of those who make the system that deserves our attention.[40] Indeed, if we are to believe scholar and strategist David J. Rothkopf, a small number (circa 6,000) of largely unelected powerful people around the globe have shaped the world during the past decades in ways that made the financial meltdown possible.[41]

As reported earlier, in the United States, the level of inequality is medieval. Together with Gar Alperovitz, we are interested in finding out what the "prehistorical possibilities of the next great change may be."[42]

From my work on humiliation, I am aware that historically, dictators always hijacked systems. Adolf Hitler hijacked the German state institutions, Siad Barre did the same in Somalia, to name just two examples. While they proceeded, they created smokescreens to hide their actions. As alluded to earlier, the walls of the Forbidden City in Beijing represented a straight-forward cover; at present, the cover seems to be provided by the complexity of "expert" language selling supposedly "modern innovation" and "progress." These "innovations" leave most citizens—even first-class thinkers—at a loss of understanding.

Futurologist Robert Jungk (1913–1994) wrote about the link between large-scale economies, particularly that of atomic energy, and the danger of totalitarian statehood, and contrasted this scenario with the hope that a new global movement will counteract it.[43] Japanese artist Isao Hashimoto has recently created a time-lapse map that Jungk would find interesting, a map of the 2053 nuclear explosions which have taken place between 1945 and 1998.[44]

It is fascinating to see how relevant Robert Jungk is today (translated by the author):

> It is not often that members of a profession warn the public against their own colleagues. That is what happened in August 1977, when over 28 outstanding physicists from 32 countries expressed the following opinions against the influence of physicists in the nuclear debate, after a colloquium of the "Scuola Internazionale Enrico Fermi" on Lake Como: "The most serious problem is that the discussion of these matters is not really taking place among citizens, but is dominated by an elite of professionals... The operators of nuclear energy accept only those scientists who support the government's nuclear program... We urge the public to look at the views of these experts very critically, and not blindly follow the affirmations of all those who claim to know everything.[45]

> In this [new global movement], real participation is possible, as required by the anti-nuclear movement in political life. This includes mutual learning, thorough listening to one another and conversing with each other. In professional life and politics, the drafting of own proposals is encouraged, not just the parroting of others'. Everyone is an irreplaceable "expert" of their own needs and wants. "Participation" is understood not only as having a voice, but also as a co-creation. This takes time, which no longer exists in a society that is characterized by the clock,

rationalization, the quest for speed, and the production of ever larger amounts of stuff.[46]

Jungk continues by saying that this new movement will work in new ways. They will avoid the problem of the past when dominant opinion leaders and opinion makers, through their rule, caused the original creativity of their colleagues to disappear. Jungk foresees that a constant stream of energy, from many minds and hearts, will be liberated: It will be *human creative power* instead of *nuclear power*. He continues:

Modesty, justice, love of nature and beauty, acceptance of emotionality, participation and liberation of imagination, these are some of the values of a more humane future that are present in the supposedly "only negative" and "destructive" movement against nuclear industry and nuclear state.[47]

New independent and self-governing cooperative forms of production that stay clear of artificially driven growth and profit, are emerging in many places, particularly where the failing old economy has led to unemployment.

It is, however, still possible that the penetration of the atomic state will force the new non-violent International [global movement] temporarily in the catacombs. But the technological tyranny is both more powerful and more vulnerable than previous tyrannies. Ultimately, water will be stronger than stone.[48]

We usually hear from economists that inequalities are unavoidable for "modern innovation" and "progress" to flourish. Yet, through his work in the impact of inequality, Richard G. Wilkinson, scholar of social epidemiology and expert in public health, along with his colleagues, provides an in-depth treatment of relevant research on the destructive consequences of inequality.[49]

In chapter 11, the success of the "Scandinavian model" will be referred to, and the work of Karl Ove Moene at the Centre of Equality, Social Organization, and Performance (ESOP).[50]

Interestingly, if people are asked directly, they prefer an equal distribution of resources to an unequal distribution. Michael I. Norton and Dan Ariely carried out a survey in the United States, where respondents "dramatically underestimated the current level of wealth inequality" in the U.S. Even more interesting, both Republicans and liberals preferred a wealth distribution that resembles that of Sweden over that of the U.S. "All demographic groups—even those not usually associated with wealth redistribution such as Republicans and the wealthy—desired a more equal distribution of wealth than the status quo."[51]

Morton Deutsch, the "father" of the field of conflict resolution, now over 90 years old, writes:

> The limitations of "economic rationality" have been addressed in criticism of the measure of Gross Domestic Product (GDP). The GDP is a flawed economic measure of the economic value of the goods produced nationally in a given year (it doesn't include many costs of increased economic production such as the costs produced by environmental pollution) which is often taken as an indicator of the well-being of the nation's citizens, individually and collectively. Thus, Stiglitz, Sen, and Fitoussi (2010) argue, in *Mismeasuring Our Lives: Why GDP Doesn't Add Up*, that the GDP is a deeply flawed indicator of well-being.[52] Also, Nussbaum (2011), in her recent book, *Creating Capabilities, The Human Development Approach*, [53] indicates that equating doing well (for a nation) with an increase in GDP per capita, distracts attention from the real problems of creating well-being for all members of a society by suggesting that the right way to improve the quality of life is by economic growth alone (i.e., increased GDP).[54]

From the large-scale geohistorical perspective that I use in my work, I have tried to understand the circumstances that stimulate raiding cultures to emerge.[55] I learned a lot when I did my doctoral research in Somalia (chapter 7). Nobody should be surprised that Somalia's warrior culture provides the world with pirates. "When plunder becomes a way of life for a group of men living together in society, they create for themselves, in the course of time, a legal system that authorizes it and a moral code that glorifies it" said French economist Frederic Bastiat (1801–1850).[56]

European raiding culture has been identified as a backdrop for the current economic crisis.[57] Lundgren, Moene, and Hartmann have been reported earlier as speaking about Anglo-Saxon culture in this way.[58] It is telling that it is the business practice of *corporate raiding* that has been associated with values of "greed is good."[59] Indeed, the plunder of American workers' retirement funds is perhaps the most insidious raid perpetrated throughout the past years.[60]

In the course of my doctoral research, I studied how Somali warlords provide their militia with drugs and sex (chapter 12). I was not astonished to read that testosterone can be linked with money trading,[61] and that investment bankers have a penchant for expensive drug and sex parties.[62] The 2010 documentary *Inside Job* featured Jonathan Alpert, a New York therapist whose clients include many high-level Wall Street executives, saying: "These people are risk-takers; they're impulsive. It's part of their behavior, it's part of their personality. And that manifests outside of work as well. It's quite typical for the guys to go out, to go to strip bars, to use drugs. I see a lot of cocaine use, a lot of use of prostitution."[63]

Raiding is high-intensity fun for raiders; it is "dazzling." Jon Stevens Corzine, a former CEO of Goldman Sachs, became chairman and CEO of MF Global Inc., a financial services firm specializing in futures brokerage in 2010. He had to file for bankruptcy protection in October 2011. This was a shock, and it brought Goldman Sachs into the limelight. William D. Cohen's 2011 book *How Goldman Sachs Came to Rule the World* received wide attention.[64] Corzine was an "aggressive trader," and that was meant as a compliment in the stock market's heydays. Robert Rubin, present United States Secretary of the Treasury, for instance, "joined Citigroup as a senior adviser and board member in 1999. A dazzling trader when he was at Goldman, he counseled Citigroup that the firm should take more risk."[65]

What do we learn? A geohistorical cultural context enables a raiding culture to flourish, it allows elites to hijack institutions (the 6,000 people Rothkopf refers to, that Hartmann analyzes, using the strategies that Tremblay summarizes), and to develop new innovate economic "weaponry" (Collateralized Debt Obligations or CDOs, and Credit

Default Swaps or CDSs, see also Warren Buffett's comments). This new weaponry gains this elite unparalleled power, at least for the short term, even if at the long-term detriment of all, including those elites' children and their children's children. This means that current economic crises that further enrich a few, create utterly unsustainable conditions for the entirety of our socio- and ecosphere.

A certain geohistorical cultural context
⬇
that enables a "raiding" culture to flourish
⬇
and to hijack institutions
⬇
with innovative tools and interventions
⬇
leads to domination and exploitation
⬇
and if this happens at a global scale, it means the destruction of the entire socio- and ecosphere.

This is where we are now. What is the solution?

The transition we need now requires a multi-thronged approach with two core moves (using Max Weber's *ideal-type* approach[66]). Let me call it *dignity transition*. It must be a hybrid bottom-up and top-down approach. A simple combination of bottom-up and top-down would not suffice, because we cannot wait for the majority of the world's citizens to become Mandelas from the bottom up. We can also not wait for the politicians of our time to implement necessary changes from the top down (see more in chapter 10).

Before we embark on a mission for global unity, we might need to face our fears. Many people Linda and I talk to fear that calling for global systemic change is nothing but dangerous striving for the perfection of utopia and will only lead to global Orwellian dictatorship. This fear is warranted.

History shows many examples of overlords uniting fragmented countries. I know Norway particularly well. Until around 860, Norwegian territories were ruled by jarls. In about 860, Harald Hårfagre united the territories, creating the Kingdom of Norway. Wherever such unification processes occurred in history, they usually brought a bright side and a dark side: there was unity, but there was also oppressive uniformity crowding out diversity. It often began with rather egalitarian relationships, then one ruler became a *primus inter pares*, yet, over time, rulers succeeded in amassing central power. Colonization followed this script: In many places it started with trade that treated all players as equals. Then economic power was translated into political power.

Nowadays, we experience something similar at a global level. A fragmented world is being united. The promising side is that it brings people together. "For the first time since the origin of our species, humanity is in touch with itself" said anthropologist William Ury.[67] Anthropologists call it the *ingathering* of the human tribes. However, globalization also has a dark side; for instance, it has created global corporate uniformity. The "king who unites" is now the global corporation, and the destructive aspects flowing from a global raiding culture that ravages ecological and social commons.

In my work, I call on us, the human family, to "humanize globalization with egalization." *Egalization* connotes the true manifestation of equality in dignity for all. I then draw both words together into *globegalization*.

Liberté, égalité, fraternité was the motto of the French Revolution in 1789 (liberty, equality, brotherhood, today we would add sisterhood) or a free community of equals.[68] Globegalization points at liberté and égalité, with fraternité still somewhat missing. Therefore, I wrote my 2010 book on *Gender, Humiliation, and Global Security*, to include loving solidarity.

When we join hands, when we cooperate, when we collaborate, we use the prefix "co" to connote "together." I coined the word *co-globegalization* to bring liberté, égalité, and fraternité into one word (see also chapter 3).[69]

What do I mean by co-globegalization? I mean that we need to become ever more aware that we are *one* human family and that a family is a good family when its members are connected in *liberté, égalité, and fraternité*.

I would describe my personal consciousness as a *postindividual consciousness*,[70] a *unity consciousness*[71] or a *planetary consciousness*.[72] As I wrote in the preface, I resonate with 14th century Persian Sufi poet Hāfez-e Šīrāzī's saying: "I have learned so much from God that I can no longer call myself a Christian, a Hindu, a Muslim, a Buddhist, a Jew. The truth has shed so much of itself in me that I can no longer call myself a man, a woman." My religion is love, humility, and awe for a universe too large for us to fathom. I speak of a *literacy of love*.[73]

I suggest that we all, in the spirit of love and humility, reflect on global governance solutions, such as *cosmopolitanism* or *world federalism*, not as rigid constructions but as fluid systems, not as global Orwellian dictatorship, but as a path to nurture global flourishing.[74] A democratic system is more flexible than a dictatorship—the bloody downfall of Libyan ruler Muammar Gaddafi brought this fact home very recently. But democratic practices are not yet flexible enough. We still have a long way to go to being truly civilized.

Economist Jeremy Rifkin calls for an *empathic civilization* to emerge.[75] Empathic civilization is the opposite to the perfection of utopia, since empathy flows from our frailties and imperfections. But an empathic civilization means also systemic change, it is aware that piecemeal interventions are not sufficient.

This brings us back to the significance of dignity. "Every human being is born with equal rights and dignity," this is the first sentence of Article 1 of the Human Rights Declaration. Since the adoption of this declaration in 1948, political rights have been foregrounded.

Now is the time to give dignity more attention. And human dignity entails the ethics of care (chapter 4).[76] Seyla Benhabib is a professor of political science and philosophy. She recently wrote a book titled *Dignity in Adversity: Human Rights in Troubled Times*.[77] Cosmopolitanism, according to Benhabib, foregrounds moral sympathy and turns the abstraction of humanity into "concrete others."

How can we overcome our fears of global utopia, of global Orwellian dictatorship, and consider the possibility of global flourishing? Asking deeper questions may help, rather than simply shrinking away from global systems thinking.

In a spirit of love and humility, we may want to consider to accept that we, as a human species on this planet, may not represent the "crown" of creation, but rather the cause of its destruction. The Norwegian philosopher Arne Næss, "father" of *deep ecology*, developed the notion of the "depth of intention," the "depth of questioning" or "deepness of answers." Næss writes "our depth of intention improves only slowly over years of study. There is an abyss of depth in everything fundamental."[78] Greater depth means continuing to ask questions at the point at which others stop asking.[79]

Linda and I, together with our colleagues, wish to continue asking questions. We wish to approach everything, including the role of economics and monetary structures for *right relationships*, with the necessary humility, but also with due candor.

In the rest of the book, I will offer a brief analysis of some of the humiliating effects of contemporary economic and monetary arrangements, and end with a "global vision" section.

Let us end this chapter with emphasizing, once again, how important it is that we all join hands and think up solutions that work for the entire human family and its habitat. The 99 percent and the 1 percent, we all have children who will not find a decent planet to live on if we do not get beyond finger-pointing and humiliation entrepreneurship now. Cycles of humiliation only cloud our minds and foreclose necessary transitions.

Let us remember that the Nobel Peace Prize 1993 was awarded jointly to Nelson Mandela and Frederik Willem de Klerk, two former enemies who worked together to create a better world for all South Africans.

Usually, terrible things that are done with the excuse that progress requires them are not really progress at all, but just terrible things.

—Russell Baker

Chapter 3
Where Might We Go? Toward a Dignity Transition

You can't cross the sea merely by standing and staring at the water.

—Rabindranath Tagore

A bird cannot know where the sorghum is ready to harvest unless it flies.

—Kinyarwanda proverb[1]

This chapter begins with a letter penned by economics professor Kamran Mofid, founder of the Globalisation for the Common Good (GCG) initiative,[2] on May 20, 2011:

Friends,
Do you remember Margaret Thatcher, the so-called Iron Lady! She told the Brits that she was going to put the "Great" back into "Great" Britain. Do you remember? Then, she told us this can only happen if we accept and implement the "Washington Consensus," the so-called neo-liberalism. She told us that there was no alternative. She told us we will all prosper and develop more fairly and equitably. She won election after elections. Everything was privatised, deregulated, self-regulated. Industry, manufacturing (the real economy) was destroyed. Instead, the banks and the bankers were encouraged to rule the world. The

economists with no principles and values were "bought" and business schools, such as Harvard and Columbia, were showered with money to act as "Cheer Leaders" for the neo-liberalism (see the *Inside Job* for evidence). Communities were dismantled and disorganised. We were told that there is no such thing as a society and community. We are all in it just for ourselves, we were told. Destructive competition at the expense of life-enhancing cooperation, collaboration and dialogue was greatly prompted. We were told to say no to love, kindness, generosity, sympathy and empathy and say yes to selfishness, individualism and narcissism, as these values will fire the engine of capitalism and wealth creation! In short, to hell with the common good, we were encouraged to believe.[3]

The Future of Market Capitalism HBS Centennial project,[4] has been exploring the evolution of capitalism—the value it has generated, and the threats that may be arising that could impede its future value creation. For this project, business leaders around the world have been interviewed to document their sense of what some of the potential threats are—and what to do about them. What is your opinion?

In many countries, the gap between the rich and the poor has grown and will continue to widen. Some say growing inequality may be an unfortunate consequence of economic growth, but isn't a real problem as long as everyone's income is improving. Others say the growing inequality will undermine the foundations of our democracies and hence our economies. What is your opinion?

There has been a great deal of discussion recently about environmental degradation, and particularly about global climate change. Some believe that capitalism, by its nature, will seek to reduce or avoid environmental regulation, exacerbating environmental damage and endangering the future health of the planet. Others see for-profit firms as increasingly recognizing the importance of environmental issues, and as working to minimize their negative impacts on the environment and to invent new technologies that will make business more sustainable. How do you see it? Is market capitalism the problem—or the solution?

If we were to analyze the situation as Kamran Mofid so eloquently decries it, what would be the core problems? Three problematic practices seem to stand at the core of current economic difficulties:

1. A first problematic practice appears to be connected to the fact that money is created as debt. The United States government, for example, writes bonds. Money is created in bank books to buy these bonds and the government promises to honor these bonds by paying back their debts over time. This creates several dilemmas. A core difficulty is connected with what is called *consideration*. Consideration is a concept of legal value in contract law defined as a promised action or omission of action. A famous court case, the First National Bank of Montgomery versus Jerome Daly, illustrates the problem. On December 9, 1968, in the Justice Court State of Minnesota, the judge ruled in favor of the debtor Jerome Daly, who had failed to honor his mortgage. Because of *failure of a lawful consideration*, the bank was prohibited from taking Daly's assets. The judge deemed it to be illegal for a bank to lend money it does not have, but has simply created virtually in its books.

    "Another important problem with the government writing bonds is that doing so, the government/society consumes today the future surplus from economy (collected in form of taxes). That is like the farmer eating the grains he would need to seed next spring," comments techno-economics analyst Ulrich Spalthoff.[5]

2. A second difficulty seems to flow from the fractional reserve system. This system is explained, for example, in the leaflet *Modern Money Mechanics* by the Federal Reserve Bank of Chicago.[6] Fractional reserve banking is a banking practice in which banks keep only a fraction of their deposits in reserve. This practice is universal in modern banking.

3. A third problematic practice has to do with how money and debt are connected. Paul Grignon explains:

> In the debt money system, money is just a promise to pay the same or more money back. New money = new debt. Debt forces people to be productive and create value to pay off their debts, including the interest, but their new production does not create new money by some magic alchemy, as many people seem to believe. New value = new money makes intuitive sense and is how self-issued credit currencies work. But in our mainstream system new debt to a bank = new money. All money is bank credit, just a promise to pay fiat cash on demand. Therefore every dollar (or whatever currency) has an appointment to be paid back to the bank that created it (demand one). But if it has been loaned again or otherwise invested for gain, it is expected to grow forever (demand two). The two opposing demands can only be reconciled if, directly or indirectly, the investment money is spent to hire the borrower, the money is paid back to the bank, and the borrower's productivity creates new money-value (not money) in the equity belonging to the investor. However, I think that there is an arithmetic problem here. This system is only compatible with endless growth. Bank credit money is loaned again either in hard returns as a loan or soft returns as an investment. This makes a perpetual debt—the bank can only be paid off by borrowing from the second lender, the second lender by another loan from a bank ad infinitum. This makes it impossible for this debt to ever be extinguished or even reduced without default. It can only grow. So any attempt to "live modestly" by reducing economic throughput (see chapter 1) will cause financial collapse. We need to change the mathematics of the system so it can adapt to shrinkage just as gracefully as to growth. I have a very detailed proposal how to do so."[7]

Later, Grignon added that some Islamic countries and some South American countries resist the current trend to global "debt slavery," including Malaysia, Brazil, Argentina, and Bolivia.[8] Grignon's *Digital Coin* concept has not been tried yet. Alternative currencies are widespread but as of yet, still marginal.[9]

What are the historical roots of the present situation? Anthropologist William Ury drew up *a simplified depiction of history* (whose core elements are widely accepted in anthropology):

1. *simple hunter-gatherers* (first 95 percent of human history, if the starting point is set at 200,000 years ago)
2. *complex agriculturists* (last 10,000 years, evolving from around 12,000 BCE to 5,000 BCE, representing the recent five percent of human history)
3. *knowledge society* (presently in the making)[10]

Human behavior is, at least partly, learned behavior, and can therefore be unlearned when cultural contexts change (see a discussion of the argument of nature versus culture in chapter 3 of *Gender, Humiliation, and Global Security*[11]). It is, therefore, important to analyze the interplay of context and human adaptations throughout human history:

Ad 2. Roughly 10,000 years ago, *circumscription* began to make itself felt—to say it very briefly, while early animists migrated freely and were surrounded by untouched abundance, at some point, "the next valley" was taken by other people.[12] Complex agriculture represented a form of adaptation by *Homo sapiens* to the changing conditions. As a result, beginning circa 10,000 years ago, until recent times, the *security dilemma* became overwhelmingly significant and the definitorial for every detail of life. The term *security dilemma* is used in political science[13] to describe how mutual distrust can bring states that have no intention of harming one another into bloody war. The security dilemma is tragic because its "logic of mistrust and fear" is inescapable: "I have to amass weapons, because I am scared.

When I amass weapons, you get scared. You amass weapons, I get more scared."

The security dilemma was predicated on one *duality* and created a second:

> 2.1. the security dilemma is predicated on a horizontal duality of *inside/outside*: in-group friends are differentiated from potential out-group allies/enemies.
> 2.2. the security dilemma pushes for the vertical duality of *up/down* that underpins stratified male-dominant "strong-man" dominator models[14] of collectivistic and ranked honor societies: domination/submission has characterized stratified societies of collectivist ranked honor (including gender segregation) beginning around 10,000 years ago. The "art of domination"[15] subsequently refined this system, with the result that the domination/submission structure became ever more covert, stealthily maintaining traditional elites and creating new elites, with the cultural imperative of profit maximization as its latest expression (see a discussion in *Emotion and Conflict* and *Making Enemies*,[16] and further publications listed in www.humiliationstudies.org).

Ad 3. At the current point in history, humankind finds itself in the middle of a transition that is as radical as the one that began 10,000 years ago. Human rights ideals represent a normative u-turn against the dominator culture of the past ten millennia. The human rights ideal of equality in dignity for all is a new ethical frame. The notion of humiliation offers a historical marker: in the English-speaking world, humiliation was defined as a hurtful violation of dignity for the first time in 1757.[17] The ideal of equality in dignity for all flows from, and in turn facilitates, the emergence of an experience of *one world*. This is mediated, not least, through various insights and experiences that call for humility.[18] Ultimately, the more interdependence manifests in a world of *one* human family, the more the security dilemma of "we against them," with its primary and secondary effects, is bound to weaken. During the first transition that began 10,000 years ago, worthiness became ranked—higher beings presided over lower beings in dominator societies and this was regarded as highly legitimate. The presently unfolding transition delegitimizes the first one and unranks human worthiness into equal dignity for all.

The presently unfolding transition—away from the dominator period of the past five percent of human history toward the partnership model of the future—is fraught with confusion. In my book *Making Enemies: Humiliation and International Conflict*, I use traffic as a metaphor to illustrate this transition:

We see that as long as there was ample space, everybody moved along without taking much notice of the other drivers. Under conditions of abundance, hunters and gatherers enjoyed pristine pride. In early agricultural empires with denser populations, however, the powerful usurped the right to pass first. Honor dictated that big vehicles drove through first at a crossroad, while the smaller ones waited in due reverence. A master regarded it as legitimate to push out the smaller ones, who accepted this treatment as divinely ordained. Occasionally somebody attempted to acquire a larger vehicle. If he succeeded, he was the new master with all the rights of a master, since revolutions toppled the masters, but not the system. However, apart from the threat of revolution, a threat that required constant attention from the masters, this system rendered a certain extent of public stability, calm, and order. At some point, around the time the word humiliation began to connote violation, a discussion arose (to stay with the metaphor) about managing traffic more effectively by using traffic lights. Equal dignity for all means that every driver, irrespective of the size of the vehicle, has the same rights before the new traffic lights. The size of the vehicle, its color, and its price do not affect the driver's status or rights.[19]

Human rights build on the French Revolution's notion of liberty, equality, and fraternity (brotherhood and sisterhood, see chapter 2). Freedom, or liberty, can be defined as "absence of restraint" (absence of traffic rules) or it can be interpreted as a "level playing field" (traffic lights regulating crossroads, see also chapter 1, Bo Lundgren's analysis). The first definition is prevalent, for example, in the United States of America, perhaps deriving its fervor from American national pride about its successful rebellion against British control.

Removing restraints, however, produces freedom for only a short while, then it begins to undermine it. Freedom so defined legitimizes *might* as *right*, which soon curtails freedom. Those who are more successful invest their newly-won resources to protect their advantages against free market forces. They begin to coerce and coopt the less mighty, including political actors, through lobbying or funding political parties. They "capture" the state and push for institutions (traffic rules and signs) that preserve their advantages. The removal of restraints, in other words, quickly leads to a very uneven playing field. Traffic lights need to be planned, placed, and maintained in concerted systemic way. In a captured state, the owners of big cars simply get priority and replicate the very dominator model they set out to be freed from.

Evidence is ubiquitous, as already discussed in chapter 1. More examples can be found everywhere. Most elite universities in the United States, for instance, replicate privilege by giving preference to the children of alumni, sometimes even to their grandchildren and siblings. In case of Princeton's class of 2015, 33 percent of those offered a place were the children of alumni, for Harvard it was 30 percent, and for Yale, 20 to 25 percent."[20] "College graduates have become good at passing down advantages to their children. If you are born with parents who are college graduates, your odds of getting through college are excellent. If you are born to high school grads, your odds are terrible... Over the past several decades, the economic benefits of education have steadily risen," writes David Brooks. [21] He speaks of *red* and *blue* inequality and suggests that we overlook the inequality that hurts most, namely red inequality. Blue inequality is the inequality between the top one percent and the bottom 99 percent. Red inequality is between those with a college degree and those without one.

The differences between the hierarchical societies of the past millennia and present world-wide arrangements are much less dramatic than modern freedom rhetoric may indicate. In the past, individuals were only more "frozen" into fixed institutions (such as feudalism and the divine right of kings). Modern ranking mechanisms are more often based on an elective use of science by those who benefit (Adam Smith's "invisible hand," for instance, has been quoted so frequently so that it has become a generally-recognized term,[22] but it is largely unknown that Smith also discussed regulations, or what could be called the "visible hand"[23]).

Both past and present hierarchies are often legitimized by invoking eternal divine forces. In the past, absolute rulers claimed that their power was God-given. It is not unusual for today's wealthy to view their prosperity as a sign of God's approval as well. Sociologist Max Weber (1864–1920) connected the religious teachings of John Calvin with the rise of capitalism:

> Calvin emphasized the doctrine of *predestination*—the belief that even before they are born, all people are divided into two groups, the saved and the damned, and only God knows who will go to heaven (the elect) and who will go to hell. Because people cannot know whether they will be saved, they tend to look for earthly signs that they are among the elect. According to the Protestant ethic, those who have faith, perform good works, and achieve economic success are more likely to be among the chosen of God… The wealthy can use religion to justify their power and privilege: It is a sign of God's approval of their hard work and morality."[24]

In the course of my international life, I have observed the almost divine status of money (rather than traditional status) being most pronounced at the West Coast in the United States (with a New Age taste) and in China (in the Chinese tradition of wishing for "wealth and a long life").

Glen T. Martin, professor of philosophy and religious studies and chairperson of the program in Peace Studies at Radford University in Virginia, read my traffic metaphor. He reacted with the following comment to its statement that "large and small vehicles (capitalism allows for such differences) all have to stop for the traffic light… the driver of the Rolls Royce as well as the pedestrian has a say (democracy)":

The model, of course, is an excellent one for democracy and the rule of law but it appears to ignore that fact that the *political* equality afforded in traditional liberal democracy (you cite Locke: one vote each for the driver of the Rolls Royce and the pedestrian) masks the fact that the driver of the Rolls Royce may have immense political power lacking to the pedestrian. This power is routinely and systematically used to manipulate the laws governing the economic system in his own interests in ways that result in the immense humiliation of global poverty.

The irony may be that the person controlling huge concentrations of private wealth may not be a racist or caught in cultural or other forms of in-group and out-group patterns of humiliation. Our world is dominated *behind the scenes* (see Ellen Brown's book[25]) by immense structural forces of exploitation that have created the horrific world in which 50 percent of the global population live on less than $2 U.S. dollars per day and the richest 225 persons on Earth have a combined wealth equivalent to this bottom 50 percent. I realize that you know these facts well, but my question is how can they be integrated into the interpretative framework of dignity versus humiliation?[26]

What to do? What is at the core of systemic humiliation? Article 1 of the Universal Declaration of Human Rights (UDHR) always reminds us: "All human beings are born free and equal in dignity and rights. They are endowed with reason and conscience and should act towards one another in a spirit of brotherhood." Why are these ideals still waiting to be fully realized?

Is it possible that a cultural and legal context that gives primacy to profit maximization is intimately connected with the confusion about the term freedom? Is the need to maximize profit built into the monetary system as soon as this system is based on money-as-debt that must be repaid?

The result of such a system is that the well-being of people is placed second to monetary gain—by design, not by individual choice. A business enterprise will go out of business if it prioritizes ethical considerations that hamper profitability. Trust is undermined systemically, since one can never be sure which products may be offered merely for profit rather than to enhance the well-being of the people and their environment. Scarcity is created and maintained by design, since abundance is not saleable—only scarce products fetch payment (Part III).

Is it possible that the monetary practices listed above cause historical pyramid systems to evolve into global pyramid schemes by design? That such systems give power to what has been called *corporatocracy*, or a system that overlooks, or even callously risks, environmental destruction and human suffering? Such systems of covert coercion could perhaps be also be called *monetary-ism*, a context that creates freedom and liberty only as an illusion. Dignity is then violated by design; the culture masks the real system of profit-driven humiliation. As in an apartheid system, no relationship within such a frame can escape its humiliating effects as long as there is no alternative system available.

Achieving a sustained level playing field may require to differentiate between legitimate and illegitimate restraints and to understand which restraints are necessary to guarantee economic fairness for all, and which undermine it. This would mean implementing the right amount and the right kinds of social and societal institutions, including economic and monetary institutions (traffic laws).

Perhaps all can agree that a world of economic homeostasis will involve careful nurturing to maintain its balance in continuously dynamic recalibrating processes. Greed as an individual psychological phenomenon may not be the problem. The real problem may be the submerging of human activity in institutions that prioritize greed in a systemic way. Profit-maximization as a primary world-defining principle may be unsustainable.[27]

Many voices have already been heard in this book, and renowned scientists Paul and Anna Ehrlich are among them, when they warn that the world's population is undermining our life support—our ecosystems—in favor of enterprise. They point to Jared Diamond's argument that civilizations collapse as a result of one factor: the mismanagement of natural resources.[28]

What to do? Where to go from here? What would be the appropriate core elements of better arrangements of human affairs on planet Earth?

Unity in diversity offers itself as an appropriate principle for a balanced world.[29] Unity in diversity means avoiding oppressive uniformity on one side, and violent division on the other side. As the examples of, for instance, North Korea and Burma show, when government gets too big, oppressive uniformity looms and diversity is lost. No one wants to put in place an Orwellian global model. Oppressive uniformity is a degradation of the unity pole of the principle of unity in diversity that must be avoided.

The degradation of the other pole, however, is just as dangerous. When public institutions fail, violent divisions threaten the potential of diversity to be enriching and inspirational. An examples is war-torn Somalia, where violent warlords have been allowed to abuse the country's power vacuum for the past two decades. Likewise, the power vacuum at the global level was exploited by financial players during the past years, leading to the economic crisis that began in 2007 and washed over the world in 2008.

Intercultural communication scholar Muneo Yoshikawa has developed a *nondualistic*[30] *double swing* model (unity is created out of the realization of differences), which shows how individuals, cultures, and intercultural concepts can blend in constructive ways.[31] This model can be graphically visualized as the infinity symbol, or Möbius strip (∞). Yoshikawa brought together Western and Eastern thought by drawing on Martin Buber's idea of "dialogical unity—the act of meeting between two different beings without eliminating the otherness or uniqueness of each"—and on *Soku*, the Buddhist nondualistic logic of "Not-One, Not-Two," described as the twofold movement between the self and the other that allows for both unity and uniqueness.[32] Yoshikawa calls the unity that is created out of such a realization of differences *identity in unity*: the dialogical unity does not eliminate the tension between basic potential unity and apparent duality.[33]

Linda and I were impressed when we heard Dorothy (Dot) J. Maver, co-director of the National Peace Academy, speak about *right relationships* at the Hollyhock Summer Gathering, July 26–31, 2009, on Cortes Island, BC, Canada. Dorothy came up with particularly concise formulations, such as "Great turning points can be great learning points!" Here are some of Linda's notes about Dot Maver's presentation:

Dot is looking for signs of right relationships. She refers to the Earth Charter entailing a message about living with oneself and others. She talks about transforming all system breakdowns into all system breakthroughs. Moving from safe and healthy communities to a safe and healthy planet. From stakeholder to careholder. WMD means: We Must Disarm!

Dot Maver explained that she works on a "science of right relationships." She said: "I do not wish for peace, I live for peace. Peace is not the goal, it is the outcome. We are the connective tissue."

Yes, Linda agrees, "we need to transcend policies and institutions that cause the sellout of dignity, that 'exclude people from access to dignified lives, both socially and economically.'"[34]

Dot Maver reported on Senate Bill 263 in Vermont, a bill that addresses what Paul Grignon describes: "CEO's are required by law to maximize returns for shareholders. They could even go to jail for purposely not doing so. Nothing else can trump this priority. Until this law is changed nothing else will."[35] Senate Bill 263 was approved on Friday, March 12, 2010, by the Committee on Economic Development, Housing and General Affairs.[36] It is expected that this bill might disrupt hundreds of years of corporate law and culture by empowering domestic corporations to charter themselves as *for benefit* corporations, a new legal designation for socially responsible businesses. Benefit corporations combine non-profit and for-profit aspects and make it legally possible for companies to consider the needs of customers, workers, the community, and the environment without chief executives risking being sued for not maximizing profits. There are many voices with similar messages. Business journalist Marjorie Kelly, for example, speaks of transitioning to for-benefit business.[37]

A new standard for urban and community accounting was ratified in early 2007. United Nations and Local Governments for Sustainability (ICLEI) ratified the triple bottom line approach, abbreviated as "TBL" or "3BL." This approach is also known as "the three pillars" of "people, planet, profit" or "economic, ecological and social." TBL became the dominant approach to accounting for the full costs of institutional activity in the public sector, see also the ecoBudget standard for reporting ecological footprint. In the private sector, a commitment to corporate social responsibility implies some form of TBL reporting.

Linda and I, like Dot, are striving for right relationships, which we believe means ending humiliating practices and advancing human dignity. Like Dot, we are generating our own special HumanDHS-informed science of right relationships. Below are Linda's thoughts on right relationships:

1. I think it is important to realize that we are not conceptualizing "right relationships" in Western, dualistic terms (good/bad relationships). We are striving for a more complex under-standing of "right relationships."

2. For me, right relationships facilitate the healthy growth and development of all involved. Based on my work with Jean Baker Miller, I believe right relationships are characterized by mutual empathy, mutual empowerment, and movement toward mutuality. By "mutuality," I do not mean relationships that involve exchange or reciprocity. Rather, mutuality means both or all people in the relationship are growing, even though they may be growing in very different ways. A lack of "movement toward mutuality" in a relationship is a clue that the relationship is not a right relationship.

3. I also think that right relationships are relationships characterized by a sense of equal dignity, equal worth. All people in the relationship feel valued and there is an understanding that each has something to contribute to the other person, to the relationship, and to the situation, even though people con-tribute in different ways.

4. Right relationships make it safe for people to be real, to be authentic, to bring more of themselves into the relationship. In right relationships, people do not have to hide large parts of themselves to stay in the relationship.

5. All people in a right relationship feel a sense of empowerment; empowerment means feeling that one can have an impact on the other person, the relationship, and the situation.

6. Right relationships energize both or all people in the relationship. This is in contrast to one-way relationships in which one person gains energy (power, benefits, etc.) at the expense of others.

7. Right relationships cultivate optimal function of both or all people in the relationship. Right relationships are not just a nice idea, they are a supremely practical way to build a better world for all of us. When people are not drained by ongoing efforts to protect and defend themselves against hurtful relationships, they can use their energy to create solutions to address the enormous problems we face today.[38]

How can humankind craft right relationships? Where do we have to look? What should be done?

Howard Richards, scholar of peace and global studies and philosophy, suggests thinking in terms of basic cultural structures derived from Roman law to identify the specific features of global modern Western historical development that need to be corrected:

- *Suum cuique (to each his own)* needs to be corrected by socially functional forms of land tenancy and socially functional forms of property in general.
- *Pacta sunt servanda (agreements must be kept)* needs to be corrected by reciprocity and responsibility for one another's welfare regardless of whether there is a contract. Externalities need to be acknowledged as normal, not exceptional, and human action should seek to promote positive externalities and to avoid negative ones.
- *Honeste vivare (to live honestly)* needs to be corrected by recognizing that our very identity is relational.

- *Alterum non laedere (not hurting others by word or deed)* needs to be corrected to promote an ideal of service to others, above and beyond the obligation not to harm them.

Richards posits that these corrections will avoid rebuilding the present one-size-fits-all global regime of capital accumulation, but will generate multiple ways of integrating factors of production to provide goods and services that support life.

The modern state system emerged from the 1648 Treaties of Osnabrück and Münster (better known as Peace of Westphalia). The relationship between citizens and the state have followed Thomas Hobbes,[39] John Locke,[40] and Jean-Jacques Rousseau[41] and their ideas about a "social contract" between the ruler and the ruled. This contract revolved around rights and duties, with citizens as more or less passive objects and the state as active subject. At present, with the marginalization of the state in favor of markets—a passive citizenry and a passive state—all are ruled by an active market.

In global institution building, Adam Smith's "invisible hand" needs many "visible hands" to make the invisible hand useful in the long term and for all, rather than for small elites for a short while. Economist Kamran Mofid puts Smith's legacy right:

We should recall the wisdom of Adam Smith, "father of modern economics," who was a great moral philosopher first and foremost. In 1759, sixteen years before his famous *Wealth of Nations*, he published *The Theory of Moral Sentiments*, which explored the self-interested nature of man and his ability nevertheless to make moral decisions based on factors other than selfishness. In The *Wealth of Nations*, Smith laid the early groundwork for economic analysis, but he embedded it in a broader discussion of social justice and the role of government. Today we mainly know only of his analogy of the "invisible hand" and refer to him as defending free markets; whilst ignoring his insight that the pursuit of wealth should not take precedence over social and moral obligations, and his belief that a "divine Being" gives us "the greatest quantity of happiness." We are taught that the free market as a "way of life" appealed to Adam Smith but not that he distrusted the morality of the market as a morality for society at large. He neither envisioned nor prescribed a capitalist society, but rather a "capitalist economy within society, a society held together by communities of non-capitalist and non-market morality." As it has been noted, morality for Smith included neighbourly love, an obligation to practice justice, a norm of financial support for the government 'in proportion to [one's] revenue', and a tendency in human nature to derive pleasure from the good fortune and happiness of other people.[42]

Asymmetry is inherently unstable. One set of players satisfies their desire for recognition by denying full recognition to another.[43] In an asymmetric world, particularly when norms such as human rights advocate the opposite and the pressure of the security dilemma wanes, the dynamics of humiliation permeate all aspects of social life.[44]

A decent dignified world of social harmony, both locally and globally, a world of *nondomination*,[45] of "good conflict," requires equal entitlement to respectful and dignified and dignifying treatment for all its members.

Philosopher Avishai Margalit wrote *The Decent Society*,[46] in which he calls for institutions that do no longer humiliate citizens—*just* societies no longer suffice; the goal should be *decent* societies that transcend humiliation. *Decency* reigns when dignity for all is made possible.

Jean Baker Miller, a pioneer in women's psychology, suggests that conflict is a necessary part of growth and change. She stipulates that conflict is not the problem—the way we engage in conflict is. Miller encourages learning how to "wage good conflict."[47]

Diversity can best be protected and nurtured through everybody uniting around the task of respecting equal dignity for all. As discussed earlier, I have coined the term *egalization* to denote equality in dignity through unity in diversity. I call on us to humanize globalization with egalization and have drawn both words together into *globegalization*.

Globegalization points at liberté and égalité, with fraternité still missing (chapter 2). My 2010 book *Gender, Humiliation, and Global Security* therefore focuses on *big love*, love in the spirit of Gandhi's *satyāgraha* (nonviolent action), a term that is assembled from agraha (firmness/force) and satya (truth-love).[48] I coined the word *co-*

globegalization to draw liberté and égalité with fraternité into one word.[49]

I first hesitated to turn to love. Love has been commoditized and emptied of its force. Federico Hewson, in his Valentine Peace Project, rightly calls on us to refuse accepting blood diamonds as symbols of love.[50] He wishes us to consider that many "commercial symbols and gifts of love actually come out of conflict."[51]

After initial hesitation, I turned to love because of its force. *Strength to Love*, is the title of a book by Martin Luther King Jr.[52] He calls on the "creatively maladjusted" to refrain from using hatred to affect change. He calls on us to use the force of love. At his funeral, he wished that it should be mentioned that he tried to "love and serve humanity."[53]

Since the United States emerged as a nation through resisting oppressive British taxation and governance, many Americans are particularly nervous about the concept of unity in diversity, since they tend to misinterpret it as advocating for oppressive uniformity. Co-globegalization is the antidote.

Love can provide the strength that is necessary for change. This is how I explain it in my book on love:

> If our forefathers, people from what we call the "dark ages," could travel to our time and see today's sophisticated ways of creating and utilizing energy—if they could see all the fancy equipment that runs on electricity—they would be flabbergasted. Before electricity was captured, people knew about it only from phenomena such as the lightning descending from thunder clouds or the rays radiating from the sun. Lightning and sunshine were the preserve of the weather gods. People in the dark ages would have shaken their heads in disbelief, had anybody told them that they had it in their power to tap the resources of the weather gods to make light.[54]

Today, we live in dark ages with respect to love. We leave its paradigm-shifting potential to change entire systems unused. Our ancestors treated lightning or sunshine as natural wonders. We still treat love like that. We hope that love will befall us, or that we will fall into it. We pray that it will grace us and make us happy, and spare us its potential for destruction. We have not yet learned to recognize and harness the force of love, at least not in sophisticated ways. We leave its potential untapped and its mystery uncelebrated.

Table 3.1 gives a highly idealized graphical impression (using Ury's historical model and applying the Weberian *ideal-type* approach[55]) of the core historical shifts (that also affect gender relationships). It shows on the left side, how, prior to ten thousand years ago, hunter-gatherer groups had ample space to roam (1). There was no need for organized war and they could maintain untouched pristine pride and essentially egalitarian societal structures. Then Earth became more populated and circumscription set in. Where soil and weather allowed for it, hierarchical societies of ranked honor based on agriculture formed (Rwanda is a good contemporary example). Where climatic conditions were less favorable, more mobile raiding cultures emerged (Somalia is a present-day illustration). In the context of the security dilemma, women and children were usually kept inside, while men were sent out to defend the borders and expand the territory. For ten millennia, larger empires swallowed up smaller communities, then fell apart again. Unity in diversity was perverted into uniformity and division—uniformity without diversity and division without unity.

Anthropologist Alan Page Fiske describes basic *relational models*.[56] Fiske found that people, most of the time and in all cultures, use just four elementary and universal forms or models for organizing most aspects of sociality. These models are: (1) communal sharing, CS, (2) authority ranking, AR, (3) equality matching, EM, and (4) market pricing, MP. Family life is often informed by communal sharing. Trust, love, care, and intimacy can prosper in this context. Authority ranking involves asymmetry among people who are ordered along vertical hierarchical social dimensions. Equality matching implies a model of balance such as taking turns, for instance, in car pools or babysitting cooperatives. Market pricing builds on a model of proportionality with respect to ratios and rates.

Table 3.1: A Dignity Transition Toward Co-Globegalization[57]

(1) First 95 percent of human history: pristine pride	(2) Past five percent of human history: collectivistic ranked honor	(2–3) Present-day global village: humiliating globalization	(3) Future equality in dignity: co-globegalization

Building a decent dignified world society where good conflict is waged means embedding Fiske's four models in ways that safeguard unity in diversity, avoiding oppressive uniformity as much as divisive fragmentation. Unity in diversity protects dignity against big oppressive government that forces everybody to become uniform or "the same." It also protects against under-regulation that obliterates diversity through the freedom of *might* is *right*, a definition of freedom that reintroduces the humiliation of the abuse of rank, or *rankism*, a term coined by Robert W. Fuller.[58]

Table 3.2 suggests how a *dignity transition* toward *co-globegalization*, could be envisioned through new ways of embedding Fiske's CS, AR, EM, and MP.

Table 3.2: A Dignity Transition Toward Co-Globegalization

(1) First 95 percent of human history:	(2) Past five percent of human history:	(2–3) Present-day humiliating globalization:	(3) Future co-globegaliza-tion:
CS defines AR	AR defines CS	MP defines AR	CS defines AR

In practice, globegalization means creating institutions at the global level that safeguard space for diversity at local levels. Globegalization means that those institutions have the common good of all humanity at heart and are informed by the communal sharing paradigm (CS). Within such a frame, authority ranking (AR) allows only functional hierarchies, not hierarchies built on the abuse of rank, or rankism. Equality matching (EM) and market pricing (MP) are embedded in ways that serve the greater common good.

Ten thousand years ago, when humankind faced changing circumstances, the knowledge to develop complex agriculture was already there to be developed and honed—people knew how to plant and how to harvest.

The knowledge needed for co-globegalization to be realized is already with us today, too.

In my work, I suggest that we, the human family, harvest all cultural mindsets and skills from all around the world, past and present, that can help us now, in the hour of crisis and change.[59] Gar Alperovitz, introduced earlier in this book, professor of political economy, is one of many other scholars who embark on a quest to "harvest" from the diversity of economic arrangements and practices that already exist.[60]

Howard Richards is doing the same with his scholarship and activism.[61] Environmental epidemiologist Rosalie Bertell focuses on the most global level of engagement in working for the protection of the biosphere, the overall basis of human life.[62]

When Steve Jobs passed away, I was in Portland, Oregon, on the West Coast of the U.S.A. The news were filled with collective awe at Jobs' creativity, and how his path had encapsulated the American Dream and impressed the entire world. Media coverage exposed intimate details of Steve Jobs' life and opinions. For instance, Jobs seemed to have looked down on Bill Gates for lacking visionary creativity. Yet, we must admit that both, Steve Jobs and Bill Gates, were ruthless defenders of their territories, that they were formidable empire builders, and that they epitomize the image of entrepreneurship being connected to money as an almost sacred symbol of success.

Many of my American friends do not understand when I question their admiration of money. Some feel criticized and humiliated by my lack of enthusiasm for money, and my contention that true creativity, to flourish, needs much more freedom, freedom that is not to be had within the current paradigm of what we believe to be "reality." In Part II, I will explore some of the humiliating effects of contemporary economic and monetary arrangements.

What we need now is creativity, and space for creativity to thrive. New peer-to-peer models (P2P) already rearrange the order of priority of the *relational models* described by Fiske. They are supported by new information and communication technologies (ICTs) and part of a global reality of nonmarket practices.[63]

Author, educator, and activist Parker J. Palmer is all over the internet with the following quote:

> Democracy is a non-stop experiment in the strengths and weaknesses of our political institutions, local communities, and the human heart—and its outcome can never be taken for granted. The experiment is endless, unless we blow up the lab, and the explosives to do the job are found within us. But so also is the heart's alchemy that can turn suffering into compassion, conflict into community, and tension into energy for creativity amid democracy's demands.[64]

Martin Luther King, Jr. lived to "love and serve humanity."[65] To build creative bridges of loving mutual understanding, I make the effort to write this book. "Loving service to humanity" is what Linda and I work for together with our global network. This will also be the banner under which we, as humankind, we believe, will have to get together, unless we want to imperil our survival as a species. Love can provide the vigor that is necessary for change.

> *All progress is precarious, and the solution of one problem brings us face to face with another problem.*
> —Martin Luther King, Jr.[66]

Part II

Dignity or Humiliation?
That Is the Question!

Chapter 4
When Scarcity and Environmental Degradation Become Systemic

The sun, the moon and the stars would have disappeared long ago... had they happened to be within the reach of predatory human hands.

—Havelock Ellis[1]

When I grew up, I learned that capitalism is the best system, preferable to communism. The primary reason I was taught was that capitalism takes human nature seriously. I learned that we will take care of land, or of artifacts and objects, only when we feel a personal sense of ownership, and that this sense can only be created through the mediation of a market. I also was made to understand that the most important advantage of owning something is that "you are free" and "you can do what you want" with it. These were some of the *a priori* beliefs I learned to take for granted. Over the years, I came to wonder: what if these beliefs do not match reality, at least not in its fullness?

I recently saw documentary material about Ayn Rand (1905–1982) and her influence on Alan Greenspan and his colleagues, and her role for the global financial crisis.[2]

Ayn Rand, in her interviews, praises the 1917 February Revolution in Russia and the spirit of liberation from oppression that carried it. Then came the October Revolution, which hijacked the process and coopted people back into oppression. It did so, among other methods, by abusing the argument of altruism and asking people to offer themselves to the state. This is why Ayn Rand came to reject altruism and highlight the virtue of uninhibited self-interest. And her philosophy became "mainstream" due to her influence on some of the most powerful shapers of frames for human endeavor on the globe, including people like Alan Greenspan.

Clearly, Ayn Rand is a highly intelligent woman. When she speaks, she seems to replay her resistance to a painfully oppressive mother, something that might have made her somewhat defensive, hard, even arrogant, and opposed to and disdainful not just of oppression, but also of warmth and solidarity. Her arrogance may have been misperceived as mastery by her followers. When "mainstreamed," this misperception might have helped lend legitimacy to coldness throughout society.

Ayn Rand is quoted as saying "We can evade reality, but we cannot evade the consequences of evading reality." This lesson has been inflicted on her followers and on the world as a whole by the economic crisis. As economist Robert J. Shiller says: "We think we've got a good quantitative framework which takes care of all the risks, but it's missing something. It's a case where people believe the theory too much, and they were willing to make huge bets based on a theory that really wasn't right."[3]

The Arab Spring, the Occupy Wall Street movement, and all similar movements would benefit from learning from Ayn Rand's insights and her path. There are several lessons to be learned. The first lesson is that revolutions are vulnerable. As the February Revolution shows, together with many other revolutions before and after, liberation movements are at risk of being hijacked by the traditional dominator mind-set and their representatives, and this can happen very quickly, from February to October so to speak.

This lesson is important. For instance, the human rights revolution is continuously in danger of being hijacked. As discussed throughout this book, the ambiguity of the term freedom, unfortunately, "invites" hostile take-over, since it can be defined in so radically different terms. There is the Kantian and the Lévinasian interpretation of human rights.[4] The Lévinasian interpretation of human rights emphasizes care and respect for the other.[5] The International Covenant on Economic, Social and Cultural Rights that was signed 1966, and is in force since 1976,[6] for instance, is in resonance with the ethics of care.

If political rights of the individual person are foregrounded—and this effect is compounded when even corporations are treated as persons[7]—the Kantian interpretation of human rights as an abstract principle is highlighted. The recent ruling in the United States that corporate political spending is protected by the First Amendment right to free speech follows this line of thought. U.S. Congresswoman Donna F. Edwards pointed out that corporations are not people and do not have the right to buy elections: "We can have democracy in this country, or we can have great wealth concentrated in the hands of a few, but we can't have both."[8]

Also the Arab Spring is in danger. My Egyptian friends are worried. The system is still a Nasserist regime and the Arab Spring has yet to succeed, they say (preface). And the danger looms not just from outside a movement, also from inside. True believers are the ones most in danger. True idealists use to be among the first victims when power hijacks values. Joseph Stalin provides a ruthless example of "cleansing" efforts among the most dedicated of his own allies. Of many revolutions we remember only foulness; the memories of the idealism at their beginnings are crowded out.

A second lesson to learn from Ayn Rand's path is that liberation efforts often entail two steps, of which the first may be appropriate, the second much less so. It is here that Ayn Rand fell short. Often people's grievances and goals are valid, yet their proposed solutions are not. Often people identify ills correctly, such as the unacceptability of oppression. However, the path from being *against* perceived ills to shaping a comprehensive vision *for* a better life is a different matter altogether.

It is particularly critical when the path toward solutions is hampered by the emotional outfall of angry confrontation. Tunnel vision is not a helpful advisor. After watching Ayn Rand speak, I turned to Brooksley Born (see more in chapter 10).[9] Here was another extraordinary woman, standing up *for* a better world, yet, in a mature warm and inclusive manner. Ayn seems to have gone from a sense of dependence to independence, while Born made it into interdependence: Ayn went from dependence in an oppressive system to the independence of ruthless individualism, while Born attained relational interdependence.

The third lesson pertains to the metaphor of traffic lights (chapter 3). In the absence of traffic lights (no government), the strong take over. *Might* becomes *right*. Ayn Rand had sympathies for the 1917 February Revolution in Russia. She saw with her own eyes how quickly partnership movements for the common good can be hijacked by the dominator model. To use the traffic metaphor, the February Revolution was prevented from installing traffic lights that treated everybody equally; it was pushed aside by the October Revolution that implemented traffic lights that gave priority to particularly privileged party leaders. How could Rand believe that the solution would be to remove all traffic lights? How could she not see that whoever accumulated *might* would then push through their own rules?

The lesson I myself draw is that it is important to be cautious with whatever is "mainstream." I will never forget that Adolf Hitler was mainstream, for a while, in Germany. I have learned a lot from research in the field of intercultural communication. When cultural assumptions are called into question, a "stress-adaptation-growth" process unfolds.[10] Intercultural research indicates that creativity is enhanced through *interactions of mutually contradictory but equally compelling forces*.[11] Beth Fisher-Yoshida and Adair Linn Nagata have taught me much about *disorienting dilemmas*, dilemmas that unsettle our fundamental beliefs and call our values into question, something that can bring about transformative learning.[12]

When I began to study psychology and medicine, I learned "mainstream" psychology and medicine. I was in awe—and still am—of practices such as peer reviewing that define and maintain what is acceptable as mainstream. But I also lived a global life, was becoming part of many cultures. As a result, disorienting dilemmas mounted in my life. I asked myself questions like linguist Anna Wierzbicka, who wondered how it is possible to define "fundamental human emotions"[13]: Why does the Polish language, for example, not have a word for *disgust*? What if Polish was the language of psychologists working on the "fundamental human emotions" rather than English? Indeed, "it is puzzling why a language would fail to provide a single word for an important, salient, discrete, and possibly innate category of experience—if such exists."[14]

"Mainstream psychology," today, is Western psychology. I started learning Chinese in 1974, when I was twenty years old. I asked myself: What if China had continued with the immense naval expeditions of the Ming Dynasty sponsored between 1405 and 1433, long before Europe was even near Chinese levels of development? [15] China could have colonized the planet and we could live in a world colored by Chinese culture. Psychologist Tony Fang tries to explain this point in his work.[16]

Western "mainstream" psychology is now beginning to recognize its own biases and conceding the validity of non-Western viewpoints. The field of psychology detects that a culture of individualism, for instance, can go too far, and that a psychology that replicates a cult of individualism may not be very helpful (chapter 10).[17]

Indigenous psychology is an intellectual movement across the globe, based on the following factors:

1. A reaction against the colonization/hegemony of Western psychology.
2. The need for non-Western cultures to solve their local problems through indigenous practices and applications.
3. The need for a non-Western culture to recognize itself in the constructs and practices of psychology.
4. The need to use indigenous philosophies and concepts to generate theories of global discourse.[18]

Louise Sundararajan is a scholar in indigenous psychology. She suggests three innovative approaches to belief systems: first, emotion as meaning, second, cognition as dialogue, and, third, an aesthetic model of meaning making (based on Susanne Langer's integrative approach to feeling and form[19]).[20] Sundararajan looks for Charles Sanders Peirce[21] to weave these three threads into an integrative theory of belief, emotion, and health.

I have grappled with questions of this kind for the last forty years. Traditional societies are often characterized by oppressive ranked collectivism. Clearly, this is stultifying, and liberating people from these traditional beliefs increases health and well-being. However, collectivism also entails elements of social cohesion that merit preservation.

I lived and worked for seven years in Egypt, a society that might be labeled collectivist, and I deeply appreciate the love, solidarity, and sense of belonging that the social and psychological webs woven by large extended families can provide. My European clients usually suffered from loneliness, many agonized that nobody would care if they died; none of my Egyptian clients presented such problems.

I always was saddened when I saw "mainstream" psychology be slow to acknowledge that relationships are among the most important pillars of mental and physical health. It pains me when I observe that relationship building is still being ridiculed as "soft" in contrast to "earning money" that is supposedly a "hard" enterprise.

Jean Baker Miller's thinking was far ahead of its time. Linda Hartling worked closely with Jean Baker Miller.[22] Linda and I agree that among the most hurtful cultural myths of the West is the myth of the "lone hero." A lone hero can be a savior, however, also a raider, and an entire raiding culture may feel empowered by that idol.

In the following six chapters, I walk through some of the humiliating effects that seem to flow systemically from the present economic setups: (1) scarcity and environmental degradation, (2) ubiquitous mistrust, (3) abuse as a means, (4) debilitating fear, (5) false choices, and (6) psychological damage.

We begin with scarcity and environmental degradation. The Intergovernmental Panel on Climate Change (IPCC) is a scientific intergovernmental body that reviews and assesses scientific, technical, and socio-economic information relevant to climate change.[23] The IPCC shared the 2007 Nobel Peace Prize with former vice president of the United States Al Gore. The *Stern Review on the Economics of Climate Change* is the largest and most widely known and discussed report of its kind.[24] Economist Nicholas Stern is the chair of the Grantham Research Institute on Climate Change and the Environment at the London School of Economics and chair of the Centre for Climate Change Economics and Policy (CCCEP) at Leeds University and LSE. The review states that climate change is the greatest and widest-ranging market failure ever seen, presenting a unique challenge for economics.

Value in a market economy depends on scarcity.[25] The air we breathe is not sold to us. As the Cree quote at the outset of this book suggests, many indigenous peoples define the entire ecosphere as a commons that is "not for sale." Chief Joseph (1840–1904), chief of the Wal-lam-wat-kain (Wallowa) band of Nez Perce and renowned as a humanitarian and peacemaker, said, "The Creative Power, when he made the Earth, made no marks, no lines of division or separation on it," [26] and the Earth was "too sacred to be valued by or sold for silver or gold."[27] "Living Well" is an indigenous social system that is being mentioned throughout this book. It focuses on reciprocity between people and Earth.[28]

Why did Chief Joseph's philosophy not prevail, if it is so beneficial? Unfortunately, there is something called the *commons dilemma*. Common goods can only be protected when all participants commit to share the burden. Commons only remain commons when nobody rides free for personal gain. Colonizers did precisely that; they did not respect indigenous commons.

Ecologist Garrett James Hardin wrote a seminal article in 1998, in which he went as far as contending that the difficulties of protecting commons made it unfeasible to even try.[29] (We are beginning to understand today that commons can be protected if all of the vulnerabilities are taken into account, and the feasibility of protecting shared commons increases in conjunction with growing intercon-nectedness.)

In a context where protecting the commons has no social and societal value, but making money from sales has, scarce goods and services that are in high demand will yield the highest profit. This kind of scarcity can be "engineered" artificially.

I write these lines while daily news bring ever more shocking stories of American corporations hoarding urgently needed medical drugs in order to fetch higher profits.[30] Many more stories can be told, ranging from rather harmless to extremely harmful in their effects. Diamonds are a shiny example of rather harmless instances. Diamonds' hardness is natural, but not their value.[31] "If you don't support the price," said Andrei V. Polyakov, a spokesman for Alrosa, "a diamond becomes a mere piece of carbon."[32] In 1888, the diamond company De Beers stockpiled diamonds to keep prices high. In 1938, De Beers hired American public relations firm N. W. Ayer to sell the idea that "a diamond is forever" (entering the lexicon 1949) and a nonnegotiable symbol of courtship, prestige and love. Today, De Beers' grip has been broken by antitrust rulings. But the Alrosa corporation has taken its place.

The Cochabamba protests of 2000, also known as the "Cochabamba Water Wars," were a series of protests that took place in Cochabamba, Bolivia's third largest city, between January and April 2000. The government had sold the public water to Aguas del Tunari, a subsidiary of the transnational corporation Bechtel, in 1999. The company immediately announced an increase of 35 percent in water prices, which for many Bolivians meant that water was no longer affordable.[33]

Thomas F. Valone, engineering physicist with twenty-five years experience in emerging energy sciences, says the profit motive has cost humankind at least one hundred years of progress. Some (disputed) historical sources indicate that the profit motive hampered the work of inventor and mechanical and electrical engineer Nikola Tesla (1856–1943). John Pierpont Morgan (father of today's JPMorgan Chase financial institution) is reported to have refused to finance research on free energy. If such reports are correct, he only financed research that would enable him to "put a meter" on a product and sell it. In other words, tapping free energy (Tesla's aim) for the common good of all of humankind was not acceptable to Morgan and other proponents of the profit motive.

Engineers doubt the practicality of Tesla's visions, but he was never encouraged to develop or test those notions comprehensively. Astrophysicist Adam Trombly, at the International Tesla Symposium in Colorado Springs in July 1988, pointed out that if society had followed up on the inventions Nikola Tesla envisioned at the turn of the 20th century, there would be no fossil-fuel economy today.[34] Valone said, "The travesty is that the global warming we are experiencing is entirely unnecessary—if we would just pursue these alternatives that have been available for so long"[35]

Even if the details of Valone's and Trombly's analyses are subjected to the most rigorous reservations and might be altogether untrue and in need of being discarded, the gist of their message remains valid. Artificial scarcity in the service of the profit motive risks foreclosing appropriate technological adaptations and creates, perpetuates, and intensifies environmental degradation.[36]

The mere possibility that global warming could have been avoided if not for the profit motive, makes me feel deeply ashamed. It humiliates my very humanity. A *Zeitgeist* that blindly adheres to solutions that risk being destructive, ignores my dignity.

Not only research in engineering has a tendency to work within the confines and limitations of the *Zeigeist* in which it is embedded.[37]Academic research in general, including research in the field of economics, is affected as well.

In 2010, economist Richard T. Carson warned that environmental economists have "lost a decade or more" on the assumption that increased wealth automatically leads to an improved environmental situation.[38] The debate over the income-pollution relationship, Carson explains, encouraged developing countries to ignore their environmental problems while they develop, although it is clear that they could have taken many actions.[39]

When I reflect on this, I can understand that it is difficult for proud proponents of a *Zeitgeist* that supports the profit motive and its maximization to acknowledge they may be wrong. For some, the shame and humiliation of such an admission may be too great. Herbert Marshall McLuhan has been quoted earlier with his saying, "Only the small secrets need to be protected. The big ones are kept secret by public incredulity."[40] Perhaps secrets are also protected by unacknowledged shame and humiliation (see the research of Thomas Scheff[41]). To overcome mutual finger pointing and shaming, I suggest we ponder David Korten's words: "Today's borderless global economy pits every person, community, and firm in a relentless race to the bottom, as private economic power extends out and governments compete to attract jobs and investment by offering the biggest subsidies and the lowest regulatory standards."[42]

As I wrote earlier, the current state of world affairs humiliates me personally. As a result, I work for a new world. I make a point of working *for* new visions for a more viable future, rather than *against* outdated solutions of the past. I wish to invite everybody into this project. I believe that the future should not be sacrificed to combating wrongs and wrongdoers; it has to be won by proactively prioritizing the creation of *right relationships* for the future.

I suggest, it is time we begin to act in concert, not just locally, in the service of "we against them," but globally, in the spirit of "all of us." Morton Deutsch's research on cooperation (which is more than six decades old) has never been needed more than now.[43]

This is not to say that righteous anger is uncalled for. Anger can provide energy for constructive action, not just for destructive action. Buddhism teaches that the positive side of anger is that it is a "cleansing" emotion, allowing us to see clearly what must be done. *Conscientization* needs energy. As Frantz Fanon and Paulo Freire have explained, conscientization is a process by which individuals and groups refrain from imitating their superiors, refrain from "mimicry," and choose to build a common critical consciousness that enables political transformation.[44]

In the spirit of conscientization, Nelson Mandela did not use his righteous anger to get aggressive and humiliate his adversaries. Nor did he turn his anger inwards to let apathy or depression guide his life. He used it to spur his oppressors to respect him as an equal.[45] He honored what Mahatma Gandhi once formulated, "Hate the sin, love the sinner," or as philosopher Arne Næss put it: "There are no murderers, only people who have murdered."[46]

In Rwanda, the traditional Hutu servants—*Hutu* means *servant*—perpetrated a genocide against the former Tutsi aristocracy. In contrast, after 27 years in prison, some of Mandela's prison guards became his friends, assisting him as he led his country on a path of social and societal transformation.

Morton Deutsch is over 90 years old now. He has seen a lot. "Given the possibility of the prevalence of rage or fear among low power groups, it would be the goal of change agents to harness the energy created by feelings of rage and fear and convert it into effective cooperative action," these are Morton Deutsch's words.[47]

Oh beautiful for smoggy skies,
insecticided grain,
for strip-mined mountain's majesty
above the asphalt plain.
America! America!
Man sheds his waste on thee,
and hides the pines with billboard signs,
from sea to oily sea.

—George Carlin

Chapter 5
When Mistrust Becomes Ubiquitous

I'm not upset that you lied to me, I'm upset that from now on I can't believe you.

—Friedrich Wilhelm Nietzsche

Ralph Richard Banks, professor at Stanford Law School, wrote a book about why African-American women have difficulties finding marriage partners.[1] Banks explains that economically successful black men are relatively rare, which amplifies their "power" on the dating market so that they can "play the field" indefinitely, negatively impacting marriage.[2] The book was reviewed in the *New York Times Book Review* by Imani Perry, who observes that this book "is an alarm bell warning of the failure of American partnerships." Perry commends Banks for alerting us "to the consequences for families," because "the alarm rings beyond marriage, to a broader social collapse that includes distrust of neighbors, weakened social networks and community institutions, evictions, foreclosures, diminished opportunity, hostility toward those we deem different and skepticism toward enduring human connection. In short, the ties that bind need tightening."[3]

On July 20, 2011, Ireland's prime minister accused the Vatican of downplaying the rape and torture of Irish children by clerical sex abusers.[4] Kamran Mofid wrote:

I have read these articles [5] with great sadness. I suppose it saddens anybody who wishes to believe in the wisdom, beauty and relevance of religion/Catholicism to everyday life. Very sad indeed. Who may we have trust in today? The politicians, the bankers, the media, the press, the police, the judges, the priest...? Who? The teacher, the lecturer, the professor, the doctor, the surgeon, the dentist, the drug companies, the food suppliers and manufacturers, the car mechanic, the builder...? Why have we turned our world so untrustworthy and for what reason, and can we find happiness, joy and peace when we can trust nobody?[6]

Kathleen Morrow, while reading this manuscript, felt moved to contribute with her own personal experience (she gave me permission to share it here):

My father grew up poor, Irish and Catholic in Waco, a small Texas town (the site in the early 1990s of the Branch Davidian massacre), a member of a minority. As an adult, my father became rather successful, crediting much of his success to the concern and mentoring he got from the priest at his childhood church. That pastor was a part of my childhood. I knew him as a highly eccentric (he had a bad case of body odor, a problem that I remember the older members of my family devoting a great deal of time to trying to remedy) but very beloved older man, a part of my family's mythology. When my father was dying, we did our best to avoid Father Romer, who had a habit of accosting us in the hospital corridors to say a Rosary for my father's recovery. It was very touching and a source of solace and some humor among those of us who were watching someone we loved die. It grieves me to see this kind of trust destroyed.[7]

Vital questions: Who can we trust today? Which mistrust is unavoidable, simply because human nature is imperfect, and which mistrust has systemic roots that could be avoided by creating better systems?

Who is my doctor working for? Do I really need this medical treatment or drug and is it really safe? How can I be sure that he does not put profit first?[8] Why are baby bottles toxic?[9] Why are baby food advertisements so misleading?[10] Why do psychiatrists on drug makers' payrolls promote bipolar disorder in young children, a condition that was once thought to affect only adults and adolescents?[11] Why does nobody question the "medical community's enthusiasm for pathologizing entirely natural emotional responses to (among other things) humiliating experiences"?[12] The list is much, much longer.

Allow me to share what a friend recently disclosed to me. He had a serious medical ailment, and, protected by a substantial private health insurance, believed he was receiving the best of treatments. It took him many years to understand that his insurance had done him a great disservice. Had he not been such a lucrative patient, his ailment might have been a minor disturbance in his life. As it turned out, he did not receive the optimal treatment, but one that turned his acute condition into a painful decade-long condition. He simply had been too good a source of income to lose for his physician.

In a setting that gives primacy to profit maximization, systemic mistrust is called for. A culture that gives primacy to maximizing profit undermines ethical behavior.[13] It erodes the very reason for trust. And it does this systemically.

Yet, living in a world that forces mistrust upon its citizens by design, is inhumane and humiliating. It is not something we, as a society should allow to happen. It is destructive, not least since social trust is directly linked to health.[14] We understand that slavery causes a legacy of depression transmitted down the generations.[15] One might expect that the African-American *post traumatic slave syndrome* is the last of its kind. But research shows that as the Western world has become wealthier, instances of clinical or major depression have grown.[16] This suggests that a culture of ruthless individualism, where everybody races for maximum profit, brings more than what Forrester calls "economic horror."[17]

Interestingly, there seems to be a historical correlation between market economy and addiction. Mass alcoholism in Europe was not a problem during the Middle Ages. Yet, it began to rise with the beginnings of free markets after 1500. After 1800, when a free market culture became dominant, it became an epidemic.[18]

It is an ultimate irony that the pharmaceutical industry maximizes profit by feeding on the damages that flow from a culture that gives priority to maximizing profit. Indignity and humiliation are compounded by bandages that deepen it. "The Illusions of Psychiatry," is the title of a review of a related books.[19]

How could a culture emerge that creates systemic mistrust? Author Philip Delve Broughton wrote about his two years at Harvard Business School:

> In 1968, the *Harvard Business Review* published an article by Albert Z. Carr titled "Is Business Bluffing Ethical?"[20] It generated a slew of critical letters. Carr compared business to poker, in which bluffing, short of outright cheating, was a perfectly legitimate activity. He said that many successful business people lived by one set of ethical standards in their private lives and a quite different set in their professional lives. The explanation, he said, was that they perceived business not as an arena for the peacock-like displays of high ethical standards, but as a game with specific rules. Knowing that you could win the game of business playing all manner of tricks that you would never inflict on your spouse, children, or friends made for a calm, unstressed, uncomplicated life. But to some, it seemed to be an acknowledgment that business was fundamentally unethical.[21]

During the past decades, a culture of cynical disdain for high ethical standards as futile and vane "peacock-like display" expanded beyond the preserve of business schools in the United States. Lying and bluffing were increasingly regarded as "just a game" in many parts of the world, legitimized by the contention that this was acceptable since all knew it was being played. As a result *just world* thinking (the belief that winners deserve to win and losers, to lose, see also chapter 6)[22] and *blaming the victim*[23] became rife, and those who did not lie and bluff were disparaged as dim-witted.[24] The *lone hero* figure (chapter 4) had transmuted from savior to raider.

In postmodern America and Britain, writes physicist Jeff Schmidt in *Disciplined Minds*,[25] a new class of Americanized managers was bred, "to run the private and public sectors: the banks, the main parties, corporations, the BBC."[26]

Professionals are said to be meritorious and non-ideological. Yet, in spite of their education, writes Schmidt, they think less independently than non-professionals. They use corporate jargon—"model," "performance," "targets," "strategic oversight." In *Disciplined Minds*, Schmidt argues that what makes the modern professional is not technical knowledge but "ideological discipline." Those in higher education and the media do "political work," but in a way that is not seen as political.[27]

Author and activist Raj Patel joins this discussion with his book, *The Value of Nothing: How to Reshape Market Society and Redefine Democracy*.[28] "We've come to believe that the only way we can value things is by sticking them in a market," Patel says. "The trouble is, as we've seen through this recession, that markets are a tremendously bad way of valuing things, tremendously fickle."[29]

Indeed, "sticking things in a market" has been a strong thrust throughout that past decades. James Murdoch, son of global media baron Rupert Murdoch, "in a lecture to the Edinburgh Television Festival in 2009, attacked the publicly-owned BBC, declaring that 'the only guarantee of independence is profit.'"[30]

Murdoch is right. Prioritizing the maximization of profit does lead to independence, but only for a few, with dependence for the rest. If freedom means lack of regulations, profit compounds profit, and inequality ensues, trapping the majority in the power games of a few.

Richard G. Wilkinson was mentioned earlier. With epidemiologist Kate Picket, he showed "why more equal societies almost always do better."[31] Their conclusion is that bigger income differences create bigger social distances along the status hierarchy, and that increasing feelings of superiority and inferiority add to status competition and insecurity. Some of the causal links are the effects of chronic stress on the immune and cardiovascular system. They are increasingly well understood and underpin the relationship of income inequality to health. Similarly, the reason violence increases in more unequal societies is because inequality makes status even more important and the most common triggers to violence are loss of face, disrespect, and humiliation."[32]

Wilkinson and Picket write further:

Although people have often regarded inequality as divisive and socially corrosive, that did not prepare us for what we found. The frequency of all these problems was systematically related to income inequality. The bigger the income differences between rich and poor in each society, the worse these health and social problems became. And rather than things being just a bit worse in more unequal countries, they were very much worse. More unequal countries tended to have three times the level of violence, of infant mortality and mental illness; teenage birth rates were six times as high, and rates of imprisonment increased eight-fold.

The sense that inequality is divisive was shown by the fact that in more unequal countries, only about 15 percent of the population feel they can trust others, compared to around two-thirds in the more equal ones. That evidence was supported by relationships with social capital and levels of violence—all showing that inequality damages the social fabric of society.[33]

Many argue that profit maximization and equality are not mutually exclusive. Since a wealthy person is able to do good and give to charity, for instance, she decreases inequality. If this contention were true, the argument would be valid. Yet, headings such as "The Charitable-Giving Divide" point at a different reality:

> For decades, surveys have shown that upper-income Americans don't give away as much of their money as they might and are particularly undistinguished as givers when compared with the poor, who are strikingly generous. A number of other studies have shown that lower-income Americans give proportionally more of their incomes to charity than do upper-income Americans.[34]

Psychologist and social scientist Dacher Keltner says "the rich really are different, and not in a good way: Their life experience makes them less empathetic, less altruistic, and generally more selfish."[35]

John T. Cacioppo, director of the University of Chicago Center for Cognitive and Social Neuroscience, found in his research that only people who feel socially isolated tend to behave in concord with the

Homo economicus model of pure self-interest. People who feel socially integrated do not adhere to this model. People who feel socially integrated tend to forego pure self-interest when the common good is violated. "Altruistic punishment" is a term that signifies that "people are deriving personal pleasure from foregoing their rational self-interests and pursuing what is in the interest of the collective."[36]

In other words, the "two cornerstones of classic economic theory," namely the assumptions that individuals are "rational decision makers" and that individuals have "purely self-regarding preferences," "fly in the face of most psychological theories, where individuals are characterized by bounded rationality if not also by bounded self-interests." [37]

Philosopher Paul R. Diesing differentiated five forms of rationality: *technical* (efficient achievement of a single goal); *economic* (efficient achievement of a plurality of goals; *legal* (rules or rule following); *political* (referring to the rationality of decision making structures); and *social* rationality (integrating forces in individuals and social systems which generate meaning and allow action to occur).[38] Political scientist Robert V. Bartlett, added a sixth type of rationality, *ecological rationality.*[39]

Morton Deutsch and his colleagues suggest extending the concept of social rationality to include community or *global rationality.*[40] "*Complete rationality* would go beyond economic rationality and would require the integration of economic rationality with social (global) rationality and other forms of rationality as is appropriate to the specific situation of decision-making."[41]

In conclusion, economic theory builds on concepts of human nature that fit only those who, through a background of social isolation, fail to value and protect social cohesion. Current economic theory is misguided at best; at worst, it promotes social dissolution by rewarding behavior that exacerbates it. Social isolation and mistrust, in a malign spiral, are systemically brought to the fore.

Kamran Mofid asks the big questions that need to be posed in this situation:

> What is education? What is knowledge? What is wisdom? What is
> a university? What is the source of true happiness and well-being?
> What is the good life? What is the purpose of economic life?

What does it mean to be a human being living on a spaceship with finite resources? Is "sustainability" a buzz word? Is it simply fashionable to talk about a sustainable future, a sustainable education? How can the global financial system become more responsive and just? What paths can be recommended to shift the current destructive global political-economic order from one of unrestrained economic growth, profit-maximisation and cost minimisation, targets and bonuses to one that embraces material wealth creation, but also preserves and enhances social and ecological well-being and increases human happiness and contentment? How should we deal with individual and institutionalized greed? What are the requirements of a virtuous economy? What role should universities play in building an integrity-based model of business education? What should be the role of the youth? How might the training of young executives be directed to supply insights into the nature of globalisation from its economic, technological and spiritual perspectives, to build supporting relationships among the participants that will lead toward action for the common good within their chosen careers? What needs to happen next for sustainability to become more integrated into the ethos of business schools? What distinct roles should students, business leaders and business schools themselves take in advancing this trend? Who is leading this agenda and what elements of best practice can be shared from their example?[42]

We're never so vulnerable than when we trust someone—but paradoxically, if we cannot trust, neither can we find love or joy.

—Walter Anderson

Chapter 6
When Abuse Becomes a Means of "Getting Things Done"

Abuse often starts with praise.

—Japanese proverb

As discussed earlier, anthropologist William Ury's *simplified depiction of history*, widely accepted by the academic community, includes: (1) *simple hunter-gatherers*, (2) *complex agriculturists*, and (3) *knowledge society*.

In Ury's system, prior to 10,000 years ago, humans populated the world as wanderers and roamers. These hunter-gatherers lived in coexistent and open networks, within which conflicts were negotiated, rather than settled through coercion. The abundance of wild food represented an expandable pie of resources that did not force opponents into win-lose paradigms.

Ten thousand years ago, due to specific circumstances (such as *circumscription*, see chapter 3), complex agriculture emerged. Because land represents a fixed pie—land is either mine or yours—as soon as land became the basis of livelihood, a set of conditions arose that created a malign win-lose situation.[1]

As a result, the security dilemma became definitorial. The term *security dilemma* was coined by international relations scholar John H. Herz[2] (and has been expanded by many authors[3]) to explain why states that have no intention of harming one another may end up in competition and war. The very essence of the security dilemma is one of tragedy, forcing bloody competition to emerge out of mutual (and inevitable) distrust. Meeting the threat of preemption with preemption is the ultimate and seemingly inevitable outcome.

The win-lose frame and the security dilemma pushed agriculturalists into closed hierarchical pyramids of power. Riane Eisler, social scientist and activist, describes how otherwise widely divergent societies followed what she calls a *dominator* model rather than a *partnership* model during the past ten millennia.[4] From the samurai of Japan to the Aztecs of Meso-America, people lived in very similar hierarchies of domination and under a rigidly male-dominant "strong-man" rule, both in the family and state. Hierarchies of domination were maintained by a high degree of institutionalized and socially accepted violence, ranging from wife- and child-beating within the family to aggressive warfare at the larger tribal or national level.

Hierarchical pyramids of power were kept in place by codes of ranked honor. Each strata in such a pyramid has its own honor. The honor of aristocrats is different from the honor of underlings. In all cases superiors have rights that inferiors do not have.

A range of options is on offer when elites wish to subjugate underlings. The use of brute force is one option. However, over the course of the past 10,000 years, more "artful" methods of domination evolved—I call it "the art of domination"[5]—replacing brute force with more subtle and covert approaches. One such art was for masters to let nobody forget the fear entailed in the security dilemma. They instrumentalized this fear for their own advantage. Masters routinely instilled dread and apprehension in underlings and threatened them with violence and terror, from torture to killing. Over time, incessant humbling, shaming, and humiliating (honor humiliation, the form of humiliation that was seen as legitimate during the past millennia) became "sufficient" when underlings had learned to feel ashamed at failing their master's expectations. Sociologist Norbert Elias highlights in his *theory of civilization* how rough knights became noble gentlemen in this way.[6]

Kathleen Morrow, while reading this manuscript, thought of how American farmers first fled from bondage only to get caught later:

Farmers in the America of yesteryear were primarily free yeomen, independent and honored for that independence and for their contributions. I would posit that many of this country's early settlers were running from the agricultural hierarchical pyramid. It has only been in the past few decades that the emergence of corporate farming has oppressed the American small farmer.[7]

If we calculate that *Homo sapiens* emerged around 200,000 years ago, the era of complex agriculturalism represents the last five percent of human history, the past 10,000 years. At the current point in history, humankind finds itself in the middle of a second transition. For this transition, many factors flow together, factors that both drive the transition and are being driven by it.

As part of this second transition, the normative adaptation of the first is delegitimized. Human rights ideals represent a normative u-turn—no longer is the subjugation of the socio- and biosphere by small dominator elites regarded as "God-given"; the new ideal is respect, mutuality, balance, and dialogue among partners considering each other as equal in dignity.

The transition toward a world informed by the human rights ideal of equality in dignity is still waiting to be fully achieved. Humankind finds itself in the middle of an unfinished paradigm shift that sometimes proceeds one step forward, only to fall back again. It is as if the world is hanging in-between, clinging to old practices, while trying to reach out to new ideals, sometimes caught in the double standards of empty human rights rhetoric that merely serves as a cover for human rights violations.

The Western culture of ruthless individualism of the *lone hero* (chapter 4), for instance, can be conceptualized as an extension of the traditional hierarchical system, under the cover of human rights rhetoric of individual freedom. Distorting human rights rhetoric represents the most covert application of the "art of domination" hitherto achieved. Coopting underlings not only to accept and maintain their own bondage voluntarily, but to misrecognize it as "freedom" is the ultimate refinement of the art of domination.[8] An analysis of Ronald Reagan's policies in the United States of America can illustrate this strategy.[9]

In contexts that promote extreme individualism, the boundaries of the security dilemma are shrunk down to each individual's personal life. Through this shrinkage, every person is separated from her fellow beings. Everyone is forced into the Machiavellian "hominus hominem lupus est "("man is a wolf to man" or, more colloquially, "dog-eat-dog") relationships that in honor contexts are reserved to the power elites.

Ruthless individualism, ironically, is a collectivist project, rigidly enforced by the overall cultural context. Freedom does not entail the choice *not* to partake in this culture of individualism. There is no freedom to wish, for instance, for a society where people are encouraged to serve the collective. Freedom has shrunk to the freedom to partake in individualism.

I do admit that I smile when I hear Slovenian philosopher Slavoj Žižek use the close-door button in elevators as a symbol for the true range of freedom in the "political illusion-making machine" of Western individualism: the elevator doors do not shut faster, but the person who pushes this button has the illusion of using her freedom of choice.[10]

A culture of extreme individualism causes character to corrode, as sociologist Richard Sennett explains.[11] It weakens empathy—the glue that keeps societies together, as psychologist Jean M. Twenge's research shows.[12] Extreme individualism systemically creates narcissism, the narcissism of packaging oneself into a competitive saleable "product" in the spirit of "personal branding."[13]

Hans-Jürgen Classen, international management consultant, working mainly in Europe and Japan, comments on an article in *Financial Times* about the Narcissistic Personality Disorder (NPD)[14] as follows:

> Reading the article I found that this explains about all the things I have encountered in my job so far. My rough guess is that more than 50 percent of senior management in corporations is affected by this. In fact I now suspect that this disease is their primary motivational factor for climbing the corporate ladder. In politics, the ratio might be a lot higher still. If true, this is a scary thought, as it would mean that we are managed and governed mostly by people whose mental state is not appropriate to being in such positions in the first place.[15]

In the *Financial Times* article, a recruitment consultant for City of London companies, explains: "Narcissists are prime candidates in finance, because they are able to make quick, bold decisions without any thought for the consequences these might have on other people."[16] Indeed, a study shows that share traders are "more reckless than psychopaths": most recently, UBS trader Kweku Adoboli, for instance, allegedly made unauthorized trades that cost the Swiss investment bank billions.[17]

Faced with this situation, we may ask: Why does everybody agree dutifully when experts warn that "the best and brightest" will leave if they cannot amass money? Let them leave! They are *not* the best and brightest. We need to define excellence in entirely new ways.

Research shows that the damage voluntary bondage inflicts on people, though not as directly traceable as the damage of involuntary bondage, is still significant. During the past millennia, people in servitude often suffered physical abuse—from beating to torture to death. As the gap between rich and poor widens,[18] the "irrelevant externalities" of poverty and environmental degradation represent the physically and psychologically painful reality for the majority of the world's population.

Unfortunately, the resources and motivation for change are almost inaccessible in a culture of extreme individualism, particularly for those at the top of the global pyramid of wealth, where the pain is less palpable. However, psychological pain does occur, even among the most privileged. As mentioned earlier, clinical or major depression has grown as the Western world has become wealthier.[19] This may partly be due to new methods of diagnosing and documenting depression, it may also be due to people responding to drug company advertisements,[20] however, still it may qualify for what Philosopher Charles Handy calls "the corporate sin."[21]

While richer countries do tend to have happier citizens than poorer ones, once people have a home, food, and clothes, extra money does not make them happier.[22] Interdependent relationships of mutuality—rather than dependence or independence—make for purposeful lives of happiness; connectedness in mutually respectful relationships produces genuine satisfaction. A study indicates that individuals need at least £50,000 to compensate for not being socially connected with friends.[23]

In recent years, there have been numerous attempts to define and measure happiness, by disciplines ranging from neuroscience and psychology to philosophy, economics and social policy.[24] The U.S. National Bureau of Economic Research has just published data from a new survey showing that although many objective measures of the lives of women in the United States have improved over the past 35 years, measures of subjective well-being have declined both absolutely and relative to men.[25] This result is found across various datasets and measures of subjective well-being and is pervasive across demographic groups and industrialized countries. A new gender gap is emerging, with higher subjective well-being for men, replacing the gap of the 1970s when women reported higher subjective well-being.

To be used as a means, as pawns in a system that pretends to serve human well-being but does not, is profoundly humiliating for the humanity of all involved, even those who profit.

"What can the Ancient Greeks do for us?" is a question that draws the reply: "Socrates refused to be paid for his philosophical teachings. Just as charging for beauty, he argued, is prostitution, so it is that money cannot be exchanged for wisdom."[26]

Philosopher Immanuel Kant (1724–1804) insisted that a person must not be used as a *means*; a person must always be treated as an *end* in itself. He wrote in 1785: "Der Mensch aber ist keine Sache, mithin nicht etwas, das bloß als Mittel gebraucht werden kann, sondern muß bei allen seinen Handlungen jederzeit als Zweck an sich selbst betrachtet werden."[27]

Philosopher Martin Buber (1878–1965) developed a *philosophy of dialogue*.[28] It views human participation in two fundamentally different kinds of relationships—*I-It* and *I-Thou*. An I-It relationship is the normal everyday relation of a human being toward the things surrounding her. This can also include fellow human beings when they are used as means at a distance, or as parts of an environment. An I-Thou relationship, in contrast, is one into which a human being enters with her innermost and whole being, producing genuine encounters and dialogues. The latter approach dovetails with Kant's notion of treating other people as ends and not as means.

A culture of ruthless individualism undercuts all these reflections. It encourages a host of malign biases to distort mainstream culture. As soon as people adhere to a *just world* belief, for instance, they begin to blame the victim.[29] The belief in a just world provides an alibi for being blind to the sufferings of others, because "everybody deserves what they get." Since they see no injustice, people who hold the just world belief are indifferent to social injustice, even if they are genuinely interested in issues of justice.[30]

Loss aversion, the tendency of people to dislike losses significantly more than they like gains, plays into these psychological preferences. People do not mind sharing equally in the future, but they do not like to lose what they have gained in the past—fairness in the future is judged differently from fairness in the past. Experiments show that, contrary to the assumption that it is in the nature of human beings to grab as many resources as possible, people are willing to share resources equally.[31] In other words, those of us who have more, tend to justify this inequality. We define fairness as equal sharing as long as the sharing lies in the future; when we have accumulated more than others, we tend to believe we deserve it. These psychological phenomena strengthen conservative stances, leading us to regard those who argue for another distribution of resources as aggressors.

The Irresistible Pull of Irrational Behavior is the telling title of a book by Ori and Rom Brafman.[32] They explain how rational action is often undermined. In a system defined by the need to maximize profit, underpinned by a culture of ruthless individualism, it is to be expected that irrational behavior is portrayed as rational and realistic, while rational analysis is vilified as irrational and unrealistic. *What Is the Matter with Kansas*, is a book that dissects how voting against one's own interests is possible.[33]

A recent film, *Inside Job* by Charles Ferguson (2010), analyzes the dynamics behind the financial crisis, pointing at a cocktail of financial deregulations and near-psychotic behavior. It is the first comprehensive film about the economic crisis that broke in 2008.

The documentary *Home* has carried the Green Party in France to unprecedented strength.[34] The film served as a wake-up call, not least because it uses breathtakingly beautiful imagery to depict the dire state of our planet. The film recommends a new culture of moderation, intelligence, and sharing.

Home underscores the message that stakeholder value must come first—involving all stakeholders of the socio- and biosphere.[35] Shareholders must serve that primary value as *careholders*[36] and *sharegivers*,[37] because the inverse prioritization ultimately destroys everybody's habitat. Nature does not negotiate. It acts. Nature does not care about the discussion whether shareholder value has lifted people out of poverty or only enriched a few for a short while.[38]

The idea of stakeholder value, though old, has lost nothing of its relevance. Thirty years ago in Youngstown, Ohio, US Steel was going to shut down a major facility. Historian and civil rights activist Staughton Lynd led a protest movement by advocating the principle that stakeholders should have the highest priority.[39] His efforts failed.

It is time for new global and local efforts to protect all stakeholders, all members of the human family.

UA MAU KE EA O KA 'AINA I KA PONO O HAWAI'I
(rough translation: The constant, wet Rain Gives Life to the land and brings goodness/change to Hawai'i)

If just for a day our king and queen
would visit all these islands and saw everything
How would they feel about the changing of our land
Could you just imagine if they were around
and saw highways on their sacred grounds
How would they feel if they 'bout this modern city life

Tears would come from each others eyes as
they would stop to realize
that our people are in great, great danger now...

—"Hawai'i 78 Introduction" by Israel Kamakawiwo Ole'[40]

Chapter 7
When Fear Becomes Overwhelming and Debilitating

A politics of hope instead of a politics of fear...

—Barack Obama

Professor of psychology and industrial relations for 45 years, Vincent Lombardi (not to be confused with the American football coach), wrote in a personal message:

After 44 years of teaching at Michigan State University and now professor emeritus, I see the growing fear, anger, and loss of hope among our youth. Generally, citizens are more and more deprived of all personal power over the material world... of things necessary to sustain their lives and the lives of their families. No limits are placed on the pace of introducing new technology in the workplace, increasing economic efficiency by displacing labor and giving rise to increasing structural unemployment. At the same time, many hold a false ideology of an unlimited and absolute right to property that has given rise to pernicious levels of material inequalities. The loss of economic freedom in the lives of many is spawning a furtive revolutionary mentality suffused with confusion about the nature of social, economic, political, and moral reality. Envy, malice, and vindictiveness are rising. The crisis is worldwide.[1]

The crisis is worldwide. Evidence emerges from many sources and in many forms. Even if only ten percent of what Roberto Saviano or John Perkins have to say is true, it is profoundly worrying, reason for deep fear.[2] If the profit motive is so strong that it spurs its adherents to step on human lives, fear is called for per design. For a drug addict, getting the next fix is paramount, and even the addict's loving family relationships are betrayed. If the profit motive mindset of people in influential positions becomes similar to an addict's, it must come as no surprise when the outcome is disastrous.

As the present financial crisis broke, former Federal Reserve chairman Alan Greenspan famously said he was "in a state of shocked disbelief" and had been wrong in thinking that relying on banks to act in their self-interest would be sufficient to protect shareholders and their equity.[3] According to the thinking of David J. Rothkopf, a scholar and strategist referred to earlier, Greenspan's observation describes a system rather than individual aberrations. A small number (circa 6,000) of largely unelected powerful people have shaped the world during the past decades in ways that made the financial meltdown possible.[4] Their power considerations neglected long-term survival to the degree of self- and other-destruction.

Fear is mandatory in such a system, the only rational response.

While fear is on the increase, its lifesaving utility goes unused. Fear, even when it represents lifesaving caution, in a context of domination and raiding, is typically denigrated as a personal psychological problem, a personal weakness. Contemporary definitions of risk, courage, and rationality betray the sad fact that the human capacity to use the energy of fear to seek safety may have been damaged by the cultural training within the dominator societies of the past millennia. A male-dominant raiding culture means fearlessness, to the point of fearlessly engaging in casino capitalism with risky speculation, callous plundering of natural resources, or, as the nuclear power plant in Fukushima attests, even the risk of nuclear power disaster.

The response to terrorism is particularly complex. Taking the threat of terrorism seriously is derided as hysterical fear, for example, when the risk from nuclear power plants' insufficient protection against terrorist attacks is to be downplayed. The risk of terrorism may also be exaggerated when it serves to strengthen a raiding culture through military expenditure. Thus the risk flowing from terrorism is both dangerously played down *and* dangerously played up. If these dynamics ended in a reasonable balance, it would be acceptable. However, this is not the case. The result is that what should be done, is not done, and what should not be done, is done. What should be done, is neglected, namely the weaving of a healthier web of global social cohesion. What should be avoided, is not, namely, instrumentalizing terrorism as a pretext for artificially re-stoking the security dilemma and legitimizing a raiding culture.

Interestingly, the atmosphere in a raiding culture is that of terror.

I would like to quote from my doctoral dissertation and use the raiding culture of Somalia as an illustration:

> Consider an interview with Muusa Bihi Cabdi, Somaliland's Interior Minister until 1995, a man in his fifties, a tough man with a life experience that hardly any Western man or woman would have survived. He is a former nomad who trained as a small child to survive in one of the harshest environments of the world, Somali semi-desert. He recounted how he learned as a six-year-old boy to never really sleep, to always be alert to danger... and... to discern the traces of dangerous animals and enemy clans. Later, he left the desert, became a MIG airplane bombardier and studied in Russia. In the Ogaden war in 1978 he participated in the bombing of Ethiopia... Russia abandoned Somalia during this war and sided with Ethiopia, inflicting a humiliating defeat on Somalia. Somalia was subsequently supported by the United States and he studied also there at a military academy. When his Isaaq clan was threatened with eradication in the 1980s, he joined the guerrilla forces and became a commander, responsible for the lives and deaths of many. Later he became a minister in the government of Somaliland. I asked him what he would change if he could live again. He answers that he would change everything: "I was always in war, tribal war; looting each others' camels; as a kid I was raised in terror; I was six years old when I saw the first person being killed; when I joined army, there was always fighting, and I saw a lot of my friends being killed. If I could live again: not all these wars!"[5]

This quote illustrates how a raiding culture leads to a psychological atmosphere of terror that permeates the entire society. Terror is not just felt by the farmers who are raided by pastoralists, but also within a pastoralist culture. Somalia is a useful example also because it demonstrates that it is not the evil nature of its people—my Somali friends are wonderful people—but the overall cultural frame that is "guilty."

I felt this atmosphere of terror keenly when I did my doctoral research in Somalia. Alliances are fickle, promises are worth little, continuous mistrust is essential for survival. Nobody should be surprised that Somalia provides the world with pirates. If all adult males are noble warriors and raiders, they are all both perpetrators and victims, and fear and fearlessness define their lives. Nobody can escape it. The security dilemma plays out not only between clans, but between all adult males. And their women, even those who have a critical view of this kind of culture, have little room to escape and to develop alternative cultural experiences.

A culture of extreme Wall Street capitalism has similar effects. Continuous mutual mistrust and fear are called for, while it is taboo to draw the necessary consequences from this fear. The necessary consequence would be a joint effort to transform the entire cultural and institutional frame for the better. What happens, instead, is that everybody participates "fearlessly," thus increasing the terror instead of diminishing it.

The present overt and covert take-over of society by a raiding culture is to be observed in many walks of life. The take-over of business schools were perhaps the earliest manifestation (chapter 5, Philip Delve Broughton[6]). Juliet B. Schor, co-founder of the Center for a New American Dream, reported at the 31st Annual E. F. Schumacher Lectures in New York City, on November 5, 2011,[7] how Martin Feldstein, who had served in the Reagan administration, came to Harvard in 1984 and reshaped the introductory economics class "Social Analysis 10: Principles of Economics" (commonly referred to as "Ec 10") to implement neo-liberal teaching as mainstream economic dogma.

The recent trajectory of conservationist work is among the most fear-inducing examples. In an article titled "A Challenge to

Conservationists," anthropologist Mac Chapin describes the flow of corporate and government funds into the three big international organizations that dominate the world's conservation agenda—World Wildlife Fund (WWF), Conservation International (CI), and The Nature Conservancy (TNC)—and how "their programs have been marked by growing conflicts of interest—and by a disturbing neglect of the indigenous peoples whose land they are in business to protect."[8]

What Chapin summarizes in his article is a mirror of what has happened in many other segments of society during the past decades. Many agendas, not just the conservation agenda, have been taken over by corporate profit maximization interests.

Humanitarian aid, for instance, has been in the limelight. The list of criticisms is long. *Living on the Edge of Emergency: Paying the Price of Inaction* is the title of the most recent CARE International report by Amber Meikle and Vanessa Rubin (2008). Another provocative title is *Do No Harm: How Aid Can Support Peace—Or War* by Mary B. Anderson (1999).

When I carried out my field work in Africa, every humanitarian worker I met, particularly "old hands," had read the book *The Road to Hell: The Ravaging Effects of Foreign Aid and International Charity* by Michael Maren (1997). This book describes the slow destruction of a humanitarian worker's ideals and life.

Also education is being turned into a commodity. In the introduction, I mentioned that the total amount of outstanding student loans in America will exceed $1 trillion in 2011, and that Americans now owe more on student loans than on credit card debt.[9] "Academic Publishers Make Murdoch Look Like a Socialist," is the provocative title of an article that discloses that many academic publishers charge vast fees to access research.[10] Equally provocative is the documentary *College, Inc.*[11]:

Even in lean times, the $400 billion business of higher education is booming. Nowhere is this more true than in one of the fastest-growing—and most controversial—sectors of the industry: for-profit colleges and universities that cater to non-traditional students, often confer degrees over the Internet, and, along the way, successfully capture billions of federal financial aid dollars.[12]

The health sector is not exempted from being commoditized. Harriet A. Washington, a scholar of medicine and ethics, analyzes the pharmaceutical industry in her 2011 book as *Deadly Monopolies*.[13] "Gene Patenting Produces Profits, Not Cures" is the telling title of one of her texts.[14]

Childhood is being "sold," as Juliet B. Schor explains in her book *Born to Buy*.[15] As mentioned in the introduction, "desperate" marketers from Disney to Versace are aggressively targeting babies up to three years olds.

As to women's sexuality, I wrote in my book on *Gender, Humiliation, and Global Security*:

> Although women's sexuality is no longer a taboo subject in Western culture, we may question whether the sexualization of women's bodies in Western culture is liberating.[16]

> Mary Roach asks: When did sex research shift from prudish to freewheeling to corporate-controlled? How did this happen, and why?[17]

This is also the question I ask myself when I walk by news stands that "bruise my soul with the glossed-up pictures of naked female skin for the sake of the male portemonnaie."[18] I feel cold and fearful in such a world, and I think fear is the best and most rational reaction.

> *One of the things which danger does to you after a time is—, well, to kill emotion. I don't think I shall ever feel anything again except fear. None of us can hate anymore— or love.*
>
> —Graham Greene[19]

Chapter 8
When False Choices Crowd Out Important Choices

The hardest thing to learn in life is which bridge to cross and which to burn.

—David Russell

Social scientist and activist Riane Eisler calls for new social categories. She advises to go beyond conventional dichotomies such as religious versus secular, right versus left, capitalist versus communist, Eastern versus Western, or industrial versus pre- or post-industrial. We could extend this list with realism versus idealism, altruism versus egoism, self-interest versus common interest, collectivism versus individualism, unity versus diversity, big versus small government, visible hand versus invisible hand,[1] women versus men, globalization versus localization,[2] and so forth.

Unsuitable dichotomies create what psychologist Jean Baker Miller calls *false choices*.[3] What is needed, instead, is what Miller calls *alternative arrangements*.[4]

Philosopher Frithjof Bergmann has this to say about choices:

There is, in the foundational walls of New Work, two questions that stick out like knives: Yes or no, does freedom mean having choices, and if so are those choices as we experience them now hopelessly, abysmally less? Imagine you give a vegetarian the choice between pork and beef: just how much freedom have you bestowed with that choice? Any at all? Could picking political candidates only too often be like a choice between pork and beef? And when we shop, do we walk down long aisles and choose among a proliferation of junk that we do not want? I hope these questions throw a shaft of sunlight onto the question that so many, in one massed chorus, have asked: Free? Really? For the last 200 years? If we are free, then freedom has certainly not lived up to the expectations it once so gleamingly raised."[5]

False choices are created and kept alive in many ways. While the world collapses, many go shopping. *Panem et circenses*, "bread and circuses" (or "bread and games") was how the Romans diverted themselves from what really was at stake. Kathleen Morrow, when reading this manuscript, asked: "Evelin, are you aware that President Bush's advice to Americans after 9/11 was 'Go shopping. Don't let this horrendous event destroy our economy'?"[6]

Presumably, most people would agree it is not a good idea to succumb to being duped into powerlessness—and that whoever is guilty should stop playing the role of a useful idiot. We should assume our responsibilities, we, as humankind as a whole, if we are guilty.[7]

First, we need to better understand where false choices come from, and why we are so easily fooled.

False choices can be created and kept alive, among others, through the dynamics of humiliation. The heat of humiliation is not amenable to balanced moderation. It foments hot feelings and hot feelings lead to tunnel vision.[8] Cycles of humiliation can create dogma and enmity. They can create false choices between *positions*, obscuring that there might be important shared *interest* (negotiation theory teaches that *interest* may bring us together, when *position* separates us,[9] see also chapter 10). In this way, past humiliation can cloud contemporary deliberations and lead to faulty outcomes, which, in turn, have humiliating effects on everybody's future. One of the most toxic outgrowths of humiliation is what James Edward Jones, professor of World Religions and African Studies, calls the *post victim ethical exemption syndrome*[10] of "if they humiliate me, I can humiliate them."

An initial predilection to buy into narratives of humiliation may flow from personal experiences—childhood experiences of humiliation that color subsequent experiences. Collective experiences come on top—for instance, memories of the reciprocal humiliation that permeated Cold War times. Dogma and enmity, in turn, can be instrumentalized for divide and rule strategies. Adolf Hitler did this, as did the Hutu *genocidaire* in Rwanda.[11] Under the cover of remedying national and ethnic humiliation, they embarked on hijacking their countries' institutions.

In this book, we speak a lot about revolutions and how they may begin with a yearning for freedom and then derail. What we call "revolution" could be interpreted as an expression of a *Zeitgeist* shift that is in the making. Usually there is an avant-garde, then there is a majority who is undecided, and there are those who lag behind. A revolution is often propelled by the avant-garde. This avant-garde can, however, damage their own goals, when they push these goals too hastily and too aggressively. Liberation movements that are driven too combatively and too confrontationally risk unleashing cycles of humiliation that may discredit and throw back even the most urgently needed transition.[12]

My world-encompassing life has given me a first row seat for watching *Zeitgeist* shifts since my global embeddedness has provided me with a deep understanding of many cultural realms. In our Human Dignity and Humiliation Studies network, I often allude to the human rights revolution as "the first continuous revolution" in history, and also the first revolution that can't contend itself with only dismantling dominators. It must build systems of dignity, and it must do so with dignity.[13] Linda and I call it *walking the talk*.

History provides many examples of cycles of humiliation that have caused significant damage through creating false choices. I collected a number of cases in one of my books.[14] Among the most glaring and most far-reaching recent examples at the international level—far-reaching with respect to cruelty and suffering—is the humiliation Americans felt in response to a notorious incident in Somalia in 1993. The dead body of an American soldier was dragged through the streets of Mogadishu by an angry crowd. This incident turned America's intention to help the Somali people into a national humiliation. Consequently, America pulled out of the country.[15] Ultimately, this humiliation cost more than 800,000 people their lives (the number could be much higher). When the genocide started in Rwanda in 1994, the international community left Rwandans to slaughter each other because nobody wanted a "second Somalia."[16] Intervention versus non-intervention became a false choice through the dynamics of humiliation.

Dynamics of humiliation may also have informed the battle of "good against evil" that permeates American history from its early days and colors American behavior in the international arena.[17] American readiness to stand up against oppression is widely admired and welcomed when the oppression is real; it can be disastrous when the oppression is imagined. A sometimes blindly hateful American "dukes up" attitude may have its roots in trauma that has been transmitted throughout generations.[18] In many cases, the reasons many early American immigrants left "Old Europe" entailed personal experiences of humiliation. And American school children learn that the American Revolution was a liberation from British oppression.[19]

In one of my books, I dedicate large sections of one chapter to addressing American people and inviting them into collaboration with the rest of the world. When I worked as a clinical psychologist and counselor in Egypt, many American clients came to me (who happened to live there or travel through). I was astonished to learn about the great suffering that lies accumulated in American collective memory, not just of America's former slaves and indigenous peoples, but also of its white population. I paraphrase and summarize what I heard from my clients about this legacy:

Our forefathers did not emigrate to the United States because they needed a casual summer outing. They escaped from places in which they were unwelcome, misunderstood or even humiliated. By extraordinary bravery and perseverance they built a better world, a world that has become the target of global envy; envy entailing both negative and positive connotations. Anti-Americanism is the negative fall-out of this envy, while imitating America is its positive aspect. Both reactions confirm American pre-eminence. Our forefathers were once humiliated and victimized, but they prevailed. When we are humiliated and victimized now, we will prevail again. We regard those around the world who are able to appreciate our achievements as our friends, those who can't are weak souls or enemies.[20]

Readers in Europe often believe that Europe and America see eye to eye and together form the bulk of "the West." They may fail to be aware to what extent Europe may be despised as "Old Europe" (many will remember Donald Rumsfeld's remarks at the run-up to the 2003 Iraq war) and as "socialist Europe." Mitt Romney, candidate for the 2012 Republican Party U.S. presidential nomination, said, "What President Obama is, is a big-spending liberal. And he takes his political inspiration from Europe, and from the socialist-democrats in Europe. Guess what? Europe isn't working in Europe. It's not going to work here. I believe in America. I believe in the opportunity and in the freedom that is in America, opportunity and freedom. I believe in free enterprise and capitalism."[21]

Not just the international level is affected, humiliation can negatively impact also national cohesion. In the United States, feelings of humiliation feed *Southern honor*, and they hamper the relationship between its conservatives and progressives. Feelings of humiliation caused a "white backlash—especially Southern white backlash—against the civil rights movement… creating the opportunity for a major push to undermine the New Deal," write Paul Krugman and Robin Wells.[22]

The American civil war may have been fed by, and still feeds the *Southern Honor* that historian Bertram Wyatt-Brown describes in his work,[23] and explains in our annual "Workshop on Transforming Humiliation and Violent Conflict."[24] Social psychologists Richard Nisbett and Dov Cohen study the psychology of violence in the culture of honor in the southern part of the United States.[25] They examine the effect of culture on aggressive responses by comparing white non-Hispanic male violence in the American South with the North. The honor which Cohen and Nisbett observe is the kind that operates in the more traditional branches of the Mafia or, more generally, in blood feuds. David Hackett Fischer reports that Southerners in America "strongly supported every American war no matter what it was about or who it was against."[26] Recent American foreign policy, from the Reagan to the George W. Bush administrations, was legitimized by American Southern honor, or by the implicit logic "because they want to humiliate us, we must prepare to humiliate them." Indeed, Henry Kissinger is quoted as saying, "They want to humiliate us and we have to humiliate them."[27]

As to the relationship between American conservatives and progressives, Jean V. Hardisty has much to say. She is the founder and president emerita of Political Research Associates (PRA), a center that analyzes right wing, authoritarian, and anti-democratic trends. She has written a book titled *Mobilizing Resentment: Conservative Resurgence From the John Birch Society to the Promise Keepers.*[28] Hardisty found that conservatives yearn for one thing: respect. Many conservatives feel that arrogant intellectuals deny them this respect. The partisan rancor of the Tea Party movement, the speeches of American radio host and conservative political commentator Rush Limbaugh, or the Americans for Prosperity Foundation's annual RightOnline Conference (chapter 2) express a venomous resentment that appears to be fed by the dynamics of humiliation of the past, misprojected onto present problems and future fears. As a result, the United States are destabilized from within.

Incidentally, "socialism" and "capitalism" share considerable common ground. Historian Thomas Parke Hughes studied the Soviet Union in the 1920s and 1930s, and he shows that concepts such as the Five-Year Plan and the centrally planned economy were based on American Fordism and Taylorism.[29] Hughes describes how the common ground between America and the Soviet Union was later denied for the sake of the rivalry of who is better at humiliating the other.[30]

Still today, feelings of humiliation, including feelings of triumph over the collapse of the Soviet Union—triumph over having successfully humiliated a humiliator—might keep contemporary thought frozen in past choices and foreclose urgently needed thinking about radically different futures.

What is required now is global leadership that is aware of these dynamics and is capable of transcending them. United Nations Secretary General Ban Ki-Moon identified the world's single most destructive problem, when he said "the biggest crisis is a lack of global leadership." His speech was titled "A Call to Global Leadership." [31] Yet, as former president of the United States, Bill Clinton reported: "What works in real life is people getting together with different perspectives and figuring out how to solve problems. Cooperation works. What works in politics is conflict."[32]

Lack of global leadership is why nothing short of collective action from a global community can save us at the present juncture. New Rosa Parks and Nelson Mandelas must come together, carried by the *global street* (see preface and chapter 12). David A. King, from 2000 to 2007 the UK's chief scientific adviser, now director of the Smith School of Enterprise and Environment at the University of Oxford, emphasizes the uniqueness of this challenge, the need for global collective action.[33]

Morton Deutsch supported us in founding our Journal of Human Dignity and Humiliation Studies.[34] He wrote in 2006:

> The key problem with regard to the Universal Declaration of Human Rights is *implementation*. In part, lack of implementation results from oppressive-humiliating relations, where those in dominating power fear that they will suffer considerable material loss, as well as degradation, if the oppressive relations are replaced by cooperative-egalitarian ones. In part, lack of implementation results from the lack of awareness that relations need not be oppressive or humiliating, that such relations are not an inevitable and natural state of being which must be accepted. The lack of awareness, a political consciousness that a better relationship is possible, often exists among both the oppressed and the oppressors. In part, it results from our lack of knowledge of how to bring about the changes which would facilitate the peaceful, humane transitions from entrenched oppressive-humiliating relationships to more cooperative, egalitarian ones.
>
> Oppressive-humiliating relations exist at all levels—among and within nations, among and within religious and ethnic groups, between the sexes and within our various institutions (the family, school, workplace, political, healthcare, etc.). It need not be extreme and involve the legal system (as in slavery, apartheid or the lack of a right to vote) nor violent (as in tyrannical societies). It may take the form of "civilized" oppressive-humiliating relationships. Such "civilized" humiliations occur as a consequence of unconscious assumptions and reactions of well-

meaning people in ordinary interactions that result from unquestioned norms, habits, symbols and the embedded rules and stereotypes that exist in various institutions.[35]

When false choices threaten to undermine our future, the path to envision is the humble recognition of our limits, the path of humility in the spirit of the Buddhist notion of *abandonment of self*. Louise Sundararajan and the concept of cognition as dialogue were introduced in chapter four. Humility means recognizing that we are all part of a larger conversation, and that when we feel something is "right," this does not mean it is right, it only means that it makes sense in a certain context in a certain historical time period. The problem with beliefs is that they have two functions, says political scientist Robert Jervis.[36] First, we need beliefs to understand the world and test reality. Second, we need them to live with ourselves and with others.[37] The result can be dissonance—the emperor has no clothes and we don't dare to see it, let alone say it.[38]

Humility is what I advocate in all of my work. In my case, life itself has humbled me; displacement and a global life have stripped me, often painfully, of whatever arrogance I may have harbored. I humbly admit that falling for false choices is quickly done. Linda and I have a pact: we help each other see. Because nobody can escape the fact that we are all blind to our own blindness, per definition.

When false choices abound, it seems timely to ask, humbly, what the truly hard choices may be. Perhaps the truly hard choices are about a culture of raiding, since, if given space, it is so unusually "successful," at least in the short term? Free riding only needs callousness on the part of the raiders, and some degree of blindness or unwitting complicity on the part of the raided.

It seems timely that we, the family of humans on planet Earth, open our eyes and no longer are complicit in the game of raiders. As highlighted in many places in this book, raiding is bound to lose its feasibility as a strategy for success the more interdependent the world grows. Raiding "works" best in a fragmented world where victims are divided. In other words, there is a chance to do something about it now—if we unite.

It may be time to become aware that power elites all over the world use to resemble each other, whatever ideology they advocate, precisely because many of them are first and foremost raiders. First, they raid resources, and then they employ them to elevate themselves over the rest, while ideology provides the cover. The result is not happiness, not for the raiders, at least not in the long term, and not for the raided.

Indeed, we can observe elites of whatever color surrounding themselves with the trappings of aristocratic privilege, even if only in secret. Recently, Hitler's tax papers were found, showing that while he pretended to live the frugal life of an idealist, he was a multi-millionaire who refused to pay even minimum taxes.[39] In 2009, I wandered through the Waldsiedlung near Berlin, where Erich Honecker, German communist leader of the German Democratic Republic, while supposedly serving his people in modesty, took secret pleasure in luxury goods from the capitalist enemy. In the same year, I admired the impressive villas on Maui in Hawai'i. I saw that some of the wealthy have indeed understood what real quality of life is, and that they use their influence to stay away from the toxicity of mass produced imitations of luxury. In the case of Maui, the beach in front of the villas is left untouched, intentionally avoiding Waikiki glitz.

Again, perhaps the truly hard choices are about preventing a raiding culture to manifest, and insisting on dignity instead? Perhaps the truly significant choices are about refusing would-be raiders to rule through diversion and division? Perhaps it is time that we truly grasp the opportunity we face when an increase in global interdependence opens a window for us to guard the dignity of us all and our planet?

Gar Alperovitz, at the 31st Annual E. F. Schumacher Lectures in New York City, on November 5, 2011,[40] explained that as long as he talks about real grievances on the ground, people from all walks of life and political convictions tend to agree because they see their shared interest. The problem starts when he speaks about ideology. Then, we may add, dynamics of humiliation cloud clear analysis and create divisive ideological positions (and dynamics of humiliation may have been instigated to achieve precisely this aim).

Heeding Alperovitz' lesson means stepping back from ideological positions and considering our shared interest in giving our children a world worth living in. The significant fault lines do not run between anything like socialism and capitalism, but between a majority and a minority that uses the masses for their ends, plundering the commons.

Hitler used Aryan domination in response to national humiliation as bait for the masses. Casino capitalism is more direct; it advocates plundering as its main purpose and invites everybody to take their share of the spoil, making all believe that being among the victors, both as raiders and consumers of spoils, is serving the common interest. This is done under the banner of freedom for everybody not to be hindered by any "oppression" from above, be it an autocratic monarch, or a communist leader, or "big government." And this narrative feels particularly "right" in the United States, on the background of American historical experiences.

I recently witnessed the pride of the American sense of freedom in a split second: I was arranging fruit on a plate for a gathering. Instead of throwing away a slightly brownish but still eatable fruit, I ate it. I do not wish to waste valuable resources. My American friend cried out: "I would never do that! I am American! I do not have to eat food that is not perfect!"

I do understand Ayn Rand's visceral rejection of oppression. I also understand Americans' visceral rejection of the restrictions of "Old Europe" and any socialist or communist oppression. I am American when in Europe and European when in America—I see the need for more action when in Europe and the need for more planning when in America. And I understand how a government can become a hated enemy rather than "one of us." In continental Europe the government is "part of us" mostly in the North and this progressively wanes the further south one comes, until one arrives in Greece or Italy, where the government is typically not trusted. The exception is Britain. Anglo-Saxon culture is somewhat apart of Continental Europe. [41] Novelist Elizabeth Gaskell's book *North and South* makes palpable the imperialist raiding spirit of British aristocracy which seems to inform the City of London.[42]

What is the path for the future?

Perhaps it is time to acknowledge that whenever a society, including the global community, is not able to create governance structures that guard it traffic lights, to use the traffic metaphor (chapter 3), the result is structural indignity and humiliation[43] in an *indecent* world?[44]

Consumers, believing to be enjoying the spoils of the raid, may need to face the truth of the matter, namely that *they are the product*; social platforms like Facebook have made an art of this approach. And all this is kept in place by *panem et circenses* and an individualism that makes sure that the ruled stay divided.

Perhaps it is time to acknowledge that there are no easy choices. There is *complexity*. Yves M. Musoni from Goma, Congo, sent us the Kinyarwanda proverb "A bird cannot know where the sorghum is ready to harvest unless it flies" (chapter 3). He wrote to us about complexity (T. Irene Sanders has widely written on that topic[45]):

> Irene Sanders' book is like my bible. I can't separate myself from it. Since I read it, I learnt how to fly and understand deeply my community, my country, my region, my continent, and our global open world. To me, it is not questionable to think about researchers and academicians essentially, in terms of modern-day explorers in our terra incognita. I strongly agree with her that not one of us has ever lived in the kind of world we live in today, and none of us have ever been to the future, so like every explorer, each of us, in our own way, has something to share with others.[46]

For complexity to be respected and factored in, we need to open up space for *collective fantasizing* (Charles Villa-Vicencio on November 12, 2011, in New York City, see chapter 12). In that space we need to collect as many ideas as possible, and then test them. No longer should we allow rigid ideological dogmas be imposed on us. It is time now to look out for the relevant choices and not be misled into false ones.

How can we do that? Chapter 10 recommends what Linda calls *listening into voice*. Chapter 12 points at indigenous approaches to inquiry and consensus building.

Yesterday, I sat with Claudia E. Cohen, Associate Director of the International Center for Cooperation and Conflict Resolution at Teachers College, Columbia University. What she told me about the concept of the *wounded healer*, the need to avoid elevating "we, the helpers" over "you, the recipients of help," the need to deeply question mainstream categories and measures of "success" sounded like a template of healing for an impaired world at large.[47] Claudia works with formerly incarcerated in New York, and I was struck by the similarity with Carmen Hetaraka's work with incarcerated Maori in New Zealand.[48] What Claudia and Carmen have in common is deep questioning. They create new language and new concepts, since the reality of fragile communities who have fallen outside of mainstream categories does not fit conventional ideology.

Claudia Cohen is an expert of *participatory action research* (PAR), as is Maggie O'Neill. Maggie works with individuals, groups, and communities using *ethno-mimesis* to create change.[49] Maggie is a member in the global advisory board of our Human Dignity and Humiliation Studies network[50]: Maggie has a reputation for developing innovative culture work to imagine new ways of understanding and articulating the experiences of crime and victimization, that breach disciplinary boundaries and expand and enliven the methodological horizons of cultural criminology. Her theoretical concept of ethno-mimesis (the inter-connection of sensitive ethnographic work and visual re-presentations) is a methodological tool as well as a process for exploring lived experience, displacement, exile, belonging and humiliation.

Approaches such as ethno-mimesis may help us to constructively face feelings of humiliation. Feelings of humiliation which fueled the backlash among whites in the South of the United States, along with the feelings of humiliation left over from the Cold War, may destroy the future for all of humanity if we don't work through them. False choices, such as the alleged choice between socialism and capitalism, between left and right, or between big and small government must be transcended. Is it not rather suggestive that North Korea's government is too big and Somalia's government too small? Must not both, *too much* and *too little*, be avoided? There is no "choice" between one or the other.

A call for clarity seems timely: Let us stop having our views clouded by *panem et circenses* and by artificially stoked-up dynamics of humiliation. Let us refuse invitations into diversion and division. Let us refuse overlooking the truly relevant choices.

Let us humbly invest in collective questioning of which choices may be false and which imperative, and let us stay in this exploration. Rather than re-act in frantic re-actionism, let us act long term and wise. Let us stand for something.

Unless we stand for something, we shall fall for anything.
—Peter Marshall

Chapter 9
When Our Souls Are Injured by the *Homo Economicus* Model

The test of a democracy is not the magnificence of buildings or the speed of automobiles or the efficiency of air transportation, but rather the care given to the welfare of all the people.

—Helen Keller[1]

What is psychological damage? Can a whole society be sick? Is it possible that an entire society can be psychologically damaged? Can a society damage its members?

All of us, "we participate in a culture where one thing is preached and another thing done," writes author and psychotherapist Carol Smaldino.[2] Carol is a deep thinker, and she always reminds our Human Dignity and Humiliation Studies network of our *shadows*, and of the need, if we want to grow, to face our shadows rather than gloss over or turn our backs on them.[3]

Yves M. Musoni, another deep thinker in our Human Dignity and Humiliation Studies network from Goma, Congo,[4] wrote to us:

In Rwanda, before 1994, more than 60 percent of the population called themselves Christians. However, in the Tutsi genocide, many—if not the majority, including the "men of God" (Priests, Bishops, Pastors, etc.) who used to preach love—failed to build the bridge between words and actions. Many killed Tutsis essentially, even in the church. As I see it, the Tutsi genocide was more than a festival. It was like a national party which took more than one hundred days off. It is not questionable that many Rwandans, including religious leaders enjoyed to kill the victims of the dynamic genocide of Tutsis like Girumuhatse who confessed to Philip Gourevitch[5] that for him, it became a pleasure to kill. The first time he said, it was to please the government. After that, he developed a taste for it:

> I hunted and caught and killed with real enthusiasm. It wasn't like working for the government, it was like working for myself." He said, "I was very, very excited when I killed. I remember each killing. Yes, I woke every morning excited to go into the bush. It was the hunt-the-human hunt." And he said, "The genocide was like a festival. At day's end, or any time there was an occasion, we took a cow from the Tutsis, and slaughtered it and grilled it and drank beer. There were no limits any more. It was a festival. "We celebrated."[6]

Musoni concluded his message by stating that he strongly believes that, globally, we need to change our ways of thinking if we want to prevent our many conflicts, wars, genocides, or international terrorism, if we want to protect ourselves from *hegemocide*. He coined this term to explain one of the many reasons the majority of Hutus might think that *identicide*,[7] or wars against Tutsis or "Nilotic people" in the Great Lakes Region of Africa, may be justifiable.

What Musoni alludes to is *méconnaissance* (misrecognition), *naturalization*,[8] and the *penetration* that results from "implanting the top dog inside the underdog,"[9] or what I call the "art of domination."[10] To illustrate this, I often use the example of Chinese foot binding, a practice that is now outlawed: for an entire millennium, Chinese women were willing to mutilate themselves for the sake of a ruling elite's preference for lotus-shaped feet.

The art of domination's sad "success" is glaringly manifested in such horrific atrocities as in Rwanda, but it also affects the "normal" lives of citizens in parts of the world that consider themselves "developed." It may not always be as shockingly evident as in Rwanda, but this must not mislead us to overlook it. This is a quote from a recent article in the *New York Times*:

> Unfortunately, many companies now keep head counts and resources to a minimum and this makes progress a struggle for employees. Most managers don't understand the negative consequences of this struggle. When we asked 669 managers from companies around the world to rank five employee motivators in terms of importance, they ranked "supporting progress" dead last. Fully 95 percent of these managers failed to recognize that progress in meaningful work is the primary motivator, well ahead of traditional incentives like raises and bonuses.[11]

People say that "incentive matters" and that nobody would work if not pushed or pulled—either humiliated into compliance or rewarded with incentives.

I resonate with Mohammad Yunus when he says that thinking of humans as largely self-interested, resource-maximizing beings is too narrow (see also chapter 5).[12] His view is in line with philosophers Martin Buber's work on the *philosophy of dialogue*, Emmanuel Lévinas (1906–1995) work on the *face of the other*,[13] or Victor Frankl's emphasis on *meaning*.[14]

As alluded to in the preface, I feel personally humiliated when I am expected to act one-dimensionally, as mere *Homo economicus*.[15] I am multi-dimensional and, first and foremost, I am a *Homo amans*, a loving being.[16] My happiness does not increase with more money. My psyche works according to the *Easterlin Paradox* (observed by economist Richard Easterlin[17]) that posits that more money does not necessarily create more happiness. For me, it is sufficient to attend to basic material needs. I do not draw any motivation and any meaning from striving for more *status* through rank or monetary remuneration. I strive for more *stature* as a human being, embedded into our human community, and in its service.

Author Charles Eisenstein wrote:

> Wherever I go and ask people what is missing from their lives, the most common answer (if they are not impoverished or seriously

ill) is "community." What happened to community, and why don't we have it any more? There are many reasons—the layout of suburbia, the disappearance of public space, the automobile and the television, the high mobility of people and jobs—and, if you trace the "why's" a few levels down, they all implicate the money system.[18]

Seymour M. (Mike) Miller is an economic-political sociologist and activist. He wrote to Linda Hartling: "My book of 40 years ago (with Pam Roby), *The Future of Inequality*, was one of the first books to broaden the discussion of poverty, long before Noble Prize economic winner Amartya Sen (who was initially opposed to that broadening)."[19]

Miller is the co-author of *Respect and Rights*, author of *The Fourth Way*, and co-founder and board member of United for a Fair Economy.[20] He is also the director of the Project on Inequality and Poverty at the Commonwealth Institute, Cambridge, Massachusetts, and a member of the advisory board of our Human Dignity and Humiliation Studies network. He is deeply worried about his country, America:

If it is widely accepted that expanding one's household's consumption is the dominant need and goal, then aiding those less fortunate by paying taxes used for social programs gains less support. If a major concern is competitively out-doing one another in home, furnishings, dress etc, then it is difficult to think about the deterioration that is occurring outside our somewhat privileged enclaves. If Americans aspire to buy more and more personal things, they will be reluctant to support taxation to enhance the public structures and amenities of the nation.

The materialist urge is likely to overwhelm societal and thereby political attention to broad national needs and interests. Politicians are reluctant to draw attention to issues that will not receive high positive responses. Materialism focuses people away from national needs to personal acquisitions.

It contributes to the atmosphere of financial speculation and instability that economist Hyman Minsky stressed as one of the great dangers of the current stage of capitalism. The over-spent American, to use Juliet Schor's phrase, may threaten the stability of the economy. The high-spending of materialist consumption may result not only in boom periods but in deep or prolonged recessions ... American life is distorted by dreams of McMansion life. Qualities of cooperation, mutual support, and connections among people are driven to the background as people believe that the achievement of big money and luxury living resolves most issues. The accumulation of goods threatens the goal of lessening inequalities. For inter-household comparisons of accumulations do not promote the idea that all people should be more rather than less similar in conditions.

Particularly disturbing, says Miller, is that so much attention goes to the consumption of popular culture. The result is diminishing action on important issues. He refers to the book *Bowling Alone*, where its author Robert Putnam charges television-watching (and now internet and cell phone addictions) as drawing people away from the civic involvement that characterized earlier generations. Miller continues:

High consumption of goods also interferes with efforts to improve environmental conditions, an important objective. It threatens the environment because of what and how goods are produced, distributed, serviced and disposed. High consumption resulting from materialist feelings is a major obstacle to improving the environment.

Commercialism, merchandising, advertising are the offspring of materialism. The flood of advertising, the reliance of the media on advertisers, the insidious penetration of commercial ways of thinking into all realms corrupt American society. (In the U.S. over a trillion dollars a year are devoted to advertising, a sizable slice of GDP.) It encourages thinking in terms of oneself and family, not of our joint needs, interests and obligations to others. (Poet John Milton in *Il Penseroso*: "Hence, vain deluding joys.")

Are materialism, commercialism and popular culture rivaling ancient Rome's use of *bread and circuses*? Are materialism and pervasive popular culture involvements dampening democratic, grass-roots actions?[21]

Why do people accept a humiliating culture? Philosopher, sociologist, and historian Michel Foucault coined the term *governmentality*[22] to describe a novel kind of governing that emerged in Europe during the sixteenth century when feudalism (an earlier form of governmentality) was failing. Governmentality was made possible again through the creation of specific (expert or professional) "knowledges" as well as the creation of experts, institutions and disciplines (for example, medicine, psychology, psychiatry).

As it seems, governmentality proceeded from overt oppression to covert cooption, through the "art of domination" mentioned above.[23] Writer, journalist, and political commentator Walter Lippmann (1889–1974) called the "manufacture of consent" a "new art" in the practice of democracy.[24] His contemporary, Sigmund Freud's nephew Edward Louis Bernays (1891–1995), spoke of "engineering of consent." [25] He combined Freud's psychoanalytical concepts with the work of Gustave LeBon on crowd psychology and Wilfred Trotter's ideas on the instincts of the "herd."[26] To expand the market for cigarettes, for instance, he persuaded women to smoke, using images of women smokers as models of women's freedom. He became one of the founders of the PR industry. Sociologist and economist Thorstein Veblen (1857–1929) coined the phrase "conspicuous consumption."[27]

In chapter 8 of my book *Emotion and Conflict*, I summarize:

The success of covert manipulation rests on the human dependence on tacit knowledge, which, in turn, makes humans inherently vulnerable to méconnaissance. And méconnaissance can be efficiently enforced by the manipulation of emotions and meta-emotions. Whoever has sufficient power-over leverage will find it advantageous to introduce ranked honor as master manipulation, because it makes might seem right, and inferiors susceptible to more manipulation. If done cleverly, these manipulations will penetrate, and underlings will debase their dignity, damage their health, and risk death "voluntarily." The overall strength of emotions and the human need for belonging and recognition figure as powerful liabilities in this process…This need makes people vulnerable to being malignly and stealthily turned into handicapped and …harmless inferiors in ranked systems—if people believe that they can increase their sense of belonging by climbing up the ladder in a ranked system, even at the cost of mutilating themselves, they may fall for this trap and do so (foot binding as stark example). I call this process voluntary self-humiliation to highlight that it can be unmasked and undone, even though I am aware that it would be more correct to say that people are unwittingly manipulated into self-humiliation.[28]

The situation can also be viewed from other perspectives. Children are taught by adults to forgo too short-term and too self-centered gratification. Good parenting means training one's children to widen their horizon and to think in ways that are more socially inclusive and long term. "Growing up," or "being an adult," means being able to act responsibly in the long term not just for oneself but also for one's loved ones. At the societal level this "parental" mentoring work is partly delegated to the judiciary and affiliated services. Their role is to nudge or even force citizens to act in ways that society at large considers to be "mature" and "grown up."

Clearly, the judiciary can only fulfill its role if society stands behind it. Nazi Germany demonstrated how societal standards can be depleted when its citizens do not stand *up*, but stand *by*.[29] During the Nazi years in Germany, a small group of leaders manipulated their followers into believing that everybody had to sacrifice for the *Endsieg* ("final victory"). At some point the judiciary was affected. From the population at large to willing judges to the legal system, everybody and everything was manipulated in a malign direction.

If we wish to avoid going down similar paths today, it is important to understand the justifications used for manipulation. Elsewhere in this book, the dominator culture of the past 10,000 years was described. In a context of collectivist ranked honor, domination is valued as something that brings recognition; victory is equivalent to having achieved domination. During the past millennia, success in domination, in the contexts of strong-men societies, was "proven" by showing off the dominator's ability to amass resources, be it by building ever more and ever bigger palaces, be master over ever larger animal herds, or filling a *harem* with ever more women.

In such a context, the most radical way to participate is to topple one's superiors and become the new top-dog. Another way is to imitate one's dominators' ways towards one's own inferiors, for instance, beat one's wife, children, and other subordinates. Yet another way is to obtain or imitate elite symbols. Through all these means, one can signal being part of the elite and try to participate in the recognition elites receive.[30]

Many examples illustrate how far imitation can go and how costly it can be. The above-mentioned outlawed Chinese tradition of foot binding is among the most evocative examples. It shows the price in terms of health and quality of life that people are willing to pay for status. Because a ruler liked the lotus-shaped feet of one of his dancers, for an entire millennium, Chinese women suffered.

I myself have witnessed many related examples during close to 40 years of global life. When I lived in Egypt, a good Egyptian friend had come to some wealth. When I first met him, together with his wife and their ten children, they lived in the midst of a maze of buildings that had organically grown in the village near the pyramids of Giza. The family was part of a large web of neighborly relationships. His wife, daughters, and neighbors used to sit in the courtyard of the house and cook their communal meals together. He and his family were accustomed to lounging on cushions and soft padding on the floor in their living room in the evenings, watching television together.

Yet, with money came a subaltern sell-out of quality of life. The new house was removed from the village, in a compound behind high walls, with a guarded gate. It was a concrete "box" filled with pitiful imitations of Western furniture, Louis XIV or XV styles, still a status symbol left over from the time of French colonizers passing through Egypt (in the rest of the world, "international" hotels betray a similar subservience to the most recent "high" culture, that of Versailles). The new house was packed with chairs and fauteuils that nobody of the family ever sat on. The master of the house, my friend himself, sat in front of the furniture, on the carpet. This was his usual custom, also when he received Western guests, whom he proudly placed in his fancy sofas. The only purpose of this furniture was to cater to and impress Western guest. The new house had a modern kitchen, but it soon fell into disrepair because it stood for an alien concept of preparing meals. And for their evenings, the family had no alternative but to huddle in the small, windowless corridor on their carpets to recapture some of the life they were used to living, misplaced in their own fine new house. What was I to say, when my friend proudly showed off his new house, that he had created for the likes of me?

In the street where I lived in Cairo, there was a woman with many children, who was very poor. Like many Egyptians, she did not have sufficient resources to buy meat. She and her family had beans for protein. She ate fewer beans and let her children starve, to save money to buy a little bottle of Coca-Cola once a month. Drinking Coca-Cola gave her the feeling of being part of the rich West. "Coca-Cola tastes sweet and gives status," she explained to me. In her eyes, the satisfaction she gained from this monthly bottle of Coca-Cola offset the damage she inflicted on her own health and the health of her children.

When I worked at the American University in Cairo as a therapist, a young Libyan student came to me. He was depressed. His father had just lost his oil fortune. Now the young man could no longer afford to be with his friends. They would do things like decide in a split second to get a Learjet to hang out in a top discotheque in New York. I asked him whether he had actually enjoyed this kind of jet set life. No, he said, it was shallow, boring, and stultifying; it was literally a golden cage. It caged its victims in cult-like rituals that had to be crazy and pricey to maintain the sense of superiority that bound them together. So, he did not miss the glitz so much, he said. But he could not bear his friends' contempt as he could no longer buy their status. His bottle of Coca-Cola had been sex and drugs in a golden cage so to speak, and it had tasted sweet and it had bought him status.

Something similar seems to have happened during the past decades with our economy (see Rodrigue Tremblay's concise chronological summary[31]). Catering to the childlike desire for quick gratification is very tempting. It tastes sweet. Gamblers fall for that temptation, even though they know that gambling is dangerous to financial and social health, just as consuming too much sugar may trigger diabetes or drugs may destroy the body.

World society, during the past decades, was manipulated into believing that gambling can be sustainable. This manipulation was brought about by the abuse of the term freedom or liberty (namely freedom for gamblers and their "innovative" financial "products"). "Greed is good!" Oliver Stone's film *Wall Street* made the motto of the *corporate raid* known to the world.

The manipulation of the past three decades dovetailed with whatever remnants were left from the traditional dominator culture of the past millennia. As a result, we see now the success of (at least) two cultural manipulations:

- during the past 10,000 years, it was legitimate to try to gain recognition through domination by means of overt oppression and covert manipulation;
- during the past 30 years, overt oppression has become less legitimate, while covert manipulation has established a culture of "freedom for the casino".

The resulting set of values could be summarized as "domination is good," and "domination achieved through gambling is even better," which, in many ways, became the value guiding the business schools and lobbyists who pushed it into law.[32] In this way, even though we are not binding our feet, we are binding our entire existence on planet Earth.

Imitating elites, scrambling for their recognition and favors, competing for who appears to be part of them best is as unwise as Chinese foot binding. It is doubly unwise. First, it damages health, and second, elites do not regard imitators as genuine elite members. Frantz Fanon describes his path from trying to be more French than French to realizing that the French will never accept him even if his imitation is perfect.[33] Clamoring for elite recognition is not only costly, it is also futile.

When certain values, benign or malign, are enshrined in culture and enough people are successfully coopted, it is difficult to introduce change. It may take major catastrophes to unmask malign values, such as the demise of Nazi Germany or the present economic crisis. Therefore, the first sentence in my book *Gender, Humiliation, and Global Security* went as follows: "The economic crisis that broke in 2008 has changed the path of this book."[34]

There is no alternative—humankind must create new visions for arranging life on Earth. Economist Kamran Mofid issued a *Call to Action* on November 17, 2011. He reminds us of a time during the American Revolution, when things looked very dire and impossible, and when Tom Paine wrote: "These are the times that try men's soul's. The summer soldier and the sunshine patriot will, in this crisis, shrink from the service of his country; but he that stands it now, deserves the love and thanks of man and women. Tyranny, like hell, is not easily conquered; yet we have this consolation with us, that the harder the conflict, the more glorious the triumph..." Mofid continued, in the spirit of many voices around the world: "This is another of those times. Our souls are being tried. This is our opportunity to stand firm, to show our perseverance and fortitude. This is a time our children and grandchildren will sing about. Their ballads will praise us for bringing them the world we all deserve."[35]

What is there to do? In the previous chapter, we spoke about acknowledging *complexity*, using *ethno-mimesis, listening into voice*, and *collective fantasizing*.

Michael Britton draws our attention to the role of *empathy*. He is one of the directors of our World Dignity University initiative. He has lectured internationally on the implications of neuroscience for our global future, and provides training for conflict resolution specialists on applications of neuroscience to their work. He draws a map of the neurological aspects of the shift from competition to nurturing that is needed and how it is incomplete as long as empathy is missing:

> What is required is not just a shift within the instinctual brain from competition on behalf of dominance, and from scrambling for position in a resource-controlling hierarchy, to a nurturing feel for each others' lives, it requires a shift in the way our distinctly human brains go about being smart: a shift from looking for opportunities for ourselves to grasping the lives of others as they themselves know their lives. The nurturing instinct without empathy is blind and therefore likely of little use to anyone.[36]

Part of practicing empathy could be to make a list of the people to whom we will have to apologize in 30 years—or in one generation. For what will we have to apologize to our children? For what will we have to pay reparations?[37] It took the Catholic Church three hundred years to apologize to Galileo Galilei (1564–1642). Finally, on October 31, 1992, Pope John Paul II expressed regret for how the affair with Galileo and his heliocentric model had been handled and officially conceded that the Earth was not stationary.[38]

Apologies may be due for fraudulent credit ratings.[39] Bankers owe humankind apologies. UK city minister Lord Myners said it was "unrealistic" that bankers should expect to be paid million-pound bonuses. He told bankers "to come back into the real world" (after Royal Bank of Scotland directors threatened to resign over bonuses).[40] Shareholders may need to apologize to stakeholders. Stakeholder value must come first—involving all stakeholders of the entire socio- and biosphere. As discussed earlier, shareholders must serve that primary value as careholders and sharegivers, because otherwise everybody's habitat is in danger. An apology may be due for the destructive consequences caused altogether by the profit-maximizing paradigm sold to us under the guise of Adam Smith's "invisible hand."

In sum, apologies may be due from all those who exploit the long-term common good for their own short-term gain and from those who hinder alternative arrangements.

Change is on its way. Judith E. Glaser, author of Creating We,[41] has just reviewed five "best books of 2010,"[42] and concluded: "In the past, in mainstream publishing, you could not mix business topics with personal effectiveness topics. But these books confirm that the barrier has fallen. By integrating research from the fields of neuroscience and psychology into books about business challenges, their authors give us a new lens through which we can more effectively and successfully navigate our complex, unpredictable world."[43]

Seymour M. (Mike) Miller's advice for America is as follows, an advice that other parts of the world could heed:

> Politicians are more oriented to election and reelection than to supporting what is in the best interest of the nation. What

structural changes in electioneering (e.g., limits on contributions, public finance of campaigns, free TV time for campaign presentations) might support moral behavior by politicians as well as deepen democracy?

James B. Quilligan was a policy advisor to former German Chancellor Willy Brandt. He has been an international economic consultant for three decades. As director of the Centre for Global Negotiations, he is the American coordinator for the Convention on the Global Commons. He shared the results of the UN Conference on the World Financial and Economic Crisis, June 24–26, 2009:

> The immediate crisis we are facing is to shift from seeing energy, nature, food and water as monetized commodities to recognizing them as reserve values that are essential for our survival and well-being. Only then shall we understand that money is a cultural creation expressing the intrinsic value of these commons—and not a function of the marketplace or of a Central Bank. The creation of a new international monetary system is just around the corner and global value must be integrally informed by human beings, culture, the environment and energy, which means a complete rethinking of all our values for a fair, inclusive and sustainable globalization supported by an authentically new and resilient multilateralism.[44]

Miguel d'Escoto Brockmann has been the president of the 63rd session of the United Nations General Assembly since September 16, 2008. He was tasked with organizing the UN High-Level Conference on the World Financial and Economic Crisis and Its Impact on Development, which was called for by participants at a financing for development meeting held in Qatar in late 2008. He emphasized that the outcome document "will make it or break it," urging that the text should not be another kind of "international charade" that will come to nothing.[45]

Yes, we will make it or break it.

While there is "substantial evidence that post material value changes have occurred"—these are sociologist Anthony Giddens' words in his book *The Third Way*[46]—will they continue when economic difficulties shape the 21st century?

Or is a *Fourth Way* needed, as Mike Miller sketches it out for America?[47] Miller writes:

> Can anti-commercialism, anti-materialism, pro-environmental issues become political as well as moral questions? Involvements in activities, closer relations with others, may reduce the concern with buying, displaying, comparing, emulating. Can community activities build attachments to others?

> The changing situation of the United States should lead to an even more challenging set of goals than extending, defending and improving New Deal and Great Society objectives and programs, important as they are. Floors, doors and connections parts of the *Fourth Way* point the way to new policies and a better America.

> Conservatives, progressives, independents, the Republican and Democratic parties widen your sights! The quality of life counts. Even politically.[48]

After this journey through the labyrinth of some of the consequences of current economic arrangements, intended and unintended consequences, Part III will open up the stage for the future.

As Mike Miller says: "The quality of life counts. Even politically." To extend Judith Glaser's conclusion, we will see more barriers falling in the future. What we call "a company" is part of a larger context. This larger context is our true capital. Our true capital is the *We*, where we all are *in company* with each other.

We must all learn to live together as brothers or we will all perish together as fools. We are tied together in the single garment of destiny, caught in an inescapable network of mutuality. And whatever affects one directly affects all indirectly.

—Martin Luther King, Jr.[49]

Part III

What Should We Do?
Let Us Unite As a Human Family!

Chapter 10
We Need a Panoply of New Strategies for Dignism!

Never doubt that a small group of thoughtful, committed citizens can change the world. Indeed, it is the only thing that ever has.

—Margaret Mead

Sony Kapoor, former investment banker and derivatives trader, now an analyst of the economic crisis, said in a keynote speech:

> We must remember the story of emperor Midas, who had the famous "Midas touch," where everything he touched became gold. The only problem was, he couldn't eat gold, he couldn't drink gold. He tried sleeping on gold, it wasn't very comfortable. I would say the same thing of the financial industry. Except it is more accurate to say that everything they have touched has become dust. But the fact remains, you cannot eat finance, you cannot drink finance, you cannot sleep on finance, you cannot drink and drive finance. Finance only exists to serve the real economy. Let us put it back where it belongs and make it work.[1]

Who could put the real economy back where it belongs?

Attorney Brooksley Born is an exceptional woman. From 1996 to 1999, she was the chairperson of the Commodity Futures Trading Commission (CFTC), the U.S. federal agency that oversees the futures and commodity options markets. Her story is brought to a wider audience in a 2009 Frontline documentary titled *The Warning*. This film breathtakingly follows Born's thwarted efforts to regulate the derivatives market. Born's predictions for the future are a wake-up call: "I think we will have continuing danger from these markets and that we will have repeats of the financial crisis—may differ in details but there will be significant financial downturns and disasters attributed to this regulatory gap, over and over, until we learn from experience."[2]

Present-day institutions, particularly global institutions, as it seems, are adapted to a bygone past, not fit for the interconnectedness of the present world, and not helpful for the creation of a socially and ecologically sustainable future. The ecosphere is troubled by dangerous climate change, while the sociosphere is troubled by debilitating inequality. The cumulative cost of climate change (the estimate is $3.75 trillion in the UK by 2050) and the cumulative cost of high levels of inequality (the estimate is $6.75 trillion for the UK in 2050) are prohibitive.[3]

Vandana Shiva, scientist, environmentalist, and food justice activist, was named one of the seven most influential women in the world by *Forbes* magazine. She has been "fighting corporate takeover in every area in her native India, combating a nuclear plant one week and patented, genetically modified seeds another."[4] She calls on the American people to "see that corporations have abandoned them long ago" and that "the people will have to rebuild democracy as a living democracy."[5] She agrees with Albert Einstein that "problems cannot be solved with the kind of thinking that created them."[6]

Vandana Shiva is only one among many voices that get ever louder in reminding us that everything is related and in resonance—relationships, processes—that nothing is separate and separable, and that this is what we have to learn to respect. We have to overcome the "corporate state" and embed business into the human community, the Earth community, Vandana explains. Gandhi's key concepts of *swaraj*, *swadeshi*, and *satyāgraha* are the way to live peacefully, equitably, and sustainably on this fragile planet. *Swaraj* means "self governance," *swadeshi* "the ability to make and to produce," and *satyāgraha* "the courage to say no to unjust law"—satyāgraha is a term that combines *agraha* (firmness/force) and *satya* (truth-love).

If we look at our present world and should describe it to a visitor from another planet, how would we describe it? Perhaps as follows:

> Primacy is given to investors. Investors are "excited" about projects that offer prospects of good return on their investment. Investors look out for "feeling a kick" from new horizons for new investments opening up, in other words, investors get excited by maximizing profit. This is, after all, what being an investor means. Projects are "made possible" through funding. Funders decide what is possible. Projects that funders deem unworthy of support, will not be possible. Even lifesaving projects will not be possible. What is *work* and what is *dream* is decided by funders.

Do we really want to deliver ourselves and our world to funders? Are they the best leaders of our world? Is this the best way to manage our affairs on our planet? Will this provide us with a healthy life on a healthy planet? What if we all get excited, jointly, by the prospects of working together for maximizing the common good, for a worthy and dignified future for our children?

The economy should exist in order to serve human beings

That the economy should exist to serve human beings and not the other way round is an ethical claim supported by ethical schools from all around the globe, present and past. It is supported, for instance, by the traditional African philosophy of *ubuntu*, "I am because you are: I am human because I belong, I participate, I share." *Ubuntu* resonates with many other philosophical and religious thought, among them the *integral human development* of the social teachings of the Roman Catholic Church. Nobel Prize winning economist Amartya Sen confirms that the market is one instrument among others, and not always the best instrument, for achieving human development.[7]

Artur Manfred Max-Neef, a Chilean economist and environmentalist, explained that "you would be inclined to think that … greed … should be of people who have nothing. No, quite the contrary. The more you have, the more greedy you become."[8] He advises teaching the following principles to young economists:

1. The economy has to serve the people; people should not serve the economy.
2. Development is about people and not about objects.
3. Growth is not the same as development and development does not necessarily require growth.
4. No economy is possible in the absence of equal system services.
5. The economy is a subsystem of a larger finite system, the biosphere, hence permanent growth is impossible.[9]

Economism is the belief in the primacy of economics. "Ensnared in an economic cosmos, we increasingly draw on economic theory, or economism, to explain reality and guide our choices. Indeed, economism even colors the language of science as researchers employ its terms to communicate concepts to the public." This is what Richard B. Norgaard, professor of energy and resources and of agriculture and resource economics at the University of California in Berkeley writes.[10] His vision for the future includes:

Our challenge is to develop a new vision for the way we conduct ourselves on earth—something as different from industrial civilization as it was agricultural civilization before it. A new ecological awareness is critical to this new vision, and for this reason the term ecological civilization resonates well. The concept of social justice has proven robust in spite of the spread of economism, and we need to maintain its centrality in our ecological civilization. While the notion of the public good has not withstood economism, the notion of "the commons" has, and it needs to be developed more fully as part of our new vision. The rise of ecological awareness has trained us to recognize complex systems, which are at the heart of a future ecological civilization. But complexity does not imbue us with the sense of humility and reverence we will also need to undertake the shaping of a new civilization—that reverence we experience on seeing the night sky in all its starry grandeur. In a sense, the whole effort to counter the devastating effects of economism is like searching through the smog for a clear expanse of night sky that enables us to witness once again the brilliant shining stars. [11]

In a previous chapter of this book, Stéphane Frédéric Hessel, French wartime resistance hero was quoted. He "cried out" against Nazism in the 1940s. Today, he calls on people to "cry out against the complicity between politicians and economic and financial powers" and to "defend our democratic rights."[12]

On February 8 and 9, 1943, members of the "Weiße Rose," a group of young intellectuals who aimed to overthrow Hitler, formulated three principal theses:

- The war is lost for Germany.
- Hitler and his followers continue with the war only for the sake of their personal safety and are prepared to sacrifice the German people for that goal.
- All opposing forces must mobilize to end this war as fast as possible.[13]

If we replace the word "war" with the phrase "onslaught on the world's socio- and biosphere," and "Germany" with "humankind," then we might have the description of current affairs that Stéphane Hessel perceives.

Juliet B. Schor, co-founder of the Center for a New American Dream,[14] spoke at the 31st Annual E. F. Schumacher Lectures in New York City, on November 5, 2011.[15] She explained that the most important task at hand is to "avoid ecological overshoot." Yet, she asked, how can we reduce ecological impact and at the same time create jobs? Is not this an unsolvable dilemma? Schor presented three possible pathways—simplified as (1) optimistic, (2) pessimistic, and (3) in between. She explained that to her view, optimists (1) who believe that the dilemma can be solved by green growth, such as *cradle-to-cradle* approaches,[16] may be overly optimistic. Yet, on the other side, pessimists may be overly pessimistic. It is not true that "nothing works," she said, since, small countries in Europe did achieve some growth with green energy. The new economy approach is that of "savvy economists," somewhere in the middle, standing for a new economic model and a new way of living, namely a *plenitude economy*. Away from overworking and overspending—not least since less working hours increase quality of life and decrease ecological overshoot—toward *do it yourself* (DIY), sharing, bartering, neighborhood exchange, re-use, re-sale, altogether toward we, the people, building social capital instead of a borrow-and-spend consumer culture.

As a result, Schor concluded her talk, "we can treat one another and the planet with the respect we all deserve."

In drawing on philosopher Frithjof Bergmann, Schor advocates *high-tech self provisioning*.

> We can reduce reliance on the market by meeting basic needs (income, food, housing, consumer goods, energy) through a series of creative, smart, high productivity technologies: growing food (using permaculture and vertical gardens), creating energy on a small scale (convert a Prius to a plug-in and double gas mileage), building homes with free labor and local, natural materials and using new Fab-Lab technologies (small, smart machines that make almost anything). Schor looks at examples of people already practicing self-provisioning and converting their skills into money-making ventures.[17]

Author Charles Eisenstein formulates his vision for a better future somewhat similar to Juliet Schor. He contends that "community is nearly impossible in a highly monetized society like our own."[18] The reason being that "community is woven from gifts, which is ultimately why poor people often have stronger communities than rich people."[19] Since, "if you are financially independent, then you really don't depend on your neighbors—or indeed on any specific person—for anything. You can just pay someone else to do it."[20]

Geneviève Vaughan has spoken out for a gift economy since a long time (chapter 11).[21] A gift culture is now rising in the social realm. "Many of us no longer aspire to financial independence, the state in which we have so much money we needn't depend on anyone for anything," formulates Eisenstein.[22] I could not agree more with him. After all, the rediscovering of communal love is the core message of my *Gender, Humiliation, and Global Security* book. Eisenstein explains:

> Today, increasingly, we yearn for community. We don't want to live in a commodity world, where everything we have exists for the primary goal of profit. We want things created for love and beauty, things that connect us more deeply to the people around us. We desire to be interdependent, not independent. The gift circle, and the many new forms of gift economy that are emerging on the Internet, are ways of reclaiming human relationships from the market.[23]

Eisenstein observes that we actually see a gift culture emerge every time there is an economic recession. People can no longer pay for various goods and services and they begin to rely on friends and neighbors instead:

> Where there is no money to facilitate transactions, gift economies reemerge and new kinds of money are created. Ordinarily, though, people and institutions fight tooth and nail to prevent that from happening. The habitual first response to economic crisis is to make and keep more money—to accelerate the conversion of anything you can into money. On a systemic level, the debt surge is generating enormous pressure to extend the commodification of the commonwealth. We can see this happening with the calls to drill for oil in Alaska, commence deep-sea drilling, and so on. The time is here, though, for the reverse process to begin in earnest—to remove things from the realm of goods and services, and return them to the realm of gifts, reciprocity, self-sufficiency, and community sharing. Note well: this is going to happen anyway in the wake of a currency collapse, as people lose their jobs or become too poor to buy things. People will help each other and real communities will reemerge.[24]

Eisenstein admits that withholding natural or social resource from being converted into money will hasten economic collapse, however, on the other side, he suggest, it will also mitigate its severity.

> Any forest you save from development, any road you stop, any cooperative playgroup you establish; anyone you teach to heal themselves, or to build their own house, cook their own food, make their own clothes; any wealth you create or add to the public domain; anything you render off-limits to the world-devouring Machine, will help shorten the Machine's lifespan. Think of it this way: if you already do not depend on money for some portion of life's necessities and pleasures, then the collapse of money will pose much less of a harsh transition for you. The same applies to the social level. Any network or community or social institution that is not a vehicle for the conversion of life into money will sustain and enrich life after money.[25]

Economist Gar Alperovitz, at the 31st Annual E. F. Schumacher Lectures in New York City, on November 5, 2011,[26] confirmed the point that is also central to this book, namely that is of crucial importance to refrain from demonizing those who believe that neo-liberal solutions are useful. We need to accept, he explained, that many noble and honorable people are deeply convinced that the neo-liberal path is the only useful and effective one. Yet, as also mentioned in chapter 2, the most hard-line neo-liberal must consider, Alperovitz suggested, that the present distribution of wealth is medieval: The richest one percent of households owns nearly half of all investment assets, and five percent have 70 percent.

In agreement with Juliet Schor, Alperovitz sees a future in which we work less. Interestingly, he reports, this is a point his students do not like to envision at all. Working only ten hours per week? What should they do with their lives?! Likewise, his students do not wish to think of planning, he reported, and that he has to invest much energy into explaining that systemic change is necessary (see also chapter 12). Indeed, he was asked the same question from the audience after his lecture, "Why is systemic change needed, when creating local cooperatives is possible?" He explained that local cooperatives are being destroyed by the market. He suggested considering the example of the Basque Mondragon initiative and how they struggle to survive.[27]

Alperovitz called on progressive liberals in the US and social democrats in Europe to place community first and turn away from losing energy in the Band-Aids of within-the-system regulatory efforts and short-term "projectism."[28] Alperovitz concluded with putting forth a *pluralist commonwealth* as the answer, with urban land trusts, conservation land trusts, community-supported agriculture, community gardens, community development corporations, public pension funds, and municipal part-ownership.

Howard Richards was introduced earlier in this book. He suggests an *ethical economy* or a *plural economy*. He writes: "Any ethical criterion defines what should be, and thus implies or states norms and goals. Norms and goals are at some times best served by one institutional form, and at other times best served by a different institutional form."[29] He proposes:

> Let us think about micro-enterprises, micro-credit, trainings, businesses owned and managed by their own employees, the social responsibility of business, stakeholders, socializing natural resources, popular education, education for peace and justice, the organization of grassroots communities one neighbourhood at a time, non-profit day care centres, fair trade, organizing unions, permaculture, urban agriculture, social entrepreneurship, barter networks, local currencies, ethical banking, consumer cooperatives, credit unions, production cooperatives, health cooperatives, funeral and burial societies, joint buying, joint bread-baking, economic empowerment of women, municipal enterprises, NGOs and non-profit foundations, social movements, community gardening, public social safety nets, putting to use unused lands and buildings, recovering indigenous and peasant lands illegally stolen, restoring ancient traditional forms of cooperation and sharing, the defence of the public sector and in some cases reversing privatizations for example of water supplies. These are typical practices of social humanism in Latin America today.[30]

Howard Richards follows Charles Taylor (1993) in using the idea of *constitutive rules*—see also John R. Searle (1969)—and characterizes the *constitutive rules of the modern world-system*—see Immanuel Maurice Wallerstein (1974)—as the rules of a *bargaining society*.[31] Richards summarizes:

> Transformation as distinct from reform changes the constitutive rules. *Ubuntu*, a traditional philosophy of Africa which according to Desmond Tutu holds that "I am because you are: I am human because I belong, I participate, I share," is cited as a source of different and transformed constitutive rules of a type badly needed to empower humanity to escape the grip of *systemic imperatives* (Ellen Meiksins Wood (2003), *irrational rationality* (Herbert Marcuse (1968), and what John Maynard Keynes called "confidence" (John Maynard Keynes (1936), chapter 12). The very constitutive rules of our society drive us ever deeper into social chaos and ecological catastrophe because there is a rationality gap: a gap between a so-called "rationality" constrained by the laws of economics, and a wider rationality of cultural creativity constrained only by the physical laws of nature. These same points could be made in terms of "paradigm"(Thomas Samuel Kuhn (1962), or "basic cultural structure" (Howard Richards and Joanna Swanger (2006) but here I make them in terms of "constitutive rules." Humanizing methodologies in teaching and in social research play an indispensable role in working for the deep culture shift that is needed."[32]

Form must follow function

How can a transition be brought about? *Form* must follow *function*. Or, as negotiation theory expresses it, *interest* must guide negotiations, not *position*.[33]

"Form must follow function" is the guiding principle for international environmental governance. *Decision 25/4* on international environmental governance was adopted by the Governing Council of the United Nations Environment Programme (UNEP) on February 20, 2009.[34] As a result of *Decision 25/4*, the Governing Council established a regionally representative, consultative group of ministers and high level representatives, which convened on June 27 and 28, 2009, in Belgrade, and on October, 28 and 29, 2009, in Rome. The meetings were co-chaired by Stefania Prestigiacomo, minister for environment, land and sea of Italy, and John Njoroge Michuki, minister for environment and mineral resources of Kenya. The co-chairs' summary was titled "Belgrade Process: Moving Forward with Developing a Set of Options on International Environmental Governance."

The work of the consultative group was set out in paragraph seven of the Belgrade Process, guided by the following basic concepts:

- Any reform to international environmental governance should be based on the principle that form should follow function;
- Consultations on functions will lead to a discussion on forms that could range from incremental changes to broader institutional reforms;
- The international environmental governance debate should be addressed in the broader context of environmental sustainability and sustainable development;
- Developing a set of options for improving international environmental governance should follow from a fresh examination of multiple challenges and emerging opportunities;
- Incremental changes to international environmental governance can be considered alongside other more fundamental reforms;
- The work of the consultative group should continue to be political in nature.[35]

What the Belgrade Process illustrates is the need for more truly *functional* psychological, social, and cultural mindsets in the world community. These new mindsets, in turn, should inform the implementation of systemic change that can provide the world with global *decency*.[36]

The transition now required must be a multi-thronged *dignity transition* (chapter 3) with at least two core moves (using Max Weber's *ideal-type* approach,[37] see also chapters 2 and 3). First, the rift between the two branches of what Paul H. Ray and Sherry Ruth Anderson call the *cultural creatives* movement must be overcome.[38] Those who turn their attention *inward* to gain new levels of consciousness, and those who turn it *outward* as activists need to transcend their former mutual antagonism. People who contend that peace starts within, and that we need to first develop our inner consciousness before we can go out into the world and work for peace there, need to understand that there is not enough time. We cannot wait until a significant majority of the world's citizens has become Thích Nhất Hạnhs bottom-up. We should also not pin our future on the unlikely probability for a few gifted Mandela-like individuals to emerge by chance and lead us. And we can certainly not wait for the politicians of our time to implement necessary changes top-down. A simple bottom-up and top-down approach would not suffice, it must be an intertwined bottom-up and top-down approach.

Peace within is only the beginning: now it is time for action. Part of that action will be to take those who resist—Ray and Anderson call them the *traditionals* and the *moderns*—into the future.

For the *dignity transition*, a large enough group of committed citizens (1), in the spirit of Margaret Mead's words quoted at the outset of this chapter, must muster sufficient awareness of global responsibility to implement new global institutional frames (2) of *inclusionism* and *dignism*. This group of committed citizens (1) must come from all levels, ranging from civil society to the gatekeepers of political and economic institutions, and must implement new global institutional frames (2) that give new *form* to global institutions, form that is *functional* for an interdependent world and that serves the *interest* of all of humankind, not only the *position* of a few (to use the language of negotiation[39]), in short, frames that can produce a *decent* global society.[40]

The development of decent institutions (2) is paramount because they can drive feedback loops that foster global cooperation in a systemic rather than haphazard way. Any subsequent move will have the advantage of enjoying support from the system, rather than depending on the unpredictable emergence of Mandela-like social change agents.

The first loop, the initial implementation of new institutions, would be helped if the world had more "non-violent revolutionaries,"[41] more Nelson Mandela-like individuals who could "nudge" the world's systems into more constructive frames in the spirit of Margaret Mead's words.[42] Nobel Peace Laureate Jody William's campaign to ban landmines, for example, expressed this spirit. The International Campaign to Ban Landmines (ICBL) organization ultimately achieved its goal in 1997 when an international treaty (Ottawa Treaty) banning anti-personnel landmines was signed in Ottawa in 1997 (though some nations, notably the United States, China, and Russia refrained).

Also the Occupy Wall Street movement expresses this spirit with their insistence on being leaderless. On November 16, 2011, a flyer with the following text was being distributed at Zuccotti Park: "Occupy Wall Street is a leaderless movement with people of many colors, genders, and political persuasions. The one thing we all have in common is that we are the 99% that will no longer tolerate the greed and corruption of the 1%. We are using the revolutionary Arab Spring occupation tactics to achieve our ends and we encourage the use of nonviolence to maximize the safety of all participants."[43]

The important role of systemic structures is increasingly acknowledged in many fields of inquiry. Peace psychologist Daniel J. Christie (2006) reports that peace psychology "emerged as a distinct area of research and practice during the Cold War, when the pre-eminent concern was the prevention of nuclear war."[44] "In particular, three themes are emerging in post-Cold War peace psychology: (1) greater sensitivity to geohistorical context; (2) a more differentiated perspective on the meanings and types of violence and peace; and (3) a systems view of the nature of violence and peace."[45]

Organizational analyst Peter M. Senge emphasizes that systems thinking has the distinction of being the "fifth discipline" since it serves to make the results of the other disciplines work together.[46] His colleague Claus Otto Scharmer speaks to Margaret Mead's adage when he emphasizes *crystallizing* as the process whereby a small group of key persons commits itself to a project that they have *presenced*. He explains that this core group functions as a vehicle for the whole to manifest, through the power of their intention, attracting people, opportunities, and resources that make things happen.[47] The next steps in this process are then *prototyping* and *performing*.

In "How to Construct Stable Democracies," Jack Goldstone and Jay Ulfelder explain that liberal democracy enhances a country's political stability. Economic, ethnic, and regional effects have only modest impact on political stability within nations.[48] Stability is rather determined by a country's patterns of political competition and political authority. The authors call for more research into "how some emerging democracies manage to foster free and open competition without descending into factionalism and why some leaders are more willing to accept meaningful constraints on their authority."[49] Goldstone and Ulfelder recommend that "the focus must be shifted from arguments over which societies are ready for democracy toward how to build the specific institutions that reduce the risk of violent instability in countries where democracy is being established."[50] This advice gives important support to those who speak out for global systemic change, since also a global society will draw stability from having the right kind of institutions.

Behavioral game theory uses variations of the prisoner's dilemma game to study human behaviors; Morton Deutsch has been a pioneer of this research.[51] In this game, the participants have the choice to cooperate or to cheat on one another. When psychologist Lee D. Ross and his colleagues asked students to play the prisoner's dilemma game, and they told them that this was a community game, the students cooperated. However, they cheated on each other when told that the same game was a Wall Street game. Ross thus demonstrated the power of *framing*: we do not need to wait for people to change from within, since the same people can behave radically different in different frames.[52]

Also psychologists such as Stanley Milgram and Philip Zimbardo have shown through their experiments how important it is to create systems that provide frames to people to behave ethically, rather than limit our efforts to attempts to reform individuals within unsupportive systems.[53] Zimbardo explains how "a system" creates "a situation," which brings "good" people to behave "badly."[54]

From what these scholars have to say, it appears wise to nurture at the systems level Mandela-like behavior. We can no longer afford to wait for exceptional personalities to emerge by chance against all odds. It is wiser to heed Jean Baker Miller's advice and create *alternative arrangements* rather than accept false choices.[55] It is wiser to systematically promote an alternative climate of trust rather than accept a systemically enforced climate of fear.[56] *Right relationships* are needed, and they must be expressed in the right kinds of institutions, not just locally, but globally. *Too little* institution building must be avoided as much as *too much* of it, oppressive *uniformity* must be prevented as much as destructive *division*, so that a balance of *unity in diversity* can flourish.

Yet, new systems are not everything. The *how* is just as important as the *what*. As was alluded to in the preface and will be discussed more in chapter 12, it is not enough to move from one rigid paradigm to another rigid paradigm. We need to move away from rigidity altogether, away from monolithic immutability toward co-created fluid process. Away from inflexible structures toward organic coming-into-being, growing like trees grow. Away from massive institutions toward a global movement that is carried by passion and enthusiasm. Away from a competitive *dominator* world (Riane Eisler), with people as little cog wheels, toward global *partnership* of rich diversity. Japanese architect Kisho Kurokawa calls it the shift from a "machine principle" to a "life principle," and it happens not just in architectural designs.[57] Touching reflections on this issue were recorded by American philosopher Alan Wilson Watts (1915–1973).[58]

The concept of *nudging* is important.[59] Morton Deutsch has discussed extensively *persuasion strategies* and *nonviolent power strategies*.[60] Nudging and persuading are best done by way of nurturing relationships with what researcher Mary F. Belenky calls *connected knowing*.[61] In connected knowing "one attempts to enter another person's frame of reference to discover the premises for the person's point of view."[62] Win/lose debate—inciting anger that makes for marketable drama—illustrates *separate knowing*. Separate knowing attempts to objectify experience, emphasizing "logical" arguments, "objective" criteria, and a "critical" examination of propositions. It emphasizes impersonal rules and procedures.

Connected knowing means *listening into voice*. This is explained by Linda Hartling as follows:

The expression "listening into voice" draws our attention to the fact that human communication is a bi-directional experience. It is a phrase that encourages us to attune to the fundamental relational nature of speaking. It reminds us to look beyond the individualist myth that speaking is a one-way experience in which the speaker is solely responsible for communicating effectively. Speaking is interactive. It is a two-way experience in which both (or all) people participating in the relationship can chose to listen and engage in a way that will help others to effectively express and clarify their ideas.[63]

Around the world, there are many indigenous approaches to consensus building that include various aspects of listening into voice (chapter 12). As has been reported earlier, Carmen Hetaraka is a bearer of oral Maori tradition, and he was one of the "pillars" of our 17th Annual Conference in Dunedin, New Zealand.[64] Alvin Cota, a Native American Yoeme from Arizona, has brought his historical knowledge to us.[65]

Morton Deutsch recommends Ramsey and Latting's fourteen competencies that can be applied to working across social differences such as race, ethnicity, religious identity, or nationality.[66] Reflection and action interact at multiple levels of a system, at the level of the individual, the group, the organization, and the environmental context. Through self-reflection and action, effective relationships can be created with others, relationships within which critical consciousness is enhanced, and systemic patterns are recognized and worked through. Mental models can thus be reframed, multiple perspectives be emphasized alongside, the personal can be connected to the cultural and social, and systemic change can be advocated and engaged in.[67]

"Unmasking Covert Manipulation" is the title of a section in one of my books.[68] There I discuss the change that is underway:

To pick a few examples among many, *social identity complexity* is currently gaining legitimacy.[69] In the past, such complexity was unwelcome. Social identity was supposed to be monolithic, shaped by power elites.[70] Social psychologists Sonia Roccas and Marilynn B. Brewer show how our identity structures become more inclusive and our tolerance of out-groups increases when we acknowledge and accept social identity complexity.

Philosopher Michel Serres advocates mixing and blending.[71] He suggests that it is not by eliminating and isolating that we grasp *the real* more fully; it is by combining, by putting things into play with each other, by letting things interact. Serres uses the metaphor of the "educated third," which, to his view, is a "third place" where a mixture of culture, nature, sciences, arts, and humanities is constructed.

Peace educator Michalinos Zembylas explains, "this 'educated third' will blend together our multiple heritages and will integrate the laws; he/she will be the inventor of knowledge, the eternal traveler who cares about nature and his/her fellow human beings."[72]

Philosopher Kwame Anthony Appiah makes a "case for contamination."[73] He says "no" to purity, tribalism, and cultural protectionism, and "yes" to a new cosmopolitanism. Emmanuel E. Lévinas highlights the *Other*, whose face forces us to be humane.[74] Terms such as *métissage*, or *intermingling*, mean that both "I" and the "other" are changed by our contact. Werner Wintersteiner, a peace educator in Austria, builds on Lévinas and uses the term of métissage in his *Pedagogy of the Other*.[75] Wintersteiner suggests that the basis for peace education in the future must be *the stranger*, and that we must learn to live with this *permanent strangeness* as a trait of our postmodern human condition and culture.

I agree with Wintersteiner and his colleagues. During the seven years I worked in Egypt as a clinical psychologist and counselor, I learned to caution people against drawing too much confidence from *How-to-Do in X-Land* handbooks or seminars and overlook that living with *permanent strangeness* is the call of the day. Many Westerners who had relied on "intercultural training" arrived as clients at my door, shaken by what they called "culture shock." My conclusion was as follows:

> The training handbooks or seminars, which compare "their" behavior to "ours," often damage the cause more than promote it. What such handbooks or seminars should teach is humility, self-control strategies, and the ability to build relationships while tolerating insecurity and fear. It is impossible to learn everything about another culture, especially in one brief training course.

Imagine your own homeland and how many seminars would have to be drawn up to cover the whole cultural richness. People in the countryside react differently than people in cosmopolitan cities, one valley may be very different from its nearest neighbor, and so forth. You probably do not really understand your parents, your spouse, your children, and sometimes you wonder about yourself. In short, it is an illusion to believe you ever could learn enough to behave perfectly with all these people at all times.[76]

A panoply of new strategies for *inclusionism* and *dignism*

New strategies are needed to bring form and function into congruence. We need, first, the nondualistic principle of *unity in diversity* as the philosophical underpinning of our new political systems. This principle is helpful in avoiding two malign distortions—oppressive *uniformity* on one side (for example, coercive communism or consumerism), and hostile *division* on the other side (for example, a culture of ruthless individualism).

Experience from past *hyperpowers* shows that the *inclusivity* of "tolerance" is a superior strategy[77] for achieving unity in diversity. As discussed above, *function* and *interest* must trump *form* and *position*. *Output* rather than *input* must be emphasized.[78] Cultural and social practices and institutions need to give priority to *communal sharing* (Alan Page Fiske, chapter 3). *Subsidiarity* is the suitable path for forging complex syntheses that can manifest unity in diversity.[79] A subsidiarity approach can help combine communal sharing with elements of market economy into new layers of local and global institutions. To bring about these changes and grasp the opportunities entailed in crisis, and this is the message of my 2010 book, *women and men* must recalibrate their contributions to society.[80]

A world of unity in diversity, implemented through the subsidiarity principle, requires humankind to build new institutional layers at the global level, just as national institutions unite federal states without effacing their diversity. This requires rethinking the classical *nation-state* concept.

States, however, are hesitant to give up sovereignty. Those who identify with the state system and earn their livelihoods through it resist the weakening of this system (there exists the well-known human weakness of *loss aversion*, chapter 6). The unifying process, therefore, meets strong resistance whenever institution building is seriously considered.

Large-scale crises often help overcome resistance and stimulate waves of change. The United Nations, for example, was founded after WWII and the Holocaust. However, such waves typically suffer from subsequent backlashes (chapter 4), as could be observed when a neoliberal rollback began around thirty years ago.

It seems that a *long unfinished revolution* cries out to be carried into the future (chapter 2). The conversation on how to build good world governance and institutions is in dire need of revival. The global economic crisis would serve humanity well if it could renew enthusiasm for the implementation of new global institutions.

At the UN Monetary and Financial Conference in Bretton Woods in July 1944, John Maynard Keynes proposed the establishment of a world "reserve currency" administered by a global central bank. Keynes believed this would have created a more stable and fairer world economy by automatically recycling trade surpluses to finance trade deficits. Both deficit and surplus nations would take responsibility for trade imbalances.[81]

Perhaps it is time to include ideas like these into a global sharing of ideas, reflections, and visions, a global "brainstorming" about the future of humankind?[82]

Paul Grignon has developed a very concrete vision for a new monetary system:

> My proposal is for a self-generating system that could arise spontaneously from a severe collapse of the existing system OR by voluntary acceptance, bottom-up, top-down or both at once. Many of these types of systems are operating now as community currencies, and *particularly successful* are the "business-to-business barter networks." Businesses may not be 100% reliable but they

are much more so than individuals, even if that is simply by being a collective enterprise not disabled by any event happening to a single person. That is why *corporate self-issued credit* that can be used as third party money by everyone is the essential backbone of my proposal, what I consider the realistic vision, although anyone, even the neighborhood babysitter, would be FREE to issue credit to *those who would accept it.* The movement for state banking led by Ellen Brown and for issuing Federal debt-free government money led by the American Monetary Institute are essentially about self-issued credit as well. But their vision is LIMITED to the state and federal levels respectively and are currently *at odds with each other!!*[83]

Grignon believes that the principle of money as a "single uniform commodity in limited supply" (gold, silver, government-authorized fiat cash) is the ROOT problem with money because *the value of money* is based on the relative *scarcity of money* and such money is a "supply" and therefore *subject to control.*[84] He writes:

In the past, precious metal coins of gold and silver were necessary for long-distance trade because money had to be *physically portable,* that is *valuable in small quantities.*
The use of precious metal coins is what gave rise to the generally unquestioned concept of money as a "single uniform commodity in limited supply."
But long before precious metal coins were invented, money was more often a *written credit* for "*something specific from someone specific,*" often grain from a local farmer.
Credits for local products and services are "money" as a redeemable claim on *real value* but, until recently, the usefulness of such credits was *geographically limited* by primitive transport and communication technologies.
Technological progress now makes it practical to re-invent this ancient concept of money as a *global* money system, and this evolutionary advance has already begun in self-issued credit systems like Time Dollars, worldwide LETS, and a host of

business-to-business barter networks, using *self-issued credits* for specific products and services as "money" among participants.[85]

Grignon proposes that everyone, from individuals, to business, to governments at all levels, be enabled through *proven demand* for their goods and/or services to issue credits for those goods and/or services expressed in a *common money unit.* Just as we measure time in minutes, length in meters, and weight in tons, we would *measure* these promises of real goods and services in "money" which would allow us to use them as money. He continues:

> But unlike the government-banking system money of today, which is either fiat cash printed by the central bank or, predominantly, checkbook promises of cash that does *NOT* exist created from promises to pay this NON-existent cash back...all "money" in a *self-issued* credit system is *redeemable for real goods and services* from a *specific supplier* at advertised prices. Thus it is defined in value, and independent of the total "supply" of credits. And since it is issued by the producers of real value, it is *free of any central control.*[86]

Currently, global institution building is seldom scrutinized as thoroughly as Grignon and like-minded thinkers would like it to have. As mentioned in chapter 2, Douglas Hurd, a former diplomat and conservative foreign secretary in the UK, explained in an interview,[87] as well as in his 2010 book, that multilateral institutions are failing.[88] The opportunity to create big enough institutions in service of world concerns was missed in 1989, is his warning. The last great settlement in 1945 failed to provide viable institutions for the world community to deal with climate change and to determine when to intervene in other people's affairs and when to stay out. This must be settled now, Hurd urges.

The website of the International Institute for Sustainable Development (IISD) reads:

> At present there are about 13 global Multilateral Environmental Agreements (MEAs) and/or conventions and about 500

international treaties or other agreements related to the environment. This proliferation of agreements has created concern among international and national communities regarding overlap and duplication of goals and programs. Lack of coherence results in high transaction costs and inefficiencies in achieving convention objectives and the need for coherence is obvious. While several MEA initiatives have yielded a more integrated approach towards environmental management, little is currently being done to find coherence between environmental agreements and development initiatives, especially the recently designed Millennium Development Goals (MDGs).[89]

All members of the human family need now to join in a period of idea collection and vision creation for a better future. We need to determine which large-scale global umbrella systems we must put in place to make our future worth living. The insight that "we sink or swim together" is not sufficiently expressed in our institutions. Form does not reflect function.

When it comes to global idea collection and vision creation, it is important to avoid projectism (chapter 2). It is also crucial to refrain from aborting ideas by "it can't be done." It is, furthermore, imperative to stay clear of introducing new, or holding on to old cycles of humiliation: maligning other people's analyses and suggestions for solutions is counterproductive (see earlier discussions of humiliating effects).

Glimpses of global idea collection and vision creation for creative and novel solutions are emerging. This book does not advocate any *one* solution, but wishes to contribute to a creative conversation among all of humankind that considers all available ideas.

> *If ... the machine of government ... is of such a nature that it requires you to be the agent of injustice to another, then, I say, break the law.*
>
> —Henry David Thoreau[90]

Chapter 11
We Need to Humanize Globalization with *Egalization*!

All learning takes place through the orderly loss of information.

—Kenneth Boulding

What we do know, we do not know in a way that serves our needs. So, we need to know in different ways, and we need to build new knowledge through new ways of knowing. The new knowledge is in the area of designing new realities, which is likely to be done by speculative and creative thinking that would be communally shared and reflected for common formulation that would be tested in a continual process of social invention.

—Betty A. Reardon[1]

More people are stepping up to the challenge of engaging in creative analysis and exploring action. *Where Good Ideas Come From: The Natural History of Innovation*, by science writer Steven Johnson, is a book we all may wish to read.[2] We should also be acquainted with the work on *tipping points* and *outliers* by author Malcolm Gladwell.[3] These works will help us learn how to shift paradigms.[4] Physicist Paul D. Raskin's important essay "Great Transition" is also a must-read.[5]

In chapter 3, I reflect on "humanizing globalization through egalization" and call this process *globegalization*. I suggest giving primacy to *communal sharing* rather than *market pricing* (Alan Page Fiske's coinage).

I suggest that *liberté, égalité, and fraternité* (chapter 2), the motto of the French Revolution of 1789, must guide institution building, locally and globally. A global systemic frame must guarantee liberté and égalité through justice informed by equality in rights and dignity for every world citizen, and this must be held together by the mutual love of fraternité.[6] I call for a *dignity transition* toward *co-globegalization*.

How could that aim be achieved in practical detail?

On March 8, 2011, the Global Development and Environment Institute presented the 2011 Leontief Prize to Nicholas Stern. In his acceptance speech, he quoted Chris Freeman, a historian of technology. Stern described Freeman's catalog of five past major technological transformations. These include: (1) mechanisation of textiles (late 18th century); (2) steam and rail (mid 19th century); (3) steel and electricity (end 19th century); (4) oil, automobiles and mass production (early 20th century); (5) information and communication technologies, ICT (end of the 20th century and continuing).

"One can quibble with timings or definitions but the key aspect of the story is clear. We now require a sixth: to our advantage it will overlap with the fifth, ICT. This sixth wave of low-carbon technologies must, in contrast to all or most of the others, be driven by public policy."[7]

The dignity transition that is called for in this book, the great transition that Raskin and Stern demand, can only be brought about by public policy spurred by *people pressure*.[8] Anthropologist Alan Page Fiske's work on the four basic modes of sociality (chapter 3) suggests that *communal sharing* must be given primacy over the other three modes.[9] Not dependence, not independence, but *interdependence* is the new buzzword. What is important is, furthermore, *quality* rather than quantity. The characteristics of the new paradigm are *complex* and *multifaceted* and they represent the *real wealth of nations* described by Riane Eisler.[10]

First, however, we need to learn how to "leave behind the instinct for organizing ourselves into *resource hierarchies*," writes Michael Britton, while reading Christopher Hedges' work,[11] to allow us to use the full potential of our resources. Linda Hartling adds, "we may want to replace the notion of hierarchy with *heterarchy*, or multiple nodes."[12] Authors Malcolm Hollick and Christine Connelly explain that some hunter-gatherers organize through heterarchy, with members of the group sharing responsibility for decisions:

> Leadership changes fluidly so that the person best able to deal with the needs of the moment assumes the lead. This ad hoc, short-term delegation makes best use of available knowledge, skills and experience, and is an effective means of handling complex situations. Consensus and heterarchy work well if there is unity of purpose, backed by the commitment of all members to the stability of the group.[13]

Sociocracy is a related concept. A sociocracy is manifested when consent-based decision-making among equivalent individuals informs organizational structures of governance that follow cybernetic principles.[14]

In this book, we focus on global economic institutions. In the context of creative analysis and tentative action, global economic institutions are a particularly important topic, since they provide the largest global defining frame (both in their presence and their absence).

Economic institutions of the historical past were, for instance, the introduction of paper currency as a by-product of Chinese block-printing. It started in the Tang dynasty (618–907 CE) and became institutionalized as a governmental policy by the Song dynasty (960–1279 CE). The first written insurance policy appeared on a Babylonian obelisk monument with the code of King Hammurabi carved into it. The Hammurabi Code was one of the first forms of written law. It offered basic insurance; a debtor did not have to pay back a loan if some personal catastrophe made it impossible (such as disability, death, or flooding).

The following list of initiatives is meant to inspire global idea collection and vision creation for future innovations. It is too long for just providing a few examples, and it is too short to give a representative global overview. Its purpose is to provide an impression of the breadth of social, societal, and political initiatives from which new thinking is emerging. The list is (roughly) chronological (well-known initiatives are listed without longer explanatory texts):

- Plato (c.428–348 B.C.E. recommended justice, wisdom, courage, and *moderation* (*sophrosyne*), a sense of limit, moral sanity, self-control, and moderation guided by true self-knowledge. Aristotle (384–322 B.C.E.) highlighted *practical wisdom* (*phronesis*, Latin *prudentia*).[15] Faith, hope, and love were added later, together constituting the seven cardinal virtues. A longer, more recent list entails eight core values: love, truthfulness, fairness, freedom, unity, tolerance, responsibility and respect for life.[16] Interestingly, Norway has emerged from the economic crisis that broke in 2008 relatively unscathed, not least due to its artful *moderation.* Philosopher Henrik Syse has advised Norwegian banks and he emphasizes *sophrosyne.*[17]

- About a century ago, theoretical economist and social activist Silvio Gesell thought that money is a public good—like the telephone or bus transport—and that a small fee should be charged for using it.[18] Through such a "demurrage charge," a monetary system could be designed that gives an incentive to long-term thinking, rather than a short-term exploitation of resources. He considered himself a world citizen and believed the Earth should belong to all people, regardless of race, gender, class, wealth, religion and age, and that borders should be made obsolete.

- "Living Well" is the indigenous social system that focuses on reciprocity between people and the Earth.[19] As Riane Eisler, author of *The Real Wealth of Nations: Creating a Caring Economics*, models, we can learn important lessons from indigenous people.[20]

- Bhutan, a small nation in South Asia, focuses on Gross National Happiness (GNH) rather than Gross National Product (GNP). "I believe that Gross National Happiness today is a bridge between the fundamental values of kindness, equality, and humanity and the necessary pursuit of economic growth," announces King Jigme Khesar Namgyel Wangchuck of Bhutan on his Facebook page.[21]

• Also in Scandinavia and Costa Rica alternative paths of economic and political strategies have been tried.[22] As mentioned above, philosopher Henrik Syse has advised Norwegian banks emphasizing *sophrosyne*. See also the work of Norway's Centre of Equality, Social Organization, and Performance (ESOP) described further down.

• An early initiative was *Our Common Future*, a report of the World Commission on Environment and Development, chaired by Norwegian prime minister Gro Harlem Brundtland in March 20, 1987.[23]

• In 1994, Thai Buddhist monk Prayudh A. Payutto warned that the study of economics has avoided questions of moral values and considerations of ethics, even though it is becoming obvious that in order to solve the problems that confront us in the world today such considerations will be necessary:

> If the study of economics is to play any part in the solution of our problems, it can no longer evade the subject of ethics. Nowadays environmental factors are taken into account both in economic transactions and in solving economic problems, and the need for ethics in addressing the problem of conservation and the environment is becoming more and more apparent."[24]

Ove Jacobsen, professor at the Centre for Ecological Economics and Ethics in Bodø, North Norway, explains:

> Payutto states that ethics is the connection between the inner and outer reality. He points to wisdom,

compassion and moderation as important characteristics of an economy that will promote individual and social development within the framework of a sustainable nature. Payutto explains Buddhist economics as based on the concepts Tanhā and Chanda. Tanhā refers to a selfish pursuit of material like experiences. As the needs of light experiences are endless, they often lead to greed, hatred and selfishness. Chanda represents wisdom and ethical values that are central to the quest for true happiness and quality of life. The road to Chanda goes through reflection on life experiences. According Payutto we will eventually discover that mental condition, moral behavior and economics are linked together through a stream of actions. The goal is to develop an overall understanding that changes conflicts of interest to an experience of community of interest between individuals, society, and nature…In terms of economic value he distinguishes between true value (Chanda) leading to 'wellbeing,' and artificial value (Tanhā), which only helps selfish greed activities… Payutto differentiates dependent happiness, independent happiness and harmonious happiness. Dependent happiness is linked to external objects and is thus dependent on things in the material world. Independent happiness is linked to internal conditions such as 'peace of mind'. Independent happiness is more stable than the happiness that is dependent on the presence of external objects. Harmonic happiness is based on an altruistic attitude where the goal is to help other peoples 'well-being.' Harmonic happiness is linked with Buddhism and aims to cultivate the experience of the relationship between 'I' and 'we' or a 'the extended self.' Trust and solidarity (with all living creatures) are thus indicators of true happiness. The best interest of communities is associated with the absence of poverty more than with the maximization of production and consumption. In Buddhist economics, work has intrinsic value because it is to seek common goals through collaboration with other people contributing to personal development while it combats selfishness (Chanda). Work that has been reduced to only be a means to raise money for consumption of goods and services are motivated by Tanhã. This means that we want to work the least possible and consume as much as possible. Also at this point Payutto recommends a balance between extremes... Payutto argues that competition is an effective means to maximize production and consumption of goods and services (Tanhã). When economic actors are working together to achieve greater market power, he uses the term 'artificial cooperation.' If the goal is to promote a development that leads to the community he recommends genuine cooperation. True collaboration occurs as a result of the insight that everything is connected and is motivated by Chanda."[25]

- Innovative initiatives have emerged from past movements, such as the Rudolf Steiner Foundation, RSF Social Finance,[26] and the Praxis Peace Institute.[27] For twenty-five years, RSF Social Finance has been building the emerging field of social finance. RSF developed the Transforming Money Network, which includes those working across the full spectrum of financial approaches, from private equity to complementary currencies. Several groups and initiatives have emerged as a result of this network including: The Sequoia Principles for Transforming Money; the Fund for Complementary Currencies; Money, Race, and Class Conversations; and, Intuition and Money gatherings. RSF's Fund for Complementary Currencies supports replicable pilot projects in new forms of currencies, including BerkShares, TimeBanks, and GETS (Global Exchange Trade System), and research and innovation with respect to the means of economic exchange. The Praxis Peace Institute

has established itself since its founding in 2001 as a vehicle
for inquiry, practical workshops, and civic education.

- Statistician W. Edwards Deming (1986) is known as the
"father" of Total Quality Management, out of which grew
the concept, for instance, of the Aldridge and European
Foundation for Quality Management (EFQM). Ulrich
Spalthoff wrote:

> Unfortunately, according to my observation, this
> balanced approach suffered a rollback, as the notion of
> shareholder value dominated MBA courses. As we see
> now, this was highly devastating to the economy as well
> as to most people. The problem now is to find a new
> paradigm. Just starting again with the theories of some
> 20, 30 years ago in my opinion is not sufficient. This
> would pose a high risk that shareholders will continue
> to dominate economics. I would be highly interested in
> the readers' thoughts about how to define an improved
> framework for quality organizations, which not only
> reduces the risk that usurpations seize too much power
> but also secures a good combination of economical
> efficiency, equal participation of all stakeholders and
> sustainable management of natural resources. The last
> point was somehow neglected in Aldridge and EFQM
> practices, but is crucial now.[28]

- Mathematician, statistician and economist Nicholas
Georgescu-Roegen introduced the concept of entropy from
thermodynamics into economics (as distinguished from the
mechanistic foundation of neoclassical economics drawn
from Newtonian physics), and did foundational work,
which later developed into *evolutionary economics*. His work
contributed significantly to *bioeconomics* and *ecological
economics*.[29]

- The transdisciplinary field of *ecological economics* is an important emerging area of academic research that aims to address the interdependence and co-evolution of human economies and natural ecosystems over time and space.[30]

- Economic innovator Dee Ward Hock formed the Chaordic Commons, a non-profit organization, with the aim to develop, disseminate, and implement new concepts of organization that result in more equitable sharing of power and wealth, improved health, and greater compatibility with the human spirit and biosphere.[31]

- Economist Bernard Lietaer's *The Future of Money* is a classic.[32] He argues that complementary currencies can protect against the destructive effects of major currency crashes.[33] In *The Money Fix*, Lietaer explains that money is a "medium of exchange," a "measurement of value," all of which are descriptions of what money does, not what money is. "Money is an agreement."[34]

- Monetary theory and history is explained by Stephen A. Zarlenga, director of the American Monetary Institute, an institute dedicated to monetary reform in the United States, in *The Lost Science of Money*.[35]

- The Earth Charter provides a template for global analysis and action.[36] The mission of the Earth Charter Initiative is to promote the transition to sustainable ways of living and a global society founded on a shared ethical framework that includes respect and care for the community of life, ecological integrity, universal human rights, respect for diversity, economic justice, democracy, and a culture of peace.[37]

- Ashoka: Innovators for the Public is a non-profit organization supporting the field of social entrepreneurship, founded by William Drayton in 1981. Its goal is to identify and support leading social entrepreneurs through a Social Venture Capital approach to elevate the citizen sector to a competitive level equal to the business sector.[38]

- The Caux Principles are grounded on two moral concepts, the Japanese concept of *kyosei*, which means living and working together for the common good, and the concept of *human dignity*. Both these statements give a central place to respect for human rights in business activity.[39]

- The European Business Ethics Network EBEN, founded in 1987 as a non-profit association, is a cross-national network dedicated to the promotion of business ethics, broadly defined, in academia, business, public sector and civil society.[40]

- Global Corporate Citizenship ("GCC") emerged in management and business scholarship in the 1990s. Similar terms are corporate social responsibility ("CSR"), corporate conscience, corporate social performance, or sustainable responsible business, all connoting the deliberate inclusion of public interest into corporate decision-making, and the honouring of a triple bottom line: people, planet, profit.[41]

- The formulation of the Millennium Development Goals (MDGs) provides a guideline for global action.[42] Its merit is to point out shortcomings. Yet, as Howard Richards, scholar of peace and global studies and philosophy, who was given the floor in chapter 2, contends, the entire system might have to be reshaped and all attempts to bring people out of poverty by bringing them into the money market as it is defined today, are doomed.[43] Anthropologist Mac Chapin might agree with Richards: the conservationist agenda was not helped by shifting rhetoric toward "the poor." Chapin explains:

Just as the once widely recognized possibilities for native stewardship have been largely dismissed, the terms "indigenous" and "traditional" have largely dropped out of the discourse of the large conservationist NGOs—replaced mainly by "marginalized" or "poor." (The more neutral terms "rural" and "local" have also spread more widely in the literature and are commonly used by both sides.) This linguistic shift robs the dignity of indigenous peoples. Who is interested in saving the culture of marginalized people? What is the value of the traditional ecological knowledge of the poor? People who are viewed as having no distinctive culture, assets, or historic claims to the land they occupy end up being, in a very real sense, a people with no value.[44]

- The United Nations Global Compact, also known as Compact or UNGC, is a United Nations initiative to encourage businesses worldwide to adopt sustainable and socially responsible policies and to report on their implementation.[45]

- The Model Economy Community is a forum for the rapidly growing group of people who believe that the dominant monetary systems need to be changed.[46]

- ISO, the International Organization for Standardization, has decided to launch an International Standard providing guidelines for social responsibility (SR), named ISO 26000 or ISO SR, which was released on November 1, 2010.

- Nobel prize winning economist Robert Alexander Mundall, who laid the groundwork for the introduction of the Euro, advocates developing a *world currency*.[47]

- PayPal is, in many ways, a new world currency. Peter Thiel, its founder, would merit having his name alongside such names as Bill Gates or Steve Jobs. PayPal's vision is to harness a global consciousness through the web, through a money service that allows the free movement of money around the world. Money can be moved across national borders through cyberspace. In 2008, it was handling 16 billion dollars in transactions per year. This was meant to give people new sovereignty over their money.

> Unfortunately, as Ulrich Spalthoff reports, over time, these lofty aims were not fulfilled. As PayPal uses its influence to exert global corporate domination, many people are rather deprived of sovereignty over their money. The same is valid for Visa, MasterCard, and Western Union. Cuban cigars, for instance, can no longer be sold in Germany by using PayPal.[48]

> In chapter 2, the colonization campaigns of the past were described as often starting out with trade. At first, this may have been politically neutral and trading partners were treated as equals. Then, when a certain amount of economic clout had been accumulated, it was used for power-over strategies. It was then that raiding, conquering, and thorough colonizing set in.

- Peter Thiel was also a key early investor of Facebook, which, if it were a country, would now have the world's third-largest population. Also Facebook faces increasing criticism for turning customers' input into a resource for profit maximization. The user is the product. The popular web vehicle "is teaming up with companies that distribute music, movies, information and games in positioning itself to become the conduit where news and entertainment is found and consumed." [49] Its new partners include Netflix and Hulu for video, Spotify for music, *The Washington Post* and Yahoo for news, Ticketmaster for concert tickets and a host of food, travel, and consumer brands. "This will let Facebook reap even more valuable data than it does now about its users' habits and desires, which in turn can be used to sell more fine-tuned advertising."[50]

LinkedIn made $58,000,000 last quarter delivering data about their members to companies who paid for it.[51]

Conclusion: It would be a cultural achievement if people who were formerly constrained by history and geography, could reach across boundaries and challenge existing power structures of nation states and corporations with global social media systems that don't commoditize their customers. As it stands now, social media seem to want to replace national power structures with new corporate ones.

• David A. King, director of the Smith School of Enterprise and Environment at the University of Oxford, urges the global community to be courageous enough to face the uniqueness of the need for global collective action, and to realize the feasibility of *green growth*.[52] (In chapter 10, Juliet B. Schor had the floor and she expressed skepticism with respect to the notion of green growth.)

• Peer-to-peer (P2P) processes (including Free Software and Open Source, the open access, the free culture movements, among others) represent an emerging field, supported by new information and communication technologies (ICTs). They increasingly form a global reality of nonmarket practices. In the project Oekonux the economic and political forms of Free Software are discussed.[53] People like Lawrence Lessig, founding board member of Creative Commons,[54] and peer-to-peer theorist Michel Bauwens aim to develop a conceptual framework for these new social processes.[55] Michel Bauwens writes that a *commons-based political economy* would be centered around peer to peer, but it would co-exist with a re-invigorated sphere of reciprocity (gift-economy). It would be centered around the introduction of time-based complementary currencies, and a reformed sphere for market exchange, the kind of "natural capitalism" described by Paul Hawken,[56] David C. Korten,[57] and Hazel Henderson,[58] where the costs for natural and social reproduction are no longer externalized, and which abandons the growth imperative for a *throughput* economy as described by Herman Daly.[59]

- Britain's New Economics Foundation publishes a Happy Planet Index, which shows that it is possible for a nation to have high well-being with a low ecological footprint.[60]

- The Beyond GDP conference in the European Parliament in 2009 discussed a new approach to measuring Quality of Life, beyond culturally biased happiness concepts.[61]

- The Franco-German Ministerial Council decided on February 4, 2010, to ask the French Conseil d'Analyse Économique (CAE), and the German Council of Economic Experts (GCEE) to follow-up on the outcome of the Commission on the Measurement of Economic Performance and Social Progress (Stiglitz-Sen-Fitoussi Commission, or SSFC).[62] In Germany, the Enquete-Kommission Wachstum, Wohlstand, Lebensqualität began its work on January 17, 2011.[63]

- The Gallup Poll provides polling data in 170 countries on percentage of people thriving.[64]

- The Human Development Index (HDI) looks at life expectancy, literacy, education, and standards of living worldwide.[65]

- The UNU-WIDER World Income Inequality Database (WIID) collects and stores information on income inequality for developed, developing, and transition countries.[66]

• The Commission on Key National Indicators was founded in 2010 by the United States Congress to provide oversight and advice for a new Key National Indicators System for the United States. The first ever, bipartisan Commission on Key National Indicators is complete, following appointments by then-speaker of the house Nancy Pelosi and minority leader John Boenher.

> The eight members of the bipartisan Commission on Key National Indicators were selected by congressional leaders in the House and the Senate to oversee implementation of a Key National Indicator System to help the American people better assess the nation's progress. The indicator system—enabled by an innovative public/private partnership—will select a limited number of key measures on the most important issues facing the country and make information about them freely available via the web using the best quality public and private data sources. The system will be implemented by the National Academy of Sciences in partnership with a non-profit institute, the State of the USA. A total of $70 million in public financial support is authorized for KNIS over nine years to complement contributions by the private sector, nearing $15 million to date.[67]

• The non-profit Center for the Advancement of the Steady State Economy, in Arlington, VA, USA, explains that "continuous economic growth on a finite planet is wishful thinking."

• The first North American De-Growth conference took place in 2010 in Vancouver, BC. The goal is a steady-state economy of reasonable incomes for all human beings in a more humane society that preserves the planet and promotes human happiness.

- A Green New Deal report was published on behalf of the Green New Deal Group by the new economics foundation (nef).[68]
- The European Green Party (EGP) and the European Free Alliance (EFA) developed a program for a *New Green Deal: Climate Protection, New Jobs and Social Justice*, by Reinhard Buetikofer and Sven Giegold.[69]

- The Declaration on Degrowth is the product of a workshop held at the Conference on Economic Degrowth for Ecological Sustainability and Social Equity held in Paris April 18–19, 2008. It reflects the points of view of the conference participants and articulates the vision of the Decroissance movement.[70] See also the Declaration of Tilburg.[71] Both declarations call upon a radical re-orientation of our economies.

- Paul Krugman received the Nobel Memorial Prize in Economics in 2008 for his contributions to new trade theory and new economic geography.[72]

- Elinor Ostrom received the Nobel Prize for Economics 2009. She is considered one of the leading scholars in the study of common pool resources. Her work emphasizes the multifaceted nature of human–ecosystem interaction and argues against any singular "panacea" for individual social-ecological system problems.[73]

- The global governance of financial systems is being discussed, among others, by John Leonard Eatwell, a British economist and the current President of Queens' College, Cambridge.[74]

- Berthold Huber, leader of the largest German union, IG-Metall, calls for *truth commissions* to work through the causes of the economic crisis that broke in 2008.[75]

- Ellen Hodgson Brown wrote about the *Web of Debt*[76]:

  > Our money system is not what we have been led to believe. The creation of money has been "privatized," or taken over by private money lenders. Thomas Jefferson called them "bold and bankrupt adventurers just pretending to have money." Except for coins, all of our money is now created as loans advanced by private banking institutions—including the privately-owned Federal Reserve. Banks create the principal but not the interest to service their loans. To find the interest, new loans must continually be taken out, expanding the money supply, inflating prices—and robbing you of the value of your money.[77]

- Community economist Thomas Henry Greco, Jr. explains alternatives to *money*" in *The End of Money and the Future of Civilization*.[78]

- The work of independent scientist, environmentalist, and futurologist James Lovelock (2009) has been foundational. His work is carried forward, among others, at the Schumacher College, by Stephan Harding (2006). Ben Brangwyn and Rob Hopkins co-founded the Transition Network, aspiring to implement a fast developing transition model.[79]

- Physicist Paul Raskin is the Founding Director of the Tellus Institute. It has conducted over 3,500 research and policy projects throughout the world on environmental issues, resource planning, and sustainable development. Paul Raskin's seminal essay "Great Transition" has had widespread international influence.[80]

- The documentary *Home* was very influential in France's last elections.[81]

- Many more influential films would merit mention here, among them the recent documentary by Charles Ferguson *Inside Job* (2010).

- More films are listed in note [82].
- Concepts of cosmopolitan constitutionalism and cosmopolitan sovereignty are emerging in many shapes and forms. *Cosmopolitanism* allows for differences in processes and procedures among states, while providing for graduated authority in judicial authority.[83]

- An economic model for the future, a *common welfare economy*, develops in Austria.[84]

- Argentina has become known for a *solidarity economy*.[85] It was referred to repeatedly in the Occupy Wall Street Youth Panel of the 2011 Schumacher Lectures in New York City (chapter 2).[86]

- A total paradigm shift in economic arrangements within less than three years is predicted by economy professor Franz Hörmann.

> The economic system of western societies (as the result of so-called "globalization" in fact nearly the economic system of the whole world) is the result of historically grown thought patterns that emerged around a few very limited premises at the core....We only need to learn how to change economic models and century-old thought patterns that are so engraved on our minds (after all, we learn how to count money already in primary school), that those common beliefs are never questioned. "You can't spend more money than you've got!" and similar sayings transform economy in our minds into a zero-sum game. But zero-sum games can only be won by one player—his opponent is doomed to lose, and, most of all, he is doomed to be an

opponent right from the start. If we succeed in changing the mental engrams of economy in the global mind, only then will humanity prosper and flourish again.[87]

- Economist Kamran Mofid has been mentioned throughout this book. He has founded the Globalisation for the Common Good (GCG) initiative.[88]

- Götz Wolfgang Werner is the founder, co-owner, and member of the advisory board of dm-drogerie markt, a German drugstore chain, and, since October 2003, the head of Cross-Department Group for Entrepreneurial Studies at the Karlsruhe Institute of Technology. He is one of the most influential advocates of *basic income* in Germany.[89] Werner explains in an interview:

> "I'm saying: we don't need a right to work, at least not to instructed, social security contributing salary work. It's no longer up to date. We need a right to income. To an unconditional basic income." Question: "You want to give 1,500 Euros to every person. Just like that. Month by month. From birth to death." Werner, "Yes. We need to give money to every person. A citizen income. The basic income needs to be enough to live modestly, but in dignity. It needs to be more than a minimum for existence—a minimum for culture."[90]

- In Germany, a group of wealthy individuals calls for higher taxes for the wealthy.[91] Retired physician Dieter Lehmkuhl, for example, says that it is time the wealthy came to the aid of their country. Lehmkuhl "reckons that if the 2.2 million Germans who have personal fortunes of more than €500,000 ($750,000) paid a tax of five percent this year and next, it would provide the state with €100 billion."[92]

- In the United States, along with United for a Fair Economy, the new Tax Wealth Like Work Campaign by Responsible

Wealth[93] focuses attention on the discrepancies in the tax system that reward income from wealth over income from work.

> As Congress and cash-strapped states struggle to balance budgets, these wealthy people are urging that the income from their investment portfolios be taxed at the same rate as work income. That was done in the late 1980s under Presidents Reagan and Bush, and restoring the rates would raise $84 billion in 2011. The campaign is also building support for Congresswoman Jan Schakowsky's Fairness in Taxation Act which would tax capital gains and dividend income as ordinary income for taxpayers with income over $1 million, and create higher income tax brackets for millionaires and billionaires.[94]

- Business journalist Marjorie Kelly speaks of the transitioning to *For-Benefit Business*.[95]

- Helena Norberg-Hodge is an analyst of the impact of the global economy on cultures and agriculture worldwide, and a pioneer of the *localisation* movement.[96]

- Scholars and activists around the world promote and develop *fair trade*. A book by Joseph E. Stiglitz is one manifestation.[97] Mitch Teberg is a young activist writing a blog while conducting research to write a book on Fair Trade.[98]

- Ragnhild Nilsen, a writer, artist, coach, and member of the global advisory board of our Human Dignity and Humiliation Studies network,[99] founded the Global Fair Trade initiative.

- The international Global Zero movement, launched in December 2008, includes more than 300 political, military, business, faith, and civic leaders—and hundreds of thousands of citizens—working for the phased, verified elimination of all nuclear weapons worldwide. The signatories of the declaration range from Hans Blix to Horst Teltschik, from Gro Harlem Brundtland to Jimmy Carter to Zbigniew Brzezinski.[100] This initiative emerged on the background of the dramatic rise of the production of military equipment since the end of the Cold War.

- Increasingly, efforts emerge that promote generosity, kindness, mindfulness, and the bridging of spirituality and action in the spirit of the *cultural creatives* movement described by Paul H. Ray and Sherry Ruth Anderson.[101] See among many others, the online magazine, *Wild River Review*, that "seeks to raise awareness and compassion as well as inspire engagement through the power of stories."[102] The Love Foundation has been founded by Harold H. Becker to "inspire people to love unconditionally."[103] KarmaTube is "dedicated to bringing inspirational stories to light, using the power of video and the internet to multiply acts of kindness, beauty, and generosity."[104] Contemplative education at the Garrison Institute is "exploring the intersection of contemplation and engaged action in the world."[105]

- Behavioral game theory uses variations of the prisoner's dilemma game to study human behaviors. In this game the participants have the choice to cooperate or to cheat on one another. Results show that humans are behaving in much more cooperative ways than the *Homo economicus* concept indicates. Results are relevant also for humiliation theory, namely, by demonstrating how people, in the face of humiliation, may want to pay back and retaliate, even at the cost of hurting themselves.[106]
Political scientist Robert Axelrod[107] explored computer models of the iterated prisoner's dilemma game (which gives two players the chance to cooperate or betray one another)

and formalized the *evolutionary tit-for-tat strategy*. Axelrod's key finding is that the evolutionary tit-for-tat strategy—also known as *reciprocal altruism*—is remarkably successful and defeats all other strategies, increasing the benefits of cooperation over time and protecting participants from predators.

In the field of social psychology Morton Deutsch is a pioneer in prisoner's dilemma research.[108] Deutsch lays out what he calls *Deutsch's crude law of social relations*. This law says that "characteristic processes and effects elicited by a given type of social relationship (cooperative or competitive) tend also to elicit that type of social relationship." In short, "cooperation breeds cooperation, while competition breeds competition."[109]

- Many environmental problems have been positively addressed by internalizing *externalities* (in many countries a decrease can be observed, for example, in acid rain, or in emissions of lead, mercury, copper, DDT, sulfur, etc).[110] However, other problems, such as climate change, are more complex. To solve the prisoner's dilemma in a cooperative way, at the level of local communities, people have the advantage of knowing each other and can communicate to achieve cooperation. At higher levels of institutional organization, however, this can only be achieved when the mandate of a societal institution is relatively congruent with the scope and level of the problem. For example, noise pollution is usually comparatively easy to address, because political and institutional influence patterns coincide with the scope and level of the problem. As for climate change, global structures that could play this role are weak or lacking.

  Economist Richard T. Carson (chapter 4) concludes that there might have been "a lost decade or more during which environmental economists failed to focus on other potential driving forces behind changes in environmental quality within a country" than the income–pollution relationship.[111]

He warns that the debate over the income–pollution relationship made developing countries ignore their environmental problems until they develop and become wealthier, even though it is clear that developing countries can take many actions.[112]

- The Nordic countries seem "to violate" what the economics profession views as necessary requirements for an economy to prosper: "They have too small wage differences, too high taxes, too large public sectors, too generous welfare states, and too strong unions. Despite of these violations, they have for decades been doing extremely well. What most economists see as a recipe for serious economic trouble seems, in the Nordic countries, to be consistent with high growth, low unemployment, low inequality, and a fairly efficient allocation of resources."[113] How come? Has economics got it wrong? "Or, is it rather a question about timing and luck? If the Nordic success stories are just luck, the renewed interest for the 'Scandinavian model' in Europe and elsewhere is misguided. If economics has got it wrong, it is important to know how and why." [114]
The Centre of Equality, Social Organization, and Performance (ESOP) is a research center funded by the Research Council of Norway (RCN) as a Centre of Excellence (CoE) at the Department of Economics of the University of Oslo, Norway. [115] ESOP was established January 1, 2007. ESOP aims at exploring the links between equality, social organization, and economic performance, both in rich and poor countries. The ambitions are:

- to confront economic theory with the Nordic lessons: Do we need to change the basic behavioral and institutional assumptions or can the Nordic lessons be explained in a standard economic approach when only the details get right?

- to understand the linkages between economic performance, distribution, and social disparities: What are the costs and benefits of more equality?
- to explore the sustainability of generous welfare states and the viability of egalitarian market economies: What determines their performance and their economic and political feasibility?
- to understand the interaction between policies, institutions and long term development: What set of policies and institutions may generate an egalitarian development path within a consistent arrangement?
- to bring these research topics to the international research frontier: What are the general lessons for economics?

Economist Karl Ove Moene leads ESOP. In his work, he explains that welfare spending and wage coordination both generate equality:

Equality can multiply due to the complementarity between wage determination and welfare spending. A more equal wage distribution fuels welfare generosity via political competition. A more generous welfare state fuels wage equality further via its support to weak groups in the labor market. Together the two effects generate a cumulative process that adds up to an important social multiplier. We focus on a political economic equilibrium that incorporates this mutual dependence between wage setting and welfare spending. It explains how almost equally rich countries differ in economic and social equality among their citizens and why countries cluster around different worlds of welfare capitalism—the Scandinavian model, the Anglo-Saxon model and the Continental model. Using data on 18 OECD countries over the period 1976–2002 we test the main predictions of the model and identify a sizeable magnitude of the equality multiplier. We obtain additional support for the cumulative complementarity between social spending and wage equality by applying another data set for the US over the period 1945–2001.[116]

- In May 2007, an Education Commission was created in Norway (*Dannelsesutvalg*) to examine international cutting edge thinking about higher education and to develop recommendations for Norway. The report was published in 2009.[117] The commission argues that liberal arts education is of utmost significance for the creation of responsible citizenship. It explains why liberal arts education is not simply "a luxury for elites." The commission calls for liberal arts education to be strengthened in all relevant curricula.[118]

- BerkShares is a local currency and one of the few privately issued scrips in the US. It has drawn much attention; hits to the BerkShares website have averaged 21,000 daily.[119] BerkShares are a local currency designed for use in the Berkshire region of Massachusetts. It is issued by BerkShares, Inc., a non-profit organization working in collaboration with participating local banks, businesses, and non-profit organizations "A good community insures itself by trust, by good faith and good will, by mutual help. A good community, in other words, is a good local economy," is a quote from Wendell Berry summarizing the spirit of this endeavor.[120]

- BitCoin is proof that a peer-to-peer money system is feasible.[121] Yet, as Paul Grignon comments, "BitCoin is created as an unstable, unbacked single uniform commodity of limited quantity (20 million BitCoins)."[122] Grignon comments further:

> According to my analysis, which is presented in *Money as Debt III, Evolution Beyond Money*, the "single

uniform commodity" principle of money is the ROOT of all of our problems with money and therefore not the model I would endorse.[123]

> We must change the paradigm of money from "debt of money as a thing in itself" to "credit for real value expressed in money units."[124]

- Digital Coin is a proposal developed by Paul Grignon, whose voice has been given room throughout this book.[125]

- Positive Money is a not-for-profit UK campaign group which aims to raise awareness of the fractional-reserve banking system and to lobby the UK government and parliament to introduce legislation to replace the existing banking system. The group has produced draft legislation for such a replacement.

- Slow Money is a movement that takes its name from the Slow Food movement. It organizes investors and donors to steer new sources of capital to small food enterprises, organic farms, and local food systems.[126]

- A *gift economy* is emerging.[127] Author Geneviève Vaughan writes:

> Many people especially in the so-called "First World" live in denial or ignorance of the devastating effects our countries' and corporations' policies have on the so-called "Third World." Even when we are conscious of these effects we feel we have no power to change them or to change similar situations within our own countries. We usually feel we do not know why these things are happening, or we attribute them to "human nature," greed, and "man's inhumanity to man." There is a way to understand what is happening which allows us to address it both on the individual and group level

and on the level of national and corporate policy. In the last decades feminists have challenged the "construction of gender," questioning male and female roles and sexual identities.... [128]

- Some people attempt to live *without money*. See, for example, Heidemarie Schwermer.[129] Note also Mark Boyle, who gave up using cash and is the founder of the Freeconomy Community.[130] (I myself live with an absolute minimum of money.)

- John Gerard Ruggie, the United Nations Special Representative of the Secretary-General on Human Rights and Transnational Corporations and Other Business Enterprises uses the approach of *principled pragmatism*, which means being guided by principle to strengthen the current human rights regime, while being pragmatic on how to get there. The Ruggie report, *Protect, Respect and Remedy: A Framework for Business and Human Rights*, was released in April 2008, and unanimously accepted by the Human Rights Council in June. In less than a year after its release, the framework has gained wide attention among business and human rights groups, corporations, and governments. I can attest to its influence; I participated in the Öffentliche Anhörung des Ausschuss für Menschenrechte und humani-täre Hilfe über Menschenrechtliche Verantwortung internationaler Unternehmen, in the German Parliament in Berlin on April 6, 2011.[131] The Ruggie report rests on three core principles:

  1. the state duty to protect against human rights abuses by third parties, including business;
  2. the corporate responsibility to respect human rights;
  3. and greater access by victims to effective remedies.[132]

- *The World Development Report 2011: Conflict, Security and Development* calls for bringing security and development together to break the cycles of fragility and violence, as they affect more than one billion people. The report transcends current typologies of wars and violence and states that "organised violence" has become the major problem, such as civil wars, communal violence, gang-based violence, and organized crime. The distinction between political and criminal violence is no longer seen as valid and the relevant institutions are called on to collaborate in radically new and radically more effective ways and envision fundamental restructuring. The report warns that rebuilding a society from cycles of violence usually takes a generation. However, such long time frames are usually not considered in the design of programs.[133]

- Martin Wolf, one of the world's most influential writers on economics and a member of the UK's Independent Banking Commission, said in 2011 that having the average taxpayer underwrite the huge transactions by investment banks "is just insane."[134]
  In his blog "Will China's Rise Be Peaceful?" of November 16, 2010,[135] Wolf draws attention to the potential advantages of the transformation now underway for the world population to share in prosperity and contribute its ideas and energy to securing a better future for everybody. He sees three possible scenarios (which resonate with the scenarios in Paul Raskin's "Great Transition" essay):

> First, the "positive sum" view wins out. Awareness of the absence of any deep ideological conflict, of mutual economic dependence, of a shared planetary destiny and of the impossibility of war in a nuclear age force adequate levels of global co-operation. For this to happen there must also be a profound commitment to co-operation, not much evident recently in such areas as climate change or global imbalances. Second, the "negative sum" view wins out. Power is relative. The incumbent and the rising powers compete

for dominance. Resources, similarly, are finite. In this world, economic disarray and the struggle for scarce resources lead to a retreat from globalisation, while balance of power politics dominate international relations. We may see the emergence of a balancing coalition against China, consisting, at the least, of the US, Europe, India and Japan, possibly joined by other powers.

Third, we muddle through, with a mixture of the above two approaches: globalisation and a degree of economic co-operation survive, but classic balance of power politics become more significant, as China becomes more assertive of its rank in the world system. This, roughly speaking, was the world before the First World War—not an encouraging precedent.

This list of initiatives, organizations, and campaigns, clearly, shows only a very small fraction of relevant activities that emerge all around the globe. Many more need to be mentioned.

What this list shows, however, is that many people are aware of the problems at hand and are willing to work for a better future. Yet, as has been pointed out earlier, there is a problem: global cooperation is lacking.

The most significant present-day challenge is to join forces and forge global coordinated proactive activity.

As the world shrinks, so our capacity for effective moral action grows.

—Peter Singer[136]

Chapter 12
We Need Many More Voices and a Clear Direction!

We do not inherit the earth from our ancestors, we borrow it from our children.

—Native American Proverb

We, the human family on planet Earth, find ourselves in unique times of opportunity. Michio Kaku, renowned physicist, states that the generation now alive is "the most important generation of humans ever to walk the Earth."[1] He writes:

Unlike previous generations, we hold in our hands the future destiny of our species, whether we soar into fulfilling our promise as a type I civilization [meaning a civilization that succeeds in building a socially and ecologically sustainable world] or fall into the abyss of chaos, pollution, and war. Decisions made by us will reverberate throughout this century. How we resolve global wars, proliferating nuclear weapons, and sectarian and ethnic strife will either lay or destroy the foundations of a type I civilization. Perhaps the purpose and meaning of the current generation are to make sure that the transition to a type I civilization is a smooth one. The choice is ours. This is the legacy of the generation now alive. This is our destiny.[2]

Yet, we, the human family fail to recognize our unparalleled opportunities and responsibilities, and instead, we choose to create unparalleled crises.

This is why collective action from the *global street* is needed at the present historical juncture, not just the *Arab street*. New Rosa Parks, new Nelson Mandelas are called on to emerge, in numbers, and move us, in the spirit of Margaret Mead's saying that opened chapter 10: "Never doubt that a small group of thoughtful, committed citizens can change the world. Indeed, it is the only thing that ever has."

Democracy is the *master antidote against hubris*, says John Keane, professor of Politics at the Centre for the Study of Democracy in London.[3] "Reimagining Democratic Societies: A New Era of Personal and Social Responsibilities," was a conference that some of our Human Dignity and Humiliation Studies network members and I had the privilege of being part of at the University of Oslo in Norway, June 27-29, 2011.[4] A few days earlier, on June 24, 2011, we had launched our World Dignity University (WDU) initiative also at the University of Oslo, hosted by its Vice-Rector, philosopher Inga Bostad, one of WDU's founding members.

As has been repeatedly discussed throughout this book, increasingly, ever more people around the world agree that what is needed now is *people pressure*, as suggested by analysts like Paul Hawken, not just locally, but globally.[5] What is needed is what Jeremy Rifkin calls a global *pro-democracy revolution* that uses *lateral power*.[6] We must consider Timothy Garton Ash's *refolution* at a global scale. Gar Alperovitz's *evolutionary reconstruction*,[7] and Paul Raskin's *great transition*[8] are at stake at global levels, not just locally and nationally. In this book, we call for a global *dignity transition*.

We would like to invite the reader to think deeply about the fact that our ancestors never saw pictures of our Blue Planet from the perspective of an astronaut. Our ancestors were unable to *see*, as we do, how we humans are *one* species living on *one* little planet. Our ancestors had no access to a similarly comprehensive knowledge base, knowledge that—if we decide to use it—is substantial enough to tackle all our challenges.

Perhaps it is time now that we grasp that we, members of the human species, have never before in history been offered a window of opportunity as wide as now? Perhaps it is time that we accept this challenge? It might be time to stop looking back and engaging in ideological warfare fed by old cycles of humiliation (see chapter 8), thus stop feeding new cycles of humiliation. Old and new cycles of humiliation will hamper whatever global cooperation is needed for us to address the global challenges we face.

The dinosaurs died out. We have not yet survived as long as they did and already we are in a situation just as dire as the one they faced at the end of their time on Earth. We resemble the Titanic just before sinking. Instead of seeing that we are in existential danger, and that we might turn the situation around if we dared to, we defend our little territories, our little cabins on Titanic, and choose to overlook that the entire ship is sinking.

What a sad picture when the wealthy scramble ever more frantically for "wealth protection," while the less wealthy fade into *panem et circenses* ("bread and games") if they can still afford it, or into desperate apathy if they cannot. How sad that we choose to risk that none of our children, the wealthy included, will inherit a planet worth living on. All this at a time when unprecedented historical conditions open up that enable us to save our future.

Why are we so lost? I had the privilege of attending the *Morton Deutsch Legacy* book launch event on November 10, 2011, at the International Center for Cooperation and Conflict Resolution (ICCCR) at Columbia University, New York City. Psychologist John T. Jost had co-authored a chapter in Morton Deutsch's legacy book about the *soporific* (sleep inducing) effects of system justification.[9] Jost listed various reasons for why people justify systems that do not serve their interests. *The Irresistible Pull of Irrational Behavior* is another telling title that was already mentioned in chapter 6.[10] We seem to be caught in *legitimizing myths* that serve interests other than we believe they serve (psychologists Jim Sidanius, and Felicia Pratto coined this phrase[11]).

This is why I recommend self-critical humility and careful caution as to blind trust in concepts just because they appear coherent or represent "mainstream" thought (chapter 4). "It feels right," says our left brain, our "interpreter,"[12] yet, it might not be right. We have a conscious awareness of coherence only because the left hemisphere is providing us with "a running narration." We pick up fragments of information and our brain fills in the gaps with assumptions. Michael S. Gazzaniga, cognitive neuroscientist, says, "It only took me 25 years to ask the right question to figure it out."[13]

Emotions are not timeless or history-independent. On the contrary, the way emotions are felt, conceptualized, and organized is interdependent with the overall worldview of the community into which people are embedded. Emotions are not felt in a vacuum. Metaemotions, or how people feel about feelings, steer how feelings are felt.[14] Metaemotions depend on our cultural scripts, which, in turn, are embedded into large-scale geopolitical framings.

Hate "feels right" and perfectly coherent to some. Revenge feels justified to others. For the followers of Osama bin Laden holy rage feels so right that they see themselves called to violent Jihad. Ayn Rand has been referred to in chapter 4.[15] She was deeply convinced that her narrative was more coherent than that of all others. I recommend observing her body language, in contrast to Brooksley Born with her very warm and rather humble and self-reflective expressions.[16] As Michael Britton writes in chapter 9, if we have a wish to be helpers and nurturers, and this wish is not connected with empathy and warmth, it might not be truly nurturing.[17] Louise Sundararajan's integrative theory of the connection between belief, emotion, and health was introduced in chapter 4.[18]

People sometimes react with *humiliated fury*[19] when put down, but they may also accept subjugation as "honorable medicine." Underlings even create *cultures of subservience* and transmit them to their children. Sometimes being put down elicits genuine humility and acts as a source of *civilized* behavior.[20] Sometimes humiliation leads to rage, hot and cold. Adolf Hitler was a humiliation entrepreneur able to enact rage through shrewd long-term planning. Nowadays, we need a way to enable feelings of humiliation in the face of all the violations of dignity around the world to feed the kind of *conscientization* (chapter 4) that foments Mandela-like social change.

We need new narratives, narratives that might come closer to the reality of our interdependent world of the 21st century. We cannot do without narratives. We need narratives that anchor us in the world. This is what is so attractive about religions. They provide such narratives, as do family legends, or national and ideological myths. We learn where we come from and where we are going. This is not trivial. People are willing to die for these narratives. Suicide bombers give their lives for a meaning that reaches beyond their earthly existence into eternity. Whole nations feel humiliated when they perceive their religion to be insulted (the Danish cartoon controversy is just one example).

Modern secular Western science does not provide us with similar long-term narratives about where we come from, where we are going, and what our true significance is. Physicists are still looking for a grand unifying theory. Do concepts such as *democracy, communism, capitalism, modernity, postmodernity,* or *information age* help?

To construct new narratives that explain the human past in ways that help create a decent future, we need conversation, discourse, dialogue, joint inquiry, shared exploration. Many more voices should be heard. They are indigenous voices, the voices of women and children, the voices of minorities, the list is long. These oft-forgotten people may have just the input needed to develop clear direction for globally coordinated action.

In my work, I treat concepts such *democracy, communism, capitalism, modernism, postmodernism,* and *modern information age* as *epiphenomena, side effects* of deeper *logics,* which are inscribed in a time frame that encompasses the entire history of modern humans as it began circa 200,000 years ago.

In one of my books, I suggest there are four logics at the core of the human condition:

1. The question of whether and to what extent resources are expandable (*game theory,* as developed by the discipline of philosophy),

2. The question of whether the *security dilemma* is weaker or stronger (*international relations theory,* developed by political science),

3. The question as to what extent long-term or short-term horizons dominate (as described in many academic disciplines, among others *cross-cultural psychology*), and

4. The question of how the human capacity to tighten or loosen fault lines of identification is calibrated (*social identity theory,* developed by social psychology).[21]

Psychological mindsets and emotions, such as *pride, honor, dignity, humiliation,* and *humility,* are dependent on and intertwined with these *logics.* Two hundred thousand years ago, anatomically modern humans emerged on our planet and began colonizing Africa and the rest of the world. Here is a snap shot of my narrative.:

> For 90 percent of human history, our species was never disappointed by Mother Earth. New valleys of abundance could be found by simply wandering a bit farther. The game was a gracious win-win, because the cake of resources could always be expanded.
>
> However, the party had to end. Once the easily accessible parts of the world were populated, there were no more known "empty" valleys to populate. The Earth has limits.
>
> Today, we find ourselves at the end of the second, much more somber "party" of the last 10,000 years, and at the beginning of the second round of globalization (which Thomas Friedman divides into three phases[22]). There are no "new" continents whose populations can be conquered and exploited. This time, humanity is not only indirectly affected by the limitations of our planet, we are consciously aware of them. Pictures from space of planet Earth cannot be ignored or forgotten. Modern technology powers the current round of globalization, creating a *single global village*— whether we want it or not—eliciting a vision of a future *global village* of diversity, embedded into relationships that are characterized by respect for equal dignity for all.
>
> The security dilemma characterizes a world of several *villages.* The good news is that its basis in reality disappears when there is only *one village.* Humankind can relax in the hope that one village will render a more *benign* reality. Male courage is no longer needed to defend the village's walls; traditional *wars, soldiers,* and *victories* lose their anchoring in reality. Humankind can hope for a more benign future, less prone to "cardiac failure." Since knowledge is a more *expandable* resource than the geographical surface of the

Earth, the world regains some of the friendly win-win character that it had among early hunters and gatherers. Again, humankind can devote itself to *maintaining* and *policing* the global village. The past ten thousand years were ferocious, but we may be sailing into more benign times.

Yet there are problems which, if not mitigated, may preempt these *benign* prospects. The Earth is on the verge of reaching its ultimate limit. The future of the global village hangs in the balance. Will it be a sustainable village where every citizen has equal dignity? Or will it be a pyramid of power with small elites exploiting the rest? [23]

It is time to develop a global culture of *public deliberation*.[24] This chapter will model this approach in its contents and its presentation, by sharing some of the dialogues that I have had the privilege of conducting with scholars from around the world. This chapter breaks with the "impersonal" style of academia and its pretense of detached objectivity even more than earlier chapters. The aim is to model the need for conversation and joint exploration in the place of confrontational debate. It takes seriously that the dynamics of humiliation are not a fertile ground for clarity in inquiry.

As for *unity in diversity*, we have too little of both these days, particularly at global levels: we have too little unity with regard to values and practices, and too little diversity with regard to the range of voices being heard. Dignity is not yet a mainstream value that unifies the human family. The true realization of equality in dignity is openly opposed or covertly undermined by traditional dominator societies and by *might is right* market culture. There is insufficient unity in values. Not least global corporations highjack unity for profit.

A few more names will be given the floor in the following paragraphs, to help us see what is happening in the area of diversity.

Joseph Preston Baratta, historian and co-founder of the Center for Global Community and World Law, is among those who have recently taken up the discussion of global political structures.[25] He is particularly interested in the implementation of a new *human right to peace*, which means the right for solidarity, for all humanity, the right to a decent environment. This is the third generation of rights. The first generation includes the civil and political rights, also known as the "rights of the police station," the so-called negative and enforceable rights. The second generation consists of economic, social, and cultural rights, or the "rights of the breakfast table," positive, non-enforceable rights. According to Baratta: "As the rights of the police station are designed to protect the people, and the rights of the breakfast table are designed to promote the conditions by which the people can pursue their whole life, the rights of solidarity envision the better world of peace and justice for all humanity in the future."[26]

The Earth Federation Movement includes the World Constitution and Parliament Association (WCPA). Chapters and independent organizations, such as the Institute on World Problems (IOWP), affirm the creation of a non-military, democratic Earth Federation under the Constitution for the Federation of Earth. Professor of philosophy and religious studies, and chairperson of the program in Peace Studies at Radford University in Virginia, Glen T. Martin, serves as secretary general of the WCPA, as president of the Institute On World Problems (IOWP), as president of International Philosophers for Peace (IPPNO), and he is a member of the global advisory board of our Human Dignity and Humiliation Studies network.[27]

Glen Martin provides a summary of the history of related initiatives in his book titled *A Constitution for the Federation of Earth—With Historical Introduction, Commentary, and Conclusion*.[28] Martin calls for *planetary maturity* that involves a general awakening of human beings to authentic communicative speech, compassion, and mutual respect. He doubts that this can evolve fast enough on a cultural level and believes that a global body-politic of planetary democracy must be established.[29] Martin writes:

> Of all the constitutions written to date, and of all the world federalist initiatives undertaken during the past 60 years, none except the *Earth Constitution* comes even close to actualizing this 'third generation of human rights' promised and 'foreshadowed' by Article 28 of the U.N. Universal Declaration of Human Rights.[30]

Unity in diversity is a major theme for the Earth Constitution. It aims at creating *the holistic dynamic of unity in diversity essential to our survival.*

To speak of a holism of human relationships on Earth without the universal democratic rule of law constitutes a naïve idealism of the worst kind. Holism must be institutionalized and embodied in our political and economic systems, just as presently fragmentation and division are institutionalized in our non-democratic planetary systems.[31]

Glen Martin's book carries the title *Triumph of Civilization*. It calls for a conversion to holistic principles, not only of thought, but also of economics and politics. It calls for the founding of an *Earth community*.

Glen Martin is representative of many voices advocating a systems view of the global change required at the current juncture. Many movements and initiatives on democratic world governance structures merit attention.[32] As long ago as the 1930s, Rosika Schwimmer (1877–1948) set out to create a world government, co-founding the World Centre for Women's Archives in 1935.

In 1948, Garry Davis became a peace activist and creator of the first "World Passport," which he kindly presented to me.[33] Davis suggests that it is important to look into the writings of Emery Reves (Hungarian Révész Imre, 1904–1981), an advocate of world federalism, and pay ongoing attention to futurist R. Buckminster Fuller (1895–1983). He furthermore commends human rights activist and lawyer Luis Kutner (1908–1993), who helped found Amnesty International in 1961, and then Anthony Stafford Beer (1926–2002), best known for his work in the fields of operational research and management cybernetics. He recommends reading Derek Benjamin Heater, co-founder of the Politics Association and author of many works on world citizenship. Davis is opposed to a world federalism of sovereign nation-states.[34] He fears federalism would be too weak to handle global problems and rein in parochial interests and, therefore, he highlights the need for "enforceable world law as the corollary of world peace."[35]

Linda Hartling wrote about the approach of the Human Dignity and Humiliation Studies network: "We dignify our work by practicing a 'lean-green' approach to finances in which economic resources *serve,* rather than *lead* our efforts. Moreover, we actively practice the principles of dignity and humiliation theory by appreciating the full value of both economic *and* relational resources."[36] Indeed, she states, our financial structure incorporates many aspects of what Manish Jain and Shilpa Jain describe here as a "gift culture":

> In these challenging times of dominating multinational corporations, collapsing neo-liberal economies, and the commodification of everything, it seems vital to explore a different form of relationship and exchange. "Gifting", and the culture it draws from as well as evokes, provides a welcome oasis of hope from the hackneyed debates around capitalism vs. communism and the paralysis of TINA (There Is No Alternative). We put this intercultural dialogue together to try to share some of the important concepts, beliefs, practices and dreams around reclaiming the gift culture in our different spaces and places.
>
> This is perhaps our most critical and important work to-date. We have come to understand that the ideas and practices of deep learning, self-organizing learning communities and vibrant learning ecosystems are predicated on a culture of generosity, care, trust and friendship. The gift culture is critical to decommodifying education and the learning process, that is, removing it from the realm of artificial scarcity, monopolized production and distribution, and institutionalized hierarchy and discrimination. It is sad to witness that learning processes that are essential to being human like play, laughter, Nature, storytelling, care, etc. are being commercialized and as a result, are becoming accessible only to the elite. The gift culture inspires us to see our learning resources and relationships as part of the larger commons that is accessible to all and taken care of by all.[37]

Gift culture is one name for a dignified and dignifying future, as explained by Genevieve Vaughan.[38] Howard Richards offers a list of alternative names for a global *culture of solidarity*, such as a *solidarity economy, love ethic, servant leadership, production for use, de-alienation, mobilizing resources to meet needs, a higher form of pragmatism,* or *economic democracy.*[39]

"A world in balance is a world where the economy serves the people, where people respect and care for each other and live in accordance with the natural environment," is how the website of the Center for a World in Balance describes its vision.[40]

Balance is needed, the balance of homeostasis, a dynamic balance that avoids too much and too little.

If we wish to have a world in balance, rather than the "silent spring" predicted by Rachel Carson—a world in which chemical poisons have "silenced" nature—what to do?[41]

If we wish to nurture a sense of wonder rather than worship brutal and narrow utility, what to do?

If we wish to protect unity in diversity through balanced layers of subsidiarity in our global economic and political structures, what to do?

What are the elements we need to take particular care of? Here are a few of those elements: (1) openness over silence, (2) malleability over rigidity, (3) unity in diversity over uniformity and division, and (4) oneness over fragmentation, joining hands in a global *dignity transition.*

Openness over silence

Legitimizing myths help protect power. Sociologist Pierre Bourdieu explains that in the presence of silence, when certain questions are taboo and cannot be asked, powerful legitimizing myths can thrive, and vice versa. Power creates and uses silence to keep myths legitimate.[42]

The defining legitimizing myth that frames our world today is that "the market knows best" and that "all obstacles that could impede the market ought to be removed." This was the ideology former U.S. Federal Reserve Chairman Alan Greenspan advocated. When the system broke, he was "in a state of shocked disbelief" and admitted that he had been wrong in thinking that relying on banks to act on self-interest would be enough to protect shareholders and their equity.[43]

Is there a way to open up the discussion for all, now that we stand in front of a broken myth? Can we create space for a worldwide discussion on which myths and narratives of history would be more appropriate to tell for humankind's contemporary situation and its future?

I suggest we move into a bird's eye perspective on the human condition to arrive at narratives that help us.

Archaeologist Ingrid Fuglestvedt studies Scandinavian Stone Age history. She differentiates between a *Palaeolithic economy* and a *Mesolithic economy*. The Palaeolithic way flourished during the *pioneer time* when virgin Scandinavian land, the *land beyond,* was peopled. In contrast to later Mesolithic economies, the earlier Palaeolithic way was characterized by egalitarian relationships among people and with animals.

> A Palaeolithic economy demarcates from other hunter-gatherer economies by its absence of a *true* economy of the symbolic gift. Exchange between people will rather take place in a context of sharing. Thus, a *Palaeolithic economy* may be defined by its orientation towards the exchange of spirit and matter between human and animal communities, and not human-to-human other than in contexts of sharing. This is different from gift exchange. This in fact defines the egalitarian ethos—the successful hunter shares, and even if the same person turns out to be the constantly successful hunter, and therefore the continuous "giver" of meat, whereas others are constant receivers—this asymmetry does not have social consequences, since practice circles around the pleasing of the animal master, and the strong social obligations following from it. Rather it works strengthening on egalitarian structures because people will make endeavors to reduce the potential "show-off-effect" following from hunting success.[44]

The transition from a Palaeolithic to a Mesolithic economy seems to have been interlinked with a transition from *animism* to *totemism* as dominating world views. Totemism is mostly associated with lineage-based groups who live a semi-sedentary life and are affiliated to defined and more or less confined landscapes. A totemic approach entails classifications of beings in the world; totemism often involves attitudes towards big game animals as prey and less as respected personal agents, as is typical of the animist attitude. The earlier animist way of being, in contrast, is manifested in a sense of wondering and openness to learning from nature, or "an ecological mode of being."[45]

Social anthropologist Tim Ingold explains the *ecological way of being* as openness to get to know natural powers rather than control them.[46] Getting to know non-human persons in the environment is like getting to know another human being. Animists regard animals as friends and persons.

Ingold has developed the concept of *enskilment*, a process of "embodiment" and "enmindment" where learning is not divorced from action.[47] This is how he explains it:

> Knowledge of the world is gained by moving about in it, exploring it, attending to it, ever alert to the signs by which it is revealed. Learning to see, then, is a matter not of acquiring schemata for mentally constructing the environment but of acquiring the skills for direct perceptual engagement with its constituents, human and non-human, animate and inanimate...it is a process not of enculturation but of enskilment. [48]

Robert Leonard Carneiro's *circumscription theory* is relevant here (see also chapter 3 and 6).[49] Robert Carneiro has his office across the corridor of Margaret Mead's former workplace in the American Museum of Natural History in New York City. I had the privilege of listening to his wisdom at his desk in the museum on December 1, 2010, and I look forward to welcoming him in our next "Workshop on Transforming Humiliation and Violent Conflict."

When resources are abundant, a win-win logic frames human life, which is inherently more benign than a win-lose logic.[50] When humankind's "peopling campaign" began to reach limits and be *circumscribed*, a profound shift occurred, a shift that affected everybody's lives. Even where it did not turn hunter-gatherers into agriculturalists, it was bound to have an effect. As long as early hunter-gatherers could merely wander off to virgin abundance, the entire frame of the situation was of a win-win nature, a frame that does not lend itself to pushing for deep hierarchies or engaging in aggressive border disputes.

Contrary to what many people would like to believe, it seems there is, indeed, no archeological proof of organized and systematic fighting among early hunter-gatherers; systematic war occurred later: "The Hobbesian view of humans in a constant state of 'Warre' is simply not supported by the archaeological record," writes anthropologist Jonathan Haas in 2001.[51] Haas is an anthropological archaeologist with over 30 years of field experience in both North and South America. His interests include the origins of war, the archaeology of the Southwest and Peru, and the evolution of complex society anthropology. In a personal communication on May 6, 2009, Haas confirmed that his 2001 statement has been "supported further by more recent archaeological research."

In my *Making Enemies* book of 2006, I made a short summary:

> As long as there are plenty of resources and groups of people lived far enough apart so as to remain unaware of each other, there was no problem. However, as soon as people moved geographically close enough for mutual raiding, but psychologically too far away to build good communication and trust, leaders became trapped in the security dilemma and had no choice but to invest in arms. As these *villages* now coalesce into *one global village*, the problem disappears again. The security dilemma poses grave problems only as long as villages stay in a medium distance, too close for geopolitical security and too far for human security.[52]

In other words, we may conclude that only for roughly the past 10,000 years, or the last five percent of human history, have humans been "brutish," and not due to their nature but out of necessity, forced by the security dilemma. Warriorhood is not a "natural" state. It carries a very high cost. Warlords have a reason for drugging militia youth. Soldiers come back from war so traumatized that they cannot overcome it.[53] During the past millennia, a peaceful philosopher king had little chance to survive for long before being toppled by warrior kings, from within or from outside. The dominator model, due to its strategic advantages, won out.[54]

A recent book by experimental psychologist Steven Pinker has caused some stir.[55] Linda and I, with a group of friends and members of our

Human Dignity and Humiliation Studies network, went to Pinker's presentation of his book in Portland, Oregon, on October 26, 2011. He based his argument on statistics which, according to him, showed that prehistoric violence was higher than now. His slides showed that he included studies on prehistoric violence (such as crushed skulls, traces of weapons in bones) that rated prehistoric violence from very high to very low. Pinker settled for a middle score. This score represented a higher rate of violence than today, thus forming the starting point for his argument.

I suspected that he had lumped together prehistoric periods that ought to be analyzed separately. My understanding was that violence was much lower prior to what Robert Carneiro calls *circumscription* kicking in (thus disagreeing with Pinker), that violence then increased, only to decreased again now (here agreeing with Pinker). I wrote to Ingrid Fuglestvedt and Jonathan Haas about this.

Ingrid Fuglestvedt replied: "You are absolutely right; he is lumping together an immense time span and very different periods into one big 'prehistory.' Doing this, he is also communicates to people of today that we were more 'primitive' in earlier times. This is contrary to all anthropological knowledge. He also implicitly praises progress, and consequently, progress as 'always' something positive for humankind."[56]

Jonathan Haas generously sent me two unfinished manuscripts that discuss my question.[57] He reports that recent years have witnessed a resurgence of archaeological and anthropological studies of warfare.[58] He explains that there are two basic schools of thought. One holds that warfare has deep historical origins and that warfare is an integral part of human culture. The other school sees warfare as a late-comer on the cultural horizon, "only arising in very specific material circumstances and being quite rare in human history until the development of agriculture in the past 10,000 years."[59] Haas agrees with Martin Wobst, that "the study of warfare in the human past is being constrained by the tyranny of the ethnographic and ethological records."[60] He concludes that "ultimately, we would argue that the root causes of warfare are to be found in demographic and economic pressures on specific populations at specific points in their respective history. Waves of peace can equally be explained by looking at the material conditions of life in those same historical trajectories."[61]

My reaction to Haas was enthusiastic. I expressed my excitement with his text to him on October 29, 2011, and wrote:

> Over the years, when I was reading archeology and anthropology, I was always humbled by the fact that I am not an expert in these fields. At the same time I wondered at all the shortcomings that you so poignantly summarize as "the tyranny of the ethnographic and ethological records." I always thought that it was extremely strange that the impact of circumscription, or "demographic and economic pressures on specific populations at specific points in their respective history" was overlooked. I doubted my own intellectual capacities and thought that I must miss something: why did all these brilliant people overlook such glaring aspects?
>
> It seems to me that this "tyranny of the ethnographic and ethological records" is serving a bias that may not be so dissimilar to the biases earlier colonizers were convinced of when they met "primitive" people in far-flung parts of the world, who, they concluded, needed to be "civilized"? It seems to me that there is more at work than simply ignorance, or simply a cultural bias in the West toward zooming in on the individual rather than the context, but that some ideological profit is being sought?

This brings us back to legitimizing myths and narratives.

Gro Steinsland studies the power of rulers and the ideology of rulership in Nordic societies from the Vikings through the medieval age, from about 800 until 1200 CE.[62] Christianity arrived relatively late in the North, and therefore the transition of ideologies in this region is well documented. Steinsland analyzes the eddaic poem Skirnismål and its depiction of the so-called myth of the sacred marriage (the Greek technical term is *hieros gamos*) or the erotic alliance between a god and a giant woman, which elevated the ruler and gave him and his lineage a unique position with regard to other people. With Christianity a related, medieval ideology of rulership was imported, namely the depiction of the king as an image of the Heavenly God.

Social anthropologist Fredrik Barth uses the example of Inner New Guinea to explain how cosmologies, which often serve as legitimizing myths, are created.[63]

Leading expert on contemporary Muslim thought, Ibrahim Abu-Rabi, wrote:

> Globalization has often aided the political elite in the Muslim world to spread their version of "false consciousness" by means of the mass media and given them the technological means to exercise full hegemony over society. Capitalism in the Muslim world, although concentrated in few hands, is deeply entrenched. It is part of the global capitalist system. As such, it competes with other capitalist groups or formations in the pursuit of unlimited wealth and power, when possible. Domestically, Arab capitalism assumes a relentless pursuit of power in order to protect its economic interests while constantly pursuing greater wealth. Instead of working for the progress of its society, capitalism in the Arab world seeks only the preservation of its hegemony and the expansion of its control. This expansion takes the form of a meager investment in religious institutions in order to exploit the religious feelings of the masses for its materialist ends.[64]

This brings us to the defining legitimizing myth that frames our world today, namely, that "the market knows best" and that "all obstacles that could impede the market ought to be removed," and that this myth has been shattered.[65]

As mentioned earlier, I did my doctoral research in Somalia and Rwanda.[66] Somalis have a point when they say that their culture of raiding, which is part and parcel of a pastoralist warrior culture, is very similar to the American lone hero culture and to ruthless individualism, and also to the colonial culture of raiding.

As it seems, the myth of "the market" that "knows best," combined with the American Dream of unlimited possibilities for everyone, provided the background for an almost unbelievable raiding campaign. California, for example, was until a few years ago a haven of affordable education and enabling infrastructure, but those resources were virtually

192 A Dignity Economy

destroyed by the financial crisis. And this version of the American Dream did not stay home; its campaign went around the world.

When we draw together insights from archaeology, anthropology, and history, we learn that while animists are friends of life, while agriculturalists are friends of land, nomadic warriors are friends of raiding. And raiding and gambling can be straightforwardly combined: it is easier to gamble with the possessions of others, the loot from raids, than one's own possessions.

In Somalia, warlords put militia boys on pickup trucks or pirate ships, give them weapons, keep them drugged, and sometimes reward them with young girls as sex slaves. In the City of London, for young "cityboys," [67] the equivalent to the pickup truck or pirate ship has been the investment bank and the bar; their weapons have been derivatives bought speculatively as "financial weapons of mass destruction;"[68] many thrive on cocaine; and they reward themselves with expensive sex parties.[69] As long as there is something left to raid, this scheme is a huge success—both warlords and militia boys are satisfied. As long as they have the weapons, the suffering of those they raid is not relevant to them. For the warlords' social and ecological environment as a whole, however, their success means ruin.

This chapter calls for more voices to enter into a global dialogue. Linda and I and our network members believe that we, as humankind, need to "harvest" from all cultural traditions, past and present, those beliefs and practices that help protect the dignity of unity in diversity (chapters 1 and 3).[70]

It seems fitting to conclude this section with a dialogue, since joint dialogical exploration is what this book recommends. And it is fitting to conclude it with a dialogue with an archaeologist, since this book also suggests that we consider the entirety of our human history, and that we remember that some of our ancestors prior to 10,000 years ago might have something to teach us today.

I conversed with archaeologist Ingrid Fuglestvedt in October 2011. Ingrid agrees that it is possible to conceptualize *totemism* as the first historical "application" of *legitimizing myths*, namely, to legitimize the perceived "right" of a particular group of people to a particular land, in distinction to the land of "neighbors" who might visit, but not stay, or even become "enemies." Ingrid's reply was as follows:

Indeed, totemism—as the concept is used today—involves notions of a material "kinship" between people, i.e. a given group with its land. People and land share substance, and thus this land belongs to "our" group. This sharing of substance between people and land will be a core element in their origin myth. How much room there is for other groups to stay or move in will vary. Clan groups' social attachment to a particular land can certainly be said to be a kind of "first limits" on (other) people (from outside). Yet this is a social situation that only makes the grounds for negative social consequences. Ethnography is also full of examples of clans that very easily, and with much openness and warmth, include newcomers and visitors and give them full clan membership. Therefore, attachments to a particular land territory do not necessarily have negative consequences. It is rather a situation that facilitated conflict and exclusion.[71]

Then I asked Ingrid about totemism, and whether it may be seen as the very first step of an ideology that overlays culture over nature, or as Linda would formulate it, "the beginning of the global dissociation process that ultimately leads to a loss of empathy."

Ingrid: Yes I think it can. Totemism is also about social classification on the basis of differences in nature, a mirror of categories of nature. So, implicitly this involves a line of demarcation between nature and culture. With animism, on the other hand (cf. Ingold[72]), nature—like animals—is included in the social world, and a nature-culture division is not acknowledged.

Evelin: The word *circumscription* stems from Latin *circum* (around) and *scribere* (to write), in other words, circumscription means limitation, enclosure, or confinement. The terms *territorial* or *social* circumscription address limitations in these respective areas. Is it possible that the transition from "home versus *virgin land beyond*" toward "my home versus my neighbor's home" may be a first, timid step in response to circumscription?

Ingrid: Yes, I think so. We talk about a first step towards limitations on persons' integrity, generally.

Evelin: And the agricultural revolution with its "big-man" dominator model of society (Riane Eisler) could be seen as an adaptation to an intensification of circumscription?

Ingrid: Yes, it may.

Evelin: Allow me to reflect on my own situation in connection to my work: As you know, dear Ingrid, I was born into an identity of being an "unwelcome newcomer" (I was born into a displaced family, into an identity that "where we lived was not our home and there was no home for us to go to"). The longer I live, the more I find this kind of identity to be quite useful in learning to think of oneself as a member of humankind in general. Let me explain: Remember Easter Island (I just saw a new documentary on how the ancient inhabitants of Easter Island went from abundance to circumscription to destruction). From the point of view of its fauna and flora, the arriving Polynesians were "newcomers." And they turned out to be rather unwelcome newcomers since they ravaged the island. They were newcomers who "unearned" their welcome, as Linda would say. This is what we, as a human species, have done as well. We have failed to earn our welcome on planet Earth.

An identity of "unwelcome newcomer" has the advantage of providing a humble starting point, it avoids any undue sense of entitlement. What we, as humankind, seem in need of learning is a sense of worth connected with the dignity not only of humans, but of all living beings. I personally attach my sense of worth not to status or to material possessions, or to any sense of affiliative identity, be it to an ethnic, national, religious, or gender category, except that I belong to the "newcomers" on planet Earth. I attach my sense of worth to trying my best to become ever more *enskilled* (I love the term enskilment as coined by Timothy Ingold) in awe and wonderment, in creative openness with respect to my social and ecological environments, including my own body-mind experiences in service to others and the world. In my lived life, I am very close to animists in many respects: I never look for a "place to stay" when I plan the next step in my global life, for instance, I always look for relationships of mutual friendship and love; these *relationships* are my home, not "a place."

Ingrid: I really love your standpoints and reflections on this! And my heart is with the animists.

Evelin: As you know, Linda and I believe that we, as humankind, need to "harvest" from all cultural traditions, past and present, harvest those beliefs and practices that help protect the dignity of unity in diversity.

Ingrid: I do follow you in your approach to this. At the bottom of my Stone Age interest is my political view that the egalitarian hunter-gatherers, especially the animists, are the best societies this world have ever witnessed. This is not a reference to the garden of Eden, it is to acknowledge that some systems are better than others in taking care of everybody's integrity, both human and animal.

Evelin: Bob Randall is a Yankunytjatjara Elder and a traditional owner of Uluru (Ayers Rock) in Australia. Carmen Hetaraka is a bearer of oral Maori tradition. From listening to Bob and Carmen, I would say that their world is a totemic world combined with elements of animism, is this a correct observation?

Ingrid: Yes, on general grounds, totemic societies may include an animist approach in certain respects. When operating with animism and totemism, I am always careful to express that we talk about "systems dominated by a totemic/animic world view." We should not forget that animism and totemism are analytical labels, even if successful in encircling real phenomena of how people approach the world.

Here the conversation with Ingrid ends. This little dialogue shows the possible pay-off gained from conversing about large-scale geohistorical lenses to discern where we may want to go in today's world.

Steven Pinker began his book presentation in Portland, Oregon, with Thomas Hobbes' analysis of the world in a state of anarchy,[73] then he mentioned Immanuel Kant and his work on *perpetual peace* with its pillars of democracy, trade, and international community.[74] He then moved on to referring to Peter Singer's *expanding circles*, to a widening scope of justice and widening boundaries of compassion.[75]

Pinker differentiates six historical trends, the first being the evolution from hunter-gatherers into settled civilizations, which he believes was a *pacification process*. It is followed by the *civilizing process*, the *humanitarian revolution*, the *long peace*, the *new peace*, and, lastly, the *rights revolution*.

Why are such narratives so important for this book? Why do I include them here? Again, because they can inspire us. If we want to devise new ways of living together on planet Earth, we need an idea of who we are. We rarely engage in viewing our existence on Earth from a bird's eye perspective. Yet, in times of crisis this is crucial.

The reader is by now familiar with my narrative: Our bodies and souls had circa 190,000 years to evolve in a win-win context. The animist mindset is something we can be proud of. And this view has nothing to do with romanticizing the *noble savage*, it has something to do with recognizing the power of *frames* (chapter 10). The dichotomy of Hobbes versus Rousseau is a false and outdated choice (chapter 8).[76]

The animist mindset deserves that we re-invigorate its relational and egalitarian spirit wherever we can, among others, by shaping our institutions accordingly. During most of the past 10,000 years, we did not do so well. We did not react to circumscription in the wisest of ways, yet, our excuse may be that the security dilemma is a formidable force. We were caught in dominator societies pitted against each other in mutual fear.

If we gather our wits now, we can nurture a global community that cooperates and designs win-win contexts of communal sharing and stewardship. We face a window of opportunity, whether we use it or not. And we'd better use it.

This window has been slowly opening for quite a while and has already had some positive effects (and this is in line with Pinker's description of decreasing cruelty). It was in 1757, for instance (chapter 3), that "to humiliate" for the first time appeared in the encyclopedia to imply the antisocial violation of dignity rather than a prosocial "humbling lesson."[77]

In the past, we adapted to changing conditions haphazardly. We are much less the puppets of history now. Never before have we had such a good understanding and such good tools to shape our fate in intentional ways. Nowadays, we can sit together and reflect intentionally. Let us do that.

Malleability over rigidity[78]

Life is a process. Reality is fluid and continuously malleable. If we try to "nail down" living processes, if we press them into static definitions, concepts, or institutions, inspired by the rigidity of Newtonian mechanics, we may create hardness and disharmony where softness would be more effective—we know that water is stronger than stone. Quantum physics or biological growth processes may sometimes be more suitable models if we wish to design social and societal structures that nurture harmony. *Quantum social science* has been proposed—"human beings are in effect 'walking wave particle dualities,' not classical material objects."[79]

Philosopher and social critic Ivan Illich has written on the commoditization of language, the tendency to use nouns instead of verbs. Philosopher Agnes Heller, in her theory of the consciousness of everyday life, says masculinity, on an ordinary, everyday level, reproduces itself through the interplay of individual consciousness and social structures. The traditional masculinist models of consciousness objectify world order, obfuscating how processual and continuously changeable it really is.[80]

The concept of the *reflective equilibrium* offers a way out. Philosopher Otto Neurath's metaphor of a ship can illustrate it. Formerly, scientists assumed that they only did science when they found a dry dock or at least could pretend that dry docks existed. Today, we understand that we must humbly accept and live with the fear-inducing uncertainty that human understanding of the world is limited. There is no dry dock. What we may think of as certain, will always be threatened by yet undiscovered insights and discoveries.

The solution is to circle through the reflective equilibrium and create understanding and action from this movement. This means continuously rebuilding the ship while at sea. It means creating just enough structure to keep the ship afloat, but never too much rigidity, which would cause the ship to break and sink.

Stability is dynamic.

Unity in diversity over uniformity and division

Around the world, there are many indigenous approaches to conflict resolution and consensus building. In Hawai'i it is called *ho'ho pono pono*, and similar notions are to be found in many other cultural realms, *musyawarah, silahturahmi, asal ngumpul, palaver, shir, jirga* are just a few examples (see chapter 8 for research methodologies such as *ethno-mimesis* and chapter 10 for *nudging, persuading,* and *listening into voice*).

These approaches need to be studied in more depth. Today's mainstream approaches, including contemporary concepts of democracy, are not yet adequately efficient and dignifying. Asking people to vote "yes" or "no" may lead to the manifestation of dualism where nondualism would be more fitting.

For my doctoral research, I interviewed Abdulqadir H. Ismail Jirdeh, Deputy Speaker of the Parliament in Hargeisa, Somaliland.[81] He explained that democracy, with its majority rule, violates the old nomad tradition of decision by consensus of the elders.[82] He said that majority rule has the potential to deeply offend and humiliate those who lose. He described in detail how he would prevent violent responses by approaching losers after voting, how he would express appreciation for their views and show confidence that their views would be honored at a later stage.

Muneo Yoshikawa's nondualistic double swing model was introduced in chapter 3. In an ever more interdependent world, dependence versus independence are outdated notions. Interdependence connects two entities, O and O, in a nondualistic way, ∞. *Dualism*, in contrast, means merging them into one entity, ◎, or separating them into two isolated entities, O|O. Dualism means *either* separation *or* merging; *either* agreement *or* disagreement; *either* one *or* two. *Nondualism* means separation *and* connection; agreement *and* disagreement; one *and* two.

On November 16, 2011, writer and peace scholar Janet Gerson brought me to Zuccotti Park and The Atrium in New York City, where most of the Occupy Wall Street activities took place then.[83] We discussed unity in diversity and that most people think it is a zero sum principle: most believe that if you want more unity, you have to give up diversity, and vice versa. This misconception feeds fear of global superordinate rules and regulations. Many are afraid that also global unity can only be had at the price of global uniformity, and that this will end in an Orwellian world. Yet, when unity is defined by dignity, when what unifies us are our shared values of equality in dignity, then unity in diversity means *more* unity and at the same time *more* diversity. Unity in dignity can only be manifested by nurturing diversity and letting it flourish. It is a win-win situation. Both poles, unity and diversity, must be boosted if dignity is what defines unity, and both need to be guarded: unity must be guarded against losing diversity through letting it degrade into uniformity, and diversity must be guarded against the destruction of unity when diversity degrades into division.

Janet was enthusiastic and explained that Buckminster Fuller's notion of *tensegrity* can describe the stability of this unity in diversity (the term is a contraction of tensional integrity).[84] Subsequent to our conversations, Janet felt moved to write a short paper. This is her summary:

Occupy Wall Street (OWS) is a social movement that demands economic dignity. The 99% are challenging Wall Street financiers' control of what many of us previously understood to be our democracy. Thousands of participants are coordinating sustained resistance to the current humiliating and excluding economic-political crisis, to contest what Amartya Sen calls "outrageous arrangements of injustice."[85] OWS is challenging our government to respond instead to *the plurality* of the population's concerns. But OWS's challenge to the 1%'s dominance also presents a challenge to collective norms by its democratic ethic of deliberation.

The OWS "Principles of Solidarity" document declares "We are daring to imagine a new socio-political and economic alternative that offers greater possibility of equality",[to] "reclaim our mortgaged future," and, thus strives to restore our eroded collective dignity.[86]

"Tweeps" are people with a mutual following on Twitter. *TweetNadwa* means "Tweet Symposium" and is a method that makes traditional indigenous methods possible at a large scale, enabled through latest information technology.

I lived in Cairo-Mohandessin for seven years (1984–1991), and it is great to know that in neighboring Dokki the new socio-political movement called *TweetNadwa* has emerged "to debate one of the most controversial issues of all, the role of religion in politics."[87] *TweetNadwa* operates as an online Egyptian forum developed by Egyptian grassroots organizer, Alaa Abd El Fattah.

> Hundreds of Twitter users and audience members gathered in-person to read and respond over a large screen in Dokki, Egypt. They voiced their thoughts on hot-button issues in no more than 140 seconds (for in-person attendees)—or 140 characters (for those participating online). The setting resembled a talk show studio setting except that participants, or "netizens", voiced opinions and thoughts on many levels—ranging from in-person questions to ones posed online by people sitting in front of their computers in other parts of Egypt. These "netizens" included Egyptians and expatriates, who could participate from countries like Canada or the United Arab Emirates. If audience members agreed with participants' responses, then they waved their hands in the air rather than clapped, so as not to disrupt the short response period.[88]

Fingerspelling, which is also used in deaf education, is now entering the public sphere as a new sign language for larger gatherings. Janet Gerson demonstrated it for me: the little finger is up for "information," two fingers forming a "c" means asking for "clarification." For a video demonstration, watch, for example, "Occupy Portland—Down Twinkles."[89]

These new methods have several features that old ones could not achieve. Groups that have never met in person can share views; virtual participation ensures that idea-makers are not being judged by appearance; large-scale controversial and nuanced conversations about religion and politics can be conducted peacefully; and abstract controversy is transformed into an accessible discussion available to anyone who respects constructive dialogue.

In conclusion, unity in diversity can be nurtured now in ways that were not available in former times. Unity in diversity can be manifested and protected in hitherto unattainable ways.

One global family on a path toward a *dignity transition*

Throughout the past millennia, humans lived in a fragmented world, always afraid of neighbors who could quickly turn into enemies. Adolf Hitler was set on war and killing and simply wishing for peace was not a valid protection. The security dilemma was the overarching definitorial frame for everything in its reach. Nobody who hoped for peace could escape the motto of the security dilemma: "Si vis pacem para bellum," or "If you want peace, prepare for war." The enemy was to be killed or captured and humiliated into subservience. Humiliating an enemy was seen as prosocial, as was humiliating inferiors to prevent them from rising up. The enemy was not a fellow human being. The enemy had no right to equality in dignity and rights. The masculinist culture that Agnes Heller describes has its home here, in a culture of uniformity that lacks diversity.

Article 1 of the Universal Declaration of Human Rights (UDHR) rejects this notion of an enemy in its first sentence: "All human beings are born free and equal in dignity and rights." Gandhi said: "There is no path to peace. Peace is the path." In a human rights context, humiliation is antisocial, it is a violation of dignity and rights. "To humiliate" is to transgress the rightful expectations of every human being and of all humanity that basic human rights will be respected.

Are human rights ideals utopian? Is the idea of equality in dignity for all utopia? An increasingly interconnected world offers a window of opportunity for its realization. As has been repeatedly expressed throughout this book, we live in exceptional historical times. Virtually every news broadcast on television, in any part of the world, starts with the image of a turning globe. None of our ancestors was able to see that. Never has it been so visually intelligible that we are *one* species living on *one* little planet that we inherit or borrow from our children.

What do we do now?

I call for a multi-thronged global *dignity transition* (chapters 3 and 10).

The more we understand and embrace our new situation, the more the window of opportunity opens, for the spirit of equality in dignity and unity in diversity to manifest. Space opens for a global dialogue that is non-utopian about a more dignified future for all of humankind, a future without humiliating structures and institutions.

If we grasp this opportunity, there is a chance for a future where "good" and "bad" neighbors can live together. Police may still be needed, but the notions of "enemy" and "warrior" will no longer apply. The capacity of people to feel humiliated will translate into a Mandela-like path of creating social and societal structures that dignify all. And this will increasingly be done not by fighting *against* old structures, but by working *for* a future of dignity. As mentioned above, working *for* something new is much more dignified, dignifying, and effective than the old paradigm of fighting *against* enemies, foes, or outdated concepts.

Flourishing is an emerging buzzword these days[90] that draws together threads of thought from a wide range of thought communities.[91] What negative emotions are to threat, positive emotions are to opportunity. Flourishing is more than the opposite of pathology and apathy, it means the unfolding of the best of one's potential, it means creativity, growth, and resilience, in relationship with oneself, with other living beings, and with the abiotic environment.

Barbara L. Fredrickson and Christine Branigan focus on positive emotions.[92] They offer a theoretical perspective that they call the *broaden-and-build* model. This model questions common assumptions of contemporary emotion theory,[93] namely, that emotions must necessarily entail action tendencies and lead to physical action. Rather than action, positive emotions facilitate changes in cognitive activity.

In the spirit of flourishing, a greater depth of questioning can be aimed for. The Norwegian philosopher Arne Næss was introduced in chapter 2. He developed the notion of the "depth of intention," the "depth of questioning" or "deepness of answers." Greater depth means continuing to ask questions at the point at which others stop asking.[94]

May I speak to you, the reader, directly?

My message to the "99%" and to the "1%" is as follows: Please engage in deep questioning. Begin with identifying who you are: Are you an idealist? Are you a follower? Are you a bystander? Are you a cynic?

My message to idealists: If you are an idealist, you deserve to be praised for your passion. This is an invaluable asset. Michael Britton was presented earlier in this book. He explains that people who wish to do good, who wish to be nurturing, will want to see others do well in taking care of their own lives.

Please ask yourself: are you achieving real nurturing in the work you do? Remember, even the most well-intentioned help can be counterproductive. International aid is a prime example. Resentment and violent backlashes typically shock those who thought they were doing good.[95]

May I share some of my experiences with you? When I came to Africa in 1998 for my doctoral research, my motivation was to do good with my research. Yet, I met bitter distrust:

> First you colonize us. Then you leave us with a so-called democratic state that is alien to us. After that you watch us getting dictatorial leaders. Then you give them weapons to kill half of us. Finally you come along to "measure" our suffering and claim that this will help us!? Are you crazy?[96]

Who is "right" and who is "wrong"? How should help be designed to be of benefit and not contribute to humiliation? I tried to listen more.

> You Westerners get a kick out of our problems. You have everything back home, you live in luxury, and you are blind to that. You think you're suffering when you can't take a shower or have to wait for the bus for more than two hours! Your four-wheel drive cars cover our people with dust! You enjoy being a king in our country, but you're just average at home! All you want is to

have fun, get a good salary, write empty reports to your organization back home or publish some articles, so you can continue this fraud. You are a hypocrite! You know that we need help—how glad we'd be not to need it! It would be great if you'd really listen to *us*, not just to the greedy ones among *us* who exploit your arrogant stupidity for their own good! We feel deeply humiliated by your arrogant and self-congratulating help![97]

In Africa, I continuously met descriptions of aid efforts, many of which were entirely praiseworthy, others entirely well-intentioned, yet, some came close to parody (containing elements of truth):

You helpers come along, build wells (or some other installations or services liable to be ecologically unsound or unmanageable in the longer run), create a few short-term jobs for chauffeurs, secretaries and security personnel, and then you disappear again![98]

Clearly, also recipients of help may sometimes be the ones who are "wrong." Help may be well-intentioned and well-designed, but meet recipients who show insufficient appreciation for the efforts of the helpers. Before starting my field work in Somalia in 1998, I talked with NGO personnel who had worked with Somali refugees. They told me that they would not support me in emphasizing Somali victimhood:

These people are arrogant and unappreciative. You should have seen their behavior in the refugee camps! They regard help as their right and are extremely pushy, unreasonable and choosy. They cheat us helpers wherever they can. They accuse us of humiliation. But if you want to speak to the people who are really being humiliated, then speak to us, the helpers![99]

Perhaps, rather than asking who is right and who is wrong, it is important to describe the interplay, as well as the complexity of accusations and counter-accusations? Perhaps shared humility is needed? Perhaps self-reflection is needed on all sides, rather than the brazen contention that good intentions are sufficient?

Sam Engelstad was the UN's Chief of Humanitarian Affairs (and on several occasions Acting Humanitarian Coordinator in Mogadishu in 1994). *Operation Restore Hope* was launched on December 9, 1992, by the United States. However, like the interventions that preceded it, also this one failed. As was already touched upon in chapter 8, in 1993 an angry crowd dragged a dead American soldier through the streets of Mogadishu in Somalia. The offer of help to an impoverished and ravaged country, Somalia, was greeted with acts of humiliation perpetrated against the helpers. Engelstad wrote to me (I quote with his permission):

> During my time in Somalia in 1994, humiliation was never far from the surface. Indeed, it pretty much suffused the relationship between members of the UN community and the general Somali population. In the day-to-day interaction between the Somalis and UN relief workers like ourselves, it enveloped our work like a grey cloud. Yet, the process was not well understood, and rarely intended to be malevolent.[100]

Engelstad added that "Among the political and administrative leadership of the UN mission, however, humiliation and its consequences were far better understood and were frequently used as policy tools. Regardless of intent, it was pernicious and offensive to many of us."

In November 2011, I met two highly idealistic groups of people. As reported earlier, on November 16, 2011, I was shown around in Zuccotti Park by Janet Gerson, who writes her doctoral dissertation on *public deliberation*.[101] I was deeply touched by listening to a volunteer who was standing in the pouring rain in the middle of Zuccotti Park, explaining his motivation. He had not slept for 24 hours, because he was the only volunteer with medical expertise available in the Occupy Wall Street arena. He said that "if others are missing in action," this would not shake his dedication.

Just a few days earlier, I had met another friend who had given a facilitation training to employees of Monsanto. These employees were equally dedicated; in their case they passionately wanted to "help feed the poor." They were deeply hurt by criticism from skeptics of transgenic plant products saying that their work may be less then ethically acceptable.

The desire to do good is of utmost value, wherever it occurs. Yet, people of all convictions do well to consider asking deeper questions, in shared humility, to make their dedication render optimal results (chapter 2). What Michael Britton writes here is valid for people of all ideological convictions:

> Creating a seed that does not survive a year and that only does well with the fertilizer you sell, when you have a monopoly on selling seed to farmers, means they have to come back to you every year, and have to buy your pesticide and fertilizer. They have lost the ability to function without you. They are less resourceful, less resilient, thanks to your intervention. This goes to the heart of what a nurturing attitude is all about: The impulse to nurture wants to see others more capable of making life successfully on their own, not less capable. The strategy of making people more dependent makes sense within the world as opportunity for private gain view, while making people more resilient, more capable of doing on their own, more independent of you, is self-defeating on your part in that same view. From a nurturing point of view, things are exactly the opposite. But, lest this be misleading, the point in nurturing is not to create a world of independent, self-caring loners, so much as to create a world of resilient, lively people who interact well with each other, including with you, in making a very interesting, rich, well-loved life together. It's about community, and the community of communities, a world of societies, with as much vibrance, resilience, generosity and creativity and productivity distributed throughout as possible.[102]

My message to followers and bystanders: If you are a follower or bystander, remember that there is no fence on which you can safely sit and watch the world falter. Marshall McLuhan reminds us: "There are no passengers on spaceship earth. We are all crew."

"We Must Stand Up! Not By!" is a section in one of my books,[103] which draws on the work by psychologist Ervin Staub, who argues that the significant element in the atrocities perpetrated by Nazi Germany was that bystanders stood idly *by* instead of standing *up* and getting *involved*.[104]

Ervin Staub calls for bystanders to get involved and stand *up* and not *by*.

My message to cynics: If you are a cynic, please begin by heeding the Chinese saying, "The person who says 'it cannot be done' should not interrupt the person doing it."

When you have retreated from the frontline, think about "realistic" Realpolitik. Think about business as usual and whether it is realistic or utopian. So-called realists doubt that humankind can come together and create world peace, since, they say, the world is caught in Hobbesian anarchy and condemned to endless conflict and war. So-called liberals are more optimistic, believing that international cooperation can make peace prevail over anarchy.[105] Where do you stand?

I am both more optimistic than many liberals and more pessimistic than many realists. I am more optimistic, because I believe that the historically unprecedented *ingathering* of humankind offers us benign opportunities more than ever. "For the first time since the origin of our species, humanity is in touch with itself" said anthropologist William Ury[106] (chapter 2).

At the same time, I am more pessimistic than realists because, according to my view, the dynamics of humiliation, if not taken seriously, may have such malign effects that they could cancel out otherwise benign tendencies. In one of my books, I collected "reasons for pessimism," "reasons for optimism," and then call for "transcending pessimism and optimism"[107]:

"Pessimism is a luxury we can afford only in good times, in difficult times it easily represents a self-inflicted, self-fulfilling death sentence."[108]

Consider research on the impact of team members who are "deadbeats" ("withholders of effort"), "downers" (who "express pessimism, anxiety, insecurity and irritation") and "jerks" (who violate "interpersonal norms of respect").[109] Having just one "slacker" or "jerk" in a group can bring down performance by 30 to 40 percent.

Message to my wealthy friends: If you are a member of the 1%, you are surely among the generous and loving ones, otherwise you would not read this book. Please accept my admiration. Generosity is a wonderful asset. Also you may want to ask deeper questions. Perhaps you would enjoy listening to your German counterparts mentioned earlier (chapter 11).

Please consider: When you plan to build a ship, will you give the task to a selection of well-intentioned generous wealthy friends? One of your allies might be willing to donate wonderful sails, another a wonderful engine. Is that enough? No. You need a comprehensive plan. You cannot build a ship piece by piece; it will sink. You need to think of the entire ship.

Remember the chaos in humanitarian help efforts after disasters, NGOs falling over each other in uncoordinated scrambles for "need" to become their "resource." One charity giver may have a soft spot for small children, another for women, yet another for a different category of sufferers or issues requiring attention.

If we extrapolate this situation to the global level, and we say that the human family finds itself on a sinking Titanic, it is utterly foolish to depend on charity. Those who have the resources to effect change are often not sufficiently motivated to invest them, whereas those who have the motivation lack the resources. Some wealthy donors may spot a hole in the wall of the ship close to their cabins on the luxury upper floor, yet, overlook the huge breach in the body of the ship further down where the poor are squatting.

Remember the story of traffic lights in chapter 3. If you do not trust the government, it may be a good idea that you help make one that you can trust. Invite into a big *We* and minimize "we versus them," be it "we versus the government," or "we versus any other enemy" (chapter 8).

I am writing these sentences in New York City in November 2011, hearing people from New Jersey being flabbergasted at the power cuts after the recent storm: "Are we a third world country?!" they cry out in indignation.[110] This is the result when systemic thinking lacks.

I have been invited to conferences on "wealth protection" and I made the point that I do not believe that it helps that you have solar panels on your mansion when the entire ecosystem fails.

Consider the absurdity: Why must not-for-profit organizations beg for funds from for-profit organizations to do so-called *good* work to offset the freedom of for-profit organizations to do *bad* work? Why is not fair trade the norm? Why is not all of the planet's biosphere, including its living creatures, a natural reserve?

Consider that commons "invite" free riding.[111] For ruthless individualists, communal sharing is nothing but an untapped resource for profit. The short-term advantages drawn from such free riding doubly hurt all those who oppose this abuse: first, when those who respect the commons pay for the free riders, and second, when they are derided for not being smart enough to join the free riders.

Please help protect the commons from free riders, give priority to global communal sharing, and make market economy serve this priority. Money must serve, not dominate. A banking system must serve like traffic police: asking police to make profit damages the commons. Profit must feed communal sharing, not suck it dry.[112]

Consider how, for the past millennia, vying for power was what kept the powerful occupied. The Templars were knights and bankers, and they were felled by King Philip IV of France when he was too deeply in debt to them. Vladimir Putin may be on a somewhat similar path with Mikhail Khodorkovsky. Sometimes also the financiers are winning, for instance, when they "capture" the state. In all cases, this struggle is detrimental to the common good. All must serve their communities, and, nowadays, our global community.

Consider helping create new global superordinate institutional structures that organize and protect the primacy of global communal sharing.[113] All of Fiske's universal forms of social relations (chapter 3) need to be interwoven into such new global superordinate institutional structures: Communal sharing must take precedence, with authority ranking, equality matching, and market pricing serving it. Consider contributing to shaping new global framings that teach everybody that the stewardship of our world is a common superordinate goal, a joint task, and that it is a "community game" and not a "Wall Street game" (chapter 10).

And remember that while raiding strategies were the fastest way to power and wealth in the past, in an ever more interdependent world, the cost becomes prohibitive. It is ever more difficult to silence victims.

Particularly, when human rights ideals are advocated, victims will no longer subserviently accept exploitation but perceive it as humiliation. The right to rise up against humiliation is being "democratized" by human rights advocacy (introduction). This is what happens now with the Occupy Movement. Drawing on the ambiguous meaning of freedom is no longer a strong enough glue when it becomes glaringly obvious that freedom for might to become right forecloses freedom for everybody.

And consider the zest for life that meaningful relationships with others and the world will provide you. Jean Baker Miller describes "five good things" that reward us when we succeed with forging growth-fostering relationships:[114]

1. increased zest (vitality),
2. increased ability to take action (empowerment),
3. increased clarity (a clearer picture of oneself, the other, and the relationship),
4. increased sense of worth, and
5. a desire for relationships beyond that particular relationship.

Morton Deutsch suggests that those in power positions will benefit from withdrawing from any processes of domination they might be involved in, from re-owning and resolve their feelings of vulnerability, and from undoing the projection of these feelings onto those left high and dry.[115]

Deutsch emphasizes the need to consider "the spiritual emptiness of power over others; the fulfillment of creating something that goes well beyond self benefit."[116] He suggests listening to Mary Parker Follett, who in 1924 advocated creating power *with* others rather than maintaining power *over* others.[117]

My message to all: Help wake everybody up! The window of opportunity that history has opened for us waits to be recognized and used. The security dilemma is waning, despite efforts to keep it alive artificially to protect wealth and investment. The "Arab street," those who gathered in Tahrir Square, try to bring about a dignity revolution. The *global street*, the citizens of this world, must now bring about a global *dignity transition*. This movement must place dignity before profit, and draw on the constructive potential entailed in globalization—on the ingathering of the human tribes, as anthropologists call it—to transcend the old fragmentation of our world.

Morton Deutsch's most recent call is for us all to help developing a global community. Do so, is his message to you, "by communicating to the possible members of such a community," by "helping those potential members imagine what it would be like," and "help them become active, at their local level as well as global level, in developing such a community."[118]

Our planet is a natural park, and we are its stewards. If we sell our commons to parochial interests, we, the human family, will not survive in the long term. To build a decent future, we need a global community with a global identification. A study in the United States, Italy, Russia, Argentina, South Africa, and Iran has just shown that "an inclusive social identification with the world community is a meaningful psychological construct that plays a role in motivating cooperation that transcends parochial interests."[119]

Global systems, global superordinate structures of unity in diversity, subsidiarity, continuously self-correcting adaptability, guarded by a global community, is the way to protect our planet, our commons, effectively.

Remember, in times of slavery, it was not enough to be kinder to your slaves. In times of apartheid, it was not sufficient to be charitable to those who were second-class citizens. The entire system had to be reshaped. Likewise, today, we need to think big.

We need to ask ourselves: What are our largest frames? I hear the reply: We have the Sun, the Moon, the Earth, the Earth's magnetic field and its ecosphere, and our monetary systems. Are all these elements on a par? We certainly treat them as such. But are our monetary systems really on a par with nature's laws? It might be time to be more creative than that.

"Let us create space to fantasize together" says Charles Villa-Vicencio, who played a central role in South Africa's Truth and Reconciliation Commission.[120]

In times of crisis, it is important to ask our elders. Betty A. Reardon, founder of peace education, is an elder whose voice needs to be urgently heard now. She said these very important words, which opened chapter 11:

> What we do know, we do not know in a way that serves our needs. So, we need to know in different ways, and we need to build new knowledge through new ways of knowing. The new knowledge is in the area of designing new realities, which is likely to be done by speculative and creative thinking that would be communally shared and reflected for common formulation that would be tested in a continual process of social invention.[121]

Morton Deutsch, the "father" of conflict resolution, is now over 90 years old. He is another elder whose voice has weight. He is also a good listener. I admire him for listening to me throughout the past ten years. Most people always attempt to convince me to "settle down" and stay in one locality on our globe. I have countered their pressure by explaining that building a global community is the only path to survival for our human species. Only as *one united* global community are we spared out-groups, are we safe from unexpected newcomers who may spoil our commons, our planet. Only then can we protect our commons from being used as raiding ground. And, I argued, I am among the very few—indeed, I have never met anybody who lives like me—who invest their entire life into nurturing such a global community, into regarding our entire planet as "my locality." So, instead of dissuading me, my path ought to be appreciated not just for its novelty, but for its usefulness. And Morton listened to me.

Morton Deutsch was recently asked about the Occupy Wall Street movement: "You've lived through periods of great change in the past. Are you hopeful about the outcomes this time?" Deutsch's reply:

> Yes, I am. I think these movements are coming out of a democratic impulse, and that's good. But it's very hard to produce a coherent democracy that isn't coopted all over again. I hope wise and efficient leadership develops out of this. I'm hopeful that it will, because there's a lot of intelligence now, more sophistication. The issue I'm concerned about, though, is that people must realize it takes time. The changes they want don't

happen overnight. I was in South Africa just after [Nelson] Mandela came into power. I was in touch with a lot of the groups who were active in bringing him to power. One of the problems was that some people felt everything could be achieved quickly. And some of the leaders weren't very effective after Mandela. So having a sense of the time it takes, and having people who are really committed over a sustained period to help move the group to real democratic participation, is really essential. It takes time, planning and effort.[122]

In 2011, Morton Deutsch formulated a pledge that you might wish to consider:

Imagine a global human community in which you, your children, and grandchildren as well as all the others in our shared planet and their children and grandchildren:
- ... Are able to live in dignity and are treated fairly.
- ... Have freedom from the fear of violence and war and can live in peace.
- ... Have freedom from want so that you do not ever have to live in such impoverished circumstances you and your loved ones can not have adequate care, food, water, shelter, health services, education, and other necessities for physical and emotional well-being as well as a dignified life.
- ...Have freedom of information, publication, speech, beliefs, and assembly so that you can be free to be different and free to express open criticism of those in authority individually or collectively.
- ... Have the responsibility to promote, protect, and defend such freedoms as those described above for yourself as well as for others when they are denied or under threat.
- ...Will work together cooperatively to make the world that their grandchildren will inherit free of such problems as war, injustice, climate change, and economic disruption.

Are you willing be a member of such a global human community? If you are, please make the following pledge: I pledge to promote these rights and responsibilities in my own life, in my community, and in the global community as best I can through nonviolent personal actions and working together with others.[123]

In chapter 8, I introduced Claudia E. Cohen. She is the associate director of the center that Morton Deutsch founded, and she works with formerly incarcerated in New York.[124] Carmen Hetaraka works with incarcerated Maori in New Zealand (chapter 1).[125] What Claudia and Carmen have in common is deep questioning. Can we really measure "success" by the rate of employment, Claudia asks? Is "having a job" the ultimate proof of "having made it"? Claudia and Carmen create new language and new concepts; the reality of fragile communities who have fallen outside of mainstream categories does not fit conventional ideology.

Incidentally, this is what presently happens worldwide—reality no longer fits the ideology of mainstream economics. "The market," "investment," "jobs," "consumer spending," "growth": what do these words mean when people and planet need "having a life"? Work with fragile communities, as Claudia and Carmen conduct it, therefore offers important lessons.

Global public health is at stake, the health of the global community that needs to heal from *bulimic economics* and create *a dignity economy*.

In chapter 10 I asked: If we look at our present world and should describe it to a visitor from another planet, how would we describe it? We would say: "Primacy is given to investors. Investors look for the 'kick' of new investments. This is what makes being an investor interesting, just as shopping makes having a salary interesting. Projects are made possible through funding. Funders decide what is possible. Projects that funders deem unworthy of support, will not be possible. Even lifesaving projects will not be possible. What is *work* and what is *dream* is decided by funders."

Perhaps it is time to ask: Is this the best way to manage our affairs on planet Earth? Is the excitement of investors and consumers the optimal path for us to feel that we belong? Is this a meaningful life? Will this provide us with a healthy life on a healthy planet?

It is time that we sit together in a global and mutually respectful dialogue and reflect on how we, all members of the human family, can organize our affairs on our home planet so that our children will find a world worth living in.

It is time that we all get excited, jointly, by the prospects of working together for maximizing the common good, for a worthy and dignified future for our children.

The transition now required is a global *dignity transition* that cherishes unity in diversity.

> *Nothing is more dangerous than an idea, when you have only one idea.*
>
> —Emile-Auguste Chartier[126]

Why does Humankind need a Dignity Transition?
For LIFE on Earth to be constantly revitalized
with an EGALIZATION mission

So sad to say: domination, exploitation, humiliation are
still widely spread
So very sad to see: millions of people having to survive with
less than a daily piece of bread

To face our fears, we need a new, humanizing quality
A dignifying Utopia—unity instead of uniformity—which
will always ensure the right to diversity

How can a fragmented world be united?
By educating all citizens so that their planetary co-
responsibility be permanently ignited

How can we dignify globalization?
By implementing EQUADIGNIZATION

To DIGNITY when will the world give more serious
attention?
When serving the health and well-being of all people
become more than a political intention

—Rhymed reflections on Evelin G. Lindner's *dignity transition*
by Francisco Gomes de Matos, peace linguist from Recife, Brazil,
and co-founder of the World Dignity University,
December 17, 2011

Acknowledgments

May I begin by extending my deepest gratitude to Donald C. Klein, Linda Hartling, and Richard Slaven for their loving support. Linda connected me with Jean Baker Miller and Seymour M. Miller. To our deep sadness, Jean Baker Miller passed away in 2006, and Don Klein in 2007.

I would like to thank Linda for coining the title of this book, "A Dignity Economy," and Ulrich ("Uli") Spalthoff for the subtitle "Creating an Economy which Serves Human Dignity and Preserves Our Planet."

I would also like to express my profound appreciation to Michael Britton and Uli Spalthoff. Linda, Rick, Michael, Uli and I form the core leadership team of the Human Dignity and Humiliation Studies (HumanDHS) network. Without the loving support of Linda, Rick, Michael, Uli, and our entire HumanDHS network, my work would be impossible. The Human Dignity and Humiliation Studies (HumanDHS) network, of which I am the founding president, with Linda as director, has close to 1,000 invited members and 40,000 people from more than 180 countries who read its web site www.humiliationstudies.org.

From this network, we launched the World Dignity University initiative on June 24, 2011. I have always considered myself to be a professor at a global university—and here it is! Every big project starts with a first step! Together we design the World Dignity University initiative in the new ways we believe economic systems need to evolve in the future: as self-correcting fluid processes of growth, as a movement co-created by people and their enthusiastic energy, rather than a rigid edifice into which people are pressed like little cog wheels into a larger machine. I am proud of the ever-evolving World Dignity University initiative and can't thank everybody who nurtures this initiative enough.

For close to four decades, I have lived a global life, moving freely, often to the place on the planet that most needs my work at any given time. This book draws on this global experience. My most recent work focused on dignity and humiliation. I began studying those two subjects in 1996, when I was preparing a four-year doctoral research project at the University of Oslo on *The Feeling of Being Humiliated: A Central Theme in Armed Conflicts (1997–2001)*. The project was designed to study the role of humiliation in the genocidal mass killings in Somalia (1988) and Rwanda (1994), using Nazi Germany as a background. I am deeply grateful to the Psychology Department at the University of Oslo, Royal Norwegian Ministry of Foreign Affairs, and the Norwegian Research Council for their commitment to this critical issue.

During this research, and for my subsequent work, I received generous support from hundreds of academics and practitioners in anthropology, history, philosophy, political science, psychology, and sociology.

In Norway, I would like to thank the rector of the University of Oslo (UiO), Ole Petter Ottersen, vice-rector Inga Bostad, and Jorunn Økland, who leads UiO's Centre for Gender Research. Furthermore, I received wonderful support during and since my doctoral research from Reidar Ommundsen, Jan Smedslund, Fanny Duckert, Astri Heen Wold, Hilde Nafstad, Rolv Mikkel Blakar, Finn Tschudi, Nora Sveaass, Siri Gullestad, Ingela Lundin Kvalem , Henrik Natvig, Karsten Hundeide, Per Schioldborg, Salman Türken, Anna Louise von der Lippe, Hanne Haavind, Egil Bergh-Telle, Dag Erik Eilertsen, and all the other committed faculty members of the Department of Psychology. My profound gratitude goes also to Ole Danbolt Mjøs, Dagfinn Kåre

Føllesdal, Jon Elster, late Arne Næss, Asbjørn Eide, Øyvind Østerud, Nils A. Butenschøn, Stein Tønnesson, Henrik Syse, Odd-Bjørn Fure and Maria Rosvoll, Thomas Hylland Eriksen, Bernt Hagtvet, Sigmund Karterud, Kjell Skyllstad, Bjørn Aksel Flatås, Lasse Moer, Hroar Klempe, Sigurd Støren, as well as Åge Bernhard Grutle, Leif E. Christoffersen, Erik Solheim, Stein Villumstad, and Per M. Bakken.

I owe a further debt of gratitude to my friends outside of Norway. My immense appreciation goes to Norman Sartorius, Maurice Aymard, Hinnerk Bruhns, Alain d'Iribarne, Serge Moscovici, Francisco Gomes de Matos, Michael Harris Bond, Steve Kulich, Michael Prosser, Hora Tjitra, Hilary and Ralph Summy, Kevin P. Clements, Virginia Cawagas and Toh Swee-Hin, Adair Linn Nagata, who brought me together with Patricia and Paul Richards, Kiyoko Sueda and Jaqueline Wasilewski, to Emanuela Del Re, Sibyl Ann Schwarzenbach, Avishai Margalit, David Rosen, Israel Charny, David Bargal, Arie Nadler, Varda Muhlbauer, Michael Dahan and Sam Bahour, Vamik D. Volkan, Michael G. Billig, Maggie O'Neill, Dennis Smith, Lester Kurtz, Aly Maher El-Sayed, Ashraf Salama, Samir Basta, Hizkias Assefa, Emmanuel Ndahimana, Jean-Damascène Gasanabo, Jan Øberg, George Kent, Norbert Ropers, Heidi Aeschlimann, and Didier Sornette, among many others.

In the United States, I wish to convey my profound thanks to Morton Deutsch of Columbia University for his continuing strong support. He authored the forewords for my books *Making Enemies: Humiliation and International Conflict (2006)* and *Emotion and Conflict: How Human Rights Can Dignify Emotion and Help Us Wage Good Conflict (2009)*—without his support, those works would not have been completed.

I also had the great privilege of learning from Peter T. Coleman, Claudia E. Cohen, and their dedicated team, as well as from Andrea Bartoli, Beth Fisher-Yoshida, Janet Gerson, Tony Jenkins, Robert Jervis, and Volker Berghahn through Columbia University. I learned an enormous amount from renowned and eminent scholars, thinkers, and practitioners based in the United States such as Riane T. Eisler, David A. Hamburg, Shibley Telhami, Noeleen Heyzer, Gay Rosenblum-Kumar and Alan B. Slifka, through whom I met William L. Ury, John Steiner, Zuzka Kurtz and Omar Amanat, as well as from Herbert Kelman, Milton Schwebel, Aaron Lazare, Ervin Staub, Howard

Richards, Howard Zehr, Daniel J. Christie, Jack A. Goldstone, Monty G. Marshall, W. Barnett Pearce, Clark R. McCauley, Dov Cohen, Anne M. Wyatt-Brown and Bertram Wyatt-Brown, Michael L. Perlin, George W. Woods, Jonathan Haas, Lee D. Ross, Robert B. Zajonc, Carlos E. Sluzki, Suzanne M. Retzinger and Thomas J. Scheff, Robert Fuller, Charles R. Figley, Judy Kuriansky, Maria R. Volpe, Anie Kalayjian, Donna Hicks, Adenrele Awotona, Virginia Swain and Joseph P. Baratta, Garry Davis, Daniel L. Shapiro, and David Kimball who introduced me to Elise Boulding and Helena Halperin, to name only a few.

I owe many of my psychological understanding to the clients I treated in my work as a clinical psychologist (1980–1984 in Hamburg, Germany, and 1984–1991 in Cairo, Egypt) before moving to social psychology as my main focus. I am deeply indebted to those "co-searchers for health."

I extend especially warm thanks to my interlocutors, neighbors and hosts all around the world, many of whom must struggle daily to carry on the work of peace, often under the most difficult circumstances.

The complete list of people who deserve my deep and heartfelt thanks would cover many pages. Please see www.humiliationstudies.org for our global advisory board, our global coordinating team, our global core team, our education and research teams. I beg those who are not listed here to know that I celebrate you with great gratitude!

Many of the hundreds of members of our HumanDHS network deserve my very special thanks, among them Victoria C. Fontan, Eric Van Grasdorff, Martin Stahl, Grace Feuerverger, Philip M. Brown, Amy C. Hudnall, Patricia Rodriguez Mosquera, Judit Revesz, Brian Ward, Stephanie Heuer, Tonya Hammer, Antoinette Errante, Corinna Carmen Gayer, Sophie Schaarschmidt, Sharon Burde, Zuzana Luckay, Zhang Xuan, Jiuquan Han, Abou Bakar Johnson Bakundukize, Salman Türken, Vegar Jordanger, Øyvind Eikrem, Noor Akbar Khalil, Leland R. Beaumont, Atle Hetland, Esta Tina Ottman and Lynn King.

Linda Hartling and I and our network members believe that we, as humankind, need to "harvest" from all cultural traditions, past and present, those beliefs and practices that help protect the dignity of unity in diversity. Bob Randall, a Uamlimutkatkar elder and traditional owner of Uluru (Ayers Rock) in Australia is a highly esteemed member in the global advisory board of our Human Dignity and Humiliation Studies network. Carmen Hetaraka is a bearer of oral Maori tradition, and he was one of the "pillars" of our 17th Annual Conference in Dunedin, New Zealand, brought to us so very kindly by Michelle Brenner in the context of her Holistic Communication approach. Alvin Cota, a Native American Yoeme from Arizona, is sharing his historical knowledge with us. My particular appreciation goes out to Bob, Carmen, and Alvin. Let me add here archaeologist Ingrid Fuglestvedt. She studies Scandinavian Stone Age history as it went from *animism* to *totemism*. I thank her for her deep understanding and confirmation of my stance that our "heart is with the animists."

I want to express my loving thanks to Nora Stene Preston, Ola Skuterud and Margret Rueffler, as well as the Rosenau family, the Jøntvedt family, the Frerk and Bakken families, as much as the Bakhoum, Khalil, Amer, Roick, Nagata, Tada, and Ward families—my many adoptive parents, siblings, and children, for their endless patience and concern for keeping my global life afloat.

I conclude by expressing my deep gratitude to the founding members of our World Dignity University Initiative, as they were invited by its first founding member, Francisco Gomes de Matos as per October 2011, Morton Deutsch, Betty A. Reardon, Federico Mayor Zaragoza, Arun Gandhi, Ole Petter Ottersen, Inga Bostad, Jorunn Økland, Egil A. Wyller, Kamran Mofid, Shahid Kamal, Ragnhild S. Nilsen, and Emanuela Claudia Del Re.

Finally, I would like to thank Kathleen Morrow for her invaluable help in making the manuscript readable. She most generously gave her care and support to my first three books, and having her brilliant mind also with this manuscript, is a gift beyond words. She applied her love of the English language to my work, making it more accessible to readers all over the world. I am so glad that Don Klein wrote to me on September 30, 2004, "I've talked with Kathleen Morrow, the woman who did such a wonderful job helping me with my book *New Vision, New Reality*. She is available and looks forward to discussing your work."

I would like to end by conveying my profound love and gratitude to my parents Gerda and Paul Lindner, whose personal courage gave my work and life its direction and motivation.

Appendix I: Quotes

Short Quotes Pertaining to Problems
of the Present Monetary System

"Permit me to issue and control the money of a nation, and I care not who makes its laws" (international banker Mayer Amschel Rothschild, 1744–1812 [1]).

"I am afraid that the ordinary citizen will not like to be told that banks can and do create money...And they who control the credit of the nation direct the policy of Governments and hold in the hollow of their hands the destiny of the people" (Reginald McKenna, past Chairman of the Board, Midlands Bank of England, 1863–1943 [2]).

"Money is a new form of slavery, and distinguishable from the old simply by the fact that it is impersonal, that there is no human relation between master and slave" (Leo Tolstoy, 1828–1910[3]).

"All of the perplexities, confusion, and distress in America arises, not from the defects of the Constitution or Confederation, not from want of honor or virtue, so much as from downright ignorance of the nature of coin, credit, and circulation" (John Adams, founding father of the American Constitution, 1735–1826).

Short Quotes Pertaining to a Monetary-based Economy Versus Resource-based Economy

"They hang the man and flog the woman
Who steals the goose from off the common
But leave the greater villain loose
Who steals the common from off the goose. "
                    Anonymous protest poem 1764 or 1821.

"The Government should create, issue, and circulate all the currency and credits needed to satisfy the spending power of the Government and the buying power of consumers. By the adoption of these principles, the taxpayers will be saved immense sums of interest. The privilege of creating and issuing money is not only the supreme prerogative of government, but it is the government's greatest creative opportunity" (Abraham Lincoln, 1809–1865, 16th president of the United States, assassinated[4]).

"Once a nation parts with the control of its currency and credit, it matters not who makes the nation's laws. Usury, once in control, will wreck any nation. Until the control of the issue of currency and credit is restored to government and recognised as its most sacred responsibility, all talk of the sovereignty of parliament and of democracy is idle and futile" (William Lyon Mackenzie King, tenth Prime Minister of Canada, 1874–July 22, 1950[5]).

More Quotes, Roughly Chronologically Ordered

"I believe that banking institutions are more dangerous to our liberties than standing armies. If the American people ever allow private banks to control the issue of their currency, first by inflation, then by deflation, the banks and corporations that will grow up around the banks will deprive the people of all property until their children wake-up homeless on the continent their fathers conquered" (Thomas Jefferson, 1743–1826, 3rd US President, in 1802).

"If once [the people] become inattentive to the public affairs, you and I, and Congress and Assemblies, Judges and Governors, shall all become wolves. It seems to be the law of our general nature, in spite of individual exceptions." (Thomas Jefferson, 1743–1826, 3rd US President)

"Independence is my happiness and I view things as they are, without regard to place or person; my country is the world…" (Thomas Paine, one of the Founding Fathers of the United States, 1737–1809).

[Corruption in high places would follow as] "all wealth is aggregated in a few hands and the Republic is destroyed." Abraham Lincoln (1809–1865), 16th President of the United States, assassinated)

"If you are familiar with the classical works of Adam Smith, you will know that there are two famous works of his. One is *The Wealth of Nations*; the other is the book on the morality and ethics…"The Wealth of Nations" deals more with the invisible hand that are the market forces. And the other book deals with social equity and justice. And in the other book…, he stressed the importance of playing the regulatory role of the government to further distribute the wealth among the people. If in a country, most of the wealth is concentrated in the hands of the few, then this country can hardly witness harmony and stability. The same approach also applies to the current U.S. economy. To address the current economic and financial problems in this country, we need to apply not only the visible hand but also the invisible hand (Chinese Premier Wen Jiabao, 2008[6]).

Appendix II: Selected Publications

In the following, a selection of references is presented, which the reader might be interested in. Some of these reference appeared in the text above, others not. The full references are to be found in the Bibliography further down.

General Publications

Frank Ackerman (2009), Frank Ackerman (2008), Frank Ackerman and Lisa Heinzerling (2004), Frank Ackerman (1998)

Kern Alexander, Rahul Dhumale, and John Leonard Eatwell (2006)

Gar Alperovitz (2009), Gar Alperovitz and Lew Daly (2008), Gar Alperovitz (2005), Thad Williamson, David Imbroscio, and Gar Alperovitz (2003).

Miguel Almunia et al. (2009)

Jeanette Armstrong (2007)

Robert D. Atkinson et al. (2011)

Joseph Preston Baratta (2004b)

Andrew J. Bacevich (2010)

Alan Beattie (2009)

Rosalie Bertell (2000)

Norberto Bobbio and Maurizio Viroli (2003)

Patrick Bond (2006), Patrick Bond (2004), Patrick Bond and Frantz Fanon (2002), Patrick Bond (2001)

Kenneth E. Boulding (1966)

David Boyle and Andrew Simms (2009)

Jean Bricmont (2005)

John Bunzl (2008), James Robertson and John Bunzl (2008)

Ellen Hodgson Brown (2008)

World Commission on Environment and Development and Gro Harlem Brundtland (1987)

Pierre Calame (2003b), Pierre Calame (2003a), Pierre Calame (2009)

Shaun Chamberlin (2009)

Colin F. Camerer (2003)

Ha-Joon Chang (2002), Ha-Joon Chang (2007), Ha-Joon Chang and Ilene Grabel (2004)

Raff Carmen (1996)

Michel Chossudovsky and Andrew Gavin Marshall (Eds.) 2010

Gregory Clark, Kevin H. O'Rourke, and Alan M. Taylor (2008)

José Luis Coraggio (1986)

Herman E. Daly (1977), Herman E. Daly and Kenneth N. Townsend (Eds.) 1993, Herman E. Daly, John B. Cobb, and Clifford W. Cobb (1989), Herman E. Daly and Joshua C. Farley (2010)

William Davies (2010)

Garry Davis (1984)

Diane Coyle (2011)

William Edward Dunkman (1970)

Jeffrey L. Dunoff and Joel P. Trachtman (Eds.) 2009

Richard A. Easterlin (Ed.) 2002, Richard A. Easterlin (2004)

William Russell Easterly (2006)

Henrik Enderlein, Sonja Wälti, and Michael Zürn (Eds.) 2010

Amitai Etzioni (2004), Amitai Etzioni (1996)

Adalbert Evers and Jean Louis Laville (2004)

Charles Ferguson (2010)

Niall Ferguson (2008)

Viviane Forrester (1996)

Thomas Frank (2004a)

Bruno S. Frey (Ed.) 2008,
Bruno S. Frey and Alois Stutzer
(Eds.) 2007

David Fromkin (1999)

Henry George (1879)

Silvio Johann Gesell (1916),
Silvio Johann Gesell (1958)

Ayelet Gneezy et al. (2010)

Lorna Gold (2004)

John Gray (2002)

Thomas Henry Greco Jr.
(1990), Thomas Henry Greco
Jr. (2009)

Jane Jacobs (1961), Jane Jacobs
(1984), Jane Jacobs (1992),
Jane Jacobs (2000), Jacobs 2004

Halldór Gudmundsson (2010)

Stephan Harding (2006)

Michael Hartmann (2007).

David Harvey (2010)

Paul Hawken (2007b)

Thomas Nathan Hale and
David Held (Eds.) 2011, David
Held, Angus Fane-Hervey, and
Marika Theros (2011), David
Held (2010), David Held and
Anthony McGrew (2007),
David Held and Ayse Kaya
(2007)

Hazel Henderson (1996), Hazel
Henderson and Simran Sethi
(2008)

John Holloway (2005), John
Holloway (2010), see also
www.youtube.com/watch?v=Qu
10HUCzTIQ

Hopkins 2008

Michael Hudson (1972)

Will Hutton (2008)

Christian Joerges (2010)

Charles Karelis (2007)

Steve Keen (2001)

Jörn Klare (2010)

Naomi Klein (2007)

David C. Korten (1993), David
C. Korten (2001), David C.
Korten (2009a), David C.
Korten (2009b)

Joel Kovel (2002)

Paul R. Krugman and Maurice Obstfeld (2009), Paul R. Krugman and Robin Wells (Ed.)(2009)

James Howard Kunstler (2006)

Robert E. Lane (2001)

Frances Moore Lappé (2011)

Eilis Lawlor, Helen Kersley, and Susan Steed (2009)

Philippe Legrain (2002)

Michael M. Lewis (2010), Michael M. Lewis (2011)

Bernard A. Lietaer (2001)

James Lovelock (2009)

Jeffrey Madrick (2011), Jeffrey Madrick (2009)

N. Gregory Mankiw (2004)

Glen T. Martin (2010a), Glen T. Martin (2010b)

Michael J. Mauboussin (2006)

Marcel Mauss (1924)

Paul Ekins and Manfred A. Max-Neef (Eds.) 1992, Manfred A. Max-Neef, Antonio Elizalde and Martin Hopenhayn (1991), Manfred A. Max-Neef (1992), Manfred A. Max-Neef and Amy Goodman (2010)

Elliott Maynard and Jacque Fresco (2003) (see also www.thevenusproject.com/resourse_eco.htm)

Federico Zaragoza Mayor (2010)

Bill McKibben (2007)

James E. Meade (1965)

Meinhard Miegel and Axel Börsch-Supan (Eds.) 2001

Gretchen Morgenson (Ed.) 2009

Herfried Münkler (2007)

Loretta Napoleoni (2008)

The Green New Deal Group (2008)

Richard B. Norgaard (1999), Richard B. Norgaard (2011)

Elinor Ostrom, Amy R. Poteete, and Marco A. Janssen (2010)

Tim Parks (2005)

Raj Patel (2010)

Heikki Patomäki (2002), Heikki Patomäki (2008)

Karl Polanyi (1944), Karl Polanyi (1977)

Linda Polman (2010)

John Quiggin (2010b)

Matthew Rabin (1996)

Paul D. Raskin et al. (2002), Paul D. Raskin (2008), Paul D. Raskin et al. (2002)

Paul H. Ray and Sherry Ruth Anderson (2000)

Erik S. Reinert (2007)

Carmen M. Reinhart and Kenneth Rogoff (2009)

Howard Richards (2011a), Howard Richards (2011b), Howard Richards (2010a), Howard Richards (2010c), Howard Richards and Joanna Swanger (2006)

Edwin Clarence Riegel (1976)

John Gerard Ruggie (2008)

Douglas Rushkoff (2009)

Jeffrey D. Sachs (2005), Jeffrey D. Sachs (2011)

Tagi Sagafi-nejad and John H. Dunning (2008)

Robert J. Samuelson (2009)

Galit A. Sarfaty (1009)

Ulrich Schäfer (2011)

Jeff Schmidt (2000)

George A. Selgin (1988), George A. Selgin (1996)

Amartya Kumar Sen (1999), Amartya Kumar Sen (2006), Amartya Kumar Sen (2009)

Alan Shipman (1999)

Sidney Pollard and Richard S. Tedlow (2001)

Hilary Silver and Seymour M. Miller (2006)

Andrew Simms, Victoria Johnson, and Peter Chowla (2010)

Peter Albert David Singer (1981), Peter Albert David Singer (2004), Peter Albert David Singer (2009)

Adam Smith (1968)

Frederick Soddy (1926)

Stephen Spratt et al. (2009)

Nicholas Stern (2006),
Nicholas Stern (2011)

Joseph E. Stiglitz, Aaron S.
Edlin, and J. Bradford DeLong
(Eds.) 2008, Joseph E. Stiglitz
and Narcís Serra (Eds.) 2008

Richard S. Tedlow (2010)

Gillian Tett (2009)

Transnational Institute (2008)

Vijay V. Vaitheeswaran (2003)

Genevieve Vaughan (1997),
Genevieve Vaughan (Ed.) 2007,
see also Jeanette Armstrong
(2007)

Immanuel Maurice Wallerstein
(1974)

Antonio Argandoña and
Heidetraut von Weltzien
Høivik (2009), Heidetraut von
Weltzien Høivik and Domènec
Melé (2009), Heidetraut von
Weltzien Høivik (2009),
Heidetraut von Weltzien
Høivik (2007), Heidetraut von
Weltzien Høivik (2005),
Heidetraut von Weltzien
Høivik (Ed.) 2002

Laura Westra (2011)

Florian Wettstein (2009)

Kenneth P. Jameson and
Charles K. Wilber (Eds.) 1996

Richard G. Wilkinson (2005),
Richard G. Wilkinson and Kate
Pickett (2009b), Richard G.
Wilkinson and Kate Pickett
(2009a)

Susan Wilkinson-Maposa et al.
(2009)

Sheldon S. Wolin (2008)

Donna J. Wood (1991)

Ellen Meiksins Wood (2003)

Stephen A. Zarlenga (2002)

Some Selected Authors of Publications Pertaining to New Economic Models

1. Gar Alperovitz and Lew Daly (2008)
2. Abhijit Banerjee and Esther Duflo (2011)
3. Larry M. Bartels (2008b)
4. Bitten Schei and Elisabeth Rønnevig (2009)
5. Derek Curtis Bok (2010)
6. Ben Brangwyn and Rob Hopkins (2011)
7. Ellen Hodgson Brown (2008)
8. Reinhard Buetikofer and Sven Giegold (2010)
9. John Bunzl (2008)
10. James Robertson and John Bunzl (2008)
11. Lorna Gold (2004)
12. Shaun Chamberlin (2009)
13. Ha-Joon Chang and Ilene Grabel (2004)
14. Gregory Clark (2007)
15. Ed Diener and Martin E. P. Seligman (2004)
16. Don Eberly (2008)
17. Tania Ellis (2010)
18. Richard Evanoff (2010)
19. Robley E. George (2002)
20. Anthony Giddens (2000)
21. Neva Rockefeller Goodwin (2010)
22. Stephan Harding (2006)
23. Errol E. Harris (2008)
24. Hazel Henderson (1996), Hazel Henderson and Simran Sethi (2008)
25. Steven Hill (2010)
26. Will Hutton (2010)
27. Tim Jackson (2009)
28. Trygve Haavelmo (1989)
29. Hopkins 2008
30. Berthold Huber (2010)

31. Marjorie Kelly (2001),
    Marjorie Kelly (2009)

32. Margrit Kennedy (1995)

33. Deirdre Kent (2010)

34. Stephen D. King (2010)

35. David Kinley (2009)

36. Hans Küng (1997)

37. Joel Kurtzman (1993)

38. Bernard A. Lietaer (1997),
    Bernard A. Lietaer (2001)

39. James Lovelock (2009)

40. Paul Hawken, Amory B.
    Lovins, and L. Hunter
    Lovins (1999)

41. Benoit B. Mandelbrot and
    Richard L. Hudson (2004)

42. Jerry Mander (ed.)(2007)

43. Tim Jackson and Nic Marks
    (1994)

44. Seymour M. Miller and
    Anthony J. Savoie (2002),
    Seymour M. Miller (2011),
    Seymour M. Miller (2011)

45. Karl Ove Moene and Erling
    Barth (2009)

46. Kamran Mofid (2002),
    Kamran Mofid (2010),
    Kamran Mofid (2011a),
    Kamran Mofid (2011b).

47. Helena Norberg-Hodge,
    Steven Gorelick, and Todd
    Merrifield (2002)

48. Karine Nyborg (2007)

49. Prayudh A Payutto (1994)

50. Erik S. Reinert (2007)

51. Philip Pettit (2001)

52. Paul Polak (2008)

53. Michael F. Porter (2010)

54. James Bernard Quilligan
    (2002)

55. Eric S. Raymond (1999)

56. Howard Richards (2011a),
    Howard Richards (2011b),
    Howard Richards (2010a),
    Howard Richards (2010c),
    Howard Richards and
    Joanna Swanger (2006)

57. Jeremy Rifkin (2009),
    Jeremy Rifkin (1995)

58. Richard J. Rosen (2009)

59. Claus Otto Scharmer
    (2007)

60. Ernst Friedrich Schumacher
    (1973)

61. Juliet B. Schor (2010),
    Juliet B. Schor (2004),
    Juliet B. Schor (1998),
    Juliet B. Schor and Jong Il
    You (Eds.) 1995, Juliet B.
    Schor (1992)

62. David Schweickart (2002)

63. Peter M. Senge (1990)

64. Robert J. Shiller (2000)

65. George Soros (2008), Joseph E. Stiglitz (2003), Joseph E. Stiglitz and Andrew Charlton (2006)

66. James Gustave Speth (2008), James Gustave Speth (2010)

67. Gillian Tett (2009)

68. Rodrigue Tremblay (2010)

69. Genevieve Vaughan (1997), Genevieve Vaughan (Ed.) 2007,
see also Jeanette Armstrong (2007)

70. Peter A. Victor (2008)

71. Götz Wolfgang Werner and André Presse (Eds.) 2007

72. Richard G. Wilkinson (2005), Richard G. Wilkinson and Kate Pickett (2009b)

73. Susan Wilkinson-Maposa et al. (2009). See also the Model Economy Wiki at model-economy.wikispaces.com

74. Rowan Williams and Larry Elliott (Eds.) 2010

75. Martin Wolf (2009)

76. The International Bank for Reconstruction and Development / The World Bank (2011)

77. Howard Zehr (1990)

78. Georg Zoche (2009)

79. Daniel Yergin (2011), Daniel Yergin (2008)

Some Selected Authors of Publications Pertaining to Feminist Political Economy and Economical Models

1. Riane Tennenhaus Eisler (2007)

2. Barbara Alice Mann (2000)

3. Maria Mies (2006), Maria Mies and Veronika Bennholdt-Thomsen (1999)

4. V. Spike Peterson (2003)

5. Robert B. Reich (2010)

6. Maude Barlow et al. (2011b), Maude Barlow et al. (2011a), Vandana Shiva (2006), Vandana Shiva (1997)

7. Genevieve Vaughan (1997), Genevieve Vaughan (Ed.) 2007, see also Jeanette Armstrong (2007)

8. Marilyn Waring (1988)

9. Claudia von Werlhof, Veronika Bennholdt-Thomsen, and Nicholas Faraclas (Eds.) 2001.

10. Christa Wichterich (2000), Christa Wichterich (2011)

Some Selected Authors of Publications Pertaining to Gift Culture

1. Jeanette Armstrong (2007)

2. Marc Ian Barasch (2005)

3. Dacher Keltner (2009b), Dacher Keltner (2009a)

4. Charles Eisenstein (2010), Charles Eisenstein (2011)

5. Lewis Hyde (1983), Lewis Hyde (2006)

6. Manish Jain and Shilpa Jain (Eds.) 2008

7. Marcel Mauss (1924)

8. Shikshantar (2008)

9. Alan D. Schrift (1997)

10. Genevieve Vaughan (1997), Genevieve Vaughan (Ed.) 2007, see also Jeanette Armstrong (2007)

Bibliography

Abu-Rabi', Ibrahim M. (2007). Modernization, Democracy and Human Rights. In Moten, Abdul Rashid and Noor, Noraini M. (Eds.), *Terrorism, Democracy, the West and the Muslim World*, pp. 13-35. Singapore: Thomson Learning.

Ackerman, Frank (1998). *The Changing Nature of Work*. Washington, DC: Island Press.

Ackerman, Frank (2008). *Poisoned for Pennies: The Economics of Toxics and Precaution*. Washington: Island Press.

Ackerman, Frank (2009). *Can We Afford the Future?: The Economics of a Warming World*. London: Zed Books.

Ackerman, Frank and Heinzerling, Lisa (2004). *Priceless: On Knowing the Price of Everything and the Value of Nothing*. New York: New Press.

Adorno, Theodor W. (1959). *Theorie der Halbbildung*. Frankfurt am Main, Germany: Suhrkamp.

Alagic, Mara, Nagata, Adair Linn, and Rimmington, Glyn M. (2009). Improving Intercultural Communication Competence: Fostering Bodymindful Cage Painting. In *Journal of Intercultural Communication, SIETAR Japan*, 12, pp. 39-55.

Alexander, Kern, Dhumale, Rahul, and Eatwell, John Leonard (2006). *Global Governance of Financial Systems: The International Regulation of Systemic Risk*. New York: Oxford University Press.

Almunia, Miguel, Bénétrix, Augustín S., Eichengreen, Barry, O'Rourke, Kevin H., and Rua, Gisela (2009). *The Effectiveness of Fiscal and Monetary Stimulus in Depressions*. London: Centre for Economic Policy Research, www.voxeu.org/index.php?q=node/4227.

Alperovitz, Gar (2005). *America Beyond Capitalism: Reclaiming Our Wealth, Our Liberty and Our Democracy*. Hoboken, NJ: Wiley.

Alperovitz, Gar (2009). *The Long Term Norm of the Economy Is Great Instability and High Inequality.* Presencing Institute, tc.presencing.com/sites/default/files/Interview_Alperovitz_0.pdf.

Alperovitz, Gar and Daly, Lew (2008). *Unjust Deserts: How the Rich Are Taking Our Common Inheritance and Why We Should Take It Back.* New York: New Press.

Anderson, Geraint (2008). *Cityboy: Beer and Loathing in the Square Mile.* London: Headline.

Anderson, Mary B. (1999). *Do No Harm: How Aid Can Support Peace - or War.* Boulder, CO: Lynne Rienners.

Angell, Marcia (2004). *The Truth About the Drug Companies: How They Deceive Us and What to Do About It.* New York: Random House.

Appiah, Kwame Anthony (2005). *The Ethics of Identity.* Princeton, NJ: Princeton University Press.

Appiah, Kwame Anthony (2006). *Cosmopolitanism: Ethics in a World of Strangers.* New York: Norton.

Appiah, Kwame Anthony (2010). *The Honor Code: How Moral Revolutions Happen.* New York: Norton.

Archer, Colin (2005). *Warfare or Welfare? Disarmament for Development in the 21st Century. A Human Security Approach.* Geneva: International Peace Bureau, ipb.org/i/pdf-files/Warfare_or_Welfare_Complete-versionEng.pdf.

Argandoña, Antonio and von Weltzien Høivik, Heidetraut (2009). Corporate Social Responsibility: One Size Does Not Fit All. Collecting Evidence From Europe. In *Journal of Business Ethics,* 89 (3), pp. 221-234, published online 2010, www.springerlink.com/content/6335313216485256/fulltext.pdf.

Ariely, Dan (2008). The Cost of Social Norms: Why We Are Happy to Do Things but Not When We Are Paid to Do Them. In *Predictably Irrational: The Hidden Forces That Shape Our Decisions*, pp. 67-88. New York: HarperCollins.

Aristotle (1980). *The Nicomachean Ethics*. Oxford: Oxford University Press.

Armendariz, Beatriz and Morduch, Jonathan (2010). *The Economics of Microfinance*. Cambridge, Mass.: MIT Press.

Armstrong, Jeanette (2007). Indigenous Knowledge and Gift Giving. In Vaughan, Genevieve (Ed.), *Women and the Gift Economy: A Radically Different Worldview Is Possible*, pp. 41-49. Toronto: Innana, www.gift-economy.com.

Atkinson, Robert D., Chhetri, Netra, Freed, Joshua, Galiana, Isabel, Green, Christopher, Hayward, Steen, Jenkins, Jesse, Malone, Elizabeth, Nordhaus, Ted, Pielke Jr., Roger, Prins, Gwyn, Rayner, Steve, Sarewitz, Daniel, and Shellenberger, Michael (2011). *Climate Pragmatism: Innovation, Resilience and No Regrets: The Hartwell Analysis in an American Context*. Washington, DC: Information Technology and Innovation Foundation (ITIF), www.itif.org/publications/climate-pragmatism-innovation-resilience-and-no-regrets.

Axelrod, Robert (1990). *The Evolution of Cooperation*. London: Penguin Books.

Baber, Walter F. and Bartlett, Robert V. (2009). *Global Democracy and Sustainable Jurisprudence: Deliberative Environmental Law*. Cambridge, MA: MIT Press.

Bacevich, Andrew J. (2010). *Washington Rules: America's Path to Permanent War*. New York: Metropolitan Books.

Badiou, Alain (2001). *Ethics: An Essay on the Understanding of Evil*. London: Verso.

Ballas, Dimitris and Dorling, Danny (1-12-2007). Measuring the Impact of Major Life Events Upon Happiness. In *International Journal of Epidemiology*, 36 (6), pp. 1244-1252, ije.oxfordjournals.org/content/36/6/1244.full.pdf+html.

Banerjee, Abhijit and Duflo, Esther (2011). *Poor Economics: A Radical Rethinking of the Way to Fight Global Poverty*. New York: PublicAffairs.

Banks, James A., Cookson, Peter, Gay, Geneva, Hawley, Willis D., Irvine, Jacqueline Jordan, Nieto, Sonia, Schofield, Janet Ward, and Stephan, Walter G. (2001). *Diversity Within Unity: Essential Principles for Teaching and Learning in a Multi-cultural Society*. Seattle: Center for Multicultural Education, College of Education, University of Washington, Seattle, www.educ.washington.edu/coetestwebsite/pdf/DiversityUnity.pdf.

Banks, Ralph Richard (2011). *How the African American Marriage Decline Affects Everyone*. New York: Dutton.

Barasch, Marc Ian (2005). *A Gift of Kindness: Field Notes on the Compassionate Life*. Emmaus, PA: Rodale Books, www.compassionatelife.com/.

Baratta, Joseph Preston (2004a). *The Politics of World Federation* (Volume 1. The United Nations, U.N. Reform, Atomic Control, Volume 2. From World Federalism to Global Governance). Westport, CT: Praeger.

Baratta, Joseph Preston (2004b). *The Politics of World Federation:* Vol.1: The United Nations, U.N. Reform, Atomic Control. Vol. 2: From World Federalism to Global Governance. Westport, CT: Praeger.

Barkan, Elazar (2000). *The Guilt of Nations: Restitution and Negotiating Historical Injustices*. New York: Norton.

Barlow, Maude, Shiva, Vandana, Tutu, Desmond Mpilo, Goldtooth, Thomas, Bassey, Nnimmo, Galeano, Eduardo, and Cullinan, Cormac (2011a). *Does Nature Have Rights?: Transforming Grassroots Organizing to Protect People and the Planet.* San Francisco, CA: The Council of Canadians, Fundación Pachamama, and Global Exchange, www.globalexchange.org/campaigns/greenrights/RightsofNatureReport WebENG.pdf.

Barlow, Maude, Suzuki, David, Atwood, Margaret, Galeano, Eduardo, Bassey, Nnimmo, Mooney, Pat, Kapur, Shekhar, George, Susan, Shiva, Vandana, and Tutu, Desmond Mpilo (2011b). *The Rights of Nature: The Case for a Universal Declaration of the Rights of Mother Earth.* The Council of Canadians, Fundación Pachamama, and Global Exchange.

Bartels, Larry M. (2008a). *Unequal Democracy: The Political Economy of the New Gilded Age.* Princeton, NJ: Princeton University Press.

Bartels, Larry M. (2008b). *Unequal Democracy: The Political Economy of the New Gilded Age.* Princeton, NJ: Princeton University Press.

Barth, Fredrik (1987). *Cosmologies in the Making: A Generative Approach to Cultural Variation in Inner New Guinea.* Cambridge: Cambridge University Press.

Bartlett, Robert V. (1986). Ecological Rationality: Reason and Environmental Policy. In *Environmental Ethics,* 8 (3), pp. 221-239.

Bateman, Milford (2010). *Why Doesn't Microfinance Work?: The Destructive Rise of Local Neoliberalism.* London: Zed Books.

Bauwens, Michel (2008). *The Political Economy of Peer Production.* Kaiserslautern, Germany: Project Oekonux, en.wiki.oekonux.org/Oekonux/TranslationProjects/BauwensPoliticalEco nomy#id2.

Beattie, Alan (2009). *False Economy: A Surprising Economic History of the World.* London: Viking.

Belenky, Mary Field (1997). *Women's Ways of Knowing: The Development of Self, Voice, and Mind.* 10th anniversary edition. New York: Basic Books.

Belenky, Mary Field, Bond, Lynne A., and Weinstock, Jacqueline S. (1997). *A Tradition That Has No Name: Nuturing the Development of People, Families, and Communities.* New York: Basic Books.

Benhabib, Seyla (2011). *Dignity in Adversity: Human Rights in Troubled Times.* Cambridge: Polity Press.

Bentall, Richard P. (2009). *Doctoring the Mind: Why Psychiatric Treatments Fail.* London: Allan Lane.

Benyus, Janine M. (2002). *Biomimicry: Innovation Inspired by Nature.* New York: Perennial.

Bergmann, Frithjof (1977). *On Being Free.* Notre Dame, IN: University of Notre Dame Press.

Bergmann, Frithjof and Ramsburgh, John (1999). An Interview With Frithjof Bergmann: Rethinking Work on a Global Scale. In *The Journal of the International Institute (II) at the University of Michigan,* 6 (2, Winter), interviewed by Journal editor John Ramsburgh on October 7, 1998. hdl.handle.net/2027/spo.4750978.0006.203;

Bernays, Edward (1928). *Propaganda.* New York: Horace Liveright.

Berry, Wendell (1990). *"The Work of Local Culture": What Are People for?* San Francisco, CA: North Point Press.

Bertell, Rosalie (2000). *Planet Earth: The Latest Weapon of War.* London: The Women's Press.

Betts, Richard K. (Ed.)(2005). *Conflict After the Cold War: Arguments on Causes of War and Peace.* 2nd edition. New York: Pearson.

Blanchflower, David G. and Oswald, Andrew J. (2005). The Wage Curve Reloaded. *NBER Working Paper No. 11338,* Cambridge, MA: The National Bureau of Economic Research (NBER), www.nber.org/papers/w11338.pdf.

Bloom, Allan (1987). *The Closing of the American Mind: How Higher Education Has Failed Democracy and Impoverished the Souls of Today's Students.* New York: Simon and Schuster.

Bobbio, Norberto and Viroli, Maurizio (2003). *The Idea of the Republic.* Cambridge: Polity Press.

Bok, Derek Curtis (2003). *Universities in the Marketplace: The Commercialization of Higher Education.* Princeton, NJ: Princeton University Press.

Bok, Derek Curtis (2006). *Our Underachieving Colleges: A Candid Look at How Much Students Learn and Why They Should Learn More.* Princeton, NJ: Princeton University Press.

Bok, Derek Curtis (2010). *The Politics of Happiness: What Government Can Learn From the New Research on Well-Being.* Princeton: Princeton University Press.

Bond, Michael Harris (1998). Unity in Diversity: Orientations and Strategies for Building a Harmonious, Multicultural Society. In *Trames, A Journal of the Humanities and Social Sciences,* 3 (2), pp. 234-263.

Bond, Patrick (2001). *Against Global Apartheid: South Africa Meets the World Bank, IMF and International Finance.* Lansdowne: University of Cape Town Press.

Bond, Patrick (2004). *Talk Left, Walk Right: South Africa's Frustrated Global Reforms.* Scottsville, South Africa: University of KwaZulu-Natal Press.

Bond, Patrick (2006). *Looting Africa: The Economics of Exploitation.* London: Zed books.

Bond, Patrick and Fanon, Frantz (2002). *Fanon's Warning: A Civil Society Reader on the New Partnership for Africa's Development.* Trenton, NJ: Africa World Press.

Boulding, Kenneth E. (1966). *The Economics of the Coming Spaceship Earth.* Washington, DC: Paper presented at the Sixth Resources for the Future Forum on Environmental Quality in a Growing Economy on March 8,1966, www.panarchy.org/boulding/spaceship.1966.html.

Bourdieu, Pierre and Thompson, John B. (1991). *Language and Symbolic Power.* Cambridge: Polity Press.

Boyle, David and Simms, Andrew (2009). *The New Economics: A Bigger Picture.* London: Earthscan.

Brafman, Oris and Brafman, Rom (2008). *Sway: The Irresistible Pull of Irrational Behavior.* New York: Doubleday Business.

Braithwaite, John (2002). *Restorative Justice and Responsive Regulation.* Oxford: Oxford University Press.

Brangwyn, Ben and Hopkins, Rob (2011). *Transition Initiatives Primer - Becoming a Transition Town, City, District, Village, Community or Even Island. Transition Network.* www.transitionnetwork.org/sites/default/files/TransitionInitiativesPrimer(3).pdf.

Breines, Ingeborg, Gierycz, Dorota, and Reardon, Betty A. (Eds.)(1999). *Towards a Women's Agenda for a Culture of Peace.* Paris: UNESCO.

Brewer, Marilynn B. and Roccas, Sonia (2002). Social Identity Complexity. In *Personality and Social Psychology Review,* 6, pp. 88-106.

Bricmont, Jean (2005). *Imperialisme Humanitaire. Droits De L'Homme, Droit D'Ingerence, Droit Du Plus Fort?* Brussels, Belgium: Aden.

Britton, Michael (2011). *Post-Opportunistic Economics: Are We Humans Capable of Something Better?* Highland Park, NJ: Paper written for "Strengthening the Public Good: Business, Government & Civil Society Relationships" conference at Dalhousie University, Halifax, Canada, June 25 to 28, 2012, convened by Kamran Mofid, the Founder of the Globalisation for the Common Good Initiative, management.dal.ca/news/CommonGood.

Brod, Harry (1997). Pornography and the Alienation of Male Sexuality. In O'Toole, Laura L. and Schiffman, Jessica R. (Eds.), *Gender Violence: Interdisciplinary Perspectives*, pp. 454-466. New York: New York University Press.

Broughton, Philip Delves (2008). *Ahead of the Curve: Two Years at Harvard Business School*. New York: Penguin Press.

Brown, Ellen Hodgson (2008). *Web of Debt: The Shocking Truth About Our Money System and How We Can Break Free*. 3rd revised edition. Baton Rouge, LA: Third Millennium Press.

Buber, Martin (1923). *Ich und Du*. Leipzig, Germany: Insel.

Buchan, Nancy R., Brewer, Marilynn B., Grimalda, Gianluca, Wilson, Rick K., Fatas, Enrique, and Foddy, Margaret (1-6-2011). Global Social Identity and Global Cooperation. In *Psychological Science,* 22 (6), pp. 821-828.

Buetikofer, Reinhard and Giegold, Sven (2010). *The New Green Deal: Climate Protection, New Jobs and Social Justice*. Brussels, Belgium: The European Green Party (EGP) and the European Free Alliance (EFA), in the European Parliament, reinhardbuetikofer.eu/wp-content/uploads/2010/03/Green-New-Deal-en.pdf.

Bunzl, John (2008). *People-Centred Global Governance - Making It Happen!* London: International Simultaneous Policy Organisation, www.simpol.org/en/books/PCGG%20Manuscript%203.7%20-%20Site%20version.pdf.

Butterfield, Jody, Bingham, Sam, Savory, Allan (2006). *Holistic Management Handbook: Healthy Land, Healthy Profits*. Washington, DC: Island Press.

Cacioppo, John T. and Patrick, William (2008). *Loneliness: Human Nature and the Need for Social Connection*. New York: Norton.

Calame, Pierre (2003a). *La démocratie en miettes, pour une révolution de la gouvernance*. Paris: Charles Léopold Mayer, www.pierre-calame.fr/fr/livres/democratie-en-miette.html.

Calame, Pierre (2003b). *Mission possible, penser l'avenir de la planète.* Paris: Charles Léopold Mayer.

Calame, Pierre (2009). *Essai sur l'oeconomie.* Paris: Charles Léopold Mayer.

Camerer, Colin F. (2003). *Behavioral Game Theory: Experiments in Strategic Interaction.* Princeton, NJ: Princeton University Press.

Carlat, Daniel J. (2011). *Unhinged: The Trouble With Psychiatry - A Doctor's Revelations About a Profession in Crisis.* New York: Free Press.

Carmen, Raff (1996). *Autonomous Development: Humanizing the Landscape: An Excursion into Radial Thinking and Practice.* London: Zed Books.

Carneiro, Robert Leonard (1988). The Circumscription Theory: Challenge and Response. In *American Behavioral Scientist,* 31 (4), pp. 497-511.

Carr, Albert Z. (1968). Is Business Bluffing Ethical? In *Harvard Business Review,* 46 (January-February), pp. 143-153.

Carson, Rachel Louise (1962). *Silent Spring.* Boston, MA: Houghton Mifflin.

Carson, Rachel Louise and Pratt, Charles (1965). *The Sense of Wonder.* New York: Harper & Row.

Carson, Richard T. (2011). The Environmental Kuznets Curve: Seeking Empirical Regularity and Theoretical Structure. In *The Review of Environmental Economics and Policy,* 4 (1), pp. 3-23.

Carvalho, Edward J. and Downing, David B. (Eds.)(2010). *Academic Freedom in the Post-9/11 Era.* New York: Palgrave Macmillan.

Casson, Mark (1995). *The Organization of International Business: Studies in the Economics of Trust.* Aldershot: Edward Elgar.

Chaiken, Shelly L. (1980). Heuristic Versus Systematic Information Processing and the Use of Source Versus Message Cues in Persuasion. In *Journal of Personality and Social Psychology*, 39, pp. 752-766.

Chaiken, Shelly L., Gruenfeld, Deborah H., and Judd, Charles M. (2000). Persuasion in Negotiations and Conflict Situations. In Deutsch, Morton and Coleman, Peter T. (Eds.), *The Handbook of Conflict Resolution: Theory and Practice*, pp. 144-165. San Francisco, CA: Jossey-Bass.

Chamberlin, Shaun (2009). *The Transition Timeline: For a Local, Resilient Future*. Totnes, Devon: Green Books.

Chang, Ha-Joon (2002). *Kicking Away the Ladder: Development Strategy in Historical Perspective*. London: Anthem Press.

Chang, Ha-Joon (2007). *Bad Samaritans: Rich Nations, Poor Policies, and the Threat to the Developing World*. London: Random House.

Chang, Ha-Joon and Grabel, Ilene (2004). *Reclaiming Development: An Alternative Economic Policy Manual*. London: Zed Book.

Chapin, Mac (2004). *A Challenge to Conservationists*. In *World Watch: Vision for a Sustainable World*, pp. 17-31, excerpted from the November/December 2004 WORLD WATCH magazine 17-3, www.worldwatch.org.

Chen, Emmeline S. and Tyler, Tom R. (2001). Cloaking Power: Legitimizing Myths and the Psychology of the Advantaged. In Lee-Chai, Annette Y. and Bargh, John A. (Eds.), *The Use and Abuse of Power: Multiple Perspectives on the Causes of Corruption*, pp. 241-261. Philadelphia, PA: Psychology Press.

Cheung, Fanny M., van de Vijver, Fons J. R., and Leong, Frederick T. L. (2011). Toward a New Approach to the Study of Personality in Culture. In *American Psychologist*, 66 (7, October), pp. 593-603.

Chossudovsky, Michel and Marshall, Andrew Gavin (Eds.)(2010). *The Global Economic Crisis: The Great Depression of the XXI Century*. Montreal, Canada: Global Research Publishers.

Christie, Daniel J. (2006). What Is Peace Psychology the Psychology of? In *Journal of Social Issues,* 62 (1), pp. 1-17, www3.interscience.wiley.com/journal/118601535/abstract.

Chua, Amy (2008). *Day of Empire: How Hyperpowers Rise to Global Dominance - and Why They Fall.* New York: Doubleday.

Clark, Eric (1988). *The Want Makers: Inside the World of Advertising.* New York: Viking.

Clark, Gregory (2007). *A Farewell to Alms: A Brief Economic History of the World.* Princeton, NJ: Princeton University Press.

Clark, Gregory, O'Rourke, Kevin H., and Taylor, Alan M. (2008). Made in America?: The New World, the Old, and the Industrial Revolution. *NBER Working Paper No. 14077*, Cambridge, MA: The National Bureau of Economic Research (NBER),www.nber.org/papers/w14077.

Clark, Phil (2010). *The Gacaca Courts, Post-Genocide Justice and Reconciliation in Rwanda: Justice Without Lawyers.* Cambridge: Cambridge University Press.

Clinchy, Blythe McVicker (1996). Connected and Separate Knowing: Toward a Marriage of Two Minds. In Goldberger, Nancy Rule, Tarule, Jill Mattuck, Clinchy, Blythe McVicker, and Belenky, Mary Field (Eds.), *Knowledge, Difference, and Power: Women's Ways of Knowing*, pp. 205-247. New York: Basic Books.

Clinchy, Blythe McVicker and Zimmerman, Claire (1985). Growing Up Intellectually: Issues for College Women. *Work in Progress, No. 19*, Wellesley, MA: Stone Center Working Paper Series.

Clor, Harry M. (2009). *On Moderation: Defending an Ancient Virtue in a Modern World.* Waco, TX: Baylor University Press.

Coates, John M. and Herbert, Joe (2008). Endogenous Steroids and Financial Risk-Taking on a London Trading Floor. In *Proceedings of the National Academy of Sciences,* 105 (16), pp. 6167-6172, www.pnas.org/content/105/16/6167.full.pdf+html.

Cohan, William D. (2011). *How Goldman Sachs Came to Rule the World.* London: Doubleday.

Cohen, Joshua (2010). *Rousseau: A Free Community of Equals.* Oxford: Oxford University Press.

Coleman, Peter T. (2003). Characteristics of Protracted, Intractable Conflict: Toward the Development of a Metaframework-I. In *Peace and Conflict: Journal of Peace Psychology,* 9 (1), pp. 1-37.

Collier, Peter and Horowitz, David (Eds.)(1989). *Second Thoughts: Former Radicals Look Back at the Sixties.* Lanham, MD: Madison.

Collins, Alan (2004). State-Induced Security Dilemma Maintaining the Tragedy. In *Cooperation and Conflict,* 39 (1), pp. 27-44.

Coraggio, José Luis (1986). *Nicaragua: Revolution and Democracy.* Boston, MA: Allen and Unwin.

Coser, Lewis A. (1977). *Masters of Sociological Thought: Ideas in Historical and Social Context.* 2nd edition. Fort Worth, TX: Harcourt Brace Jovanovich.

Cosgrove, Lisa, Krimsky, Sheldon, Vijayraghavan, Manisha, and Schneider, Lisa (2006). Financial Ties Between DSM-IV Panel Members and the Pharmaceutical Industry. In *Psychotherapy and Psychosomatics,* 75 (3), pp. 154-160, www.tufts.edu/~skrimsky/pdf/dsm%20coi.pdf.

Council on Communications and Media (1-7-2011). Children, Adolescents, Obesity, and the Media. In *Pediatrics,* 128 (1), pp. 201-208, pediatrics.aappublications.org/content/128/1/201.abstract.

Coyle, Diane (2011). *The Economics of Enough: How to Run the Economy As If the Future Matters.* Princeton: Princeton University Press.

Cushman, Philip (1995). *Constructing the Self, Constructing America: A Cultural History of Psychotherapy.* Reading, MA: Addison-Wesley.

d'Escoto Brockmann, Miguel (2009). *Upcoming UN Economic Summit 'Timely and Historic' - Assembly President.* New York: United Nations News Center, www.un.org/apps/news/story.asp?NewsID=30749#.

Daly, Herman E. (1977). *Steady-State Economics: The Economics of Biophysical Equilibrium and Moral Growth.* San Francisco, CA: W.H. Freeman.

Daly, Herman E., Cobb, John B., and Cobb, Clifford W. (1989). *For the Common Good: Redirecting the Economy Toward Community, the Environment, and a Sustainable Future.* Boston: Beacon Press.

Daly, Herman E. and Farley, Joshua C. (2010). *Ecological Economics: Principles and Application.* 2nd edition. Washington: Island Press.

Daly, Herman E. and Townsend, Kenneth N. (Eds.)(1993). *Valuing the Earth: Economics, Ecology, Ethics.* Cambridge, MA: MIT Press.

Dannelsesutvalg (2009). *Kunnskap og dannelse foran et nytt århundre: innstilling fra Dannelsesutvalget for høyere utdanning.* Bergen and Oslo, Norway: University of Bergen, www.uib.no/filearchive/innstilling-dannelsesutvalget.pdf, www.uio.no/om_uio/uttalelser/dannelsesutvalgets-sluttdokument.pdf.

Danner, Mark (2008). America Defeated: How Terrorists Turned a Superpower's Strengths Against Itself. In *Alternet,* March 26, www.alternet.org/story/80547

Dasgupta, Susmita, Laplante, Benoit, Wang, Hua, and Wheeler, David (2002). Confronting the Environmental Kuznets Curve. In *Journal of Economic Perspectives,* 16 (1), pp. 147-168, pubs.aeaweb.org/doi/pdfplus/10.1257/0895330027157.

Davies, James, Sandström, Susanna, Shorrocks, Anthony, and Wolff, Edwards (2006). *The World Distribution of Household Wealth.* Tokyo, Japan: World Institute for Development Economics Research of the United Nations University (UNU-WIDER), www.wider.unu.edu/events/past-events/2006-events/en_GB/05-12-2006/.

Davies, William (2010). Between Bureaucracy and Academy: The Authority of the Economic Policy Advisor. In Calhoun, Craig and Sennett, Richard (Eds.), *Creating Authority*, London: Routledge, forthcoming.

Davis, Garry (1961). *My Country Is the World: The Adventures of a World Citizen.* New York: G.P. Putnam's Sons.

Davis, Garry (1984). *My Country Is the World: The Adventures of a World Citizen.* 2nd printing edition. Sorrento, ME: Juniper Ledge.

De Rivera, Joseph, Kurrien, Rahael, and Olsen, Nina (2007). Emotional Climates, Human Security, and Cultures of Peace . In *Journal of Social Issues,* 63 (2, June), pp. 255-271.

de Waal, Frans B. M. (2009). *The Age of Empathy: Nature's Lessons for a Kinder Society.* New York: Harmony Books.

Deming, W. Edwards (1986). *Out of the Crisis: Quality, Productivity and Competitive Position.* Cambridge: Cambridge University Press.

Deutsch, Morton (1958). Trust and Suspicion. In *Journal of Conflict Resolution,* 2, pp. 265-279.

Deutsch, Morton (1960a). The Effect of Motivational Orientation Upon Trust and Suspicion. In *Human Relations,* 13, pp. 123-139.

Deutsch, Morton (1960b). Trust, Trustworthiness, and the F-Scale. In *Journal of Abnormal and Social Psychology,* 61, pp. 138-140.

Deutsch, Morton (1962). Cooperation and Trust: Some Theoretical Notes. In Jones, Marshall R. (Ed.), *Nebraska Symposium on Motivation,* Lincoln, NE: University of Nebraska Press.

Deutsch, Morton (1973). *The Resolution of Conflict: Constructive and Destructive Processes.* New Haven, CT: Yale University Press.

Deutsch, Morton (2002). *Oppression and Conflict.* Skovde, Sweden: Plenary address given at the annual meetings of the International Society of Justice Research in Skovde, Sweden, on June 17, 2002, www.cpa.ca/epw/epw/Deutsch.pdf.

Deutsch, Morton (2006). A Framework for Thinking About Oppression and Its Change. In *Social Justice Research,* 19 (1), pp. 7-41.

Deutsch, Morton, Marcus, Eric C., and Brazaitis, Sarah (2012). A Framework for Thinking About Developing a Global Community. In Deutsch, Morton and Coleman, Peter T. (Eds.), *The Psychological Components of Sustainable Peace*, New York: Springer.

Dewey, John (1902). *The Child and the Curriculum.* Chicago: University of Chicago Press.

Dewey, John (1916). *Democracy and Education.* New York: Macmillan.

Diamond, Jared (1997). *Guns, Germs, and Steel.* New York: Norton.

Diamond, Jared (2005a). *Collapse: How Societies Choose to Fail or Succeed.* New York: Viking.

Diamond, Jared (2005b). *Guns, Germs, and Steel: The Fates of Human Societies.* New edition. New York: Norton.

Diamond, Jared (2011). *Collapse: How Societies Choose to Fail or Succeed.* Revised edition. London: Penguin Books.

Diamond, Jared and Robinson, James A. (2010). *Natural Experiments of History.* Cambridge, MA: Belknap Press of Harvard University Press.

Dichter, Thomas W. (2003). *Despite Good Intentions: Why Development Assistance to the Third World Has Failed.* Boston: University of Massachusetts Press.

Dichter, Thomas W. and Harper, Malcolm (2007). *What's Wrong With Microfinance?* Rugby: Practical Action Publ.

Diener, Ed and Seligman, Martin E. P. (2004). Beyond Money. Toward an Economy of Well-Being. In *Psychological Science in the Public Interest,* 5 (1, July), pp. 1-31.

Diesing, Paul R. (1962). *Reason in Society: Five Types of Decisions and Their Social Conditions.* Urbana, IL: University of Illinois Press.

Donoghue, Frank (2008). *The Last Professors: The Corporate University and the Fate of the Humanities.* New York: Fordham University Press.

Dow, Elizabeth I. (2005). *Approaching Intercultural Communication From the Space Between.* Tokyo, Japan: Seminar given at the 20th Annual Conference of the Society for Intercultural Education, Training, and Research (SIETAR) Japan, June 26th 2005, Rikkyo University.

Dowd, Kevin (1992). *The Experience of Free Banking.* London: Routledge.

Dowd, Kevin (1993). *Laissez-Faire Banking.* London: Routledge.

Dreier, Peter (2004). Reagan's Legacy: Homelessness in America. In *NHI Shelterforce Online* (135, May/June), www.nhi.org/online/issues/135/reagan.html.

Dreyer, Edward L. (2007). *Zheng He: China and the Oceans in the Early Ming Dynasty, 1405-1433.* New York: Pearson Longman.

Drucker, Peter (1993). *Concept of the Corporation (With a New Introduction by the Author).* New Brunswick, NJ: Transaction , originally published in 1946 by John Day Company.

Drumbl, Mark A. (2007). *Atrocity, Punishment and International Law.* Cambridge: Cambridge University Press.

Dunkman, William Edward (1970). *Money, Credit, & Banking.* New York: Random House.

Dunoff, Jeffrey L. and Trachtman, Joel P. (Eds.)(2009). *Ruling the World? Constitutionalism, International Law, and Global Governance.* Cambridge: Cambridge University Press.

Duraiappah, Anantha Kumar and Bhardwaj, Asmita (2007). *Measuring Policy Coherence Among the MEAs and MDGs.* Winnipeg, MB: International Institute for Sustainable Development (IISD), www.iisd.org/pdf/2007/measuring_policy.pdf.

Easterlin, Richard A. (1974). Does Economic Growth Improve the Human Lot? In David, Paul A. and Reder, Melvin W. (Eds.), *Nations and Households in Economic Growth: Essays in Honor of Moses Abramovitz*, New York: Academic Press.

Easterlin, Richard A. (Ed.)(2002). *Happiness in Economics.* Cheltenham: Edward Elgar.

Easterlin, Richard A. (2004). *The Reluctant Economist: Perspectives on Economics, Economic History, and Demography.* Cambridge: Cambridge University Press.

Easterlin, Richard A., Angelescu McVey, Laura, Switek, Malgorzata, Sawangfa, Onnicha, and Smith Zweig, Jacqueline (2010). The Happiness-Income Paradox Revisited. In *Proceedings of the National Academy of Sciences of the United States of America,* 107 (52), pp. 22463-22468.

Easterly, William Russell (2006). *The White Man's Burden: Why the West's Efforts to Aid the Rest Have Done So Much Ill and So Little Good.* New York: Penguin Press.

Eberly, Don (2008). *The Rise of Global Civil Society: Building Nations From the Ground Up.* San Francisco, CA: Encounter Books.

Ehrlich, Paul R. and Ehrlich, Anne H. (2008). *The Dominant Animal: Human Evolution and the Environment.* Washington, DC: Island Press.

Eisenstein, Charles (2007). *The Ascent of Humanity: The Age of Separation, the Age of Reunion, and the Convergence of Crises That Is Birthing the Transition.* Harrisburg, PA: Panenthea Productions.

Eisenstein, Charles (2008). *Money and the Crisis of Civilisation.* Reality Sandwich, www.realitysandwich.com/money_and_crisis_civilization.

Eisenstein, Charles (2010). *A Circle of Gifts.* Boulder, CO: Speaking Truth to Power, us1.campaign-archive1.com/?u=b8e53c620300ae88791163048&id=c3e7f05949&e=913c0c20d4.

Eisenstein, Charles (2011). *Sacred Economics: Money, Gift, and Society in the Age of Transition.* Berkeley, CA: Evolver Editions.

Eisler, Riane Tennenhaus (1987). *The Chalice and the Blade: Our History, Our Future.* London: Unwin Hyman.

Eisler, Riane Tennenhaus (1995). *Sacred Pleasure: Sex, Myth, and the Politics of the Body.* San Francisco, CA: HarperCollins.

Eisler, Riane Tennenhaus (2007). *The Real Wealth of Nations: Creating a Caring Economics.* San Francisco, CA: Berrett-Koehler.

Ekins, Paul and Max-Neef, Manfred A. (Eds.)(1992). *Real-Life Economics: Understanding Wealth Creation.* London: Routledge.

Elias, Norbert (1982). *The Civilizing Process* (Volume I. The History of Manners, 1969, Volume II. State Formation and Civilization, 1982). Oxford: Blackwell.

Ellis, Havelock (1973). *The Dance of Life.* Westport, CT: Greenwood Press, www.gutenberg.net.au/ebooks03/0300671.txt.

Ellis, Tania (2010). *The New Pioneers: Sustainable Business Success Through Social Innovation and Social Entrepreneurship.* Chichester: John Wiley.

Elworthy, Scilla and Rifkind, Gabrielle (2005). *Hearts and Minds: Human Security Approaches to Political Violence.* London: Demos, www.demos.co.uk.

Endenburg, Gerard (1988). *Sociocracy: The Organization of Decision-Making "No Objection" As the Principle of Sociocracy.* Rotterdam, The Netherlands: Stichting Sociocratisch Centrum.

Enderlein, Henrik, Wälti, Sonja, and Zürn, Michael (Eds.)(2010). *Handbook of Multi-Level Governance.* Cheltenham: Edward Elgar.

Etzioni, Amitai (1995). *New Communitarian Thinking: Persons, Virtues, Institutions, and Communities.* Charlottesville, VA: University Press of Virginia.

Etzioni, Amitai (1996). *The New Golden Rule: Community and Morality in a Democratic Society.* New York: Basic Books.

Etzioni, Amitai (2004). *The Common Good.* Cambridge: Polity Press.

Evanoff, Richard (2010). *Bioregionalism and Global Ethics: A Transactional Approach to Achieving Ecological Sustainability, Social Justice, and Human Well-Being.* London: Routledge.

Evers, Adalbert and Laville, Jean Louis (2004). *The Third Sector in Europe.* Cheltenham: Elgar.

Fang, Tony (2005). From "Onion" to "Ocean" Paradox and Change in National Cultures. In *International Studies of Management and Organization,* 35 (4, Winter), pp. 71-90.

Fanon, Frantz (1952). *Peau noire, masques blancs.* Paris: Editions du Seul.

Fanon, Frantz (1961). *Les damnés de la terre.* Paris: Maspero.

Fanon, Frantz (1963). *The Wretched of the Earth.* New York: Grove Press.

Fanon, Frantz (1986). *Black Skin, White Masks.* London: Pluto Press.

Fanon, Frantz and Markmann, Charles Lam (1967). *Black Skin, White Masks.* New York: Grove Press.

Federal Reserve Bank of Chicago (1994). *Modern Money Mechanics: A Workbook on Bank Reserves and Deposit Expansion.* Chicago: Federal Reserve Bank of Chicago.

Felps, Will, Mitchell, Terence R., and Byington, Eliza (2006). How, When, and Why Bad Apples Spoil the Barrel: Negative Group Members and Dysfunctional Groups. In *Research in Organizational Behavior,* 27, pp. 175-222, condor.depaul.edu/dweinste/smallgroups/Felps-Badapples.pdf.

Ferguson, Charles (2010). Larry Summers and the Subversion of Economics - The Chronicle Review. In *The Chronicle of Higher Education,* October 3, chronicle.com/article/Larry-Summersthe/124790/.

Ferguson, Niall (2008). *The Ascent of Money: A Financial History of the World.* New York: The Penguin Press.

Festinger, Leon (1957). *A Theory of Cognitive Dissonance.* Stanford, CA: Stanford University Press.

Fischer, David Hackett (1989). *Albion's Seed: Four British Folkways in America.* New York: Oxford University Press.

Fisher, Roger, Ury, William, and Patton, Bruce (1991). *Getting to Yes: Negotiating Agreement Without Giving in.* New York: Houghton Mifflin.

Fisher-Yoshida, Beth (2008). Coaching to Transform Perspective. In Mezirow, Jack and Taylor, Edward W. (Eds.), *Transformative Learning in Action,* San Francisco: Jossey-Bass.

Fisher-Yoshida, Beth, Geller, Kathy Dee, and Shapiro, Steven A. (Eds.)(2009). *Innovations in Transformative Learning: Space, Culture and the Arts.* New York: Peter Lang.

Fiske, Alan Page (1991*). Structures of Social Life: The Four Elementary Forms of Human Relations - Communal Sharing, Authority Ranking, Equality Matching, Market Pricing.* New York: Free Press.

Flexner, Abraham (1930). *Universities: American, English, German.* London: Oxford University Press.

Follett, Mary Parker (1924). *Creative Experience.* New York: Longmans, Green.

Forrester, Viviane (1996). *L'horreur économique.* Paris: Fayard.

Foucault, Michel (1979). On Governmentality. In *Ideology and Consciousness,* 6, pp. 5-21.

Foucault, Michel (1991). Governmentality. In Burchell, Graham, Gordon, Colin, and Miller, Peter (Eds.), *The Foucault Effect: Studies in Governmentality*, pp. 87-104. Chicago: University of Chicago Press.

Fox, Warwick (1990). *Toward a Transpersonal Ecology: Developing New Foundations for Environmentalism.* Boston, MA: Shambhala.

Fox, Warwick (1992). Intellectual Origins of the "Depth" Theme in the Philosophy of Arne Naess. In *Trumpeter*, 9 (2), trumpeter.athabascau.ca/archives/content/v9.2/fox2.html.

Frank, Thomas (2004a). *What's the Matter With America?: The Resistible Rise of the American Right.* London: Secker & Warburg.

Frank, Thomas (2004b). *What's the Matter With Kansas?: How Conservatives Won the Heart of America.* New York: Metropolitan Books.

Frankl, Viktor Emil (1963). *Man's Search for Meaning: An Introduction to Logotherapy.* New York: Washington Square Press, Simon and Schuster. Earlier title, 1959, *From Death-Camp to Existentialism.* Originally published in 1946 as *Ein Psycholog erlebt das Konzentrationslager.*

Fredrickson, Barbara L. and Branigan, Christine (2001). Positive Emotions. In Mayne, Tracy J. and Bonanno, George A. (Eds.), *Emotions: Current Issues and Future Directions*, pp. 123-151. New York: Guilford Press.

Fredrickson, Barbara L. and Levenson, Robert Wayne (1998). Positive Emotions Speed Recovery From the Cardiovascular Sequelae of Negative Emotions. In *Cognition & Emotion,* 12 (2), pp. 191-220.

Freeman, Christopher (2008). *Systems of Innovation: Selected Essays in Evolutionary Economics.* Cheltenham: Edward Elgar.

Freeman, Christopher and Louçã, Francisco (2001). *As Time Goes by: From the Industrial Revolutions to the Information Revolution.* Oxford: Oxford University Press.

Freire, Paulo (1968). *Educação e conscientização: Extencionismo rural.* Cuernavaca, México: CIDOC/Cuaderno, no. 25.

Freire, Paulo (1970a). *Pedagogia do oprimido.* Rio de Janeiro, Brazil: Paz e Terra.

Freire, Paulo (1970b). *Pedagogy of the Oppressed.* New York: Continuum.

Frey, Bruno S. (Ed.)(2008). *Happiness: A Revolution in Economics.* Cambridge, MA: MIT Press.

Frey, Bruno S. and Stutzer, Alois (Eds.)(2007). *Economics and Psychology: A Promising New Cross-Disciplinary Field.* Cambridge, MA: MIT Press.

Friedman, Thomas L. (2005). *The World Is Flat: A Brief History of the Twenty-First Century.* New York: Farrar, Straus and Giroux.

Fromkin, David (1999). *The Way of the World: From the Dawn of Civilization to the Eve of the Twenty-First Century.* New York: Knopf.

Fromm, Erich (1981). *On Disobedience and Other Essays.* New York: Seabury Press.

Früh, Werner and Stiehler, Hans-Jörg (2002). *Fernsehen in Ostdeutschland.* Berlin, Germany: Vistas.

Fry, Douglas P. (2007). *Beyond War: The Human Potential for Peace.* Oxford: Oxford University Press.

Fuechtmann, Thomas G. (1989). *Steeples and Stacks: Religion and Steel Crisis in Youngstown.* New York: Cambridge University Press.

Fuglestvedt, Ingrid (2009). *Phenomenology and the Pioneer Settlement on the Western Scandinavian Peninsula.* Lindome: Bricoleur Press.

Fujiwara, Takeo and Kawachi, Ichiro (2008). Social Capital and Health: A Study of Adult Twins in the U.S. In *American Journal of Preventive Health,* 35 (2), pp. 139-144.

Fukuyama, Francis (1992). *The End of History and the Last Man.* New York: Avon Books.

Fuller, Robert W. (2003). *Somebodies and Nobodies: Overcoming the Abuse of Rank.* Gabriola Island, BC: New Societies.

Gadamer, Hans Georg and Smith, P. Christopher (1986). *The Idea of the Good in Platonic-Aristotelian Philosophy.* New Haven, CT: Yale University Press.

Gaertner, Samuel L. and Dovidio, John F. (1999). *Reducing Intergroup Bias: The Common Ingroup Identity Model.* Hove, UK: Psychology Press.

Galtung, Johan (1996). *Peace by Peaceful Means.* Oslo, Norway, and London: International Peace Research Institute Oslo (PRIO) and Sage.

Gandhi, Arun Manilal (2003). *Legacy of Love: My Education on the Path of Nonviolence.* El Sobrante, CA: North Bay Book.

Gaskell, Elizabeth (1855). *North and South.* London: Originally appeared as a twenty-two-part weekly serial from September 1854 through January 1855 in the magazine *Household Words*, edited by Charles Dickens.

Gaucher, Danielle and Jost, John T. (2011). Difficulties Awakening the Sense of Injustice and Overcoming Oppression: On the Soporific Effects of System Justification. In Coleman, Peter T. (Ed.), *Conflict, Interdependence, and Justice: The Intellectual Legacy of Morton Deutsch*, pp. 227-247. New York: Springer.

Gazzaniga, Michael S. (2011). *Who's in Charge?: Free Will and the Science of the Brain.* New York: Ecco.

George, Henry (1879). *Progress and Poverty: An Inquiry into the Cause of Industrial Depressions, and of Increase of Want With Increase of Wealth: The Remedy.* Garden City, NY: Doubleday, Page & Co., www.econlib.org/library/YPDBooks/George/grgPP.html.

George, Robley E. (2002). *Socioeconomic Democracy: An Advanced Socioeconomic System.* Westport, CT: Praeger/Greenwood.

Georgesçu-Roegen, Nicholas (1971). *The Entropy Law and the Economic Process.* Cambridge, MA: Harvard University Press.

German Council of Economic Experts and Conseil d'Analyse Économique (2010). *Monitoring Economic Performance, Quality of Life and Sustainability.* Wiesbaden, Paris: Joint report as requested by the Franco-German Ministerial Council, www.sachverstaendigenrat-wirtschaft.de/fileadmin/dateiablage/Expertisen/2010/ex10_en.pdf.

Gesell, Silvio Johann (1916). *Die natürliche Wirtschaftsordnung durch Freiland und Freigeld.* Les Hauts Geneveys: Selbstverlag.

Gesell, Silvio Johann (1958). *The Natural Economic Order.* Revised edition. London: Peter Owen.

Gibson, Rachel L. (2007). *Toxic Baby Bottles: Scientific Study Finds Leaching Chemicals in Clear Plastic Baby Bottles.* Los Angeles: Environment California, Research and Policy Center, www.environmentcalifornia.org/uploads/Ve/AQ/VeAQsr6MMu4xA3-2ibnr_g/Toxic-Baby-Bottles.pdf.

Giddens, Anthony (2000). *The Third Way and Its Critics.* Cambridge: Polity Press.

Gilligan, Carol (1982). *In a Different Voice: Psychological Theory and Women's Development.* Cambridge, MA: Harvard University Press.

Giroux, Henry A., Freire, Paulo and Aronowitz, Stanley (Eds.)(2001). *Theory and Resistance in Education: Towards a Pedagogy for the Opposition.* Westport, CT: Bergin and Garvey.

Giroux, Henry A. and Giroux, Susan Searls (2004). *Take Back Higher Education: Race, Youth, and the Crisis of Democracy in the Post-Civil Rights Era.* New York: Palgrave Macmillan.

Gladwell, Malcolm (2000). *The Tipping Point: How Little Things Can Make a Big Difference.* New York: Little, Brown and Company.

Gladwell, Malcolm (2008). *Outliers: The Story of Success.* London: Allen Lane.

Glaser, Judith E. (2005). *Creating We: Change I-Thinking to We-Thinking & Build a Healthy Thriving Organization and the DNA of Leadership.* Avon, MA: Platinum Press, Adams Media.

Glaser, Judith E. (2006). *The DNA of Leadership: Leverage Your Instincts to Communicate, Differentiate, Innovate.* Avon, MA: Platinum Press.

Glaser, Judith E. (2010). Best Books of 2010: You Are What You Think - The Human Mind. In *Strategy + Business,* pp. 97-102, www.strategy-business.com/article/10409f?gko=8311b&cid=enews2010 1123.

Gneezy, Ayelet, Gneezy, Uri, Nelson, Leif D., and Brown, Amber (2010). Shared Social Responsibility: A Field Experiment in Pay-What-You-Want Pricing and Charitable Giving. In *Science,* 329 (5989), pp. 325-327.

Gold, Lorna (2004). *The Sharing Economy: Solidarity Networks Transforming Globalisation.* Aldershot, UK: Ashgate.

Goldstone, Jack A. and Ulfelder, Jay (2005). How to Construct Stable Democracies. In *Washington Quarterly,* 28, Winter 2004-5 (1), pp. 9-20.

Goodale, Mark and Merry, Sally Engle (2007). *The Practice of Human Rights: Tracking Law Between the Global and the Local.* Cambridge: Cambridge Univerity Press.

Goodwin, Neva Rockefeller (2010). *A New Economics for the Twenty-First Century.* World Futures Review, neweconomicsinstitute.org/content/new-economics-21st-century.

Gornitzka, Åse and Langfeldt, Liv (2008). *Borderless Knowledge: Understanding the "New" Internationalisation of Research and Higher Education in Norway.* Dordrecht, The Netherlands: Springer.

Gottman, John Mordechai, Katz, Lynn Fainsilber, and Hooven, Carole (1997). *Meta-Emotion: How Families Communicate Emotionally.* Mahwah, NJ: Erlbaum.

Goudzwaard, Bob Rijnhout Leida, Keune, Lou, Juffermans, Jan, Somers, Esther, Hogenhius, Christiaan, Boer, Bart de, Hudig, Kees, van de Water, Marjolein, Gort, Rob, and van Vliert, Peter (2008). *Declaration of Tilburg: A Convenient Truth.* Tilburg, The Netherlands: Conference held at Tilburg University, 10 January 2008, www.worldinbalance.net/pdf/ec-dot.pdf.

Gray, John (2002). *False Dawn: The Delusions of Global Capitalism.* London: Granta Books.

Greco Jr., Thomas Henry (1990). *Money and Debt: A Solution to the Global Crisis.* Part I Political Money and the Debt Imperative: Why the Budget Can't Be Balanced circ2.home.mindspring.com/Money_and_Debt_Part1_lo.pdf Part II Freedom and the Monetary Ideal circ2.home.mindspring.com/Money_and_Debt_Part2_lo.pdf Part III Segregated Monetary Functions and an Objective, Global, Standard Unit of Account circ2.home.mindspring.com/Money_and_Debt_Part3_lo.pdf.

Greco Jr., Thomas Henry (2009). *The End of Money and the Future of Civilization.* White River Junction, VT: Chelsea Green.

Green, Robert (2010). *Security Without Nuclear Deterrence.* Christchurch, New Zealand: Astron Media and the Disamament & Security Centre.

Greene, Graham (1939). *The Confidential Agent: An Entertainment.* London: William Heinemann.

Grignon, Paul (2009). *Digital Coin - Beyond Money.* Gabriola Island, BC: www.digitalcoin.info/Digital_Coin_Draft_Proposal_Grignon_Aug16_2 009.pdf.

Gudmundsson, Halldór (2010). *Wir sind alle Isländer: Von Lust und Frust, in der Krise zu sein.* Munich, Germany: btb.

Guruge, Ananda W. P. (2008). *Buddhism, Economics and Science - Further Studies in Socially Engaged Humanistic Buddhism.* Bloomington, IN: AuthorHouse.

Guzzini, Stefano and Leander, Anna (2006). *Constructivism and International Relations: Alexander Wendt and His Critics.* New York: Routledge.

Haas, Jonathan (2001). Warfare and the Evolution of Culture. In Price, T. Douglas and Feinman, Gary M. (Eds.), *Archaeology at the Millennium: A Sourcebook*, pp. 329-350. New York: Kluwer Academic, Plenum Publishers.

Haas, Jonathan and Piscitelli, Matthew (2011). *The Prehistory of Warfare: Misled by Ethnograpy and Ethology.* Unpublished manuscript.

Haavelmo, Trygve (1989). *Econometrics and the Welfare State: Trygve Haavelmo - Prize Lecture to the Memory of Alfred Nobel, December 7, 1989.* Stockholm and Oslo: The Nobel Foundation, http://nobelprize.org/nobel_prizes/economics/laureates/1989/haavelmo-lecture.html.

Habermas, Jürgen (1962). *Strukturwandel der Öffentlichkeit: Untersuchungen zu einer Kategorie der bürgerlichen Gesellschaft.* Neuwied, Germany: Luchterhand.

Habermas, Jürgen (1981). *Theorie des kommunikativen Handelns, Band I, Handlungsrationalität und gesellschaftliche Rationalisierung, Band II, Zur Kritik der funktionalistischen Vernunft.* Frankfurt am Main, Germany: Suhrkamp Verlag.

Habermas, Jürgen (1985). *The Theory of Communicative Action, Volume 1, Reason and the Rationalization of Society, Volume 2, Lifeworld and System: A Critique of Functionalist Reason.* Boston, MA: Beacon Press.

Habermas, Jürgen (1989). *The Structural Transformation of the Public Sphere: An Inquiry into a Category of Bourgeois Society.* Cambridge: Polity Press.

Hale, Thomas Nathan and Held, David (Eds.)(2011). *Handbook of Transnational Governance: Institutions and Innovations.* Cambridge: Polity Press.

Handy, Charles and Bernhut, Stephen (2004). Leader's Edge: An Interview With Charles Handy. In *Ivey Business Journal,* March/April (Reprint # 9B04TB06), pp. 1-7, www.iveybusinessjournal.com/view_article.asp?intArticle_ID=476.

Hardin, Garrett James (1998). Extensions of "The Tragedy of the Commons". In *Science,* 280 (5364), pp. 682-683.

Harding, Stephan (2006). *Animate Earth: Science, Intuition and Gaia.* Totnes, Devon: Green Books.

Hardisty, Jean V. (1999). *Mobilizing Resentment: Conservative Resurgence From the John Birch Society to the Promise Keepers.* Boston, MA: Beacon Press.

Harris, Errol E. (2008). *Twenty-First Century Democratic Renaissance: From Plato to Neoliberalism to Planetary Democracy.* Sun City, AZ: Institute for Economic Democracy Press.

Hartling, Linda M. (2003a). Prevention Through Connection: A Collaborative Response to Women's Substance Abuse. *Work in Progress, No. 103,* Wellesley, MA: Stone Center Working Papers Series.

Hartling, Linda M. (2003b). Strengthening Resilience in a Risky World: It Is All About Relationships. *Work in Progress, No. 101,* Wellesley, MA: Stone Center Working Papers Series.

Hartling, Linda M. (2005a). *An Appreciative Frame: Beginning a Dialogue on Human Dignity and Humiliation.* Introductory text presented at the 5th Annual Conference of Human Dignity and Humiliation Studies "Beyond Humiliation: Encouraging Human Dignity in the Lives and Work of All People," Berlin, Germany, 15th - 17th September, 2005.

Hartling, Linda M. (2005b). *Humiliation: Real Pain, a Pathway to Violence.* Boston, MA: Paper presented at the 2005 "Workshop on Humiliation and Violent Conflict," Columbia University, December 15-16, 2005, www.humiliationstudies.org/whoweare/annualmeeting06.php.

Hartling, Linda M. (2007). Humiliation: Real Pain, a Pathway to Violence. In *Brazilian Journal of Sociology of Emotion,* 6 (17), pp. 466-479.

Hartling, Linda M. (2008). Jean Baker Miller: Living in Connection. In *Feminism and Psychology,* 18 (3), pp. 326-335.

Hartling, Linda M. and Luchetta, Tracy (1999). Humiliation: Assessing the Impact of Derision, Degradation, and Debasement. In *Journal of Primary Prevention,* 19 (5), pp. 259-278.

Hartling, Linda M. and Miller, Jean Baker (2005). *Moving Beyond Humiliation: A Relational Reconceptualization of Human Rights.* Wellesley, MA: Paper presented at the Summer Advanced Training Institute: Encouraging an Era of Connection.

Hartling, Linda M., Rosen, Wendy, Walker, Maureen, and Jordan, Judith V. (2000). Shame and Humiliation: From Isolation to Relational Transformation. *Work in Progress, No. 88,* Wellesley, MA: Stone Center Working Papers Series.

Hartling, Linda M. and Sparks, E. (2000). Relational-Cultural Practice: Working in a Nonrelational World. *Work in Progress, No. 97,* Wellesley, MA: Stone Center Working Papers Series.

Hartmann, Michael (2007). *The Sociology of Elites.* London: Routledge.

Harvey, David (2010). *The Enigma of Capital: And the Crises of Capitalism.* London: Profile Books.

Hawken, Paul (2007a). *Blessed Unrest: How the Largest Movement in the World Came into Being, and Why No One Saw It Coming.* New York: Viking.

Hawken, Paul (2007b). To Remake the World: Something Earth-Changing Is Afoot Among Civil Society. In *Orion Magazine,* May/June (266), www.orionmagazine.org/index.php/mag/issue/266/.

Hawken, Paul, Lovins, Amory B., and Lovins, L. Hunter (1999). *Natural Capitalism: The Next Industrial Revolution.* Boston, MA: Little, Brown and Company.

Hayashi, Kichiro (2002). Current Intercultural Issues and Challenges in Japanese Business Interfaces: Blending Theory and Practice. In *Intercultural Communication Studies,* 5 (February), pp. 23-32.

Head, Simon (2003). *The New Ruthless Economy: Work and Power in the Digital Age.* Oxford: Oxford University Press.

Heard, Gerald (1963). *The Five Ages of Man.* New York: Julian Press.

Heath, Chip and Heath, Dan (2010). *Switch: How to Change Things When Change Is Hard.* New York: Cornerstone.

Hedges, Christopher Lynn (2010). *Death of the Liberal Class.* New York: Nation Books.

Heidegger, Martin (2006). *Sein und Zeit.* 19th edition. Tübingen, Germany: Max Niemeyer Verlag.

Held, David (2010). *Cosmopolitanism: Ideals and Realities.* Cambridge: Polity Press.

Held, David, Fane-Hervey, Angus, and Theros, Marika (2011*). The Governance of Climate Change: Science, Politics and Ethics.* Cambridge: Polity Press.

Held, David and Kaya, Ayse (2007). *Global Inequality: Patterns and Explanations.* Cambridge: Polity.

Held, David and McGrew, Anthony (2007). *Globalization/Anti-Globalization: Beyond the Great Divide.* Cambridge: Polity Press.

Held, Virginia (2006). *The Ethics of Care: Personal, Political, and Global.* Oxford: Oxford University Press.

Heller, Agnes (1984). *Everyday Life.* London: Routledge.

Heller, Patrick, Baiocchi, Gianpaolo, and Kunrath Silva, Marcelo (2011). *Bootstrapping Democracy: Transforming Local Governance and Civil Society in Brazil.* Stanford, CA: Stanford University Press.

Henderson, Hazel (1996). *Building a Win-Win World: Life Beyond Global Economic Warfare.* San Francisco, CA: Berrett-Koehler.

Henderson, Hazel and Sethi, Simran (2008). *Ethical Markets: Growing the Green Economy.* White River Junction, VT: Chelsea Green.

Hersh, Richard H. and Merrow, John (Eds.)(2005). *Declining by Degrees: Higher Education at Risk.* New York: Palgrave Macmillan.

Herz, John H. (1950). Idealist Internationalism and the Security Dilemma. In *World Politics,* II, pp. 157-180.

Hessel, Stéphane (2010). *Indignez-vous!* Montpellier, France: Indigène éditions.

Hicks, Donna (2010). *A Matter of Dignity: A New Approach to Building Strong Relationships and Healing and Reconciling Relationships in Conflict.* New Haven, CT: Yale University Press.

Hill, Steven (2010). *Europe's Promise: Why the European Way Is the Best Hope in an Insecure Age.* Berkeley: University of California Press.

Hobbes, Thomas (1651). *Leviathan, or, The Matter, Forme, and Power of a Common Wealth, Ecclesiasticall and Civil.* London: Printed for Andrew Crooke, reproduction of original in Yale University Library.

Hock, Dee Ward (1999). *Birth of the Chaordic Age.* San Francisco, CA: Berrett-Koehler.

Hollick, Malcolm (2006). *The Science of Oneness: A Worldview for the Twenty-First Century.* Winchester, UK: O Books.

Hollick, Malcolm and Connelly, Christine (2011). *Hope for Humanity: How Understanding and Healing Trauma Could Solve the Planetary Crisis.* Winchester, UK: O Books.

Holloway, John (2005). *Change the World Without Taking Power.* New edition. London: Pluto Press.

Holloway, John (2010). *Crack Capitalism.* Puebla, Mexico, London: Instituto de Ciencias Sociales y Humanidades, Benemérita Universidad Autónoma de Puebla, Pluto Press.

Hoopes, James (Ed.)(1991). *Peirce on Signs: Writings on Semiotic.* Chapel Hill, NC: University of North Carolina Press.

Hopkins, Rob (2008). *The Transition Handbook: From Oil Dependency to Local Resilience.* Totnes, Devon: Green Books.

Hörmann, Franz (2009). Premises and Promises of Theory Formation in Economics. In Leidlmair, Karl (Ed.), *After Cognitivism - A Reassessment of Cognitive Science and Philosophy*, pp. 213-225. Dordrecht, The Netherlands: Springer Netherlands, www.wu.ac.at/taxmanagement/Institut/Mitarbeiter/Hoermann/new200 6/downloads/hoermann-premises-and-promises.doc.

Houkes, John M. (2004). *An Annotated Bibliography on the History of Usury and Interest From the Earliest Times Through the Eighteenth Century.* Lewiston, NY: Edwin Mellen Press.

Howard, Milford Wriarson (1895). *The American Plutocracy.* New York: Holland Publishing Company.

Howlett, Chuck and Harris, Ian (2010). *Books Not Bombs: Teaching Peace Since the Dawn of the Republic.* Charlotte, NC: Information Age Publishing.

Huber, Berthold (2010). *Kurswechsel für Deutschland: Die Lehren aus der Krise.* Frankfurt am Main, Germany: Campus Verlag.

Hudson, Michael (1972). *Super Imperialism: The Economic Strategy of American Empire.* New York: Holt, Rinehart and Winston.

Hudson, Michael (2003). *Super Imperialism: The Origin and Fundamentals of U.S. World Dominance.* 2nd edition. London: Pluto Press.

Hughes, Thomas Parke (2004). *American Genesis: A Century of Invention and Technological Enthusiasm, 1870-1970*. Chicago: The University of Chicago Press.

Humboldt, Wilhelm von (1993). *The Limits of State Action*. Indianapolis: Liberty Fund.

Humboldt, Wilhelm von (2002). *Schriften zur Anthropologie und Geschichte. Werke I*. 4th edition. Darmstadt, Germany: Wissenschaftliche Buchgesellschaft.

Hurd, Douglas (2010*). Choose Your Weapons: The British Foreign Secretary: Two Centuries of Conflict and Personalities*. London: Weidenfeld and Nicolson.

Hutton, Will (2008). *The Writing on the Wall: China and the West in the 21st Century*. London: Abacus.

Hutton, Will (2010). *Them and Us: Changing Britain - Why We Need a Fair Society*. London: Little, Brown and Company.

Hyde, Lewis (1983). *The Gift: Imagination and the Erotic Life of Property*. New York: Random House.

Hyde, Lewis (2006). *The Gift: How the Creative Spirit Transforms the World*. Edinburgh, UK: Canongate.

Ingold, Timothy (2000a). Evolving Skills. In Rose, Hilary and Rose, Steven (Eds.), *Alas, Poor Darwin: Arguments Against Evolutionary Psychology*, pp. 225-246. London: Jonathan Cape.

Ingold, Timothy (2000b). *The Perception of the Environment: Essays in Livelihood, Dwelling and Skill*. London: Routledge.

International Tesla Society (1988). *International Tesla Symposium Proceedings (1984, 1986, 1988, 1990, 1992)*. Security, CO: International Tesla Society.

Jackson, Tim (2009). *Prosperity Without Growth: Economics for a Finite Planet*. London: Earthscan.

Jackson, Tim and Marks, Nic (1994). *Measuring Sustainable Economic Welfare: A Pilot Index: 1950-1990*. Stockholm: Stockholm Environment Institute, published in cooperation with The New Economics Foundation.

Jackson, Wes (1994). *Becoming Native to This Place*. Lexington, KY: University Press of Kentucky.

Jacobs, Jane (1961). *The Death and Life of Great American Cities*. New York: Random House.

Jacobs, Jane (1984). *Cities and the Wealth of Nations: Principles of Economic Life*. New York: Random House.

Jacobs, Jane (1992). *Systems of Survival: A Dialogue on the Moral Foundations of Commerce and Politics*. New York: Random House.

Jacobs, Jane (2000). *The Nature of Economies*. New York: Random House.

Jacobs, Jane (2004). *Dark Age Ahead*. New York: Vintage Books.

Jacobsen, Ove (2010). Økonomer med fokus på miljø og samfunnsansvar: P. A. Payutto. In *Pengevirke*, 4, pp. 22-23, www.cultura.no/uploads/Pengevirke_2010-4_NO_web.pdf.

Jain, Manish and Jain, Shilpa (Eds.)(2008). *Reclaiming the Gift Culture*. Udaipur, Rajasthan, India: Shikshantar: The Peoples' Institute for Rethinking Education and Development, www.swaraj.org/shikshantar.

Jameson, Kenneth P. and Wilber, Charles K. (Eds.)(1996). *The Political Economy of Development and Underdevelopment*. New York: McGraw-Hill.

Jervis, Robert (2006). Understanding Beliefs. In *Political Psychology*, 27 (5), pp. 641-663.

Jervis, Robert, Lebow, Richard Ned, and Stein, Janice Gross (1985). *Psychology and Deterrence*. Baltimore, MD: Johns Hopkins University Press.

Joerges, Christian (2010). Unity in Diversity As Europe's Vocation and Conflicts Law As Europes Constitutional Form. *LEQS Paper No. 28/2010*, London: London School of Economics. (LSE) "Europe in Question" Discussion Paper Series, http://ssrn.com/paper=1723249.

Johnson, Steven (2010). *Where Good Ideas Come From: The Natural History of Innovation.* New York: Riverhead.

Jones, James Edward (2006). *The Post Victim Ethical Exemption Syndrome: An Outgrowth of Humiliation.* New York: Paper presented at the 3rd Workshop on Humiliation and Violent Conflict, Columbia University, December 14-15, 2006, www.humiliationstudies.org/documents/JonesNY06meeting.pdf.

Jungk, Robert (1977). *Der Atomstaat: Vom Fortschritt in die Unmenschlichkeit.* Munich, Germany: Kindler.

Kaku, Michio (2005). *Parallel Worlds: A Journey Through Creation, Higher Dimensions, and the Future of the Cosmos.* New York: Doubleday.

Kant, Immanuel (1785). *Grundlegung zur Metaphysik der Sitten zweiter Abschnitt: Übergang von der populären sittlichen Weltweisheit zur Metaphysik der Sitten.* Riga, Latvia: Johann Friedrich Hartknock.

Kant, Immanuel (1790). *Die Kritik der Urteilskraft.* Berlin and Liebau, Germany: Lagarde und Friederich.

Kant, Immanuel (1795). *Zum ewigen Frieden: Ein philosophischer Entwurf.* Königsberg: Friedrich Nicolovius, www.uni-kassel.de/fb5/frieden/themen/Theorie/kant.html.

Kant, Immanuel and Rink, Friedrich Theodor (1803). *Über die Pädagogik.* Königsberg: Friedrich Nicolovius.

Karelis, Charles (2007). *The Persistence of Poverty: Why the Economics of the Well-Off Can't Help the Poor.* New Haven, CT: Yale University Press.

Keane, John (2009). *The Life and Death of Democracy.* London: Simon and Schuster.

Keen, Steve (2001). *Debunking Economics: The Naked Emperor of the Social Sciences*. London: Zed Books.

Kelly, Marjorie (2001). *The Divine Right of Capital: Dethroning the Corporate Aristocracy*. San Francisco, CA: Berrett-Koehler.

Kelly, Marjorie (2009). Not Just for Profit: Emerging Alternatives to the Shareholder-Centric Model. In *Strategy + Business*, 54, pp. 1-10, www.corporation2020.org/new_documents/Kelly%20Not%20Just%20 for%20Profit%20-%20SB%20mag%20spring%2009.pdf.

Kelly, Raymond C. (2000). *Warless Societies and the Origin of War*. Ann Arbor, MI: The University of Michigan Press.

Keltner, Dacher (2009a). *Born to Be Good: The Science of a Meaningful Life*. New York: Norton.

Keltner, Dacher (2009b). Darwin's Touch: Survival of the Kindest. In *Psychology Today Blog Born To Be Good*, February 11, blogs.psychologytoday.com/blog/born-to-be-good/200902/darwins-touch-survival-the-kindest.

Kendall, Diana (2007). *Sociology in Our Times*. Belmont, CA: Wadsworth.

Kennedy, Declan and Kennedy, Margrit (1997). *Designing Ecological Settlements: Ecological Planning and Building: Experiences in New Housing and in the Renewal of Existing Housing Quarters in European Countries*. Berlin: Dietrich Reimer Verlag.

Kennedy, Margrit (1995*). Interest and Inflation Free Money: Creating an Exchange Medium That Works for Everybody and Protects the Earth. New revised and expanded edition*. Okemos, MI: Seva International, userpage.fu-berlin.de/~roehrigw/kennedy/english/.

Kent, Deirdre (2010). *Healthy Money, Healthy Planet: Developing Sustainability Through New Money Systems*. Carterton, New Zealand: Craig Potton Publishing.

Keohane, Robert O. (1990). International Liberalism Reconsidered. In Dunn, John (Ed.), *The Economic Limits to Modern Politics*, pp. 165-194. Cambridge, MA: Cambridge University Press.

Keynes, John Maynard (1936). *The General Theory of Employment Interest and Money*. London: Macmillan.

Kidder, Rushworth M. (1994). *Shared Values for a Troubled World: Conversations With Men and Women of Conscience*. San Francisco, CA: Jossey-Bass.

Kilbourne, Jean (2000). *Can't Buy My Love: How Advertising Changes the Way We Think and Feel*. New York: Free Press.

Kim, Young Yun and Ruben, Brent David (1988). Intercultural Transformation: A Systems Theory. In *International and Intercultural Communication Annual*, 12, 1988, pp. 299-321.

King Jr., Martin Luther (1963). *Strength to Love*. New York: Harper and Row.

King, Jr. Martin Luther (2007). *Dream: The Words and Inspiration of Martin Luther King, Jr*. Boulder, CO: Blue Mountain Arts.

King, Stephen D. (2010). *Losing Control: Why the West's Economic Prosperity Can No Longer Be Taken for Granted*. New Haven, CT: Yale University Press.

Kinley, David (2009). *Civilising Globalisation: Human Rights and the Global Economy*. Cambridge: Cambridge University Press.

Kirsch, Irving (2009). *The Emperor's New Drugs: Exploding the Antidepressant Myth*. London: Bodley Head.

Klare, Jörn (2010). *Was Bin Ich Wert? Eine Preisermittlung*. Frankfurt am Main, Germany: Suhrkamp.

Klein, Naomi (2007). *The Shock Doctrine: The Rise of Disaster Capitalism*. New York: Metropolitan Books.

Koblik, Steven and Graubard, Stephen (Eds.)(2000). *Distinctively American: The Residential Liberal Arts Colleges.* New Brunswick, NJ: Transaction Publishers.

Koestler, Arthur (1967). *The Ghost in the Machine.* London: Hutchinson.

Koestler, Arthur (1978). *Janus: A Summing Up.* London: Hutchinson.

Korten, David C. (1993). A Not So Radical Agenda for a Sustainable Global Future. In *Convergence,* 26, pp. 57-66.

Korten, David C. (2001). *When Corporations Rule the World.* Bloomfield, CT: Kumarian Press.

Korten, David C. (2009a). *Agenda for a New Economy: From Phantom Wealth to Real Wealth.* San Francisco, CA: Berrett-Koehler.

Korten, David C. (2009b). *Path to a Peace Economy.* Sonoma, CA: Paper presented at the Economics of Peace Conference, organized by the Praxis Peace Institute & RSF Social Finance, October 19, 2009, www.davidkorten.org/peaceeconomy.

Kovel, Joel (2002). *The Enemy of Nature: The End of Capitalism or the End of the World?* Halifax, NS: Fernwood Publishing.

Kronman, Anthony T. (2007). *Education's End: Why Our Colleges and Universities Have Given Up on the Meaning of Life.* New Haven, CT: Yale University Press.

Krugman, Paul R. (2007). *The Conscience of a Liberal.* New York: W.W. Norton.

Krugman, Paul R. Wells, Robin (Ed.)(2009). *Economics.* New York: Worth.

Krugman, Paul R. and Obstfeld, Maurice (2009). *International Economics: Theory and Policy.* 8th edition. Boston, MA: Addison Wesley.

Kuhn, Thomas Samuel (1962). *The Structure of Scientific Revolutions.* Chicago: University of Chicago Press.

Küng, Hans (1997). *A Global Ethic for Global Politics and Economics.* London: SCM Press.

Kunstler, James Howard (2006). *The Long Emergency: Surviving the End of Oil, Climate Change, and Other Converging Catastrophes of the Twenty-First Century.* New York: Grove Press.

Kurokawa, Kisho, in Schmal, Peter Cachola, Flagge, Ingeborg, and Visscher, Jochen (Eds.)(2005). *Kisho Kurokawa: Metabolism and Symbiosis.* Berlin, Germany: Jovis.

Kurtzman, Joel (1993). *The Death of Money: How the Electric Economy Has Destabilized the World's Markets and Created Financial Chaos.* New York: Simon and Schuster.

Lair, Daniel J., Sullivan, Katie, and Cheney, George (2005). Marketization and the Recasting of the Professional Self. In *Management Communication Quarterly,* 18 (3), pp. 307-343.

Lakoff, George P. (2004). *Don't Think of an Elephant!: Know Your Values and Frame the Debate: The Essential Guide for Progressives.* White River Junction, VT: Chelsea Green.

Lane, Robert E. (2001). *The Loss of Happiness in Market Democracies.* New Haven, CT: Yale University Press.

Langer, Susanne K. (1953). *Feeling and Form: A Theory of Art Developed From Philosophy in a New Key.* New York: Charles Scribner.

Lappé, Frances Moore (2011). *EcoMind: Changing the Way We Think, to Create the World We Want.* New York: Nation Books.

Lawlor, Eilis, Kersley, Helen, and Steed, Susan (2009). *A Bit Rich: Calculating the Real Value to Society of Different Professions.* London: nef (the new economics foundation), www.neweconomics.org/sites/neweconomics.org/files/A_Bit_Rich.pdf.

Leary DeGruy, Joy (2005). *Post Traumatic Slave Syndrome: America's Legacy of Enduring Injury and Healing.* Milaukie, Oregon: Upton.

Legrain, Philippe (2002). *Open World: The Truth About Globalisation.* London: Abacus.

Lerner, Melvin J. (1980). *The Belief in a Just World: A Fundamental Delusion.* New York: Plenum Press.

Lerner, Melvin J. (2003). The Justice Motive: Where Social Psychologists Found It, How They Lost It and Why They May Not Find It Again. In *Personality and Social Psychology Review, 7,* pp. 388-399.

Lessig, Lawrence (2005). *Free Culture: The Nature and Future of Creativity.* New York: Penguin Books.

Lévinas, Emmanuel (1961). *Totalité et infini: Essai sur l'extériorité.* The Hague, The Netherlands: Martinus Nijhoff.

Lévinas, Emmanuel (1985). Responsibility for the Other. In Lévinas, Emmanuel (Ed.), *Ethics and Infinity: Conversations With Phillipe Nemo,* pp. 93-101. Pittsburgh, PA: Duquesne University Press.

Levinson, Nanette S. (2004). *Local Globalization: Rethinking the Local and the Global.* Montreal: Paper presented at the annual meeting of the International Studies Association, Le Centre Sheraton Hotel, Montreal, Quebec, Canada, www.allacademic.com/meta/p72287_index.html.

Lewis, Harry R. (2006). *Excellence Without a Soul: How a Great University Forgot Education.* New York: Public Affairs.

Lewis, Helen Block (1971). *Shame and Guilt in Neurosis.* New York: International Universities Press.

Lewis, Michael M. (2010). *The Big Short: Inside the Doomsday Machine.* New York: Norton.

Lewis, Michael M. (2011). *Boomerang: Travels in the New Third World.* New York: Norton.

Liberman, Varda, Samuels, Steven M., and Ross, Lee D. (2004). The Name of the Game: Predictive Power of Reputations Versus Situational Labels in Determining Prisoner's Dilemma Game Moves. In *Personality and Social Psychology Bulletin,* 30 (X), pp. 1-11.

Lietaer, Bernard A. (1997). Beyond Greed and Scarcity: Bernard Lietaer Talks to Sarah Van Gelder About the Transformational Effects of Currency Redesign. In *Yes! Powerful Ideas, Practical Actions,* Money: Print your Own! (June 30), pp. 1-8, www.yesmagazine.org/issues/money-print-your-own/beyond-greed-and-scarcity.

Lietaer, Bernard A. (2001). *The Future of Money: Creating New Wealth, Work, and a Wiser World.* London: Century.

Lindner, Evelin Gerda (1999). Women in the Global Village: Increasing Demand for Traditional Communication Patterns. In Breines, Ingeborg, Gierycz, Dorota, and Reardon, Betty A. (Eds.), *Towards a Women's Agenda for a Culture of Peace,* pp. 89-98. Paris: UNESCO.

Lindner, Evelin Gerda (2000a). *Globalisation and Humiliation: Towards a New Paradigm.* Oslo, Norway: University of Oslo, Human Dignity and Humiliation Studies, www.humiliationstudies.org/whoweare/evelin02.php.

Lindner, Evelin Gerda (2000b). *Humiliation and Rationality in International Relations. The Role of Humiliation in North Korea, Rwanda, Somalia, Germany, and the Global Village.* Oslo, Norway: University of Oslo, Human Dignity and Humiliation Studies, www.humiliationstudies.org/whoweare/evelin02.php.

Lindner, Evelin Gerda (2000c). *Humiliation, Human Rights, and Global Corporate Responsibility.* Oslo, Norway: University of Oslo, Human Dignity and Humiliation Studies, www.humiliationstudies.org/whoweare/evelin02.php.

Lindner, Evelin Gerda (2000d). *The "Framing Power" of International Organizations, and the Cost of Humiliation.* Oslo, Norway, and Coalition for Global Solidarity and Social Development - Peace and Conflicts: globalsolidarity.transcend.org/articles/the.pdf.

Lindner, Evelin Gerda (2000e). *The Psychology of Humiliation: Somalia, Rwanda / Burundi, and Hitler's Germany.* Oslo, Norway: University of Oslo, Department of Psychology, doctoral dissertation in psychology.

Lindner, Evelin Gerda (2000f). *Transnational Corporations and the Global Poor: From Humiliation to Dialogue.* Oslo, Norway: University of Oslo, postdoctoral research proposal, www.humiliationstudies.org/documents/evelin/PovertyandTNCSLongV ersion2000.pdf.

Lindner, Evelin Gerda (2000g). *What Every Negotiator Ought to Know: Understanding Humiliation.* Oslo, Norway and Coalition for Global Solidarity and Social Development - Peace and Conflicts: globalsolidarity.transcend.org/articles/what.pdf.

Lindner, Evelin Gerda (2000h). *What Is a Good Life - Comparison Between Egypt and Germany.* Oslo, Norway: University of Oslo, manuscript presented at the Middle East Virtual Community (MEViC), first MEViC online Internet conference, 2000, on the basis of doctoral dissertation in medicine (1994).

Lindner, Evelin Gerda (2001a). How Research Can Humiliate: Critical Reflections on Method. In *Journal for the Study of Peace and Conflict,* Annual Edition 2001-2002, pp. 16-36,   jspc.library.wisc.edu.

Lindner, Evelin Gerda (2001b). Humiliation - Trauma That Has Been Overlooked: An Analysis Based on Fieldwork in Germany, Rwanda / - Burundi, and Somalia. In *TRAUMATOLOGYe,* 7 (1), Article 3 (32 pages), tmt.sagepub.com/cgi/content/abstract/7/1/43, or www.fsu.edu/%7Etrauma/v7/Humiliation.pdf.

Lindner, Evelin Gerda (2001c). Humiliation and the Human Condition: Mapping a Minefield. In *Human Rights Review,* 2 (2), pp. 46-63.

Lindner, Evelin Gerda (2001d). *Moratorium on Humiliation: Cultural and "Human Factor" Dimensions Underlying Structural Violence.* New York: Discussion paper presented at the Expert Group Meeting on Structural Threats to Social Integration: Indicators for Conflict Prevention, Session 2: Structural threats to social integrity 18th 20th December 2001, New York, organized by the United Nations Department of Economic and Social Affairs, Division for Social Policy and Development, Social Integration Branch, www.un.org/esa/socdev.

Lindner, Evelin Gerda (2001e). *On Globalisation and Quality of Life.* Regensburg: Submitted to the University of Regensburg, Department of Psychology, for Habilitation.

Lindner, Evelin Gerda (2002). *Humiliation, and the Building of Respect and Trust.* Oslo, Norway: University of Oslo, postdoctoral research proposal.

Lindner, Evelin Gerda (2003). Humiliation or Dignity: Regional Conflicts in the *Global Village.* In *International Journal of Mental Health, Psychosocial Work and Counselling in Areas of Armed Conflict,* 1 (1, January), pp. 48-63, www.transnational.org/forum/meet/2002/Lindner_RegionalConflicts.html.

Lindner, Evelin Gerda (2005). Human Rights, Humiliation, and Globalization. In Janus, Ludwig, Galler, Florian, and Kurth, Winfried (Eds.), *Symbolik, Gesellschaftliche Irrationalität und Psychohistorie, Jahrbuch für psychohistorische Forschung, Vol. 5, 2004,* pp. 143-172. Heidelberg, Germany: Mattes Verlag.

Lindner, Evelin Gerda (2006a). *A New Culture of Peace: Can We Hope That Global Society Will Enter into a Harmonious Information Age?* Human Dignity and Humiliation Studies, www.humiliationstudies.org/whoweare/evelin02.php.

Lindner, Evelin Gerda (2006b). Emotion and Conflict: Why It Is Important to Understand How Emotions Affect Conflict and How Conflict Affects Emotions. *The Handbook of Conflict Resolution: Theory and Practice,* pp. 268-293. Jossey-Bass.

Lindner, Evelin Gerda (2006c). *Is It Possible to "Change the World"? Some Guidelines to How We Can Build a More Decent and Dignified World Effectively: The Case of Dignifying Abusers*. Human Dignity and Humiliation Studies. www.humiliationstudies.org#evelin02.php.

Lindner, Evelin Gerda (2006d). *Making Enemies: Humiliation and International Conflict*. Westport, CT: Praeger Security International, Greenwood.

Lindner, Evelin Gerda (2007a). Avoiding Humiliation - From Intercultural Communication to Global Interhuman Communication. In *Journal of Intercultural Communication, SIETAR Japan,* 10, pp. 21-38.

Lindner, Evelin Gerda (2007b). Dynamics of Humiliation in a Globalizing World. In *International Journal on World Peace,* XXXIV (3, September), pp. 15-52.

Lindner, Evelin Gerda (2007c). In Times of Globalization and Human Rights: Does Humiliation Become the Most Disruptive Force? In *Journal of Human Dignity and Humiliation Studies,* 1 (1, March) www.humilliationstudies.upeace.org/.

Lindner, Evelin Gerda (2008a). *The Need for a New World*. New York: Paper presented at the 5th Workshop on Humiliation and Violent Conflict, Columbia University, December 11-12, 2008, www.humiliationstudies.org/whoweare/evelin02.php.

Lindner, Evelin Gerda (2008b). *What the World's Cultures Can Contribute to Creating a Sustainable Future for Humankind*. Oslo, Norway: Paper presented at the 11th Annual Conference of Human Dignity and Humiliation Studies, Oslo, Bergen, Trondheim, 23th June - 1st July 2008, www.humiliationstudies.org/whoweare/evelin02.php.

Lindner, Evelin Gerda (2008c). Why There Can Be No Conflict Resolution As Long As People Are Being Humiliated. In *International Review of Education,* Special Issue on Education for Reconciliation and Conflict Resolution, Volume 55 (May 2-3, 2009), pp. 157-184, published OnlineFirst on December 27, 2008, at www.springerlink.com/content/bg5g32x832152953/?p=61dc6cf755b14 43c83e89d49221b3e7a&pi=1, including the short version of Finn Tschudi's response and Evelin Lindner's rejoinder; long version at humiliationstudies.org/documents/evelin/ReconciliationforBirgitFinnEv elinlonginterview.pdf.

Lindner, Evelin Gerda (2009a). *Emotion and Conflict: How Human Rights Can Dignify Emotion and Help Us Wage Good Conflict.* Westport, CT: Praeger Security International, Greenwood.

Lindner, Evelin Gerda (2009b). Genocide, Humiliation, and Inferiority: An Interdisciplinary Perspective. In Robins, Nicholas A. and Jones, Adam (Eds.), *Genocides by the Oppressed: Subaltern Genocide in Theory and Practice*, pp. 138-158. Bloomington: Indiana University Press.

Lindner, Evelin Gerda (2009c). Traumatized by Humiliation in Times of Globalization: Transforming Humiliation into Constructive Meaning? In Kalayjian, Ani, Eugene, Dominique, and Reyes, Gilbert (Eds.), *Mass Trauma and Emotional Healing Around the World: Rituals and Practices for Resilience, 2 Vols,* Westport, CT: Greenwood/Praeger Security International.

Lindner, Evelin Gerda (2010a). Disasters As a Chance to Implement Novel Solutions That Highlight Attention to Human Dignity. In Awotona, Adenrele (Ed.), *Rebuilding Sustainable Communities for Children and Their Families After Disasters: A Global Survey*, pp. 335-358. Newcastle upon Tyne, UK: Cambridge Scholars Publishing, proceedings of the International Conference on Rebuilding Sustainable Communities for Children and Their Families after Disasters, convened by Adenrele Awotona at the College of Public and Community Service University of Massachusetts at Boston, November 16-19, 2008, www.rebuilding.umb.edu/rsccfd.

Lindner, Evelin Gerda (2010b). *Gender, Humiliation, and Global Security: Dignifying Relationships From Love, Sex, and Parenthood to World Affairs*. Santa Barbara, CA: Praeger Security International, ABC-CLIO.

Lindner, Evelin Gerda (2012). Fostering Global Citizenship. In Deutsch, Morton and Coleman, Peter T. (Eds.), *The Psychological Components of Sustainable Peace*, New York: Springer.

Lindner, Evelin Gerda, Hartling, Linda M., and Spalthoff, Ulrich (2011). Human Dignity and Humiliation Studies: A Global Network Advancing Dignity Through Dialogue. In *Policy Futures in Education*, 9 (1, Special Issue: The Council of Europe's *White Paper on Intercultural Dialogue*), pp. 66-73, www.wwwords.co.uk/PFIE.

Lippmann, Walter (1922). *Public Opinion*. New York: Macmillan.

Locke, John (1689). *Two Treatises of Government*. London: Awnsham Churchill.

Lovelock, James (2009). *The Vanishing Face of Gaia: A Final Warning*. London: Allen Lane.

Lugard, Frederick John Dealtry (1965). *The Dual Mandate in British Tropical Africa*. London: Frank Cass.

Lutz, Catherine A. (2009). *The Bases of Empire: The Global Struggle Against U.S. Military Posts*. Washington Square, NY: New York University Press.

Mack, Andrew and Nielsen, Zoe (2010). *Human Security Report 2009/2010: The* Causes *of Peace and the Shrinking Costs of War*. Vancouver: Human Security Report Project, Simon Fraser University, http://hsrgroup.org/human-security-reports/20092010/ overview.aspx.

Madrick, Jeffrey (2009). *The Case for Big Government*. Princeton, NJ: Princeton University Press.

Madrick, Jeffrey (2011). *Age of Greed: The Triumph of Finance and the Decline of America, 1970 to the Present*. New York: Knopf.

Mandela, Nelson Rolihlahla (1996). *Long Walk to Freedom: The Autobiography of Nelson Mandela.* London: Abacus.

Mandelbrot, Benoit B. and Hudson, Richard L. (2004). *The (Mis)Behavior of Markets: A Fractal View of Risk, Ruin, and Reward.* New York: Basic Books.

Mander, Jerry (Ed.)(2007). *Manifesto on Global Economic Transitions - Powering-Down for the Future. Toward a Global Movement for Systemic Change: Economies of Ecological Sustainability, Equity, Sufficiency and Peace - "Less and Local".* San Francisco, CA: International Forum on Globalization, the Institute for Policy Studies, and the Global Project on Economic Transitions, www.ifg.org/pdf/manifesto.pdf.

Mankiw, N. Gregory (2004). *Essentials of Economics.* Mason, OH: Thomson.

Mann, Barbara Alice (2000). *Iroquoian Women, the Gantowisas.* New York: Peter Lang.

Marcuse, Herbert (1968). Liberation From the Affluent Society. In Cooper, David (Ed.), *The Dialectics of Liberation,* pp. 175-192. Harmondsworth, UK, Baltimore, MD: Penguin, given as a lecture in London in 1967.

Maren, Michael (1997). *The Road to Hell: The Ravaging Effects of Foreign Aid and International Charity.* New York: Free Press.

Margalit, Avishai (1996). *The Decent Society.* Cambridge, MA: Harvard University Press.

Martin, Glen T. (2010a). *A Constitution for the Federation of Earth - With Historical Introduction, Commentary, and Conclusion.* Sun City, AZ: Institute for Economic Democracy Press.

Martin, Glen T. (2010b). *Triumph of Civilization: Democracy, Non-violence and the Piloting of Spaceship Earth.* Sun City, AZ: Institute for Economic Democracy Press.

Martin, Judith N., Nakayama, Thomas K., and Flores, Lisa A. (2002). A Dialectical Approach to Intercultural Communication. In Martin, Judith N., Nakayama, Thomas K., and Flores, Lisa A. (Eds.), *Readings in Intercultural Communication: Experiences and Contexts*, pp. 3-13. 2nd edition. Boston, MA: McGraw-Hill.

Maruna, Shadd and Toch, Hans (2001). *Making Good: How Ex-Convicts Reform and Rebuild Their Lives.* Washington, DC: American Psychological Association.

Masaaki, Honda (1998). The Road to a Theology of *Soku.* In *Nanzan Bulletin,* 22, pp. 59-74, paper written for the 10th Nanzan Symposium, "What does Christianity have to Learn from Buddhism? The Dialogue Among Religions, Nanzan Institute for Religion and Culture, Nagoya, Japan, www.nanzan-u.ac.jp/SHUBUNKEN/publications/Bulletin_and_Shoho/pdf/22-Honda.pdf.

Maté, Gabor (2008). *In the Realm of Hungry Ghosts: Close Encounter With Addiction.* Berkeley, CA: North Atlantic Books.

Mauboussin, Michael J. (2006). *More Than You Know: Finding Financial Wisdom in Unconventional Places.* New York: Columbia University Press.

Mauboussin, Michael J. (2009). *Think Twice: Harnessing the Power of Counterintuition.* Boston: Harvard Business Press.

Mauss, Marcel (1924). Essai sur le don. Forme et raison de l'echange dans les sociétés archaïques. In *L'Année Sociologique,* seconde série, 1923-1924 (tome I), pp. 1-106, édition électronique réalisée par Jean-Marie Tremblay le 17 février 2002, classiques.uqac.ca/classiques/mauss_marcel/socio_et_anthropo/2_essai_sur_le_don/essai_sur_le_don.pdf.

Max-Neef, Manfred A. (1992). *From the Outside Looking in: Experiences in 'Barefoot Economics'.* 2nd edition. London: Zed Books.

Max-Neef, Manfred A., Elizalde, Antonio, and Hopenhayn, Martin (1991). *Human Scale Development: Conception, Application and Further Reflections.* New York: Apex Press.

Max-Neef, Manfred A. and Goodman, Amy (2010). *Chilean Economist Manfred Max-Neef on Barefoot Economics, Poverty and Why The U.S. Is Becoming an "Underdeveloping Nation".* November 26 edition. New York: Democracy Now: The War and Peace Report, www.democracynow.org/2010/11/26/chilean_economist_manfred_max _neef_on.

Maynard, Elliott and Fresco, Jacque (2003). *Transforming the Global Biosphere: Twelve Futuristic Strategies.* Sedona, AZ: Arcos Cielos Research Center.

Mayor, Federico Zaragoza (2010). *From Subjects to Citizens: The Great Transition.* Madrid: Fundación Cultura de Paz.

McDonough, William and Braungart, Michael (2002). *Cradle to Cradle: Remaking the Way We Make Things.* New York: North Point Press.

McKibben, Bill (2007). *Deep Economy: The Wealth of Communities and the Durable Future.* New York: Times Books.

McLuhan, Herbert Marshall (1962). *The Gutenberg Galaxy: The Making of Typographic Man.* Toronto: University of Toronto Press.

McMaster, Gerald and Trafzer, Clifford E. (2004). *Native Universe: Voices of Indian America.* Washington, DC: National Museum of the American Indian, Smithsonian Institution in association with National Geographic.

Meade, James E. (1965). *Principles of Political Economy.* London: Allen and Unwin.

Meharg, Sarah Jane (2006). Identicide: Precursor to Genocide. *Working Paper 05*, Ottawa, Canada: Centre for Security and Defence Studies, Norman Paterson School of International Affairs, Carleton University, www3.carleton.ca/csds/docs/working_papers/MehargWP05.pdf.

Meikle, Amber and Rubin, Vanessa (2008). *Living on the Edge of Emergency: Paying the Price of Inaction.* London: CARE International UK.

Mesquita, Batja (2001). Culture and Emotion: Different Approaches to the Question. In Mayne, Tracy J. and Bonanno, George A. (Eds.), *Emotions: Current Issues and Future Directions*, pp. 214-250. New York: Guilford Press.

Mezirow, Jack (1991). *Transformative Dimensions of Adult Learning.* San Francisco, CA: Jossey-Bass.

Miegel, Meinhard and Börsch-Supan, Axel (Eds.)(2001). *Pension Reform in Six Countries: What Can We Learn From Each Other?* Berlin: Springer.

Mies, Maria (2006). *Patriarchy and Accumulation on a World Scale : Women in the International Division of Labour.* London: Zed Books.

Mies, Maria and Bennholdt-Thomsen, Veronika (1999). *The Subsistence Perspective: Beyond the Globalized Economy.* London: Zed Book.

Milgram, Stanley (1974). *Obedience to Authority.* New York: Harper and Row.

Mill, John Stuart (1859). *On Liberty.* London: Parker.

Mill, John Stuart (1873). *Autobiography.* London: Longmans.

Miller, Jean Baker (1976). *Toward a New Psychology of Women.* Boston, MA: Beacon Press.

Miller, Jean Baker (1986a). *Toward a New Psychology of Women.* 2nd edition. Boston, MA: Beacon Press.

Miller, Jean Baker (1986b). What Do We Mean by Relationships? *Work in Progress, No. 22*, Wellesley, MA: Stone Center Working Paper Series.

Miller, Jean Baker (2006). Forced Choices, False Choices. In *Research and Action Report*, 27 (2, Spring/Summer), pp. 16-17.

Miller, Seymour M. (2011). *The Fourth Way: Policies, Politics and Persuasion.* forthcoming.

Miller, Seymour M. and Roby, Pamela A. (1970). *The Future of Inequality.* New York: Basic Books.

Miller, Seymour M. and Savoie, Anthony J. (2002). *Respect and Rights: Class, Race, and Gender Today.* Lanham, MD: Rowman and Littlefield.

Miller, William Ian (1993). *Humiliation and Other Essays on Honor, Social Discomfort, and Violence.* Ithaca, NY: Cornell University Press.

Mills, Pauls S. and Presley, John R. (1999). *Islamic Finance: Theory and Practice.* Basingstoke: Macmillan.

Milner, Chris and Read, Robert (2002). *Trade Liberalization, Competition, and the WTO.* Cheltenham: Edward Elgar.

Moene, Karl Ove and Barth, Erling (2009). The Equality Multiplier. *NBER Working Paper No. 15076,* Cambridge, MA: The National Bureau of Economic Research (NBER), www.nber.org/papers/w15076.

Mofid, Kamran (2002). *Globalisation for the Common Good.* London: Shepheard-Walwyn.

Mofid, Kamran (2010). *Globalisation and Education for the Common Good: A Path to Sustainability, Well-Being and Happiness.* Halifax, Nova Scotia: Public lecture presented at the School of Business Administration at Dalhousie University, Wednesday, 3 November 2010, https://blogs.dal.ca/management/files/2010/11/mofid-lecture-2010.pdf.

Mofid, Kamran (2011a). *How It Began: My Story and Journey.* United Kingdom: Globalisation for the Common Good Initiative, www.gcgi.info/index.php?option=com_content&view=article&id=53&I temid=56.

Mofid, Kamran (2011b). *Student Manifesto for New Economics.* United Kingdom: Globalisation for the Common Good Initiative, www.gcgi.info/index.php?option=com_content&view=article&id=112:s tudent-manifesto-for-new-economics&catid=1:latest-news&Itemid=50.

Morgenson, Gretchen (Ed.)(2009). *The Capitalist's Bible: The Essential Guide to Free Markets - and Why They Matter to You.* New York: HarperCollins.

Mundell, Robert A., Zak, Paul J., and Schaeffer, Derek M. (Eds.) (2005). *International Monetary Policy After the Euro.* Cheltenham, UK: Edward Elgar, Conference Proceedings of the Bologna-Claremont International Monetary Conference.

Münkler, Herfried (2007). *Empires: The Logic of World Domination From Ancient Rome to the United States.* Cambridge: Polity.

Musoni, Yves M. (2003). *La problématique de la cohabitation conflictuelle entre les Banyarwanda et leurs voisins au Congo (RDC). Le cas du Nord-Kivu.* Butare, Rwanda: National University of Rwanda.

Naess, Arne (1978). Through Spinoza to Mahayana Buddhism or Through Mahayana Buddhism to Spinoza? In Wetlesen, Jon (Ed.), *Spinoza's Philosophy of Man: Proceedings of the Scandinavian Spinoza Symposium 1977,* Oslo, Norway: University of Oslo Press.

Nagata, Adair Linn (2006). Transformative Learning in Intercultural Education. In *Rikkyo Intercultural Communication Review,* 4, pp. 39-60.

Nagata, Adair Linn (2007). Bodymindfulness for Skillful Communication. In *Rikkyo Intercultural Communication Review,* 5, pp. 61-76.

Nakayama, Nobuji (1973). *Mujunteki Sosoku No Roni [The Logic of Soku].* Kyoto, Japan: Hyakka En.

Napoleoni, Loretta (2008). *Rogue Economics: Capitalism's New Reality.* New York: Seven Stories Press.

Nijstad, Bernard A. and Levine, John M. (2007). Group Creativity and Stages of Creative Problem Solving. In Hewstone, Miles, Schut, Henk A. W., de Wit, John B. F., Van den Bos, Kees, and Stroebe, Margaret S. (Eds.), *The Scope of Social Psychology: Theory and Applications,* pp. 159-172. Hove, UK: Psychology Press.

Nisbett, Richard E. and Cohen, Dov (1996). *Culture of Honor: The Psychology of Violence in the South.* Boulder, CO: Westview Press.

Norberg-Hodge, Helena, Gorelick, Steven, and Merrifield, Todd (2002). *Bringing the Food Economy Home: Local Alternatives to Global Agribusiness.* London: Zed Books.

Norgaard, Richard B. (1999). Beyond Growth and Globalisation. In *Economic and Political Weekly,* 34 (36), pp. 2570-2574.

Norgaard, Richard B. (2011). *Economism and the Night Sky.* Great Barrington, MA: New Economics Institute, neweconomicsinstitute.org/e-newsletters/economism-and-night-sky.

Norton, Michael I. and Ariely, Dan (2011). Building a Better America - One Wealth Quintile at a Time. In *Perspectives on Psychological Science,* 6 (1), pp. 9-12, www.people.hbs.edu/mnorton/norton%20ariely%20in%20press.pdf.

Nussbaum, Martha C. (1997). *Cultivating Humanity: A Classical Defense of Reform in Liberal Education.* Cambridge, MA: Harvard University Press.

Nussbaum, Martha C. (2011). *Creating Capabilities: The Human Development Approach.* Cambridge, MA: Belknap Press of Harvard University Press.

Nussbaum, Martha C. and Sen, Amartya Kumar (1993). *The Quality of Life.* Oxford: Clarendon Press of Oxfort University Press.

Nyborg, Karine (2007). Information and the Burden of Moral Responsibility. In Østreng, Willy (Ed.), *Consilience. Interdisciplinary Communications 2005/2006,* pp. 27-30. Oslo: Centre for Advanced Study, www.cas.uio.no/Publications/Seminar/Consilience.pdf.

O'Halloran, Patrick J. (1995). *Humanitarian Intervention and the Genocide in Rwanda.* London: Research Institute for the Study of Conflict and Terrorism.

O'Neill, Dan, Dietz, Rob, and Jones, Nigel (Eds.)(2010). *Enough Is Enough: Ideas for a Sustainable Economy in a World of Finite Resources: The Report of the Steady State Economy Conference*. Leeds, UK: Center for the Advancement of the Steady State Economy and Economic Justice for All.

O'Neill, Maggie (2009). Making Connections: Ethno-Mimesis, Migration and Diaspora. In *Psychoanalysis, Culture and Society*, 14 (3), pp. 289-302.

O'Neill, Maggie (2010). *Asylum, Migration and Community*. Bristol, UK: Policy Press.

Olivera, Oscar (2004). *Cochabamba: Water War in Bolivia*. Cambridge, MA: South End Press.

Olsen, Johan P. (2010). *Governing Through Institution Building: Institutional Theory and Recent European Experiments in Democratic Organization*. Oxford: Oxford University Press.

Olsen, Jørn Bue (2006). *Om doble normer i næringslivet: Etikken i tidsklemma*. Asker, Norway, Gothenburg, Sweden: University of Gothenburg, doctoral dissertation.

Opotow, Susan, Gerson, Janet, and Woodside, Sarah (2005). From Moral Exclusion to Moral Inclusion: Theory for Teaching Peace. In *Theory into Practice*, 44 (4), pp. 303-338.

Orton, Michael (2011). Flourishing Lives: The Capabilities Approach As a Framework for New Thinking About Employment, Work and Welfare in the 21st Century. In *Work, Employment and Society*, 25 (2), pp. 352-360.

Ostrom, Elinor, Poteete, Amy R., and Janssen, Marco A. (2010). *Working Together: Collective Action, the Commons, and Multiple Methods in Practice*. Princeton, NJ: Princeton University Press.

Palmer, Parker J. (2011). *Healing the Heart of Democracy: The Courage to Create a Politics Worthy of the Human Spirit*. San Francisco, CA: Jossey-Bass.

Paris, Joel (2008). *Prescriptions for the Mind: A Critical View of Contemporary Psychiatry*. Oxford: Oxford University Press.

Parks, Tim (2005). *Medici Money: Banking, Metaphysics, and Art in Fifteenth-Century Florence*. London: Profile Books.

Pascarella, Ernest T., Wolniak, Gregory C., Seifert, Tricia A., Cruce, Ty M., and Blaich, Charles F. (2005). Liberal Arts Colleges and Liberal Arts Education: New Evidence on Impacts. *Association for the Study of Higher Education (ASHE) Report*, Volume 31, Number 3. San Fransisco, CA: Jossey-Bass.

Patel, Raj (2010). *The Value of Nothing: How to Reshape Market Society and Redefine Democracy*. New York: Picador.

Patomäki, Heikki (2002). *After International Relations: Critical Realism and the (Re)Construction of World Politics*. London: Routledge.

Patomäki, Heikki (2008). *The Political Economy of Global Security: War, Future Crises and Changes in Global Governance*. London, New York: Routledge.

Pauli, Gunter A. (1991). *Double-Digit Growth: How to Achieve It With Services*. Berlaar: Pauli Publishing.

Payutto, Prayudh A. (1994). *Buddhist Economics: A Middle Way for the Market Place*. Bankok, Thailand: Buddhadmamma Foundation, www.buddhanet.net/cmdsg/econ.htm.

Perkins, John (2004). *Confessions of an Economic Hit Man*. San Francisco, CA: Berrett-Koehler.

Peterson, V. Spike (2003). *A Critical Rewriting of Global Political Economy: Integrating Reproductive, Productive and Virtual Economies*. London: Routledge.

Pettigrew, Thomas F. and Tropp, Linda R. (2006). A Meta-Analytic Test of Intergroup Contact Theory. In *Journal of Personality and Social Psychology*, 90 (5), pp. 751-783.

Pettit, Philip (1997). *Republicanism: A Theory of Freedom and Government.* Oxford: Clarendon Press.

Pettit, Philip (2001). *A Theory of Freedom: From the Psychology to the Politics of Agency.* Cambridge, UK: Polity Press.

Pink, Daniel H. (2009). *Drive: The Surprising Truth About What Motivates Us.* New York: Riverhead Books.

Pinker, Steven (2011). *The Better Angels of Our Nature: Why Violence Has Declined.* New York: Viking Adult.

Polak, Paul (2008). *Out of Poverty: What Works When Traditional Approaches Fail.* San Francisco, CA: Berrett-Koehler.

Polanyi, Karl (1944). *The Great Transformation.* New York: Farrar and Rinehart.

Polanyi, Karl (1977). *The Livelihood of Man (Studies in Social Discontinuity).* New York: Academic Press.

Pollard, Sidney and Tedlow, Richard S. (2001). *Economic History.* London: Routledge.

Polman, Linda (2010). *The Crisis Caravan: What's Wrong With Humanitarian Aid?* New York: Metropolitan Books.

Pope, Kenneth S. (2007). Ethics and Critical Thinking. In Pope, Kenneth S. and Vasquez, Melba J. T. (Eds.), *Ethics in Psychotherapy and Counseling: A Practical Guide*, pp. 16-36. 3rd edition. San Francisco, CA: Jossey-Bass. See an adaptation of this chapter at kspope.com/apologies.php.

Porter, Michael F. (2010). *As If the Future Mattered: Translating Social and Economic Theory into Human Behavior.* Medford, MA: Global Development And Environment Institute at Tufts University (GDAE).

Putnam, Robert David (1995). Bowling Alone: America's Declining Social Capital. In *Journal of Democracy,* 6 (1), pp. 65-78.

Quiggin, John (2010a). *Zombie Economics: How Dead Ideas Still Walk Among Us*. Princeton, NJ: Princeton University Press.

Quiggin, John (2010b). *Zombie Economics: How Dead Ideas Still Walk Among Us*. Princeton, NJ: Princeton University Press.

Quilligan, James Bernard (2002). *The Brandt Equation: 21st Century Blueprint for the New Global Economy*. Philadelphia, PA, PA: Brandt 21 Forum, www.brandt21forum.info/BrandtEquation-19Sept04.pdf.

Qureshi, Anwar Iqbal (1967). *Islam and the Theory of Interest: With a New Chapter on Interest Free Banking*. London: Dstributed by Luzac.

Rabin, Matthew (1996). *Psychology and Economics*. Berkeley: Department of Economics, University of California, draft prepared for Journal of Economic Literature, emlab.berkeley.edu/users/rabin/peboth7.pdf.

Ramsey, V. Jean and Latting, Jean Katambu (2005). A Typology of Intergroup Competencies. In *Journal of Applied Behavioral Science*, 41 (3), pp. 265-284, www.creighton.edu/fileadmin/user/StudentServices/StudentActivities/DAT/images_-_DAT/intergroup_competencies. pdf.

Raskin, Paul D. (2008). World Lines: A Framework for Exploring Global Pathways. In *Ecological Economics*, 65 (3), pp. 461-470.

Raskin, Paul D., Banuri, Tariq, Gallopín, Gilbert, Gutman, Pablo, Hammond, Al, Kates, Robert, and Swart, Rob (2002). *Great Transition: The Promise and Lure of the Times Ahead*. Boston: Stockholm Environment Institute (SEI), Tellus Institute, a report of the Global Scenario Group, www.gtinitiative.org/documents/Great_Transitions.pdf.

Ray, Paul H. and Anderson, Sherry Ruth (2000). *The Cultural Creatives: How 50 Million People Are Changing the World*. New York: Three Rivers Press.

Raymond, Eric S. (1999). *The Cathedral and the Bazaar: Musings on Linux and Open Source by an Accidental Revolutionary.* Sebastopol, CA: O'Reilly.

Readings, Bill (1996). *The University in Ruins.* Cambridge, MA: Harvard University Press.

Reardon, Betty A. (1988). *Comprehensive Peace Education: Educating for Global Responsibility.* New York: Teachers College Press.

Reardon, Betty A. (1993). *Women and Peace: Feminist Visions of Global Security.* Albany: State university of New York press.

Reardon, Betty A. (1995). *Educating for Human Dignity: Learning About Rights and Responsibilities.* Philadelphia: University of Pennsylvania Press.

Reardon, Betty A. (2001). *Education for a Culture of Peace in a Gender Perspective.* Paris: UNESCO.

Reardon, Betty A. and Hans, Asha (Eds.)(2010). *The Gender Imperative: Human Security vs State Security.* New Delhi: Routledge India.

Reich, Robert B. (2010). *Aftershock: The Next Economy and America's Future.* New York: Knopf.

Reinert, Erik S. (2007). *How Rich Countries Got Rich... And Why Poor Countries Stay Poor.* New York: Carroll and Graf.

Reinhart, Carmen M. and Rogoff, Kenneth (2009). *This Time Is Different: Eight Centuries of Financial Folly.* Princeton, NJ: Princeton University Press.

Richards, Howard (2008). *Paradigm Meltdown and Opportunities for Peacebuilding.* groups.yahoo.com/group/globalpolecon/message/457.

Richards, Howard (2010a). *Constructing a New Global Dispensation Beyond Economics.* Pretoria, South Africa: Keynote talk at an international conference on "Democracy, Human Rights and Social Justice in a New Global Dispensation -Challenges and Transformations," University of South Africa, 1-3 February 2010, howardrichards.org/pacem/index.php?option=com_content&task=view&id=137&Itemid=163.

Richards, Howard (2010b). *Human Development and the Transformation of the Academy.* Pretoria: Talk given at the University of South Africa, November 20, 2010.

Richards, Howard (2010c). *Humanizing Methodologies in Transformation.* Pretoria, South Africa: Lecture given at the University of South Africa, 20 July 2010.

Richards, Howard (2011a). *An Ethical Alternative to the Philosophy of Friedrich von Hayek.* Santiago de Chile: A presentation to the "Rethinking Economics" Group, 20 January 2011.

Richards, Howard (2011b). Human Development and the Transformation of the Academy. In *Journal of Developing Societies,* 27 (2, June), pp. 201-206.

Richards, Howard and Swanger, Joanna (2006). *The Dilemmas of Social Democracies.* Lanham, MD: Rowman and Littlefield.

Riegel, Edwin Clarence (1976). *The New Approach to Freedom, Together With Essays on the Separation of Money and State.* New York and San Pedro, CA: Valun Institute for Monetary Research, New York 1949; expanded new edition published by the Heather Foundation, San Pedro, CA, 1976, www.newapproachtofreedom.info/naf/index.html.

Rifkin, Jeremy (1995). *The End of Work: The Decline of the Global Labor Force and the Dawn of the Post-Market Era.* New York: Putnam.

Rifkin, Jeremy (2009). *The Empathic Civilization: The Race to Global Consciousness in a World in Crisis.* New York: J.P. Tarcher, Penguin.

Roach, Mary (2008). *Bonk: The Curious Coupling of Science and Sex.* New York: Norton.

Robertson, James and Bunzl, John (2008). *Monetary Reform - Making It Happen!* London: International Simultaneous Policy Organisation, www.simpol.org/en/books/monetaryreform.pdf.

Robinson, Fiona (1999). *Globalizing Care: Ethics, Feminist Theory, and International Relations.* Boulder, CO: Westview Press.

Rogers, Deborah S., Deshpande, Omkar, and Feldman, Marcus W. (2011). The Spread of Inequality. In *PLoS ONE,* 6 (9), e24683, www.plosone.org/article/info%3Adoi%2F10.1371%2Fjournal.pone.00 24683.

Roodman, David and Morduch, Jonathan (2009). The Impact of Microcredit on the Poor in Bangladesh: Revisiting the Evidence. *Working Paper 174,* Washington, DC: Center for Global Development.

Rorty, Richard (1979). *Philosophy and the Mirror of Nature.* Princeton, NJ: Princeton University Press.

Rosen, Richard J. (2009). How Should the Economy Be Regulated? The US System of Public Utility Commissions Provides a Model for Democratically Accountable Large-Scale Investment Making. In *Open Democracy,* September 8, www.opendemocracy.net/article/email/how-should-the-economy-be-regulated.

Ross, Lee D. and Jost, John T. (1999). Fairness Norms and the Potential for Mutual Agreements Involving Majority and Minority Groups. In Neale, Margaret A, Mannix, Elizabeth A, and Wageman, Ruth (Eds.), *Research on Managing Groups and Teams (Vol. 2): Groups in Their Context,* pp. 93-114. Greenwich, CT: JAI Press.

Ross, Lee D. and Ward, Andrew (1996). Naive Realism in Everyday Life: Implications for Social Conflict and Misunderstanding. In Brown, Terrance, Reed, Edward S., and Turiel, Elliot (Eds.), *Values and Knowledge,* pp. 103-135. Hillsdale, NJ: Erlbaum.

Rothkopf, David J. (2008). Superclass: The Global Power Elite and the World They Are Making. New York: Farrar, Straus and Giroux.

Rousseau, Jean-Jacques (1762). Du contrat social ou principes du droit politique. Amsterdam, The Netherlands: Marc Michel Rey, Archives de la Société Jean-Jacques Rousseau, un2sg4.unige.ch/athena/rousseau/jjr_cont.html.

Ruggie, John Gerard (2008). Embedding Global Markets: An Enduring Challenge. Aldershot: Ashgate.

Rushkoff, Douglas (2009). Life Inc.: How the World Became a Corporation and How to Take It Back. New York: Random House.

Russell, James A. (1991). Cultural Variations in Emotions: A Review. In Psychological Bulletin, 112 (2), pp. 179-204.

Sachs, Jeffrey D. (2005). The End of Poverty: Economic Possibilities for Our Time. New York: Penguin Group.

Sachs, Jeffrey D. (2011). The Price of Civilization: Reawakening American Virtue and Prosperity. New York: Random House.

Sagafi-nejad, Tagi and Dunning, John H. (2008). The UN and Transnational Corporations: From Code of Conduct to Global Compact. Bloomington: Indiana University Press.

Salecl, Renata (2004). On Anxiety. London: Routledge.

Samuelson, Paul Anthony (1947). Foundations of Economic Analysis. Cambridge, MA: Harvard University Press.

Samuelson, Robert J. (2009). The Great Inflation and Its Aftermath: The Past and Future of American Affluence. New York: Random House.

Sanders, T. Irene (1998). Strategic Thinking and the New Science: Planning in the Midst of Chaos, Complexity, and Change. New York: Free Press.

Sarfaty, Galit A. (1009). Why Culture Matters in International Institutions: The Marginality of Human Rights at the World Bank. In *American Journal of International Law,* 103 (4), pp. 647-683, knowledge.wharton.upenn.edu/papers/download/090210_Galit_Sarfaty _The_Marginality_of_Human_Rights_at_the_World_Bank.pdf.

Schäfer, Ulrich (2011). *Der Angriff. Wie der islamistische Terror unseren Wohlstand sprengt.* Frankfurt am Main, Germany: Campus.

Scharmer, Claus Otto (2007). *Theory U: Leading From the Future As It Emerges: The Social Technology of Presencing.* Cambridge, MA: Society for Organizational Learning.

Scharmer, Claus Otto (2009). *Theory U: Leading From the Future As It Emerges: The Social Technology of Presencing.* San Francisco, CA: Berret-Koehler Publishers.

Scheff, Thomas J. (2006). Aggression, Hypermasculine Emotions and Relations: The Silence/Violence Pattern. In *Irish Journal of Sociology,* 15 (1), pp. 24-37, www.soc.ucsb.edu/faculty/scheff/main.php?id=42.html.

Schei, Bitten and Rønnevig, Elisabeth (2009). *Vilje til endring: Sosialt entreprenørskap på norsk.* Notodden: Mother Courage.

Scheler, Max (1923). *Wesen und Formen der Sympathie.* Bonn, Germany: Friedrich Cohen, zweite, erweiterte Ausgabe von *Zur Phänomenologie und Theorie der Sympathiegefühle und von Liebe und Haß,* 1913.

Scheuch, Michael (2009). *Bankberatung trotz Krise mangelhaft: Stichprobe unter 25 Bankberatern von Verbraucherschützern und WISO.* Mainz, Germany: Zweites Deutsches Fernsehen (ZDF), WISO, 19.06.2009, wiso.zdf.de/ZDFde/inhalt/17/0,1872,7599377,00.html.

Schiff, Peter D. and Downes, John (2009). *Crash Proof 2.0: How to Profit From the Economic Collapse.* Hoboken, NJ: John Wiley.

Schmidt, Jeff (2000). *Disciplined Minds: A Critical Look at Salaried Professionals and the Soul-Battering System That Shapes Their Lives.* Lanham, MD: Rowman and Littlefield.

Schor, Juliet B. (1992). *The Overworked American: The Unexpected Decline of Leisure.* New York: Basic Books.

Schor, Juliet B. (1998). *The Overspent American: Upscaling, Downshifting, and the New Consumer.* New York: Basic Books.

Schor, Juliet B. (2004). *Born to Buy: The Commercialized Child and the New Consumer Culture.* New York: Scribner.

Schor, Juliet B. (2010). *Plenitude: The New Economics of True Wealth.* New York: Penguin Press.

Schor, Juliet B. and You, Jong Il (Eds.)(1995). *Capital, the State, and Labour: A Global Perspective.* Aldershot: Edward Elgar.

Schrift, Alan D. (1997). *The Logic of the Gift: Toward an Ethic of Generosity.* New York: Routledge.

Schultz, Ellen E. (2011). *Retirement Heist: How Companies Plunder and Profit From the Nest Eggs of American Workers.* New York: Portfolio.

Schumacher, Ernst Friedrich (1966). Buddhist Economics. In Wint, Guy (Ed.), *Asia: A Handbook*, London: Anthony Bont, www.schumachersociety.org/buddhist_economics.html.

Schumacher, Ernst Friedrich (1973). *Small Is Beautiful: A Study of Economics As If People Mattered.* London: Blond and Briggs.

Schumacher, Ernst Friedrich (1999). *Small Is Beautiful: Ecomomics As If People Mattered : 25 Years Later ... With Commentaries.* Point Roberts, WA: Hartley and Marks.

Schuster, Jack H. and Finkelstein, Martin J. (2006). *The American Faculty: The Restructuring of Academic Work and Careers.* Baltimore: Johns Hopkins University Press.

Schweickart, David (2002). *After Capitalism*. Lanham, MD: Rowman and Littlefield.

Searle, John R. (1969). *Speech Acts, an Essay in the Philosophy of Language*. New York: Cambridge University Press.

Sechrest, Larry J. (1993). *Free Banking: Theory, History, and a Laissez-Faire Model*. Westport, CT: Quorum Books.

Selgin, George A. (1988). *The Theory of Free Banking: Money Supply Under Competitive Note Issue*. Lanham, MD: Rowman and Littlefield, files.libertyfund.org/files/2307/Selgin_1544_EBk_v5.1.pdf.

Selgin, George A. (1996). *Bank Deregulation and Monetary Order*. London: Routledge.

Sen, Amartya Kumar (1980). Equality of What? In McMurrin, Sterling M. (Ed.), *Tanner Lectures on Human Values: Volume I*, Cambridge: Cambridge University Press.

Sen, Amartya Kumar (1999). *Development As Freedom*. Oxford: Oxford University Press.

Sen, Amartya Kumar (2006). *Identity and Violence: The Illusion of Destiny*. London: Penguin.

Sen, Amartya Kumar (2009). *The Idea of Justice*. Cambridge, MA: Belknap Press of Harvard University Press.

Sen, Amartya Kumar and Drèze, Jean (1995). *India: Economic Development and Social Opportunity*. Delhi, India: Oxford University Press.

Senge, Peter M. (1990). *The Fifth Discipline: The Art and Practice of the Learning Organization*. New York: Doubleday.

Sennett, Richard (1998). *The Corrosion of Character: The Personal Consequences of Work in the New Capitalism*. New York: Norton.

Serres, Michel (1997). *The Troubadour of Knowledge*. Ann Arbor: University of Michigan Press.

Shapiro, Harold T. (2005). *A Larger Sense of Purpose: Higher Education and Society*. Princeton, NJ: Princeton University Press.

Shaw, Martin (2000). *Theory of the Global State: Globality As Unfinished Revolution*. Cambridge: Cambridge University Press.

Sher, Leo and Vilens, Alexander (2009). *War and Suicide*. New York: Nova Science Publishers.

Shikshantar (2008). Reclaiming the Gift Culture. In *Vimukt Shiksha,* December

Shiller, Robert J. (2000). *Irrational Exuberance*. Princeton, NJ: Princeton University Press.

Shipman, Alan (1999). *The Market Revolution and Its Limits: A Price for Everything*. London: Routledge.

Shiva, Vandana (1997). *The Enclosure and Recovery of the Commons: Biodiversity, Indigenous Knowledge and Intellectual Property Rights*. New Delhi, India: Research Foundation for Science, Technology, and Ecology.

Shiva, Vandana (2006). *Earth Democracy: Justice, Sustainability, and Peace*. London: Zed books.

Sidanius, Jim and Pratto, Felicia (1999). *Social Dominance: An Intergroup Theory of Social Hierarchy and Oppression*. Cambridge: Cambridge University Press.

Silver, Hilary and Miller, Seymour M. (2006). From Poverty to Social Exclusion: Lessons From Europe. In Hartman, Chester (Ed.), *Poverty and Race in America: The Emerging Agendas*, pp. 57-70. Lexington, MA: Lexington Books.

Simms, Andrew, Johnson, Victoria, and Chowla, Peter (2010). *Growth Isn't Possible: Why We Need a New Economic Direction*. Totnes, London: Schumacher College and nef (the new economics foundation), www.neweconomics.org/sites/neweconomics.org/files/Growth_Isnt_Possible.pdf.

Singer, Peter Albert David (1973). *Democracy and Disobedience.* Oxford: Clarendon Press.

Singer, Peter Albert David (1981). *The Expanding Circle: Ethics and Sociobiology.* Oxford: Clarendon Press of Oxford University Press.

Singer, Peter Albert David (2004). *One World: The Ethics of Globalization.* 2nd edition. New Haven, CT: Yale University Press.

Singer, Peter Albert David (2009). *The Life You Can Save: Acting Now to End World Poverty.* London: Picador.

Skjervheim, Hans (2002). Eit grunnproblem i pedagogisk filosofi. In Hellesnes, Jon and Skirbekk, Gunnar (Eds.), *Mennesket,* pp. 103-117. Oslo, Norway: Universitetsforlaget.

Slaughter, Sheila and Rhoades, Gary (2004). *Academic Capitalism and the New Economy: Markets, State, and Higher Education.* Baltimore, NJ: Johns Hopkins University Press.

Smith, Adam (1759). *The Theory of Moral Sentiments.* London, Edinburg, UK: Printed for A. Millar, London; and A. Kincaid and J. Bell, Edinburgh.

Smith, Adam (1776). *An Inquiry into the Nature and Causes of the Wealth of Nations.* London: Strahan/Cadell, www.adamsmith.org/smith/won-index.htm.

Smith, Adam (1968). *The Money Game.* London: Pan Books.

Smith, M. Brewster, Bruner, Jerome S., and White, Robert W. (1956). *Opinions and Personality.* New York: John Wiley.

Smithin, John N. (2000). *What Is Money?* London: Routledge.

Snauwaert, Dale T. (2010). Democracy As Public Deliberation and the Psychology of Epistemological World Views and Moral Reasoning: A Philosophical Reflection. In *Journal of Peace Education and Social Justice,* 4 (1), pp. 120-126, www.infactispax.org/volume4dot1/Snauwaert.pdf.

Snyder, Jack (1985). Perceptions of the Security Dilemma in 1914. In Jervis, Robert, Lebow, Richard Ned, and Stein, Janice Gross (Eds.), *Psychology and Deterrence*, pp. 153-179. Baltimore, MD: Johns Hopkins University Press.

Snyder, Jack and Walters, Barbara (Eds.)(1999). *The Security Dilemma and Intervention in Civil Wars*. New York: Columbia University Press.

Soddy, Frederick (1926). *Wealth, Virtual Wealth and Debt*. London: George Allen and Unwin.

Soros, George (2008). *The New Paradigm for Financial Markets: The Credit Crisis of 2008 and What It Means*. London: PublicAffairs.

Speth, James Gustave (2008). *The Bridge at the Edge of the World: Capitalism, the Environment, and Crossing From Crisis to Sustainability*. New Haven, CT: Yale University Press.

Speth, James Gustave (2010). Towards a New Economy and a New Politics. In *The Solutions Journal*, 1 (5, May), pp. 33-41, www.thesolutionsjournal.com/node/619.

Spratt, Stephen, Simms, Andrew, Neitzert, Eva, and Ryan-Collins, Josh (2009). *The Great Transition: A Tale of How It Turned Out Right*. London: nef (the new economics foundation), www.neweconomics.org/publications/growth-isnt-possible.

Staub, Ervin (1989). *The Roots of Evil: The Origins of Genocide and Other Group Violence*. Cambridge: Cambridge University Press.

Staub, Ervin (2003). *The Psychology of Good and Evil: Why Children, Adults, and Groups Help and Harm Others*. Cambridge: Cambridge University Press.

Steele, David (2007). Global Society and Its Ancient Greek Antecedents. In *The European Legacy*, 12 (1), pp. 1-21, pdfserve.informaworld.com/55441_751315987_762428366.pdf.

Steiner, Claude M. (2003). *Emotional Literacy: Intelligence With a Heart*. Fawnskin, CA: Personhood Press.

Steinsland, Gro (2007). *Myth and Power in the Cultural Transformation of the Nordic Countries From Viking to Medieval Age.* Oslo, Norway: Centre for Advanced Study (CAS) at the Norwegian Academy of Science and Letters, Opening ceremony, September 4, 2007, Lecture by Professor Gro Steinsland, ILN, University of Oslo, Group leader at CAS, 2007/2008, cas.uio.no/research/0708rulership/lecture_040907.pdf.

Stern, Nicholas (2006). *Stern Review of the Economics of Climate Change.* Cambridge: Cambridge University Press.

Stern, Nicholas (2011). *How Should We Think About the Economics of Climate Change?* Lecture for Leontief Prize, 8th March 2011. Medford, MA: ase.tufts.edu/gdae/about_us/leontief/SternLecture.pdf.

Stevenson, Betsey and Wolfers, Justin (2009). *The Paradox of Declining Female Happiness.* Cambridge, MA: The National Bureau of Economic Research, www.nber.org/papers/w14969.

Stiglitz, Joseph E. (2003). *Globalization and Its Discontents.* New York: Norton.

Stiglitz, Joseph E. and Charlton, Andrew (2006). *Fair Trade for All: How Trade Can Promote Development (Initiative for Policy Dialogue).* Oxford, New York: Oxford University Press.

Stiglitz, Joseph E., Edlin, Aaron S., and DeLong, J. Bradford (Eds.)(2008). *The Economists' Voice: Top Economists Take on Today's Problems.* New York: Columbia University Press.

Stiglitz, Joseph E., Sen, Amartya Kumar, and Fitoussi, Jean-Paul (2011). *Mismeasuring Our Lives: Why GDP Doesn't Add Up.* New York: New Press.

Stiglitz, Joseph E. and Serra, Narcís (Eds.)(2008). *The Washington Consensus Reconsidered: Towards a New Global Governance.* Oxford: Oxford University Press.

Stoknes, Per Espen (1996). *Sjelens Landskap: Refleksjoner Over Natur Og Myter.* Oslo, Norway: Cappelen.

Strasburger, Victor C., Jordan, Amy B., and Wilson, Barbara J. (2009). *Children, Adolescents, and the Media*. Los Angeles: Sage.

Sullivan, Paul (2010). Clutch: *Why Some People Excel Under Pressure and Others Don't*. New York: Portfolio.

Sundararajan, Louise (2011). Belief, Emotion, and Health: Toward an Integrative Account: Commentary on John Cromby's "Beyond Belief". In *Journal of Health Psychology*, forthcoming.

Sundararajan, Louise, Kim, Chulin, Reynolds, Martina, and Brewin, Chris R. (2010). Language, Emotion, and Health: A Semiotic Perspective on the Writing Cure. In Hamel, Steven C. (Ed.), *Semiotics: Theory and Applications*, pp. 65-97. New York: Nova Science.

Sundararajan, Louise and Schubert, Lenhart K. (2005). Verbal Expressions of Self and Emotions: A Taxonomy With Implications for Alexithymia and Related Disorders. In Ellis, Ralph D. and Newton, Natika (Eds.), *Consciousness and Emotion: Agency, Conscious Choice, and Selective Perception*, pp. 243-284. Amsterdam, The Netherlands: John Benjamins.

Suskind, Ron (2011). *Confidence Men: Wall Street, Washington, and the Education of a President*. Harper.

Syse, Henrik Preben (2009). *Måtehold i grådighetens tid*. Oslo, Norway: Cappelen Damm.

T., Anne (2009). *Die Gier war Grenzenlos: Eine deutsche Börsenhändlerin packt aus*. Düsseldorf, Germany: Econ Verlag.

Tajfel, Henri and Turner, John C. (1986). The Social Identity Theory of Intergroup Behavior. In Worchel, Stephen and Austin, William G. (Eds.), *Psychology of Intergroup Relations*, pp. 204-227. Chicago: Neston-Hall.

Taylor, Charles (1993). To Follow a Rule... In Calhoun, Craig, LiPuma, Edward, and Postone, Moishe (Eds.), *Bourdieu: Critical Perspectives*, pp. 45-60. Cambridge: Polity Press, published in association with Blackwell, and written in association with the Center for Psychosocial Studies.

Taylor, Frederick Winslow (1911). *The Principles of Scientific Management.* New York: Harper and Brothers.

Tedlow, Richard S. (2010). *Denial: Why Business Leaders Fail to Look Facts in the Face - and What to Do About It.* New York: Portfolio.

Tett, Gillian (2009). *Fool's Gold: How the Bold Dream of a Small Tribe at J.P. Morgan Was Corrupted by Wall Street Greed and Unleashed a Catastrophe.* New York: Free Press.

Thaler, Richard and Sunstein, Cass (2008). *Nudge: Improving Decisions About Health, Wealth and Happiness.* New Haven, CT: Yale University Press.

The Green New Deal Group (2008). *A Green New Deal: Joined-Up Policies to Solve the Triple Crunch of the Credit Crisis, Climate Change and High Oil Prices.* London: The report is published on behalf of the Green New Deal Group by nef (the new economics foundation).

The International Bank for Reconstruction and Development / The World Bank (2011). *World Development Report 2011: Conflict, Security, and Development.* Washington DC: The International Bank for Reconstruction and Development / The World Bank, wdr2011.worldbank.org/sites/default/files/Complete%202011%20WDR%20Conflict%2CSecurity%20and%20Development_0.pdf.

Thomas, Alexandar R. (1998). Ronald Reagan and the Commitment of the Mentally Ill: Capital, Interest Groups, and the Eclipse of Social Policy. In *Electronic Journal of Sociology*, , www.sociology.org/content/vol003.004/thomas.html.

Thomas, Caroline (2001). Global Governance, Development and Human Security: Exploring the Links. In *Third World Quarterly*, 22 (2), pp. 159-175, www.jstor.org/pss/3993404.

Thoreau, Henry David, Glick, Wendell and Zinn, Howard (Eds.) (2004). *The Higher Law: Thoreau on Civil Disobedience and Reform.* Princeton, NJ: Princeton University Press.

Thoreau, Henry David and Sharp, Gene (1963). *Thoreau: On the Duty of Civil Disobedience.* London: Peace News.

Thoren, Theodore R. and Warner, Richard F. (Eds.)(1980). *The Truth in Money Book.* Chagrin Falls, OH: A Truth in Money Publication.

Todd, John and Todd, Nancy Jack (1980). *Tomorrow Is our Permanent Address: The Search for an Ecological Science of Design As Embodied in the Bioshelter.* New York: Harper & Row.

Transnational Institute (2008). *The Global Economic Crisis: An Historic Opportunity for Transformation.* Amsterdam The Netherlands: Transnational Institute, www.tni.org/archives/beijingstatementoncrisis.

Tremblay, Rodrigue (2010). *The Code for Global Ethics: Ten Humanist Principles.* Amherst, NY: Prometheus.

Tschudi, Finn (2008). Dignity Violations: An Alternative View of "Administrative Evil". In *Public Administration,* 96 (4), pp. 895-903.

Twenge, Jean M. (2006). *Generation Me: Why Today's Young Americans Are More Confident, Assertive, Entitled - and More Miserable Than Ever Before.* New York: Free Press.

Twenge, Jean M. and Campbell, W. Keith (2009). *The Narcissism Epidemic: Living in the Age of Entitlement.* New York: Free Press.

Twenge, Jean M., Konrath, Sara H., Foster, Joshua D., Campbell, Keith W., and Buschman, Brad J. (2008). Egos Inflating Over Time: A Cross-Temporal Meta-Analysis of the Narcissistic Personality Inventory. In *Journal of Personality,* 76 (4, August), pp. 875-901, www.psychology.sdsu.edu/new-web/FacultyLabs/twenge/narctimeJP.pdf.

United Nations Department of Economic and Social Affairs (2005). *2005 Report on the World Social Situation.* New York: United Nations, www.un.org/esa/socdev/rwss/media%2005/cd-docs/fullreport05.htm.

United Nations Environment Programme (UNEP)(2009). *International Environmental Governance: Outcome of the Work of the Consultative Group of Ministers or High-Level Representatives.* Nairobi: United Nations Environment Programme (UNEP), "Belgrad Process" on June 27 and 28, 2009 in Belgrade, and on October 28 and 29, 2009, in Rome, by a regionally representative, consultative group of ministers or highlevel representatives, following Governing Council decision 25/4 of February 20, 2009, on international environmental governance, www.unep.org/gc/gcss-xi/working_docs.asp.

Ury, William (1999). Getting to Peace: *Transforming Conflict at Home, at Work, and in the World.* New York: Viking.

Vaitheeswaran, Vijay V. (2003). *Power to the People: How the Coming Energy Revolution Will Transform an Industry, Change Our Lives, and Maybe Even Save the Planet.* New York: Farrar, Straus and Giroux.

Valle, Victor M. (2001). *Spiraling in Human Insecurity: The Historic Evolution of a Country.* New York: Discussion paper presented at the Expert Group Meeting on Structural Threats to Social Integration: Indicators for Conflict Prevention, Session 2: Structural threats to social integrity 18th 20th December 2001, New York, organized by the United Nations Department of Economic and Social Affairs, Division for Social Policy and Development, Social Integration Branch, www.un.org/esa/socdev.

Valone, Thomas F., Cullen, T., and Carter, Susan M. (2004). Tom Valone Reviews a Myriad of Alternative Energy Technologies: Report on Thomas Valone's Lecture at the New Energy Movement Conference, September 25, 2004, Portland, Oregon, USA. In *Pure Energy Systems News,* October, www.pureenergysystems.com/events/conferences/2004/NewEnergyMovement/6900056_ThomasValone/.

Vaughan, Genevieve (1997). *For-Giving: A Feminist Criticism of Exchange.* Austin, TX: Plain View Press.

Vaughan, Genevieve (Ed.)(2007). *Women and the Gift Economy: A Radically Different Worldview Is Possible.* Toronto: Innana, www.gifteconomy.com.

Veblen, Thorstein Bunde (1899). *The Theory of the Leisure Class: An Economic Study in the Evolution of Institutions.* New York: Macmillan.

Verba, Sidney, Schlozman, Kay Lehman, and Brady, Henry E. (1995). *Voice and Equality: Civic Voluntarism in American Politics.* Cambridge, MA: Harvard University Press.

Vetlesen, Arne Johan (Ed.)(2008). *Nytt klima: Miljøkrisen i samfunnskritisk lys.* Oslo, Norway: Gyldendal.

Victor, Peter A. (2008). *Managing Without Growth: Slower by Design, Not Disaster.* Cheltenham: Edward Elgar.

Villa-Vicencio, Charles (2000). *Transcending a Century of Injustice.* Rondebosch, South Africa: Institute for Justice and Reconciliation.

Villa-Vicencio, Charles (2009). *Walk With Us and Listen: Political Reconciliation in Africa.* Washington, DC: Georgetown University Press.

Villa-Vicencio, Charles and Du Toit, Fanie (2006). *Truth and Reconciliation in South Africa: 10 Years on.* Claremont, South Africa: David Philip.

von Weltzien Høivik, Heidetraut (Ed.)(2002). *Moral Leadership in Action: Building and Sustaining Moral Competence in European Organizations.* Cheltenham: Edward Elgar.

von Weltzien Høivik, Heidetraut (2005). *Consultants As Destructive Confidants and the Unethical Games That People Play.* Oslo, Norway: Cappelen.

von Weltzien Høivik, Heidetraut (2007). East Meets West: Tacit Messages About Business Ethics in Stories Told by Chinese Managers. In *Journal of Business Ethics*, 74 (4), pp. 457-469.

von Weltzien Høivik, Heidetraut (2009). Developing Students' Competence for Ethical Reflection While Attending Business School. In *Journal of Business Ethics,* 88 (1), pp. 5-9.

von Weltzien Høivik, Heidetraut and Melé, Domènec (2009). Can an SME Become a Global Corporate Citizen? Evidence From a Case Study. In *Journal of Business Ethics,* 88 (3), pp. 551-563.

Wadhwa, Vivek, Saxenian, AnnaLee, Freeman, Richard B., and Gereffi, Gary (2009). *America's Loss Is the World's Gain: America's New Immigrant Entrepreneurs, Part 4.* Durham, NC: Duke University, ssrn.com/abstract=1348616.

Walker, Gabrielle and King, David A. (2008). *The Hot Topic: What We Can Do About Global Warming.* Orlando, FL: Harcourt.

Wallerstein, Immanuel Maurice (1974). *The Modern World-System (Three Volumes 1974-1989).* New York: Academic Press.

Walsh, Roger (2011). Lifestyle and Mental Health. In *American Psychologist,* 66 (7, October), pp. 579-592.

Waltz, Kenneth (1979). *Theory of International Politics.* Reading, MA: Addison-Wesley.

Walzer, Michael (1970). *Obligations: Essays on Disobedience, War, and Citizenship.* Cambridge, MA: Harvard University Press.

Walzer, Michael (1992). The Civil Society Argument. In Mouffe, Chantal (Ed.), *Dimensions of Radical Democracy: Pluralism, Citizenship, Community,* pp. 89-107. London: Verso.

Waring, Marilyn (1988*). If Women Counted: A New Feminist Economics.* San Francisco, CA: Harper and Row.

Washington, Harriet A. (2007). *Medical Apartheid: The Dark History of Medical Experimentation on Black Americans From Colonial Times to the Present.* New York: Doubleday.

Washington, Harriet A. (2011). *Deadly Monopolies: The Shocking Corporate Takeover of Life Itself - and the Consequences for Your Health and Our Medical Future.* New York: Doubleday.

Weber, Max (1904). Die protestantische Ethik und der Geist des Kapitalismus. In *Archiv für Sozialwissenschaften und Sozialpolitik,* Erstveröffentlichung 1904, 20. Band, Heft 1, Seiten 1-54, sowie 1905, 21. Band, Heft 1, Seiten 1-110

Weber, Thomas (1999). Gandhi, Deep Ecology, Peace Research and Buddhist Economics. In *Journal of Peace Research,* 36 (3), pp. 349-361.

Weiss, Thomas G. (2009). What Happened to the Idea of World Government? In *International Studies Quarterly,* 53 (2), pp. 253-271, www3.interscience.wiley.com/cgi-bin/fulltext/122437391/PDFSTART.

Wendt, Alexander (2004). *Social Theory As Cartesian Science: An Auto-Critique From a Quantum Perspective.* Columbus, OH: www.humiliationstudies.org/documents/WendtAutoCritique.pdf.

Werlhof, Claudia von, Bennholdt-Thomsen, Veronika, and Faraclas, Nicholas (Eds.)(2001). *There Is an Alternative: Subsistence and Worldwide Resistance to Corporate Globalization.* North Melbourne, Victoria: Spinifex Press.

Werner, Götz Wolfgang and Presse, André (Eds.)(2007). *Grundeinkommen und Konsumsteuer. Impulse für „Unternimm die Zukunft."* Karlsruhe, Germany: Universitätsverlag, Tagungsband zum Karlsruher Symposium "Grundeinkommen: bedingungslos," digbib.ubka.uni-karlsruhe.de/volltexte/1000006351.

Westra, Laura (2011). *Globalization, Violence and World Governance.* Leiden, The Netherlands: Brill.

Wettstein, Florian (2009). *Multinational Corporations and Global Justice: Human Rights Obligations of a Quasi-Governmental Institution.* Stanford, CA: Stanford Business Books.

Whitaker, Robert (2010). *Anatomy of an Epidemic: Magic Bullets, Psychiatric Drugs, and the Astonishing Rise of Mental Illness in America.* New York: Crown.

White, Lawrence H. (1984). *Free Banking in Britain: Theory, Experience, and Debate, 1800-1845.* Cambridge: Cambridge University Press.

White, Lawrence H. (1999). *The Theory of Monetary Institutions.* Malden, MA: Blackwell.

Wichterich, Christa (2000). *The Globalized Woman: Reports From a Future of Inequality.* London: Spinifex Press.

Wichterich, Christa (2011). *The Other Financial Crisis: Poor Women, Small Credits, Big Businesses.* Brussels, Belgium: Women In Development Europe (WIDE), 62.149.193.10/wide/download/TheOtherFinancialCrisis_Microcredit_christa.pdf?id=1415.

Wickert, Ulrich (2011). *Redet Geld, schweigt die Welt: Was uns Werte wert sein müssen.* Hamburg, Germany: Hoffman und Campe.

Wierzbicka, Anna (1986). Human Emotions: Universal or Culturespecific? In *American Anthropologist,* 88, pp. 584-594.

Wierzbicka, Anna and Harkins, Jean. (Eds.)(2001). *Emotions in Crosslinguistic Perspective.* Berlin, Germany: Mouton de Gruyter.

Wilkinson, Richard G. (2005). *The Impact of Inequality. How to Make Sick Societies Healthier.* London: Routledge.

Wilkinson, Richard G. and Pickett, Kate (2009a). *The Spirit Level: Why Greater Equality Makes Societies Stronger.* New York: Bloombury Press.

Wilkinson, Richard G. and Pickett, Kate (2009b). *The Spirit Level: Why More Equal Societies Almost Always Do Better.* London: Allen Lane.

Wilkinson-Maposa, Susan, Fowler, Alan, Oliver-Evans, Ceri, and Mulenga, Chao F. N. (2009). *The Poor Philanthropist: How and Why the Poor Help Each Other.* Cape Town, South Africa: Compress.

Williams, Raymond (1961). *The Long Revolution.* London: Chatto and Windus.

Williams, Rowan and Elliott, Larry. (Eds.)(2010). *Crisis and Recovery: Ethics, Economics and Justice.* Basingstoke: Palgrave Macmillan.

Williamson, Thad, Imbroscio, David, and Alperovitz, Gar (2003). *Making a Place for Community: Local Democracy in a Global Era.* New York: Routledge.

Wilshire, Bruce (1990). *The Moral Collapse of the University: Professionalism, Purity, and Alienation.* Albany: State University of New York Press.

Wintersteiner, Werner (1999). *Pädagogik des Anderen: Bausteine für eine Friedenspädagogik in der Postmoderne.* Münster, Germany: Agenda.

Wobst, Martin (1978). The Archaeo-Ethnology of Hunter-Gatherers or the Tyranny of the Ethnographic Record in Archaeology. In *American Antiquity,* 43 (2), pp. 303-309.

Wolf, Martin (2009). *Fixing Global Finance: How to Curb Financial Crises in the 21st Century.* New Haven: Yale University press.

Wolin, Sheldon S. (2008). *Democracy Incorporated: Managed Democracy and the Specter of Inverted Totalitarianism.* Princeton, NJ: Princeton University Press.

Wood, Donna J. (1991). Corporate Social Performance Revisited. In *The Academy of Management Review,* 16 (4), pp. 691-718, www.jstor.org/stable/258977.

Wood, Ellen Meiksins (2003). *Empire of Capital.* London: Verso.

World Commission on Environment and Development and Brundtland, Gro Harlem (1987). *Our Common Future.* Oxford: Oxford University Press, en.wikisource.org/wiki/Brundtland_Report.

Wyatt-Brown, Bertram (2005). *The Changing Faces of Honor in National Crises: Civil War, Vietnam, Iraq, and the Southern Factor.* Baltimore, MD: The Johns Hopkins History Seminar, Fall 2005.

Yergin, Daniel (2008). *The Prize: The Epic Quest for Oil, Money & Power*. New York: Free Press.

Yergin, Daniel (2011). *The Quest: Energy, Security, and the Remaking of the Modern World*. New York: Penguin Press.

Yoshikawa, Muneo Jay (1980). *The "Double Swing" Model of Eastern-Western Intercultural Communication*. Paper prepared for the Seminar on Communication Theory from Eastern and Western Perspectives, East-West Communication Institute, Honolulu, Hawaii.

Yoshikawa, Muneo Jay (1987). The "Double Swing" Model of Intercultural Communication Between the East and West. In Kincaid, D. Lawrence (Ed.), *Communication Theory: Eastern and Western Perspectives*, pp. 319-329. San Diego, CA: Academic Press.

Yudkin, Michael (Ed.)(1969). *General Education: A Symposium on the Teaching of Non-Specialists*. Harmondsworth: Penguin.

Zarlenga, Stephen A. (2002). *The Lost Science of Money*. Valatie, NY: American Monetary Institute.

Zehr, Howard (1990). *Changing Lenses: A New Focus for Crime and Justice*. Scottdale, PA: Herald Press.

Zehr, Howard (2002). *The Little Book of Restorative Justice*. Intercourse, PA: Good Books.

Zembylas, Michalinos (2002). Of Troubadours, Angels, and Parasites: Reevaluating the Educational Territory in the Arts and Sciences Through the Work of Michel Serres. In *International Journal of Education & the Arts*, 3 (3, March 17) ijea.asu.edu/v3n3.

Zerubavel, Eviatar (1997). *Social Mindscapes: An Invitation to Cognitive Sociology*. Cambridge, MA: Harvard University Press.

Zimbardo, Philip G. (1971). *The Power and Pathology of Imprisonment.* Congressional Record. (Serial No. 15, 1971-10-25). Hearings Before Subcommittee No. 3, of the Committee on the Judiciary, House of Representatives, Ninety-Second Congress, First Session on Corrections, Part II, Prisons, Prison Reform and Prisoner's Rights: California. Washington, DC: Government Printing Office.

Zimbardo, Philip G. (2007). *The Lucifer Effect: Understanding How Good People Turn Evil.* New York: Random House.

Zoche, Georg (2009). *Welt Macht Geld.* Berlin: Blumenbar, weltmachtgeld.de.

Zsolnai, László and Ims, Knut J. (2006). *Business Within Limits: Deep Ecology and Buddhist Economics.* Oxford: Peter Lang.

Index

Notes

Preface

[1] 13th Annual Conference of Human Dignity and Humiliation Studies, August 20–22, 2009, see humiliationstudies.org/whoweare/annualmeeting.13.php.

[2] I thank Linda Hartling for coining the main title "A Dignity Economy," and Ulrich Spalthoff for the subtitle "Creating an Economy Which Serves Human Dignity and Preserves our Environment," ." later amended, with Linda's help, to "Creating an Economy Which Serves Human Dignity and Preserves Our Planet."
Here is a list of some of the titles that were pondered:

- A Dignity Economy: A Fundamentally New World (Evelin Lindner)
- A Dignity Economy: People and Planet Before Profit? (Evelin Lindner)
- A Dignity Economy: If not State Socialism, if not Corporate Capitalism, What Then? (Evelin Lindner, inspired by Gar Alperowitz)
- A Solidarity Economy (Evelin Lindner inspired by the example of Argentina, see, for instance, www.solidarityeconomy.net/2011/04/12/argentinas-women-and-the-solidarity-economy/)
- Dignity or Humiliation in Economic and Monetary Systems: Can We Occupy Wall Street and Transcend the Old Cs (*Communism* and *Capitalism*) through Economic Systems of

True Inclusion? What about *Inclusionism*? Or *Dignism*? (Evelin Lindner, one of the titles of the original article)

- *Dignism* (or *Dignitism*), Rather than *Communism* or *Capitalism*: Dignity or Humiliation in Economic and Monetary Systems (Evelin Lindner, one of the titles of the original article)
- Dignity or Humiliation in Economic and Monetary Systems: Toward a System of "Right Relationships," of *Dignitism* or *Dignism*, Instead of *Communism* or *Capitalism* (Evelin Lindner, one of the titles of the original article)
- Dignity or Humiliation in Economic and Monetary Systems: Toward a System of "Right Relationships" (Evelin Lindner, one of the titles of the original article)
- A Dignifying Economy (Morton Deutsch), expanded to *A Dignified and Dignifying Economy* by Evelin Lindner
- A Manifest to Tame Casino Capitalism and to Create an Economy Which Serves Human Dignity and Preserves our Environment (Ulrich Spalthoff)
- A Personal Manifest for a Humane Economy (Ulrich Spalthoff)
- Creating an Economics that Gives Dignity to All Our Lives (Michael Britton)
- Choices: Making Economics that Provide Everyone with Dignity in Life (Michael Britton)
- Rescuing Human Dignity (For All of Us) From Opportunistic Economics (Michael Britton)
- Worldwide Dignity: A New Economics Paradigm (Michael Britton)
- An Economy of Dignity (Ingrid Fuglestvedt)
- Money: From Humiliation to Dignity (Lynn King)

[3] See, among others, Jürgen Habermas (1989), Jürgen Habermas (1985), Jürgen Habermas (1981), Jürgen Habermas (1962).

[4] On November 16, 2011, writer and peace scholar Janet Gerson took me to Zuccotti Park and The Atrium in New York City, where most of the Occupy Wall Street activities took place. Janet shared with me her doctoral research and I thank her for reminding me of the significance of the notion of *grappling*. See www.humiliationstudies.org/whoweare/evelinpics11.php.#OWS.

[5] "Academic Publishers Make Murdoch Look Like a Socialist" by George Monbiot, August 29, 2011, www.guardian.co.uk/commentisfree/2011/aug/29/academic-publishers-murdoch-socialist. I thank Kamran Mofid for making me aware of this article.

[6] See www.dignitypress.org. See also Evelin Gerda Lindner, Linda M. Hartling, and Ulrich Spalthoff (2011).

[7] Gender, Humiliation, and Global Security, Evelin Gerda Lindner (2010b).

[8] "Credit Default Swaps: The next Crisis?" by Janet Morrissey, in *Time*, March 17, 2008, www.time.com/time/printout/0,8816,1723152,00.html. "Credit Rating Agencies and the Next Financial Crisis" was the title of the House Oversight and Government Reform Committee's hearing in Washington on September 30, 2009.

[9] Evelin Gerda Lindner (2010b), p. xv.

[10] Linda Hartling in a personal communication, September 18, 2011, in Portland, Oregon, USA.

[11] Jared Diamond (2011), Jared Diamond and James A. Robinson (2010), Jared Diamond (2005b). I thank Margrethe Tingstad for reminding me, on June 30, 2011, of Diamond's important work on the collapse of human civilizations and that it would merit to stand at the beginning of this text.

[12] Paul Hawken (2007a).

[13] "How the 99% Are Using Lateral Power to Produce a Global Revolution," by Jeremy Rifkin, *Huffington Post*, November 8, 2011, www.huffingtonpost.com/jeremy-rifkin/how-the-99-are-using-late_b_1081552.html?. I thank Kathleen Morrow for making me aware of this article. She summarizes Rifkin's argument as follows:

His thesis is that the first two industrial revolutions were based on energy/communications breakthroughs and that the new revolution will be based on social media combined with green energy, with consumers producing their own energy and sharing it via Internet with billions around the globe. This revolution will decentralize power and capital and put the means of production in the hands of everyone who wants to participate. He calls it a pro-democracy revolution.

For an *empathic civilization*, see Jeremy Rifkin (2009), and his 2010 RSA animate "The Empathic Civilisation," www.youtube.com/watch?v=l7AWnfFRc7g.

[14]   In an e-mail from the New Economics Institute from October 20, 2011, Alperovitz is quoted as saying that "instead of feeling confined to the binary paths of reforming the broken economic system or revolting to overthrow it, citizens are opting to create something new that will replace the current economic regime, making the old system obsolete in the process." Alperovitz calls this third way *evolutionary reconstruction*. See Gar Alperovitz (2009), Gar Alperovitz and Lew Daly (2008), Gar Alperovitz (2005), Thad Williamson, David Imbroscio, and Gar Alperovitz (2003).

[15]   Paul D. Raskin et al. (2002).

[16]   Jean Kilbourne (2000).

[17]   Mary Roach (2008). See also the life work of feminist, sociologist and political activist Barbara Ehrenreich.

[18]   "Egypt's Botched Revolution," by Michael J. Totten, September 11, 2011, pjmedia.com/michaeltotten/2011/09/11/egypt%e2%80%99s-botched-revolution/.

[19]   See neweconomicsinstitute.org.

[20]   Jared Diamond (2011), Jared Diamond and James A. Robinson (2010), Jared Diamond (2005b).

[21]   Read more on www.humiliationstudies.org/whoweare/evelin.php.

[22]   Evelin Gerda Lindner (2010b), p. xxiv.

[23]   *Pleasantville* is an Academy Award-nominated 1998 film written, produced, and directed by Gary Ross. See also *The Clonus Horror* (1979) or *The Island* (2005). As to "personal branding," see Daniel J. Lair, Katie Sullivan, and George Cheney (2005). I discussed this topic in January 29, 2007, in Harrania, near Cairo, Egypt, with Sophie Wissa-Wassef, who makes a point of protecting her artists' creativity by not disclosing to them whether their art sells or not. See

www.humiliationstudies.org/intervention/art.php#ramseswissawassef or www.wissa-wassef-arts.com/intro.htm. See also Douglas Rushkoff (2009); I thank Keith Grennan for this link.

[24] I explain this point in more depth on www.humiliationstudies.org/whoweare/evelin.php.

[25] Evelin Gerda Lindner (2010b), p. xxiv.

[26] See Philip Pettit (1997).

[27] Read more about Linda at www.humiliationstudies.org/whoweare/linda.php, and about Evelin at www.humiliationstudies.org/whoweare/evelin.php.

[28] See for publications by the entire Human Dignity and Humiliation Studies network, www.humiliationstudies.org/publications/publications.php, for Hartling's publications, www.humiliationstudies.org/whoweare/linda.php, and for Lindner's publications, www.humiliationstudies.org/evelin02.php. See for some of Lindner's texts relevant to the topic of this paper, among others, Evelin Gerda Lindner (2000c), Evelin Gerda Lindner (2000e), Evelin Gerda Lindner (2000h), Evelin Gerda Lindner (2000f), Evelin Gerda Lindner (2000d), Evelin Gerda Lindner (2000a), Evelin Gerda Lindner (2000g), Evelin Gerda Lindner (2000b), Evelin Gerda Lindner (2001b), Evelin Gerda Lindner (2002), Evelin Gerda Lindner (2001e), Evelin Gerda Lindner (2001c), Evelin Gerda Lindner (2003), Evelin Gerda Lindner (2005), Evelin Gerda Lindner (2006a), Evelin Gerda Lindner (2007b), Evelin Gerda Lindner (2007a), Evelin Gerda Lindner (2007c), Evelin Gerda Lindner (2008b), Evelin Gerda Lindner (2008a), Evelin Gerda Lindner (2008c).

[29] See www.humiliationstudies.org.

[30] See www.worlddignityuniversity.org.

[31] Evelin Gerda Lindner (2006d). For more details, see www.humiliationstudies.org/whoweare/evelin04.php.

[32] Evelin Gerda Lindner (2006b).

[33] Evelin Gerda Lindner (2009a). For more details, see www.humiliationstudies.org/whoweare/evelin041.php.

[34] Evelin Gerda Lindner (2010b). For more details, see www.humiliationstudies.org/whoweare/evelin042.php.

[35] I thank Linda Hartling for sharing her impressions of meeting Gandhi's grandson Arun M. Gandhi at the "Messages of Peace" conference, September 20, 2009, at Marylhurst University in Oregon, USA. Gandhi described the crucial lessons he learned from his grandfather about the lifelong practice of nonviolent action. He also offered a rare glimpse into how the women in his grandfather's life shaped the development of nonviolent principles and practices. "'You cannot change people's hearts by law,' Grandfather said. 'You can only change hearts by love,'" Arun Manilal Gandhi (2003), p. 91. See also arungandhi.org.

[36] Marshall McLuhan is credited with having coined the phrase "global village" in 1959, after borrowing it from Wyndham Lewis. The term appeared in Herbert Marshall McLuhan (1962).

[37] Evelin Gerda Lindner (2006d), p. 38.

[38] See the work by Paul H. Ray and Sherry Ruth Anderson (2000), and their analysis of how the two branches of what they call the *cultural creatives* movement are now coming together.

Introduction

[1] I thank Linda Hartling for making me aware of this quote.

[2] Intentional living means living with integrity in relation to one's conscience and environment. Related terms cover a vast array, starting with ethical, frugal, or sustainable living, supported by appropriate technology and informed by areas of investigation and activism as diverse as conservation, ecology, environmentalism, ethics, humanism,

humanitarianism, moralism, religion, or simply socially responsible investing.

[3] Marshall McLuhan is credited with having coined the phrase "global village" in 1959, after borrowing it from Wyndham Lewis; the term appeared in Herbert Marshall McLuhan (1962).

[4] Thomas Hobbes (1651).

[5] See Philip Pettit (1997).

[6] Evelin Gerda Lindner (2006d), pp. 171–172.

[7] See, among others, Colin Archer (2005), Scilla Elworthy and Gabrielle Rifkind (2005), Andrew Mack and Zoe Nielsen (2010), Betty A. Reardon and Asha Hans (Eds.) 2010. See also the Human Security Report Project by the Human Security Research Group, www.hsrgroup.org/human-security-reports/human-security-report.aspx.

[8] Caroline Thomas (2001).

[9] Stéphane Hessel (2010). See also www.independent.co.uk/news/world/europe/the-little-red-book-that-swept-france-2174676.html#.

[10] Please read about ideal types in Lewis A. Coser (1977):

Weber's three kinds of *ideal types* are distinguished by their levels of abstraction. First are the *ideal types* rooted in historical particularities, such as the "western city,' "the Protestant Ethic," or "modern capitalism," which refer to phenomena that appear only in specific historical periods and in particular cultural areas. A second kind involves abstract elements of social reality—such concepts as "bureaucracy" or "feudalism"—that may be found in a variety of historical and cultural contexts. Finally, there is a third kind of *ideal type*, which Raymond Aron calls "rationalizing reconstructions of a particular kind of behavior." According to Weber, all propositions in economic theory, for example, fall into this category. They all refer to the ways in which men would behave were they actuated by purely economic motives, were they purely economic men, Lewis A. Coser (1977), p. 224.

[11] "It is no secret that the relationship between President Obama and Wall Street has chilled. A striking measure of that is the latest campaign finance

reports. Mitt Romney has raised far more money than Mr. Obama this year from the firms that have been among Wall Street's top sources of donations for the two candidates," these are the first sentences in "Romney Beating Obama in a Fight for Wall St. Cash," by Nicholas Confessore and Griff Palmer, *The New York Times*, October 15, 2011, www.nytimes.com/2011/10/16/us/romney-perry-and-cain-open-wide-financial-lead-over-field.html?_r=1&hp.
See , furthermore, "Why Do We Think Corporations Are People?," by Jamie Malanowski, August 16, 2011, www.washingtonmonthly.com/ten-miles-square/2011/08/why_do_we_think_corportions_ar031572.php?page=all& print=true. I thank Kathleen Morrow for making me aware of this article.

[12] Matthias Matussek in *Der Spiegel*, 18, May 2, 2011, p. 136, original text in German:

Wir sind aufgeklärt, allerdings ist uns nicht wohl dabei. Wenn Aufklärung der Ausweg aus selbstverschuldeter Unmündigkeit ist, müssen wir zugeben: Sie ist gescheitert. Der Markt hat uns fester im Griff als je eine Kirche. Er hat uns Preisschilder angenäht und die Würde genommen, jedem von uns. Gleichzeitig ist die rationale Zurichtung der Welt unauflösbar an ein erhebliches Maß an Irrationalität geknüpft. Wir züchten die genetisch veredelte Turbokartoffel, aber jeden Tag verhungern 30 000 Menschen. Wir bohren die Meeresböden auf, wir holzen Wälder ab und lassen die Natur veröden, bis Ökosysteme kippen, Arten sterben. Ja, tatsächlich machen wir uns die Natur so sehr untertan, dass sie japsend unter uns zusammenbricht. Oder wir liefern uns einer Technologie aus, die uns vernichtet, wie wir es gerade in Fukushima erleben. Woher der Stolz auf diese Form von Vernunft rühren soll, ist mir schleierhaft.

[13] Dieter Hildebrandt is a public speaker, who, at the age of 84, tours Germany with a new program in 2011:

"'The history of the world economy has proved that nothing is so reliable as the triumph of the free market—over reason.' When Dieter Hildebrandt formulated this in the 1980s, he could not know that this quote would be almost programmatic. 'But I can not help it either' is therefore the title of his new program."

German original:

„'Die Geschichte der Weltwirtschaft hat bewiesen, dass auf nichts so Verlass ist, wie auf den Sieg des Freien Marktes—über die Vernunft.' Als Dieter Hildebrandt in den 1980ern zu dieser Erkenntnis kam, konnte er nicht wissen, dass dieses Zitat nahezu programmatisch sein würde. ‚Ich kann doch auch nichts dafür' heißt folgerichtig sein neues Programm." Quoted and translated from venyoo.de/Bad-Pyrmont/s374774-dieter-hildebrandt-ich-kann-doch-auch-nichts-dafuer.

[14] Nadine Gordimer in a BBC World News *HARDtalk* interview with Stephen Sackur, May 10, 2010, news.bbc.co.uk/2/hi/programmes/hardtalk/9481410.stm.

[15] "The Next Great American Consumer: Infants to 3-Year-Olds: They're a New Demographic Marketers are Hell-Bent on Reaching," by Brian Braiker, *Adweek*, September 26, 2011, www.adweek.com/news/advertising-branding/next-great-american-consumer-135207. According to Victor C. Strasburger, professor of pediatrics at the University of New Mexico School of Medicine, children under the age of seven are "psychologically defenseless" against advertising." "We've created a perfect storm for childhood obesity—media, advertising, and inactivity," said Strasburger, lead author of a policy statement published June 27, 2011, by the American Academy of Pediatrics (AAP) Council on Communications and Media. "American society couldn't do a worse job at the moment of keeping children fit and healthy—too much TV, too many food ads, not enough exercise, and not enough sleep," he said, quoted from aap.org/advocacy/releases/june2711studies.htm, referring to the Council on Communications and Media (2011). See also Victor C. Strasburger, Amy B. Jordan, and Barbara J. Wilson (2009). In Sweden, all advertisements aimed at children under the age of twelve have been banned. In the U.S., business is trying to prevent regulation on advertising to children, see "Will Food Industry's New Marketing Guidelines Satisfy the Feds?," by Katy Bachman, July 15, 2011, www.adweek.com/news/advertising-branding/will-food-industrys-new-marketing-guidelines-satisfy-feds-133437.
It seems that the language of "values" and "ecology" has been applied to the market in particularly blunt ways in the U.S., see the self-representation of the Right Media Exchange, the Platform for Premium Digital Advertising, www.rightmediablog.com (italics added by the author):

Right Media launched digital advertising's first exchange platform in the spring of 2005 and is currently the largest exchange in the industry. Our success stems from the principles we started with: transparent, fair, open and efficient. We've stayed true to these *values* throughout a variety of market cycles. Since Yahoo! acquired the company in 2007, we have been working to build a premium exchange with more than 300,000 active global buyers and sellers and more than 11 billion daily transactions. Today, the Right Media platform supports an *ecosystem* of leading digital advertising companies, including differentiated ad networks, direct advertisers in our non-guaranteed marketplace, data providers, technology innovators, and global agencies. Our strategy includes focusing on: premium buying and selling, data-driven valuation, audience sourcing, interoperability. As the industry changes, Right Media is evolving to change with it. The Right Media platform is designed to help all participants in the digital advertising *ecosystem* conduct business with one another in a seamless fashion, and deliver marketers the greatest number of options in how they define and reach their relevant audiences."

[16] Ibid.

[17] "Unpaid Student Loans Top $1 Trillion," by Tim Mak, *Politico*, October 19, 2011, www.politico.com/news/stories/1011/66347.html.

[18] See www2.ohchr.org/english/law/cescr.htm#art13.

[19] Morton Deutsch, Eric C. Marcus, and Sarah Brazaitis (2012). Morton Deutsch is a member in the global advisory board of our Human Dignity and Humiliation Studies network, and founding member of our World Dignity University initiative. He received the Lifetime Achievement Award of the Human Dignity and Humiliation Studies network in the 2009 Workshop on Transforming Humiliation and Violent Conflict, see www.humiliationstudies.org/whoweare/annualmeeting14.php.

Chapter 1

1 See also Claus Otto Scharmer (2009).

2 Herbert Marshall McLuhan is credited for having formulated this saying.

3 Evelin Gerda Lindner (2007a).

4 On June 5, 2008, more than one thousand representatives from indigenous communities across the Americas gathered in Lima, Peru, and agreed on a new social system, called "Living Well." See, among others, www.villageearth.org/pages/Projects/Peru/perublog/2008/06/living-well-development-alternative.html#.

5 "Why Is China Building Eerie 'Ghost Cities'?: Google Earth Photographs Reveal Towns Completely Devoid of People," by Jerome Corsi, February 6, 2011, www.wnd.com/?pageId=260645.

6 "American Indignees Put their Money in Cooperative Credit Unions," www.youtube.com/watch?feature=player_embedded&v=0YCyPYIs_qo.

7 See Evelin Gerda Lindner (2000e).

8 Herman E. Daly and Kenneth N. Townsend (Eds.) 1993.

9 Through my doctoral research in social psychology on humiliation and armed conflict, I learned to appreciate the analytical frame of health. See Evelin Gerda Lindner (2000e).

10 Linda Hartling, September 18, 2011, in Portland, Oregon, USA.

11 Howard Richards (2011a).

12 See, for instance, www.solidarityeconomy.net/2011/04/12/argentinas-women-and-the-solidarity-economy/.

13 See, for instance, europa.eu/scadplus/glossary/subsidiarity_en.htm.

[14] For essayist Arthur Koestler's theory of holons and holarchies, see Arthur Koestler (1978), Arthur Koestler (1967). I thank John Bunzl for reminding me of Koestler's work.

[15] John Braithwaite (2002). Also the brain uses regulatory feedback loops that are organized hierarchically, with *subordinate loops* embedded within *superordinate loops*.

[16] I had the privilege of listening to Phil Clark and Joanna Quinn during the "International Symposium on Restorative Justice, Reconciliation and Peacebuilding," at the New York University School of Law, November 11–12, 2011, www.iilj.org/RJRP/about.asp. They introduced me to the work of Sally Engle Merry and Mark A. Drumbl, see Mark Goodale and Sally Engle Merry (2007) and Mark A. Drumbl (2007). I learned that British colonizers set up a "relationships commission" as far back as 1898. Lord Lugard wrote about the "dual mandate" in Africa, see Frederick John Dealtry Lugard (1965). See also Phil Clark (2010).

[17] See www.uvh.nl/kosmopolisinstitute, for a discussion of pluralism. The Kosmopolis Institute explains its mission as follows:

The Kosmopolis Institute was founded in 2004 by the University of Humanistic Studies in consultation with the Humanist Institute for Development Cooperation (Hivos). ... In 2010, Kosmopolis Institute was affiliated with Harvard University for their Pluralism Project. The Kosmopolis Pluralism Project is part of the Hivos Knowledge Programs and is a collaboration of (1) Kosmopolis, (2) the Center of Religious and Cross Cultural Studies at the Graduate School of Gadjah Mada University in Yogyakarta, Indonesia, (3) The Centre for the Study of Culture and Society in Bangalore, India, (4) The Cross Cultural Foundation of Uganda in Kampala and (5) International Institute for Studies in Race, Reconciliation and Social Justice at the University of the Free State in Bloemfontein, South Africa.

[18] Ibid.

[19] Sen introduced the *capability approach to social justice* as an alternative to the prevailing utilitarian and Rawls' theory in Amartya Kumar Sen (1980). From then on he has been elaborating and clarifying this notion in a number of subsequent writings. See, among others, *The Quality of Life*, co-

edited with Martha Nussbaum, Martha C. Nussbaum and Amartya Kumar Sen (1993). In collaboration with Martha Nussbaum, development economist Sudhir Anand, and economic theorist James Foster, he inspired the creation of the UN's Human Development Index (HDI). The Human Development and Capability Association (HDCA) was launched in September 2004 with Sen as the founding president until 2006, when Martha Nussbaum became president, succeeded by Frances Stewart in 2008, see www.capabilityapproach.com/index.php.

[20] Evelin Gerda Lindner (2007a). How local governance and civil society were transformed in Brazil would be an example to consider; for instance, see Patrick Heller, Gianpaolo Baiocchi, and Marcelo Kunrath Silva (2011).

[21] See note 4 earlier in this chapter.

[22] See www.humiliationstudies.org/whoweare/board.php.

[23] See www.humiliationstudies.org/whoweare/annualmeeting17.php.

[24] See www.humiliationstudies.org/education/teamshort.php.

[25] "The Financial Crisis Inquiry Report: Final Report of the National Commission on the Causes of the Financial and Economic Crisis in the United States," 2011, c0182732.cdn1.cloudfiles.rackspacecloud.com/fcic_final_report_full.pdf.

Among the key conclusions are the following:

- "The financial crisis was avoidable. The crisis was the result of human action and inaction, not of Mother Nature or computer models gone haywire."
- "Widespread failures in financial regulation and supervision proved devastating to the stability of the nation's financial markets."
- "The Federal Reserve was the one entity empowered" to set prudent mortgage standards. "And it did not."
- Wall Street firms were ignorant of their exploding exposure to great risk. "By one measure, the leverage ratios (of major investment banks) were as high as 40 to 1, meaning for every $40 in assets, there was only $1 in capital to cover losses." This

means a small turn in the market put them at great risk of insolvency, which is exactly how it played out.

- The government was ill-prepared for the crisis and then made matters worse with its inconsistent response, bailing out Bear Stearns and AIG while allowing Lehman Bros. to fail, for instance.

[26] See www.humiliationstudies.org/whoweare/linda.php, and Linda M. Hartling and Tracy Luchetta (1999). See, furthermore, Linda M. Hartling (2008), Linda M. Hartling (2007), Linda M. Hartling (2005b), Linda M. Hartling (2005a), Linda M. Hartling and Jean Baker Miller (2005), Linda M. Hartling (2003a), Linda M. Hartling (2003b), Linda M. Hartling et al. (2000), Linda M. Hartling and E. Sparks (2000).

[27] See www.humiliationstudies.org/whoweare/evelin.php, and Evelin Gerda Lindner (2000e).

[28] Donna Hicks (2010). Donna Hicks is a member in the global advisory board of our Human Dignity and Humiliation Studies network, see www.humiliationstudies.org/whoweare/board.php.

[29] Harsh Agarwal in a personal communication, February 26, 2010.

[30] Yves M. Musoni in a personal communication, November 9, 2011. Yves M. Musoni was forced to leave his country, the Democratic Republic of the Congo, in 1996. He spent 13 years in Rwanda before immigrating to the USA as the winner of the US Diversity Visa Program. He is both a Member of the Global Research Team of our Human Dignity and Humiliation Studies, and the Peace and Collaborative Development Network. Musoni refers to "Airplane Turbulence Isn't As Dangerous As It Might Seem," by Jack Williams, www.usatoday.com/weather/wturbwht.htm. See also Yves M. Musoni (2003).

[31] Paul D. Raskin et al. (2002).

[32] I thank sociologist Ingrid Eide for making me aware (in a meeting on January 14, 2011, in Oslo) of the work of three relevant scholars, namely, Trygve Haavelmo, recipient of the Nobel Prize in Economics, see Trygve Haavelmo (1989), mathematician Benoit Mandelbrot, see Benoit B. Mandelbrot and Richard L. Hudson (2004), and economist Karine Nyborg, see Karine Nyborg (2007). The conversation with Ingrid Eide

took place in the context of the 2nd International Conference on
Democracy as Idea and Practice, Oslo, January 13–14, 2011,
www.demokrati.uio.no/arrangementer/konferanser/2011/2nd-Democracy-
as-idea-and-practice-jan-2011. This conference highlighted relevant
transdisciplinary scholarship, see, for example, Johan P. Olsen (2010).

[33] "Herman Cain: 'If You Don't Have A Job And You're Not Rich, Blame
Yourself,'" posted by CNN Associate Producer Rebecca Stewart,
www.youtube.com/watch?v=SHMEC8Xk9cg.

[34] The archbishop was speaking during a panel discussion to mark the
launch of a book, *Crisis and Recovery: Ethics, economics and justice*, edited by
Rowan Williams and Larry Elliott, the economics editor at *The Guardian*,
see Rowan Williams and Larry Elliott (Eds.) 2010. See also "Rehumanise
Economics, Says Williams," by Ed Beavan, *Church Times*, October 1, 2010,
www.churchtimes.co.uk/content.asp?id=101427. See, furthermore, an
introductory explanation at www.archbishopofcanterbury.org/2998.

[35] Evelin Gerda Lindner (2010b).

[36] See www.humiliationstudies.org/whoweare/annualmeeting17.php.

[37] See www.economicsandpeace.org. IEP is "an international research
institute dedicated to building a greater understanding of the key drivers
and measures of peace and to identifying the economic benefits that
increased peacefulness can deliver."

[38] Ulrich Wickert (2011). I thank Elfi Lindner for making me aware of this
book.

[39] „Immer Mehr ist immer Weniger. Wer bestimmt eigentlich über den
Fortschritt?" by Richard David Precht, *Der Spiegel*, 5/2011, January 31,
2011,
wissen.spiegel.de/wissen/image/show.html?did=76659530&aref=image046/
2011/01/29/CO-SP-2011-005-0128-0129.PDF&thumb=false,
pp. 128–129.

[40] Translated from the German original by the author:

Was kann der Einzelne überhaupt noch tun? Gefragt ist sein
Wohlverhalten. Sich in die Castingshows und die alimentierten
Rentensysteme so hineinfügen, dass er als Vorbild für die Angepasstheit der

anderen gilt–dies wird dann mit Sondervaluta honoriert (vgl. Boldt, 2008; Reinhardt, 2007). Ansonsten gibt es wenig Spielraum: sich hochzuklimmen zu der Regentschaft mag einzelnen Extrem-Charismatikern der Unterschicht im Einzelfall gelingen—aber selbst oben angekommen, bleiben sie Kanonenfutter. Das Abtauchen in die Revolution (dem Menschen das Menschliche zurückgeben) bleibt dann der Selbstmordidee oder einer ebenfalls hoch organisierten Terrorismus-Maschinerie vorbehalten. Wenig Platz für die 'Normalos'!, *MANUAL AAT 2009*, www.4emotions.de/aat/?page_id=16.

[41] Clearly, feelings vary in different world regions. Many people in Germany and Scandinavia, also people in China or India, for instance, are much less alarmed than, for instance, people in America or Southern Europe.

[42] Linda Hartling made us aware of "The Rise and Fall of the G.D.P.," by Jon Gertner, *New York Times*, May 10, 2010, www.nytimes.com/2010/05/16/magazine/16GDP-t.html?pagewant.

[43] "Unconventional Wisdom: A Special Anniversary Report Challenging the World's Most Dangerous Thinking," *Foreign Policy*, January/February 2011, foreignpolicy.com/articles/2011/01/02/unconventional_wisdom?page=0,0.

[44] "A Crisis of Faith in Britain's Central Banker," by Landon Thomas jr. and Julia Werdigier, *The New York Times*, February 6, 2011, www.nytimes.com/2011/02/07/business/07king.html?nl=todaysheadlines& emc=tha25.

[45] How to scale this risk back is the subject of a much anticipated independent inquiry, led by John Vickers, a former Bank of England chief economist and head of the Office of Fair Trading.

[46] By the Verbraucherzentrale Bundesverband (vzbv)(Federal Association of Consumer Centers) in co-operation with the Second Channel of German Television's (ZDF) economics and consumer program WISO.

[47] Michael Scheuch (2009).

[48] Eilis Lawlor, Helen Kersley, and Susan Steed (2009).

[49] Warren Buffet in the "Berkshire Hathaway's Annual Report to Shareholders" in 2002, www.berkshirehathaway.com/2002ar/2002ar.pdf.

[50] Warren Buffet in his "Annual Letter to Berkshire Shareholders," released on February 27, 2010. See www.berkshirehathaway.com.

[51] See, for example, "Don't Fear the Swedish Model," by Benjamin Sarlin, *The Daily Beast*, March 24, 2009, www.thedailybeast.com/blogs-and-stories/2009-03-24/dont-fear-the-swedish-model/. I have attempted to analyze Anglo-Saxon cultural mindsets in Evelin Gerda Lindner (2008b). The novel *North and South* by Elizabeth Gaskell (1855) makes this discussion palpable.

[52] "The Tyranny of the Minority," by Larry M. Bartels, *The New York Times*, September 20, 2011, www.nytimes.com/roomfordebate/2011/09/19/do-taxes-narrow-the-wealth-gap/taxes-and-the-tyranny-of-the-minority. See also Larry M. Bartels (2008a).

[53] "The Tyranny of the Minority," by Larry M. Bartels, *The New York Times*, September 20, 2011, www.nytimes.com/roomfordebate/2011/09/19/do-taxes-narrow-the-wealth-gap/taxes-and-the-tyranny-of-the-minority. See also Larry M. Bartels (2008a).

[54] Ibid.

[55] Economist Gar Alperovitz at the Thirty-First Annual E. F. Schumacher Lectures on November 5, 2011, in New York City, www.neweconomicsinstitute.org.

[56] "Complexity Equals Corruption," by Fareed Zakaria, *Time Magazine*, October 31, 2011, p. 27. See the first paragraph on www.time.com/time/magazine/article/0,9171,2097396,00.html.

[57] See www.pittsburghsummit.gov/mediacenter/129639.htm.

[58] Halldór Gudmundsson (2010).

[59] "Hedge Funds Try 'Career Trade' Against Euro," by Susan Pulliam, Kate Kelly, and Carrick Mollenkamp, *Wallstreet Journal*, February 26, 2010,

online.wsj.com/article/SB10001424052748703795004575087741848074 392.html.

[60] "Q+A—How Fear of Speculators Drives European Leaders," *Reuters*, Brussels, May 10, 2010, www.reuters.com/article/idUSLDE6480EM20100510. "Many European political leaders have blamed speculators for aggravating the rocky financial markets that forced them to agree a bumper emergency package for struggling countries on Sunday."

[61] "Revealed—the Capitalist Network that Runs the World," by Andy Coghlan and Debora MacKenzie, *New Scientist*, Issue 2835, updated October 24, 2011, www.newscientist.com/article/mg21228354.500-revealed--the-capitalist-network-that-runs-the-world.html.

[62] On The Daily Show with Jon Stewart, November 8, 2011, seen by Kathleen Morrow.

[63] See economist Karl Ove Moene's work at Centre of Equality, Social Organization, and Performance (ESOP), where he differentiates these three cultures, see Karl Ove Moene and Erling Barth (2009). Whoever wishes to acquire an intuition for the Anglo-Saxon approach, is recommended to read novelist Elizabeth Gaskell (1855), who is up-to-date with her piece *North and South*, where "gentlemen" in London like to "double in cotton." See also Evelin Gerda Lindner (2008b).

[64] Herman E. Daly and Kenneth N. Townsend (Eds.) 1993.

[65] William McDonough and Michael Braungart (2002).

[66] See gbo3.cbd.int.

[67] *BBC News*, May 10, 2010, news.bbc.co.uk/2/hi/science_and_environment/10103179.stm .

[68] Ibid.

[69] Ibid.

[70] See a graphic illustration by Bhopal disaster campaigner Satinath Sarangi in a BBC World News *HARDtalk* interview with Jonathan Charles, March 17, 2010, where Sarangi warns that the present establishment of special economic zones, such as Chemicals and Petrochemical Investment Regions

(PCPIR), where national laws do not apply, in the service of profit maximization, is setting the scene for new Bhopal-like accidents, news.bbc.co.uk/2/hi/programmes/hardtalk/8566937.stm.

[71] Juliet B. Schor at www.julietschor.org/the-book/synopsis/.

[72] Evelin Gerda Lindner (2010b).

[73] Peter Drucker (1993). Indeed, the Occupy Wall Street movement's approach to leadership is to ask everybody to step up and step back.

[74] Sean O'Casey, 1917, *The Story of Thomas Ashe*, as Sean O'Cathasaigh.

Chapter 2

[1] Reading recommendations, among others, John N. Smithin (2000), George A. Selgin (1996), Kevin Dowd (1992), Chris Milner and Robert Read (2002), Pauls S. Mills and John R. Presley (1999), Lawrence H. White (1999), Mark Casson (1995), Kevin Dowd (1993), Larry J. Sechrest (1993), Lawrence H. White (1984), Anwar Iqbal Qureshi (1967).

[2] See, for instance, Henry George (1879). See also the Henry George School of Social Science, www.henrygeorgeschool.org. I thank Harvey Newman for making me aware of this school.

[3] Edwin Clarence Riegel (1976). I thank Paul Grignon for making me aware of Riegel's work.

[4] Paul Anthony Samuelson (1947).

[5] James E. Meade (1965).

[6] John M. Houkes (2004).

[7] "Canon of St Paul's 'Unable to Reconcile Conscience with Evicting Protest Camp,'" by Alan Rusbridger, *The Guardian*, October 27, 2011,

www.guardian.co.uk/uk/2011/oct/27/giles-fraser-occupy-london-st-pauls. I thank Kamran Mofid for making me aware of this interview.

[8] The day the London Stock Exchange's rules changed, October 27, 1986, was labeled the "Big Bang."

[9] See note 7 earlier in this chapter.

[10] *Wall Street* is a 1987 American drama film released by 20th Century Fox. It was directed by Oliver Stone and stars Michael Douglas, Charlie Sheen and Daryl Hannah. It is corporate raider Gordon Gekko (played by Michael Douglas), who professes that "greed is good."

[11] I saw the Americans for Prosperity Foundation holding its second annual RightOnline Conference on C-SPAN on August 15, 2009. Speakers included Michelle Malkin and Grover Norquist. See www.c-spanarchives.org/library/index.php?main_page=product_video_info&products_id=288387-1

[12] See krugman.blogs.nytimes.com.

[13] See *The Essence of Money* at digitalcoin.info/The_Essence_of_Money.html. See then www.moneyasdebt.net. For *Money as Debt II: Promises Unleashed*, see also www.ustream.tv/recorded/4155763. For *Money as Debt I*, see, furthermore, www.youtube.com/watch?v=GrO-7awnwGs&feature=player_embedded#!, and then read about the disputed issues in this movie at paulgrignon.netfirms.com/MoneyasDebt/disputed_information.html. Read the Pdf files on www.digitalcoin.info, for example, Paul Grignon (2009). Also Money as Debt III, parts 1 and 4, are posted on YouTube, the two parts fitting together and bypassing the details of Parts 2 and 3, see paulgrignon.netfirms.com/MoneyasDebt/Money_as_Debt_YouTube_links.html

[14] Paul Grignon, www.digitalcoin.info.

[15] The E.F. Schumacher Society was founded in 1980, with the mission to promote the building of strong local economies that link people, land, and community, www.smallisbeautiful.org. See Ernst Friedrich Schumacher (1973). Susan Witt was the Executive Director of the E. F. Schumacher Society, the predecessor of the New Economics Institute, see

neweconomicsinstitute.org, and neweconomicsinstitute.org/content/susan-witt. I thank Margrit Kennedy for introducing me to Susan Witt. Susan Witt helped found the Schumacher Society in 1980 and led the development of its highly regarded publication, library, seminar, and other educational programs while at the same time remaining committed to implementing Schumacher's economic ideas in her home region of the Berkshires. The E. F. Schumacher Society has recently worked with the New Economics Foundation (nef) in London to form the New Economics Institute in North America (neweconomicsinstitute.org). David Boyle is one of the senior staff at the New Economics Foundation (nef, www.neweconomics.org), see also efssociety.blogspot.com/2009/09/david-boyle-at-launch-of-brixton-pound.html. See also David Boyle and Andrew Simms (2009).

[16] The phrase "Small is beautiful" came from Schumacher's teacher Leopold Kohr. See Ernst Friedrich Schumacher (1966), Ernst Friedrich Schumacher (1973), Ernst Friedrich Schumacher (1999).

[17] Organized by the Open Center, www.opencenter.org. The talks by Gus Speth, Neva Goodwin, and Stewart Wallis can be viewed online at vimeo.com/channels/150944.

[18] See, among others, James Gustave Speth (2008), James Gustave Speth (2010).

[19] See, among others, Neva Rockefeller Goodwin (2010).

[20] See www.neweconomics.org.

[21] See www.newdream.org and Juliet B. Schor (2010), Juliet B. Schor (2004), Juliet B. Schor (1998), Juliet B. Schor and Jong Il You (Eds.) 1995, Juliet B. Schor (1992). See also an animation that provides a vision of what a post-consumer society could look like, with people working fewer hours and pursuing re-skilling, homesteading, and small-scale enterprises that can help reduce the overall size and impact of the consumer economy at www.julietschor.org/2011/08/video-new-dream-mini-views-visualizing-a-plenitude-economy. This was originally posted on The Center for a New American Dream's site.

[22] Gar Alperovitz is professor of political economy, founding principal of The Democracy Collaborative, former legislative director in the U.S. House

of Representatives and Senate, special assistant in the Department of State, and president of the Center for Community Economic Development. See Gar Alperovitz (2009), Gar Alperovitz and Lew Daly (2008), Gar Alperovitz (2005), Thad Williamson, David Imbroscio, and Gar Alperovitz (2003). See also Thad Williamson, David Imbroscio, and Gar Alperovitz (2003). I thank Brian Trautman and Margrit Kennedy for having made me aware of Alperovitz' work already earlier.

[23] See neweconomicsinstitute.org.

[24] See Margrit Kennedy (1995), and Declan Kennedy and Margrit Kennedy (1997). See also the Gaia University (www.gaiauniversity.org/english), which "offers a unique approach to higher learning by offering students (called Associates) access to accredited Bachelors and Masters degrees and Graduate Diplomas whilst the Associate is actively engaged in self and planetary transformation. Linking your ideals with self-directed practical experience, you act as a world changer, by working for local and global sustainability and regeneration, justice and peace." Margrit and Declan Kennedy are members in the global advisory board of our Human Dignity and Humiliation Studies network, see www.humiliationstudies.org/whoweare/board.php. I thank Margrit and Declan Kennedy for receiving me in their home in Germany on October 20, 2010.

[25] See "Bernard Lietaer Urges the Growth of New Currency," *Bank Technology News*, July 1, 2004, www.highbeam.com/doc/1G1-118904906.html. See also Bernard A. Lietaer (2001), www.transaction.net/money/book, and www.lietaer.com. Linda and I thank Lynn King for drawing my attention to his 2009 TED talk at www.youtube.com/watch?v=nORI8r3JIyw and his 1997 interview with Sarah Van Gelde, see Bernard A. Lietaer (1997). I thank Margit Kennedy for making me aware of Lietaer's work.

[26] Rodrigue Tremblay (2010). See also his blog www.TheNewAmericanEmpire.com/blog.html which is being followed all around the world. Rodrigue Tremblay is a member in the global advisory board of our Human Dignity and Humiliation Studies network, see www.humiliationstudies.org/whoweare/board.php.

[27] "Economic Bubbles and Financial Crises, Past and Present: The Collapse of Subprime Mortgage-Backed Derivatives, in 2007–09, and How the U.S. Government Became the De Facto Private Government of Large Banks and Bailed them out of their Huge Gambling Debts," by Rodrigue Tremblay, Conference by Dr. Rodrigue Tremblay at the Renaissance Academy at the Florida Gulf Coast University (FGCU), Friday, March 19,2010, www.thenewamericanempire.com/FGCU.htm. See a short version at www.TheNewAmericanEmpire.com/tremblay=1123.

[28] Howard Richards is a member in the global advisory board of our Human Dignity and Humiliation Studies network, see www.humiliationstudies.org/whoweare/board.php.

[29] See howardrichards.org, Howard Richards and Joanna Swanger (2006), Howard Richards (2011a), Howard Richards (2011b), Howard Richards (2010a), Howard Richards (2010c).

[30] We were deeply disturbed when seeing the film *Caught in Micro Debt* on Norwegian state television November 30, 2010. See *Brennpunkt: Fanget i mikrogjeld* on the Norwegian video archive www.nrk.no/nett-tv/klipp/688333/. See also Milford Bateman (2010), and www.odi.org.uk/events/documents/2447-presentation-m-bateman.pdf, David Roodman and Jonathan Morduch (2009), Beatriz Armendariz and Jonathan Morduch (2010), Thomas W. Dichter (2003), Thomas W. Dichter and Malcolm Harper (2007), as well as Christa Wichterich (2000), Christa Wichterich (2011). Wichterich starts her 2011 paper as follows:

India is in the midst of a financial crisis that shows striking similarities to the US subprime crisis, both in its origins and the rescue strategies used. Just as the cheap mortgage granted to low-income households in the USA, the microcredits given to poor women in rural areas worked out as financialisation of everyday live and integration of the women into the global financial market with its return-based logic. This jeopardised the social processes and the very objectives at the heart of the initial non-profit microfinance model. The growth of this sector led to an over-supply of microcredits in villages and in turn to the over-indebtedness of women, the collapse of repayments and a capital shortage of the microfinance institutions. What seems at first sight to be a specifically Indian crisis results in fact from the market rationale of growth, overheating, and crisis, Christa Wichterich (2011).

[31] Howard Richards (2008), p. 2.

[32] See www.ashoka.org/entrepreneurforsociety and www.youtube.com/watch?v=Boh9zKQl5oc&eurl=http%3A%2F%2Fwww %2Eashoka%2Eorg%2Fentrepreneurforsociety&feature=player_embedded. I thank Wilford Welch for this lead.

[33] Douglas Hurd in a BBC World News *HARDtalk* interview with Stephen Sackur, February 23, 2010, news.bbc.co.uk/2/hi/programmes/hardtalk/8530106.stm.

[34] Douglas Hurd (2010).

[35] "Financial Reform: Unfinished Business," by Paul Volcker, *The New York Review of Books*, November 24, 2011, www.nybooks.com/articles/archives/2011/nov/24/financial-reform-unfinished-business/?pagination=false. Former Federal Reserve Chairman Paul Volcker's name is being put forward as suitable Treasury Secretary for U.S. President Barack Obama's administration. And the consumer-credit reformer Elizabeth Warren is of similar caliber. See "An Implausible Populist," by Joe Klein, *Time Magazine*, October 31, 2011, p. 24, www.time.com/time/magazine/article/0,9171,2097392,00.html. See also Ron Suskind (2011).

[36] Raymond Williams, academic, novelist, and critic, in *The Long Revolution*, wrote: "It seems to me that we are living through a long revolution, which our best descriptions only in part interpret. It is a genuine revolution, transforming men and institutions; continually and variously opposed by explicit reaction and by pressure of habitual forms and ideas. Yet it is a difficult revolution to define, and its uneven action is taking place over so long a period that it is almost impossible not to get lost in its exceptionally complicated process," Raymond Williams (1961), p. 10. I thank Tony Webb for making me aware of Williams' discussion. The *Levellers* were members of a political movement during the English Civil Wars which emphasized popular sovereignty, extended suffrage, equality before the law, and religious tolerance, all of which were expressed in the manifesto "Agreement of the People" (issued between 1647 and 1649). See

on the topic of the "unfinished revolution" also Martin Shaw (2000) and David Steele (2007).

[37] "Our Giant Banking Crisis—What to Expect," by Paul R. Krugman and Robin Wells, *The New York Review of Books,* May 13, 2010, www.nybooks.com/articles/archives/2010/apr/19/our-giant-banking-crisis/?page=1, p. 3.

[38] Ibid, p. 3.

[39] Thomas Henry Greco Jr. (1990), p. 44. See also Thomas Henry Greco Jr. (2009) and William Edward Dunkman (1970).

[40] Michael Hartmann (2007). I thank Ulrich Spalthoff for making me aware of Hartmann's work.

[41] David J. Rothkopf (2008).

[42] See the talk on "Change in America" by Alperovitz at www.youtube.com/user/Efssociety#p/u/0/WSGQ-Qf-Qt0. He speaks about the concept of land trusts and the Mondragon design.

[43] Robert Jungk (1977).

[44] See www.youtube.com/watch?v=LLCF7vPanrY&feature=player_embedded#.

[45] Robert Jungk (1977), p. 201.

[46] Robert Jungk (1977), p. 208.

[47] Robert Jungk (1977), p. 209.

[48] Robert Jungk (1977), p. 210.

[49] Richard G. Wilkinson (2005), Richard G. Wilkinson and Kate Pickett (2009b) and Richard G. Wilkinson and Kate Pickett (2009a). See also www.youtube.com/watch?v=zYDzA9hKCNQ. See, furthermore, the Equality Trust at www.equalitytrust.org.uk. I thank Linda Hartling, Finn Tschudi, Robert W. Fuller, Thomas J. Scheff, and Rick Ingrasci for making me aware of Wilkinson's work. See also Finn Tschudi (2008). The topic of systemic emotional mutilation is also central to my book *Emotion and Conflict.* See, furthermore, the work by Seymour M. (Mike) Miller further down.

[50] See www.esop.uio.no.

[51] Michael I. Norton and Dan Ariely (2011). See also Dan Ariely (2008).

[52] Joseph E. Stiglitz, Amartya Kumar Sen, and Jean-Paul Fitoussi (2011).

[53] Martha C. Nussbaum (2011).

[54] Morton Deutsch, Eric C. Marcus, and Sarah Brazaitis (2012), p. 16.

[55] Evelin Gerda Lindner (2000e).

[56] I thank Rodrigue Tremblay for this quote.

[57] Barbara Alice Mann (2000).

[58] I have attempted to differentiate cultural mindsets in Evelin Gerda Lindner (2008b). The novel *North and South* by Elizabeth Gaskell (1855) makes this discussion palpable.

[59] See note 10.

[60] See Ellen E. Schultz (2011). I thank Linda Hartling for making me aware of this book.

[61] A Cambridge University study found a direct link between the amount of money traders make and testosterone levels. See John M. Coates and Joe Herbert (2008).

[62] Sony Kapoor is a former investment banker and derivatives trader in India, the UK, and the United States. See his witness accounts in various media, among others, *"Sony Kapoor: Re-define,"* keynote speech by Sony Kapoor , May 14, 2009, Berlin, Germany, Deutscher Gewerkschaftsbund (DGB)-Kapitalismuskongress, May 14–15, 2009, www.kapitalismuskongress.dgb.de/materialien/paper_referenten/kapoor_ke ynotespeech_kapkon_14.05.09.pdf. See also *Gender, Humiliation, and Global Security*, Evelin Gerda Lindner (2010b), p. 56. See, furthermore, Geraint Anderson (2008). See, furthermore, "Share Traders More Reckless Than Psychopaths, Study Shows," September 26, 2011, www.spiegel.de/international/zeitgeist/0,1518,788462,00.html.

[63] *Inside Job* transcript, September 2010, www.sonyclassics.com/awards-information/insidejob_screenplay.pdf.

[64] William D. Cohan (2011).

[65] "It's Lonely Without the Goldman Net, as Jon Corzine Is Discovering," by Andrew Ross Sorkin, October 31, 2011, dealbook.nytimes.com/2011/10/31/its-lonely-without-the-goldman-net/.

[66] See note 10 in the Introduction.

[67] William Ury (1999), p. XVII. William Ury is a member in the global advisory board of our Human Dignity and Humiliation Studies network, see www.humiliationstudies.org/whoweare/board.php.

[68] See a recent discussion of the inspirations for the French Revolution by Joshua Cohen, director of the Program on Global Justice, Joshua Cohen (2010). I thank Janet Gerson for making me aware of Joshua Cohen's work.

[69] Evelin Gerda Lindner (2010a), p. 152.

[70] Gerald Heard (1963).

[71] Malcolm Hollick (2006) and Malcolm Hollick and Christine Connelly (2011). I thank Sigurd Støren for making me aware of this work. Sigurd Støren, Malcolm Hollick, and Christine Connelly are members in the global advisory board of our Human Dignity and Humiliation Studies network, see www.humiliationstudies.org/whoweare/board.php.

[72] See the list of the Laureates of the Planetary Consciousness Award 1996—2004 on www.clubofbudapest.org/laureats-planet-consc.php.

[73] *Emotional Literacy* is a book by Claude M. Steiner (2003), a psychotherapist who has written extensively about transactional analysis (TA). See also "Strokes, the Stroke Economy and Opening the Heart," by Claude M. Steiner, 1999, www.claudesteiner.com/economy.htm. I thank Janet Gerson of reminding me of Steiner's work and the notion of a *stroke economy*.

[74] See, among others, Michael Orton (2011).

[75] 2010 RSA animate "The Empathic Civilisation," www.youtube.com/watch?v=l7AWnfFRc7g. See also Frans B. M. de Waal (2009).

[76] Carol Gilligan (1982), Martha C. Nussbaum (2011). See also Virginia Held (2006) and Fiona Robinson (1999).

[77] Seyla Benhabib (2011). I thank Mark Singer for making me aware of this book.

[78] Arne Naess (1978), p. 143. Warwick Fox (1992) in his paper "Intellectual Origins of the 'Depth' Theme in the Philosophy of Arne Næss," explains: "The extent to which a person discriminates along a chain of precizations (and, therefore, in a particular direction of interpretation) is a measure of their depth of intention, that is, the depth to which that person can claim to have understood the intended meaning of the expression," Warwick Fox (1992), p. 5. Arne Næss was a pillar of our 2nd Annual Meeting of Human Dignity and Humiliation Studies, September 12–13, 2003, at the Maison des Sciences de l'Homme de l'Homme in Paris, see www.humiliationstudies.org/whoweare/annualmeeting02.php. Arne Næss was a member in the global advisory board of our Human Dignity and Humiliation Studies network, see www.humiliationstudies.org/whoweare/board.php.

[79] Warwick Fox (1990), chapter 4, pp. 81–118, chapter 5, pp. 119–145.

Chapter 3

[1] I thank Yves M. Musoni for making me aware of this proverb.

[2] See www.globalisationforthecommongood.info, and Kamran Mofid (2002), Kamran Mofid (2010), Kamran Mofid (2011a), Kamran Mofid (2011b). Watch the talk he gave on April 19, 2011, to the winners of the Endowment Association MGIMO student grants of the Moscow State Institute of International Relations (MGIMO-University), at their International Conference "Education of My Dream," which was devoted to investments in education and human capital. See www.youtube.com/watch?feature=player_embedded&v=F8irN9kQuFs.

Kamran Mofid is a member in the global advisory board of our Human Dignity and Humiliation Studies network, see www.humiliationstudies.org/whoweare/board.php.

[3] Kamran Mofid in a personal communication, May 20, 2011. Mofid also points at "Vince Cable: People Do not Understand How Bad the Economy Is," by Patrick Wintour, *The Guardian*, May 20, 2011, www.guardian.co.uk/politics/2011/may/20/vince-cable-economy. He then asks whether there is an alternative to the "Washington Consensus," the so-called neo-liberalism? His reply is "Yes, of course." He refers to, for example: "Small is Beautiful: The Wisdom of E.F. Schumacher," at gcgi.info/news/128-small-is-beautiful-the-wisdom-of-ef-schumacher; "Education of My Dream," at gcgi.info/news/129-education-of-my-dream; and "The Correlation Between Ethics and Economics: My Story and Journey" at gcgi.info/news/130-the-correlation-between-ethics-and-economics-my-story-and-journey.

[4] See www.hbs.edu/centennial/conversation/futureofmarketcap.

[5] Ulrich Spalthoff in a personal communication, March 19, 2010.

[6] Federal Reserve Bank of Chicago (1994).

[7] Paul Grignon in a personal communication, March 28, 2010.

[8] Paul Grignon in a personal communication, July 16, 2010.

[9] See www.communitycurrency.org.

[10] William Ury (1999), p. 108.

[11] Evelin Gerda Lindner (2010b).

[12] Latin circum = around, scribere = to write, circumscription means limitation, enclosure, or confinement. The terms territorial or social circumscription address limitations in these respective areas. See, among others, the work by Robert Leonard Carneiro (1988), the "father" of *circumscription theory*.

[13] See John H. Herz (1950).

[14] Riane Tennenhaus Eisler (1987).

[15] See the section "How the 'Art of Domination' Was Perfected in Systems of Ranked Honor" in chapter 5 of *Emotion and Conflict*, Evelin Gerda Lindner (2009a), pp. 60–64.

[16] Evelin Gerda Lindner (2009a), Evelin Gerda Lindner (2006d).

[17] William Ian Miller (1993), p. 175.

[18] See, for example, Evelin Gerda Lindner (2006d), p. 40, where I summarize the many historical events that had a humbling effect on human arrogance: Nicolaus Copernicus (1473–1543) developed the heliocentric model, with its shocking implication that the Earth is not the center of the universe. The church rejected Copernicus' model until the 1800s, when supportive evidence came from Galileo Galilei (1564–1642), Tycho Brahe (1546–1601) and Johannes Kepler (1571–1630). Charles Darwin (1809–1882) added more humbling lessons, claiming that *Homo sapiens* is just another animal, one that is not even in control of himself. Sigmund Freud (1856–1939) taught that dreams and hypnosis indicate life in our souls of which we know almost nothing.

We may not be as "sapiens" [wise, judicious] and certainly not as mighty as we once thought. Ironically, the human toolkit, meant to heighten human standing, ultimately humbles it. Telescopes dissipate the message that haughtiness on the part of *Homo sapiens* is misplaced. It is unsettling for any intelligent being to ponder whether *Homo sapiens* is chosen by God or merely lost in space. Anyone who thinks along such lines, even with the tiniest shred of doubt, is about to lose faith in fixed order. Masters are not sure anymore whether *up* is really their divinely ordained place; underlings question whether they are divinely ordained to remain down. The thought that planet Earth may be better off without humans may not be the most humbling. Perhaps we will die out like the Dinosaurs, and the world will sigh with relief. All aspects of *globalization* that highlight humanity's insignificance and vulnerability humble us, make us more cautious, less prone to *proud subjugation* and *mindless violation*, Evelin Gerda Lindner, 2006b, p. 40.

[19] Evelin Gerda Lindner (2006d), pp. 25–26.

[20] "Being a Legacy Has Its Burden," by Pamela Paul, *The New York Times*, November 4, 2011, www.nytimes.com/2011/11/06/education/edlife/being-

a-legacy-has-its-burden.html?pagewanted=all. I thank Linda Hartling for making me aware of this article.

[21] "The Wrong Inequality," by David Brooks, *The New York Times*, October 31, 2011, www.nytimes.com/2011/11/01/opinion/brooks-the-wrong-inequality.html.

[22] Adam Smith (1776).

[23] Adam Smith (1759).

[24] Diana Kendall (2007), p. 569. See also Max Weber (1904).

[25] Ellen Hodgson Brown (2008).

[26] Glen T. Martin in a personal communication, January 28, 2010. Glen Martin is a member in the global advisory board of our Human Dignity and Humiliation Studies network, see www.humiliationstudies.org/whoweare/board.php.

[27] Ulrich Spalthoff in a personal communication, March 19, 2010:

Replace "profit maximization" by "individual profit maximization"? For me it would not be a problem if some people get rich, as long as this is a side effect of the society in total getting richer... What means "profit"? Profit as such is not hoarding money like Dagobert Duck. For me it means tailoring economic processes in a way that outcome is higher than input, thus leaving a surplus which can be used to advance the society. This is a positive aspect, which should not be ignored. Of course, any society needs legal boundaries to prevent individuals from taking more than appropriate... What is appropriate? One would need a scale which tells: This much is the limit, if an individual takes more, it causes harm to the society. That's a matter of political discussion.

[28] Paul R. Ehrlich and Anne H. Ehrlich (2008). Jared Diamond (2005a).

[29] See, for example, "Unity in Diversity" by Michael Harris Bond, and "Diversity within Unity" by James A. Banks; Michael Harris Bond (1998), and James A. Banks et al. (2001).

[30] Philosophy of mind is the ontology of the mind, of mental events, mental functions, mental properties, consciousness and their relationship to the physical body. The dominant Western metaphysical orientation that

underpinned its expansion during the past centuries was *dualism*. Dualism holds that ultimately there are two kinds of substance. René Descartes' dualistic view of a mind-body dichotomy is perhaps the most widely known expression of dualism. Dualism is to be distinguished from *pluralism*, which claims that ultimately there are many kinds of substances, as well as from *monism*, which is the metaphysical and theological view that all is one, either the mental (*idealism*) or the physical (*materialism* and *physicalism*).

[31] Muneo Jay Yoshikawa (1980), Muneo Jay Yoshikawa (1987).

[32] Nobuji Nakayama (1973), pp. 24–29, as explained by Elizabeth I. Dow (2005). For the notion of *soku*, see, among others, Honda Masaaki (1998).

[33] Judith N. Martin, Thomas K. Nakayama, and Lisa A. Flores (2002).

[34] Linda Hartling in a personal communication, September 18, 2011, in Portland, Oregon, USA. Dot Maver is a member in the global advisory board of our Human Dignity and Humiliation Studies network, see www.humiliationstudies.org/whoweare/board.php.

[35] Paul Grignon in a personal communication, March 30, 2010.

[36] See blog on www.vermontnewsguy.com/corporate-values, posted on March 15, 2010.

[37] See www.thelecturebureau.com/speakers/marjorie_kelly.html, and Marjorie Kelly (2001), Marjorie Kelly (2009). I thank Neva Goodwin for making me aware of Kelly's work.

[38] Linda Hartling in a personal communication, March 11, 2010.

[39] Thomas Hobbes (1651).

[40] John Locke (1689).

[41] *The Social Contract,* Jean-Jacques Rousseau (1762). See also Joshua Cohen (2010).

[42] "Our Crises are not merely Economic but Spiritual: A Time for Awakening," by Kamran Mofid, October 24, 2011, www.gcgi.info/news/136-our-crises-are-not-merely-economic-but-spiritual-a-time-for-awakening. See also Adam Smith (1759), and Adam Smith (1776).

[43] Francis Fukuyama (1992), pp. 163, 182.

[44] Richard G. Wilkinson and Kate Pickett (2009b).

[45] Philip Pettit (1997).

[46] Avishai Margalit (1996).

[47] Jean Baker Miller (1986a). Jean Baker Miller and S. Michael (Mike) Miller are members in the global advisory board of our Human Dignity and Humiliation Studies network, see www.humiliationstudies.org/whoweare/board.php. They received the Lifetime Achievement Award of the Human Dignity and Humiliation Studies network in the 2011 Workshop on Transforming Humiliation and Violent Conflict, see www.humiliationstudies.org/whoweare/annualmeeting18.php.

[48] See note 35 in the Preface.

[49] Evelin Gerda Lindner (2010a), p. 152.

[50] See www.valentinepeaceproject.org.

[51] Ibid.

[52] Martin Luther King Jr. (1963).

[53] Jr. Martin Luther King (2007), p. 26, with an Introduction by Archbishop Desmond Tutu.

[54] Evelin Gerda Lindner (2010b), p. 163.

[55] See note 10 in the Introduction.

[56] The *relational theory model* (RTM) was introduced by anthropologist Alan Page Fiske (1991), and an introduction to the theory, overview of research, and a bibliography is to be found on www.sscnet.ucla.edu/anthro/faculty/fiske/relmodov.htm.

[57] Adapted from Evelin Gerda Lindner (2010a), p. 152.

[58] Robert W. Fuller (2003).

[59] Evelin Gerda Lindner (2007a).

[60] Gar Alperovitz (2005). See also Evelin Gerda Lindner (2007a).

[61] See note 29 in chapter 2.

[62] Rosalie Bertell (2000). See her educational video presentation at video.google.com/videoplay?docid=33751601457371140472#.

[63] See, for example, Lawrence Lessig (2005), or Michel Bauwens (2008).

[64] Parker J. Palmer (2011).

[65] Martin Luther King Jr. (2007), p. 26, with an Introduction by Archbishop Desmond Tutu.

[66] Martin Luther King Jr. (1963).

Chapter 4

[1] Havelock Ellis (1973).

[2] I thank Linda Hartling for sharing documentary material about Ayn Rand with me. See, among others, "Love and Power," the first in a BBC2 documentary series by Adam Curtis, May 23, 2011, www.bbc.co.uk/programmes/b011k45f. It explores the idea that humans have been colonised by the machines they have built. See also a review of the series "All Watched Over by Machines of Loving Grace," by Sam Wollaston, *The Guardian*, Monday 23 May 2011, www.guardian.co.uk/tv-and-radio/2011/may/23/review-machines-of-loving-grace.

[3] *Mind over Money: Can Markets Be Rational when Humans aren't?*, aired April 26, 2010, on PBS, see the transcription on www.pbs.org/wgbh/nova/body/mind-over-money.html. Economist Robert J. Shiller (2000) foresaw the economic crisis.

[4] See note 26 in chapter 1.

⁵ For the ethics of care, see, among others, Carol Gilligan (1982), Martha C. Nussbaum (2011). See also Virginia Held (2006) and Fiona Robinson (1999).

⁶ See www2.ohchr.org/english/law/cescr.htm#art13.

⁷ "Why Do We Think Corporations Are People?," by Jamie Malanowski, August 16, 2011, www.washingtonmonthly.com/ten-miles-square/2011/08/why_do_we_think_corportions_ar031572.php?page=all& print=true. I thank Kathleen Morrow for making me aware of this article.

⁸ Ibid.

⁹ I thank Linda Hartling for sharing documentary material about Brooksley Born with me. See, among others, www.pbs.org/wgbh/pages/frontline/warning/interviews/born.html.

¹⁰ Young Yun Kim and Brent David Ruben (1988).

¹¹ Kichiro Hayashi (2002).

¹² See, for example, Jack Mezirow (1991). See also Beth Fisher-Yoshida (2008). Beth Fisher-Yoshida is now the Academic Director of a Master of Science in Negotiation and Conflict Resolution at the School of Continuing Education at Columbia University, ce.columbia.edu/Negotiation-and-Conflict-Resolution/Beth-Fisher-Yoshida-Biography?context=974. It is a privilege to have her as a member in the global advisory board of our Human Dignity and Humiliation Studies network, together with Adair Linn Nagata, and also Barnett Pearce (whom we just so tragically lost). See www.humiliationstudies.org/whoweare/board.php. See also Beth Fisher-Yoshida, Kathy Dee Geller, and Steven A. Shapiro (Eds.) 2009, and see Adair Linn Nagata (2006), Adair Linn Nagata (2007), Mara Alagic, Adair Linn Nagata, and Glyn M. Rimmington (2009).

¹³ Anna Wierzbicka (1986), p. 584. See also Anna Wierzbicka and Jean Harkins (Eds.) 2001.

¹⁴ Batja Mesquita (2001), p. 223. James A. Russell (1991), p. 440.

¹⁵ See, for example, Edward L. Dreyer (2007).

¹⁶ Tony Fang (2005).

[17] A recent volume of the *American Psychologist* acknowledges this problem. See Roger Walsh (2011) and Fanny M. Cheung, Fons J. R. van de Vijver, and Frederick T. L. Leong (2011). I thank Linda Hartling for making me aware of this volume.

[18] See www.indigenouspsych.org/index.html.

[19] Susanne K. Langer (1953).

[20] Louise Sundararajan (2011).

[21] James Hoopes (Ed.) 1991, see also Louise Sundararajan and Lenhart K. Schubert (2005), Louise Sundararajan et al. (2010).

[22] See www.humiliationstudies.org/whoweare/linda.php, and Linda M. Hartling and Tracy Luchetta (1999). See, furthermore, Linda M. Hartling (2008), Linda M. Hartling (2007), Linda M. Hartling (2005b), Linda M. Hartling (2005a), Linda M. Hartling and Jean Baker Miller (2005), Linda M. Hartling (2003a), Linda M. Hartling (2003b), Linda M. Hartling et al. (2000), Linda M. Hartling and E. Sparks (2000).

[23] See www.ipcc.ch.

[24] Nicholas Stern (2006).

[25] Ulrich Spalthoff in a personal communication, March 19, 2010:

This is true, if one adds: "market economy in times of abundance." Not long ago (when I was a child), market economy was existing but there was no abundance. It was not a consumer economy, but a supply economy having the target to serve the needs of people. Basic needs from today's point of view. I remember my mother saying: "There is a new stuff in store, called yoghurt. Comes from Bulgaria. But no one needs it." That was the time when economy turned from serving needs to creating demand. Today, marketing does not care to serve basic needs. It creates a demand, often by manipulating people psychologically. And scarcity helps always, as we all have in our genes the history, where it was long time a problem just to get basics like scarce food. But these are tricks of Today's marketing, this is not the characteristic of market economy as such.

[26] Gerald McMaster and Clifford E. Trafzer (2004), p. 116.

[27] Ibid.

[28] See note 4 in chapter 1.

[29] Garrett James Hardin (1998).

[30] "Drug Shortages Open Door to Profiteering, Study Says," August 19, 2011, www.fairwarning.org/2011/08/drug-shortages-open-door-to-profiteering-study-says/.

[31] "Diamond: Its Hardness Is Natural; Its Value Is Not," *Scientific American,* September 2009, Special Edition, p. 87.

[32] "Russia Stockpiles Diamonds, Awaiting the Return of Demand," by Andrew E. Kramer, *The New York Times,* May 11, 2009, www.nytimes.com/2009/05/12/business/global/12diamonds.html?_r=1.

[33] Oscar Olivera (2004).

[34] International Tesla Society (1988).

[35] Thomas F. Valone, T. Cullen, and Susan M. Carter (2004).

[36] Ulrich Spalthoff in a personal communication, March 19, 2010:

I do not believe the statements referred to about Nikolas Tesla. Tesla did not work on energy generation, except on generators using fossil fuels as source. All messages from Valone are very debatable. I refer to this report: www.pureenergysystems.com/events/conferences/2004/NewEnergyMovement/6900056_ThomasValone/. There he claims to know various solutions to the fossil energy problem and lists them...

The argument of "artificial scarcity" for me looks like a conspiracy theory. In an economy where competition is everywhere, excessive profits can be made only for limited time and mostly in some regions. It will not take long and someone—ironically usually a greedy corporation—will find ways to introduce another technology which has a little bit less profit, but allows the new entrant to take market share away from established players, as cogently described by Clay Christensen. There are many well documented examples for that. I am sure, there is no way to prevent any alternative technology which is capable to provide a service (a service like energy utilities) at lower cost."

[37] See, for instance, Simon Head (2003).

[38] Richard Carson explains:

A more pessimistic view of the situation is that belief in an autonomous EKC relationship engendered an unfounded optimism that growth by itself would be helpful for the environment. As a result there was a lost decade or more during which environmental economists failed to focus on other potential driving forces behind changes in environmental quality within a country. The debate over the income–pollution relationship allowed us as a profession to take our eye off what really mattered. First, and perhaps foremost, it made it easy to believe that developing countries should be able to ignore their environmental problems until they develop and become wealthier. But we now know that developing countries can take many actions (Dasgupta et al. 2002) to improve their environmental conditions and that those actions can have enormously positive implications for societal welfare. Second, as a group, we largely ignored the role of population and technology, the other two factors in the IPAT equation. Third, for every dozen EKC papers, there might be one that seriously looked at how changes in the regulatory structures and incentive systems in place across different political jurisdictions could be used to improve environmental quality in places where population is increasing, income is improving, and technology from around the world is potentially available. What is needed now and in the future is work identifying factors that can translate some of the increased income from growth into improved environmental quality," Richard T. Carson (2011), p. 20. I thank Karine Nyborg for making me aware of this article.

[39] Susmita Dasgupta et al. (2002).

[40] See also George P. Lakoff (2004), where the author draws on research with environmental and political leaders, and explains how to think in terms of values instead of programs.

[41] For Scheff, bypassed shame—shame that is not acknowledged—is the motor of all violence. Psychologist Helen Block Lewis coined the phrase *humiliated fury*. See Helen Block Lewis (1971); Thomas J. Scheff (2006). Tom Scheff and his wife Suzanne Retzinger are members in the global advisory board of our Human Dignity and Humiliation Studies network, see www.humiliationstudies.org/whoweare/board.php.

[42] Korten 2006, private communication to Riane Eisler, cited in Riane Tennenhaus Eisler (2007), p. 16.

[43] See www.tc.columbia.edu/icccr.

[44] See Frantz Fanon (1952), Frantz Fanon (1961), Frantz Fanon (1963), Frantz Fanon and Charles Lam Markmann (1967), and Paulo Freire (1970b), Paulo Freire (1970a), Paulo Freire (1968).

[45] Nelson Rolihlahla Mandela (1996).

[46] Arne Næss explained his point at the 2nd Annual Meeting of Human Dignity and Humiliation Studies, September 12–13, 2003, Maison des Sciences de l'Homme de l'Homme, Paris, www.humiliationstudies.org/whoweare/annualmeeting02.php. Næss described in rich detail how he would invite convicted murderers from prison into his philosophy class at Oslo University to demonstrate to his students that even murderers deserve and need to be dignified. He was adamant that only individuals who feel secure in their connection to humanity can admit to a crime, feel guilty, and show remorse. As long as people feel less than fully human, there is no reason for them to care that they have hurt others or society. See related work by Howard Zehr (1990), Howard Zehr (2002). Howard Zehr is in the global advisory board of our Human Dignity and Humiliation Studies network, see www.humiliationstudies.org/whoweare/board.php.

[47] Morton Deutsch, Eric C. Marcus, and Sarah Brazaitis (2012), p. 18.

Chapter 5

[1] Ralph Richard Banks (2011).

[2] "Blacks, Whites and the Wedding Gap," book review by Imani Perry, *The New York Times*, September 16, 2011,

www.nytimes.com/2011/09/18/books/review/is-marriage-for-white-people-by-ralph-richard-banks-book-review.html?pagewanted=all.

[3] Ibid.

[4] See, for example, "Is This the End of Catholic Ireland?," www.newstatesman.com/blogs/nelson-jones/2011/07/ireland-vatican-church, or "Ireland Squares Up to the Vatican," at www.independent.co.uk/opinion/commentators/joan-smith/joan-smith-ireland-squares-up-to-the-vatican-2319524.html.

[5] Ibid.

[6] Kamran Mofid in a personal communication, July 24, 2011.

[7] Kathleen Morrow gave permission to share her family memories here on November 18, 2011.

[8] See, for instance, Marcia Angell (2004). See also videos.med.wisc.edu/videos/940.

[9] Rachel L. Gibson (2007).

[10] "Child Food Adverts 'Misleading," *BBC News*, December 14, 2008, news.bbc.co.uk/go/pr/fr/-/2/hi/health/7779438.stm.

[11] See, among others, "Psychiatrists Revise the Book of Human Troubles," by Benedict Carey, *The New York Times*, December 18, 2008, www.nytimes.com/2008/12/18/health/18psych.html. See also Lisa Cosgrove et al. (2006) or Joel Paris (2008). I thank Eugenia Tsao for the last two references..

[12] Eugenia Tsao in a personal communication, July 3, 2009.

[13] See, among others, Richard P. Bentall (2009), Philip Cushman (1995) and Kenneth S. Pope (2007). I thank Linda Hartling for these links.

[14] Takeo Fujiwara and Ichiro Kawachi (2008). I thank Linda Hartling for making me aware of this seminal study.

[15] DeGruy Joy Angela Leary (2005).

[16] Robert E. Lane (2001). According to the World Health Organisation (WHO, www.who.int/), major depression (i.e. severe depressed mood that

is episodic in nature and recurs in 75–80 percent of cases) is now the
leading cause of disability world-wide with a lifetime prevalence of 17
percent in the western world, thus ranking fourth among the ten leading
causes of global disease burden. In addition, the WHO states that
depression is the most common mental disorder leading to suicide and they
project that, at its present rate of growth, depression will be the second
leading contributor to global disease burden by 2020.

[17] Viviane Forrester (1996). Quoted in Evelin Gerda Lindner (2010b), p.
131.

[18] Bruce Alexander, "The Roots of Addiction in Free Market Society,"
Canadian Centre for Policy Alternatives, Toronto, April 12, 2001,
www.cfdp.ca/roots.pdf. See also Gabor Maté (2008). I thank Linda
Hartling for making me aware of this literature.

[19] "The Illusions of Psychiatry," by Marcia Angell, *The New York Review of
Books*, July 14, 2011,
www.nybooks.com/articles/archives/2011/jul/14/illusions-of-
psychiatry/?utm_medium=email&utm_campaign=July+14+2011+issue&ut
m_content=July+14+2011+issue+CID_30e963840ef16c93f2ce73f81f161ef
f&utm_source=Email+marketing+software&utm_term=The+Illusions+of+
Psychiatry. See Irving Kirsch (2009), Robert Whitaker (2010), Daniel J.
Carlat (2011).

[20] Albert Z. Carr (1968).

[21] Philip Delves Broughton (2008), p. 159.

[22] See Lee D. Ross and John T. Jost (1999); and for later work Melvin J.
Lerner (2003).

[23] See, among others, Lee D. Ross and Andrew Ward (1996).

[24] Jørn Bue Olsen wrote his doctoral thesis on the ethics in the
telecommunication business in Norway, a country proud of its
international peace work. Olsen found attitudes such as "i business er alt
tillatt" ("in business, everything is allowed"). Ethics were seen as something
to be thought of when all other "important things" had been taken care of.
See Jørn Bue Olsen (2006).

[25] Jeff Schmidt (2000).

[26] "Brainwashing the Polite, Professional and British Way," by John Pilger, *New Statesman* (UK), June 23, 2011, www.newstatesman.com/society/2011/06/professional-managers-pilger.

[27] See above note.

[28] Raj Patel (2010).

[29] Ulrich Spalthoff in a personal communication, March 19, 2010:

Here I make a distinction between individual values, which cannot be found by the market method, and social values which must emerge somehow from a chaos of competing and controversial individual values. For me, the market method (in somehow idealistic view, I admit) is the way to bring democracy into the economy. Or: Social values must compete on a marketplace. They cannot be defined from the ground up, like one can do with one's personal values based on rigid ethical motives. That is why I am not skeptical against letting a market define the value of something. Of course, the value found this way may not be in line with my personal preference. This is unavoidable and it is ok.

[30] Kamran Mofid in a personal communication, July 14, 2011.

[31] Richard G. Wilkinson and Kate Pickett (2009b).

[32] See onpoint.wbur.org/2011/01/27/inequality-societies#.

[33] Ibid.

[34] "The Charitable-Giving Divide," by Judit Warner, *The New York Times*, August 20, 2010, www.nytimes.com/2010/08/22/magazine/22FOB-wwln-t.html.

[35] "The Empathy Ceiling: The Rich Are Different—And Not In a Good Way, Studies Suggest: The 'Haves' show less empathy than 'Have-nots,'" by Brian Alexander, published on Wednesday, August 10, 2011, at www.commondreams.org/headline/2011/08/10-7. I thank Salman Türken for making me aware of this article.

[36] See psychology.uchicago.edu/people/faculty/cacioppo/index.shtml, and John T. Cacioppo and William Patrick (2008). I thank Linda Hartling for introducing me to Cacioppo's work.

[37] See psychology.uchicago.edu/people/faculty/cacioppo/index.shtml..

[38] Paul R. Diesing (1962). I thank Morton Deutsch for reminding me of the work by Paul Diesing.

[39] Robert V. Bartlett (1986). See also Walter F. Baber and Robert V. Bartlett (2009).

[40] Morton Deutsch, Eric C. Marcus, and Sarah Brazaitis (2012), pp. 15–16. See also Evelin Gerda Lindner (2012).

[41] Morton Deutsch, Eric C. Marcus, and Sarah Brazaitis (2012), p. 16. See also Evelin Gerda Lindner (2012).

[42] "Towards an Education Worth Believing In: Can Business Education and the Business Schools Advance Sustainability and the Common Good?," written by Kamran Mofid, August 29, 2011, at www.gcgi.info/news/133-towards-an-education-worth-believing-in.

Chapter 6

[1] Samuel L. Gaertner and John F. Dovidio (1999).

[2] John H. Herz (1950).

[3] See also Robert Jervis, Richard Ned Lebow, and Janice Gross Stein (1985) and Richard K. Betts (Ed.) 2005. The security dilemma is defined as one state requiring the insecurity of another. See Jack Snyder (1985) and Jack Snyder and Barbara Walters (Eds.) 1999, while a state-induced security dilemma is defined by Alan Collins (2004).

[4] Riane Riane Tennenhaus Eisler (1987). See her most recent book Riane Tennenhaus Eisler (2007). Riane Eisler is a member in the global advisory board of our Human Dignity and Humiliation Studies network, see www.humiliationstudies.org/whoweare/board.php.

[5] See the section "How the 'Art of Domination' Was Perfected in Systems of Ranked Honor" in chapter 5 of *Emotion and Conflict*, Evelin Gerda Lindner (2009a), pp. 60–64.

[6] Norbert Elias (1982).

[7] Kathleen Morrow in a personal communication, November 18, 2011.

[8] See more on the notion of misrecognition in chapter 8 of my book *Emotion and Conflict* (2009), pp. 129–137.

[9] See, for example, Alexandar R. Thomas (1998), or Peter Dreier (2004). I thank Linda Hartling for making me aware of these articles.

[10] „Der Denkautomat," *Der Spiegel*, July 5, 2010, p. 99:

His favorite form of thought is that of paradox, with the help of his psychoanalytic tools he tries to prove how liberal democracy is manipulating the people. One of his famous observations of everyday life concerns the close-door button in elevators. He has found out that they are placebos. The doors close not a second faster if you press the button. But they also do not have to; it is enough that the person who pushes the button has the illusion that she could influence something: This is precisely the way, says Žižek, functions the political illusion-making machine which is called Western democracy." Original text. „Seine liebste Denkform ist die des Paradoxons, mit Hilfe seines psychoanalytischen Rüstzeugs versucht er nachzuweisen, wie die liberale Demokratie die Menschen manipuliert. Eine seiner berühmten Alltagsbeobachtungen dazu betrifft die Tür-zu-Knöpfe in Fahrstühlen. Er hat herausgefunden, dass sie Placebos sind. Die Türen schließen keine Sekunde schneller, wenn man den Knopf drückt, aber das müssen sie auch nicht. Es reicht, dass der Drückende die Illusion hat, er könnte etwas beeinflussen: Genauso, sagt Žižek, funktioniere auch die politische Illusionsmaschine, die sich westliche Demokratie nennt.

[11] Richard Sennett (1998).

[12] Jean M. Twenge (2006), Jean M. Twenge et al. (2008), Jean M. Twenge and W. Keith Campbell (2009).

[13] See Daniel J. Lair, Katie Sullivan, and George Cheney (2005). I discussed this topic in January 29, 2007, in Harrania, near Cairo, Egypt, with Sophie Wissa-Wassef, who makes a point to protect her artists'

creativity by not disclosing to them whether their art sells or not. See www.humiliationstudies.org/intervention/art.php#ramseswissawassef or www.wissa-wassef-arts.com/intro.htm. See also Douglas Rushkoff (2009). I thank Keith Grennan for this link.

[14] "When Narcissism Becomes Pathological," by Adrian Tempany, *Financial Times,* September 4, 2010, www.ft.com/intl/cms/s/2/5ff67be2-b636-11df-a784-00144feabdc0.html#axzz1eCNfKSXx.

[15] Hans-Jürgen Classen in a personal communication, September 10, 2010. I thank Sayaka Funada-Classen and her husband Hans-Jürgen Classen very much for welcoming me in their Tokyo home. Sayaka Funada-Classen is a member in our Human Dignity and Humiliation Studies network.

[16] See note 14 earlier in this chapter.

[17] "Share Traders More Reckless Than Psychopaths, Study Shows," *Der Spiegel,* September 26, 2011, www.spiegel.de/international/zeitgeist/0,1518,788462,00.html.

[18] Paul R. Krugman (2007), United Nations Department of Economic and Social Affairs (2005).

[19] See note 16 in chapter 5.

[20] I thank Kathleen Morrow for including this reflection.

[21] "Here we are, we're supposed to be great, prosperous and successful countries and people are unhappy, not because they're badly treated, not because they're badly managed, but because they're actually not using their lives in the way that I think is fully productive. And I call this a sort of 'corporate sin,'" Charles Handy and Stephen Bernhut (2004), p. 4.

[22] See also the Easterlin Paradox, Richard A. Easterlin et al. (2010), Richard A. Easterlin (2004), Richard A. Easterlin (Ed.) 2002, Richard A. Easterlin (1974).

[23] This information has already found its way into the public eye, see, for instance, "On the Happy Trail," by Mark Honigsbaum, *The Observer,* April 4, 2004, www.guardian.co.uk/society/2004/apr/04/mentalhealth.observermagazine.

[24] See, among others, Dimitris Ballas and Danny Dorling (2007), or David G. Blanchflower and Andrew J. Oswald (2005).

[25] Betsey Stevenson and Justin Wolfers (2009).

[26] "What Can the Ancient Greeks Do for Us?," by Charlotte Higgins, *The Guardian*, August 1, 2011, www.guardian.co.uk/world/2011/aug/01/what-can-ancient-greeks. I thank Takis Ioannides for making me aware of this article.

[27] Immanuel Kant (1785).

[28] Martin Buber (1923).

[29] See Lee D. Ross and John T. Jost (1999); and for later work Melvin J. Lerner (2003). See also Lee D. Ross and Andrew Ward (1996).

[30] See Melvin J. Lerner (1980), and for his later work Melvin J. Lerner (2003).

[31] Lee D. Ross and John T. Jost (1999).

[32] Oris Brafman and Rom Brafman (2008).

[33] Thomas Frank (2004b).

[34] The movie *Home* was released on June 5, 2009. See www.home-2009.com/us/index.html, www.goodplanet.org/en, and www.youtube.com/homeproject, 2009.

[35] Ulrich Spalthoff in a personal communication, March 19, 2010:

I like the notion of stakeholder value. This is the concept behind the Total Quality Management, practices by the methods of the European Foundation for Quality Management (EFQM, I am a certified EFQM assessor). 10 to 15 years ago stakeholder value was recognized a lot, afterwards the shareholder value became more fashionable. I am happy to see this fashion being over now.

[36] I thank Dorothy J. Maver for this coinage.

[37] I thank Linda Hartling for this coinage.

[38] James Davies et al. (2006).

[39] Thomas G. Fuechtmann (1989).

[40] See
actionext.com/names_i/israel_kamakawiwo_ole_lyrics/hawaii_78.html.

Chapter 7

[1] Vincent Lombardi in a personal message, August 1, 2011.

[2] "Roberto Saviano at Zuccotti Park!," November 19, 2011,
occupywallst.org/forum/roberto-saviano-at-zuccotti-park/. For John Perkins
(2004), see an interview by Mike McCormick of Talking Stick TV in
Seattle, at www.youtube.com/watch?v=yTbdnNgqfs8. See, furthermore, a
short video cartoon narrated by John Perkins about the IMF, at
www.youtube.com/watch?v=n7Fzm1hEiDQ.

[3] "Financial Crisis 'like a Tsunami,'" *BBC NEWS*, October 10, 2008,
news.bbc.co.uk/go/pr/fr/-/2/hi/business/7687101.stm.

[4] David J. Rothkopf (2008).

[5] Evelin Gerda Lindner (2000e), pp. 150–151.

[6] Philip Delves Broughton (2008), p. 159.

[7] See neweconomicsinstitute.org.

[8] Chapin 2004, Abstract. I thank Mariana Vergara for making me aware of
this article.

[9] See note 17 in the Introduction.

[10] See note 5 in the Preface.

[11] See an introduction to *College, Inc.* at
www.pbs.org/wgbh/pages/frontline/collegeinc/etc/synopsis.html. I thank
Linda Hartling for showing me this documentary.

[12] See www.pbs.org/wgbh/pages/frontline/collegeinc/etc/synopsis.html.. The documentary features Michael Clifford, Jack Welch, John Sperling, the Apollo group, and Campus Crusade for Christ International.

[13] Harriet A. Washington (2007), Harriet A. Washington (2011).

[14] "Gene Patenting Produces Profits, Not Cures," by Harriet A. Washington, *Huffington Post*, July 14, 2010, www.huffingtonpost.com/harriet-a-washington/gene-patenting-produces-p_b_645862.html.

[15] See note 21 in chapter 2.

[16] See, among others, Harry Brod (1997). See also Peter Collier and David Horowitz (Eds.) 1989.

[17] Mary Roach (2008). See also the life work of feminist, sociologist and political activist Barbara Ehrenreich.

[18] Evelin Gerda Lindner (2010b), p. 105.

[19] Graham Greene (1939).

Chapter 8

[1] Adam Smith (1759), Adam Smith (1776).

[2] See, among others, Nanette S. Levinson (2004).

[3] Jean Baker Miller (2006). See her first, seminal book, Jean Baker Miller (1976).

[4] *Choice* is a RSA animate, where professor Renata Salecl explores the paralyzing anxiety and dissatisfaction surrounding limitless choice. Does the freedom to be the architects of our own lives actually hinder rather than help us? Does our preoccupation with choosing and consuming actually obstruct social change? See www.youtube.com/watch?v=1bqMY82xzWo

and the RSA's free public events program www.thersa.org/events. See also Renata Salecl (2004).

[5] See Frithjof Bergmann and John Ramsburgh (1999). See also Frithjof Bergmann (1977). I thank Juliet B. Schor for making me aware of Bergmann's work.

[6] Kathleen Morrow in a personal communication, November 18, 2011.

[7] See more discussion in chapter 8 of my book *Emotion and Conflict* (2009), pp. 124–137.

[8] Peter T. Coleman (2003), p. 17. The Human Dignity and Humiliation Studies network is honored to have Peter Coleman on its global advisory board, together with Morton Deutsch, Claudia Cohen, Beth Fisher-Yoshida and Andrea Bartoli, and all other, equally esteemed members of our global advisory board. See humiliationstudies.org/whoweare/board.php.

[9] See, for example, Roger Fisher, William Ury, and Bruce Patton (1991). We learn there that we need to focus on *interest* and not on *position* to attain an optimal outcome. If two people fight over an orange, for example, sharing it equally would solve the conflict, however, not optimally. The optimal solution would be to ask more detailed questions and consider, for example, that one person wishes to use the skin of the orange for a cake while the other wants to extract the juice from the fruit meat. As a result, the outcome would be that both have 100 percent of their interest served, not just 50 percent of their initial positions. Not that such a positive outfall can be guaranteed—sometimes a situation simply does not entail the potential for win-win solutions—but by not searching for such potential win-win solutions, those solutions are overlooked and untapped.

[10] James Edward Jones (2006). We have the privilege of having James Jones in the global advisory board, of our Human Dignity and Humiliation Studies network, see www.humiliationstudies.org/whoweare/board.php.

[11] See my doctoral dissertation Evelin Gerda Lindner (2000e).

[12] See a discussion in Evelin Gerda Lindner (2006c).

[13] See a discussion in Evelin Gerda Lindner (2006c).

[14] Evelin Gerda Lindner (2006d).

[15] On December 9, 1992, *Operation Restore Hope* had been launched, by the United States of America, as a response to the failure of the first United Nations operation *UNOSOM*. However, *Operation Restore Hope* failed, as did *UNOSOM II*.

[16] Patrick J. O'Halloran (1995).

[17] I discuss this point in Evelin Gerda Lindner (2006d), in the section entitled "Why Do They Hate Us?," pp. 98–105.

[18] Evelin Gerda Lindner (2006d), pp. 100–105.

[19] See, for example, the essay "British Oppression: The Cause of the American Revolution?" from February 3, 2004, for 10th grade High School students posted on www.cheathouse.com/essay/essay_view.php?p_essay_id=29116:

The American Revolution was costly and bloody war that granted the Americans the independence for which they fought. This 8-year-long revolutionary war from 1775 to 1783 is considered one of the greatest revolutions of all time in that the Americans had defeated the most powerful nation in the world at the time, Great Britain. The American Revolution is a critical event in the history of the United States and has been explored and evaluated by numerous historians of the 20th century. Whether or not the revolution is justifiable by the American colonists is a long, debatable subject. Some historians assume that the American Revolution is a result of colonial selfishness and ideology...

[20] Evelin Gerda Lindner (2006d), pp. 94–95.

[21] "Romney, Obama, and Socialism," by Stanley Kurtz, September 23, 2011, www.nationalreview.com/corner/278158/romney-obama-and-socialism-stanley-kurtz.

[22] "The Busts Keep Getting Bigger: Why?" by Paul Krugman and Robin Wells, *The New York Review of Books*, July 14, 2011, www.nybooks.com/articles/archives/2011/jul/14/busts-keep-getting-bigger-why/?utm_medium=email&utm_campaign=July+14+2011+issue&utm_co ntent=July+14+2011+issue+CID_30e963840ef16c93f2ce73f81f161eff&ut m_source=Email+marketing+software&utm_term=The+Busts+Keep+Getti ng+Bigger+Why See Jeffrey Madrick (2011), Jeffrey Madrick (2009).

²³ Bertram Wyatt-Brown (2005), p. 2.

²⁴ See www.humiliationstudies.org/whoweare/annualmeetings.php. We have the privilege of having Anne and Bertram Wyatt-Brown as members in the global advisory board of the Human Dignity and Humiliation Studies network, see www.humiliationstudies.org/whoweare/board.php.

²⁵ Richard E. Nisbett and Dov Cohen (1996). We have the privilege of having Dov Cohen as member in the global advisory board of the Human Dignity and Humiliation Studies network, see www.humiliationstudies.org/whoweare/board.php.

²⁶ David Hackett Fischer (1989), p. 843.

²⁷ Henry Kissinger said, "They want to humiliate us and we have to humiliate them," see "America Defeated: How Terrorists Turned a Superpower's Strengths Against Itself," by Mark Danner, *Alternet,* March 26, 2008, www.alternet.org/story/80547, p. 3. This essay was adapted from an address first delivered in February at the Tenth Asia Security Conference at the Institute for Security and Defense Analysis in New Delhi, Mark Danner (2008)

²⁸ Jean V. Hardisty (1999). I thank Linda Hartling for drawing my attention to Hardisty's work.

²⁹ Named after the American industrial engineer Frederick Winslow Taylor (1856–1915) who laid down the fundamental principles of large-scale manufacturing through assembly-line factories. See Frederick Winslow Taylor (1911).

³⁰ See Thomas Parke Hughes (2004). This rivalry found many expressions. For example, the Socialist Unity Party of Germany (SED) of the German Democratic Republic, believed that communism would only be able to keep up with the capitalist West, if it entertained its citizens with what Romans called *panem et circenses*, or "bread and circuses" (or "bread and games"). Interestingly, East Germans continue to prefer this kind of entertainment also after the unification of Germany. See Werner Früh and Hans-Jörg Stiehler (2002).

[31] United Nations Secretary General Ban Ki-Moon addressed the 63rd session of the General Assembly on September 23, 2008. See www.un.org/ga/63/generaldebate/sg.shtml.

[32] On The Daily Show with Jon Stewart, November 8, 2011, seen by Kathleen Morrow.

[33] David Anthony King in a BBC World News *HARDtalk* interview with Stephen Sackur, September 30, 2009, news.bbc.co.uk/go/pr/fr/-/2/hi/programmes/hardtalk/8282169.stm.

[34] See www.humiliationstudies.org/publications./journal.php.

[35] "Dignity and Humiliation," by Morton Deutsch, Morton Deutsch, November 22, 2006, www.humiliationstudies.org/publications./journal.php.

[36] Robert Jervis (2006), 641, Abstract.

[37] Jervis suggests going back fifty years, revisiting the typology introduced by M. Brewster Smith, Jerome S. Bruner, and Robert W. White (1956).

[38] Leon Festinger (1957).

[39] „Hitler und das Geld: Der "Führer": Multimillionär und Steuerbetrüger," November 13, 2011, history.zdf.de/ZDFde/inhalt/10/0,1872,8366538,00.html.

[40] See neweconomicsinstitute.org.

[41] Evelin Gerda Lindner (2008b).

[42] Elizabeth Gaskell (1855).

[43] Evelin Gerda Lindner (2010a).

[44] Avishai Margalit (1996).

[45] T. Irene Sanders (1998).

[46] Yves M. Musoni, in a personal note on November 17, 2011, See also Yves M. Musoni (2003).

[47] The meeting took place on November 21, 2011, at Columbia University in New York City. See www.fortunesociety.net for the project Claudia

works with. I thank Claudia for making me aware of the work of Shadd
Maruna and Hans Toch (2001) and his theory of change, see also
www.shaddmaruna.info/. Claudia Cohen is a member in the global
advisory board of our Human Dignity and Humiliation Studies network,
see www.humiliationstudies.org/whoweare/board.php.

[48] We recently organized our 17th annual conference in New Zealand.
Carmen Hetaraka shared his indigenous Maori knowledge. See
www.humiliationstudies.org/whoweare/annualmeeting17.php.

[49] See, among others, Maggie O'Neill (2009), Maggie O'Neill (2010).

[50] See www.humiliationstudies.org/whoweare/board.php.

Chapter 9

[1] Helen Keller, *The Home Magazine*, April 1935.

[2] "Defense at the Center: Who Is Really Listening About the Bullying?,"
by Carol Smaldino, *Huffington Post*, November 11, 2011,
www.huffingtonpost.com/carol-smaldino/defense-at-the-center-
who_b_1085375.html. I thank Yves M. Musoni for connecting his work so
impressively with Carol's work.

[3] Carol Smaldino is an avid writer for *Huffington Post*. In Jungian
psychology, the shadow or "shadow aspect" is an important part of the
unconscious mind.

[4] Yves M. Musoni (2003).

[5] "Rwanda: Will the truce hold?" by Philip Gourevitch, November 07,
2009, www.guardian.co.uk/world/2009/nov/08/rwanda-gacaca-genocide-
courts-gourevitch.

[6] Yves M. Musoni in a personal communication, November 12, 2011.
See also ref. 5 above.

[7] See Sarah Jane Meharg (2006).

[8] Concepts such as *méconnaissance* (misrecognition) and naturalization were used by Roland Barthes, Pierre Bourdieu, and Michel Foucault (among others). They address how power structures use the concealed nature of habitus to manipulate not just overtly but covertly and stealthily, making it much more difficult to rid oneself of these manipulations.

[9] Johan Galtung (1996), p. 199.

[10] Evelin Gerda Lindner (2009a), chapters 5 and 8.

[11] "Do Happier People Work Harder?," by Teresa Amabile and Steven Kramer, *The New York Times*, September 3, 2011, at www.nytimes.com/2011/09/04/opinion/sunday/do-happier-people-work-harder.html.

[12] See note 30 in chapter 2.

[13] Emmanuel Lévinas (1961).

[14] Viktor Emil Frankl (1963). Frankl played a central role for my life, see Evelin Gerda Lindner (2009c).

[15] Bruno S. Frey (Ed.) 2008, Bruno S. Frey and Alois Stutzer (Eds.) 2007.

[16] Max Scheler (1923).

[17] Richard A. Easterlin et al. (2010), Richard A. Easterlin (2004), Richard A. Easterlin (Ed.) 2002, Richard A. Easterlin (1974).

[18] Charles Eisenstein (2010), see also Charles Eisenstein (2007) and Charles Eisenstein (2008).

[19] Seymour M. (Mike) Miller in a personal message, October 26, 2011. See Seymour M. Miller and Pamela A. Roby (1970).

[20] Seymour M. Miller and Anthony J. Savoie (2002), Seymour M. Miller (2011).

[21] Seymour M. Miller (2011), pp. 18–21.

[22] Michel Foucault (1979), Michel Foucault (1991).

[23] See the section "How the 'Art of Domination' Was Perfected in Systems of Ranked Honor" in chapter 5 of *Emotion and Conflict*, Evelin Gerda Lindner (2009a), pp. 60–64.

[24] Walter Lippmann (1922).

[25] Edward Bernays (1928).

[26] See also Eric Clark (1988).

[27] Thorstein Bunde Veblen (1899).

[28] Evelin Gerda Lindner (2009a), p. 133.

[29] Ervin Staub (1989).

[30] I analyze this dynamic, among others, in my doctoral dissertation, and in my work on subaltern genocide, see Evelin Gerda Lindner (2009b), Evelin Gerda Lindner (2000e).

[31] See www.thenewamericanempire.com/tremblay=1123.

[32] See, for example, P. D. Broughton, *Ahead of the Curve: Two Years at Harvard Business School* (New York: Penguin Press, 2008

[33] Frantz Fanon (1963), Frantz Fanon (1986).

[34] Evelin Gerda Lindner (2010b), p. xv.

[35] See the full text, among others, on www.humiliationstudies.org/intervention/declarations.php#links and www.humiliationstudies.org/news/?p=6437.

[36] Michael Britton (2011), p. 6. Michael Britton is a member of the core leadership group of the Human Dignity and Humiliation Studies network, together with, among others, Linda Hartling, Ulrich Spalthoff, and Evelin Lindner.

[37] Elazar Barkan (2000). I had the privilege of listening to Elazar Barkan during the "International Symposium on Restorative Justice, Reconciliation and Peacebuilding," at the New York University School of Law, November 11–12, 2011, www.iilj.org/RJRP/about.asp.

[38] "Vatican Admits Galileo Was Right," *New Scientist,* November 7, 1992, www.newscientist.com/article/mg13618460.600-vatican-admits-galileo-was-right.html.

[39] On Wednesday, September 30, 2009, in Washington, Chairman Edolphus "Ed" Towns (D-NY) reconvened the House Oversight and Government Reform Committee's hearing to examine what role inaccurate credit ratings played in the current financial crisis, and what regulatory changes need to be implemented to prevent a future collapse. Ilya Eric Kolchinsky, Former Managing Director, Moody's Investors Service, appeared and spoke about the practices of credit rating agencies such as Standard & Poor's, Moody's or Fitch Ratings.

[40] "Bankers 'Need to Join Real World', Minister Says" *BBC News,* December 3, 2009, news.bbc.co.uk/2/hi/8392791.stm.

[41] Judith E. Glaser (2005), see also Judith E. Glaser (2006). Judith Glaser is a member of the global advisory board of the Human Dignity and Humiliation Studies network, see www.humiliationstudies.org/whoweare/board.php.

[42] "Best Books of 2010: You Are What you Think—The Human Mind," by Judith E. Glaser, *Strategy + Business,* Issue 61, November 23, 2010, www.strategy-business.com/article/10409f?gko=8311b&cid=enews20101123. The five books that Judith reviews are Michael J. Mauboussin (2006), Michael J. Mauboussin (2009), Chip Heath and Dan Heath (2010), Paul Sullivan (2010), Daniel H. Pink (2009).

[43] Judith E. Glaser (2010), p. 101.

[44] James Bernard Quilligan (2002). See www.un.org/ga/econcrisissummit/background.shtml.

[45] Miguel d'Escoto Brockmann (2009).

[46] Anthony Giddens (2000), p. 20.

[47] Seymour M. Miller (2011).

[48] Seymour M. Miller (2011), p. 53.

[49] Martin Luther King, Jr., Speech in St. Louis, Missouri, March 22, 1964.

Chapter 10

[1] Sony Kapoor (2009). See also his blog Re-Define, at www.re-define.org/blogs/sonykapoor. See, furthermore, Anne T. (2009).

[2] See www.pbs.org/wgbh/pages/frontline/warning/interviews/born.html. Former Federal Reserve Chairman Paul Volcker's name is being put forward as suitable Treasury Secretary for U.S. President Barack Obama's administration. And the consumer-credit reformer Elizabeth Warren is of similar caliber. See "An Implausible Populist," by Joe Klein, *Time Magazine*, October 31, 2011, p. 24, www.time.com/time/magazine/article/0,9171,2097392,00.html. See also Ron Suskind (2011).

[3] Stephen Spratt et al. (2009).

[4] Vandana Shiva advises American activists in "Understanding the Corporate Takeover," with Laura Flanders, published on April 30, 2011, by GRITtv, at www.commondreams.org/video/2011/04/30. See also Maude Barlow et al. (2011b), Maude Barlow et al. (2011a), Vandana Shiva (2006), Vandana Shiva (1997).

[5] Vandana Shiva advises American activists in "Understanding the Corporate Takeover," with Laura Flanders, published on April 30, 2011, by GRITtv, at www.commondreams.org/video/2011/04/30.

[6] Vandana Shiva's message is that apartheid was "the human relations version of classical physics," and that we have to expand our understanding, just as we have understood that classical physics, while valid for macroscopic systems and "normal" timeframes, don't work for atomic dimensions and ultra short timeframes.

[7] Amartya Kumar Sen and Jean Drèze (1995). p. 202.

[8] "Chilean Economist Manfred Max-Neef on Barefoot Economics, Poverty and Why The U.S. is Becoming an 'Underdeveloping Nation'," interviewed by Amy Goodman, *Democracy Now*, September 22, 2010, democracynow.org/2010/9/22/chilean_economist_manfred_max_neef_us, the transcript, November 26, 2010, democracynow.org/2010/11/26/chilean_economist_manfred_max_neef_on . I thank Linda Hartling for making me aware of this interview. See also "The Myth of 'American exceptionalism' Implodes," by Richard D. Wolff, January 18, 2011, guardian.co.uk/commentisfree/cifamerica/2011/jan/17/economics-globalre.

[9] See previous note.

[10] Richard B. Norgaard (2011).

[11] Ibid.

[12] Stéphane Hessel (2010). See also www.independent.co.uk/news/world/europe/the-little-red-book-that-swept-france-2174676.html#.

[13] „Die Weiße Rose," Referat von Jörg Hartnagel, gehalten am 16.03.2005 im Lise-Meitner-Gymnasium Crailsheim vor Schülern des „Lycée Notre Dame" aus Pamiers, winfriedschley.net/schulaustausch05/weisserose.htm. German original:

Am 8. und 9. Februar kam es zu einem Treffen in München—Falk Harnack spricht nach dem Krieg von einer „Münchener Konferenz," bei der nach seinem Bericht neben ihm Prof. Huber, Alexander Schmorell, Hans Scholl, Willi Graf und Sophie Scholl zugegen waren. Sie beschlossen, drei Thesen zu propagieren:

Der Krieg ist für Deutschland verloren.

Hitler und seine Clique setzen den Krieg nur für ihre persönliche Sicherheit fort und sind dafür bereit, das deutsche Volk zu opfern.

Alle oppositionellen Kräfte sind zu mobilisieren, um den Krieg so schnell wie möglich zu beenden.

[14] See www.newdream.org and Juliet B. Schor (2010), Juliet B. Schor (2004), Juliet B. Schor (1998), Juliet B. Schor and Jong Il You (Eds.) 1995,

Juliet B. Schor (1992). See also an animation that provides a vision of what a post-consumer society could look like, with people working fewer hours and pursuing re-skilling, homesteading, and small-scale enterprises that can help reduce the overall size and impact of the consumer economy. See www.julietschor.org/2011/08/video-new-dream-mini-views-visualizing-a-plenitude-economy. This was originally posted on The Center for a New American Dream's site.

[15] See neweconomicsinstitute.org.

[16] William McDonough and Michael Braungart (2002).

[17] See www.julietschor.org/the-book/synopsis, and Juliet B. Schor (2010), Juliet B. Schor (2004), Juliet B. Schor (1998), Juliet B. Schor and Jong Il You (Eds.) 1995, Juliet B. Schor (1992).

[18] Charles Eisenstein (2010).

[19] Ibid.

[20] Ibid.

[21] See, among others, Genevieve Vaughan (1997), Genevieve Vaughan (Ed.) 2007, see also Jeanette Armstrong (2007).

[22] Ibid.

[23] Ibid.

[24] Charles Eisenstein (2008).

[25] Ibid.

[26] See neweconomicsinstitute.org.

[27] See the talk on "Change in America" by Alperovitz at www.youtube.com/user/Efssociety#p/u/0/WSGQ-Qf-Qt0. He speaks about the concept of land trusts and the Mondragon design.

[28] Gar Alperovitz (2009).

[29] Howard Richards (2011a), p. 20.

[30] Howard Richards (2011a), p. 17.

[31] Howard Richards (2010c).

[32] Howard Richards in a personal communication, July 23, 2010, italics added by Lindner.

[33] See note 9 in chapter 8.

[34] *Decision 25/4* followed a recommendation from informal consultations of the General Assembly of UNEP on the institutional framework for United Nations environment work, dated February 10, 2009. In these informal consultations , hope was expressed that ministers of environment would "find a political compromise and entrust their delegations in New York with pragmatic, creative and constructive proposals, which allow improving the current system," United Nations Environment Programme (UNEP)(2009), p. 2.

[35] United Nations Environment Programme (UNEP)(2009), p. 2.

[36] Avishai Margalit (1996).

[37] See note 10 in the introduction.

[38] Paul H. Ray and Sherry Ruth Anderson (2000). Ray and Anderson identify three main cultural tendencies: firstly *moderns* (endorsing the "realist" worldview of *Time Magazine,* the *Wall Street Journal,* big government, big business, big media, or past socialist, communist, and fascist movements); second, the first countermovement against moderns, the *traditionals* (the religious right and rural populations); and third, the most recent countermovement, the *cultural creatives* (valuing strong ecological sustainability for the planet, liberal on women's issues, personal growth, authenticity, and anti–big business). In the United States, traditionals comprise about 24–26 percent of the adult population (approximately 48 million people), moderns about 47–49 percent (approximately 95 million) and cultural creatives are about 26–28 percent (approximately 50 million). In the European Union, the cultural creatives are about 30–35 percent of the adult population.

[39] Roger Fisher, William Ury, and Bruce Patton (1991).

[40] Avishai Margalit (1996).

[41] I thank Glen T. Martin for relating the phrase "nonviolent revolutionary" to me.

[42] As to the concept of *nudging*, see, for example, Richard Thaler and Cass Sunstein (2008).

[43] A flyer distributed at Zuccotti Park in New York City by the Occupy Wall Street movement, on November 16, 2011, transcribed by the author.

[44] Daniel J. Christie (2006), Abstract. Dan Christie is a member in the global advisory board of our Human Dignity and Humiliation Studies network, see humiliationstudies.org/whoweare/board.php.

[45] Ibid.

[46] See, for example, Peter M. Senge (1990).

[47] See, for example, Claus Otto Scharmer (2007).

[48] Jack A. Goldstone and Jay Ulfelder (2005), p. 9. Jack Goldstone is a member in the global advisory board of our Human Dignity and Humiliation Studies network, together with Monty Marshall, who brought Jack to us, see www.humiliationstudies.org/whoweare/board.php.

[49] Ibid., pp. 19–20.

[50] Ibid., p. 20.

[51] Morton Deutsch has been a pioneer in behavioral game theory research that uses variations of the prisoner's dilemma game, see Morton Deutsch (1958), Morton Deutsch (1960a), Morton Deutsch (1960b), Morton Deutsch (1962).

[52] See Varda Liberman, Steven M. Samuels, and Lee D. Ross (2004). I thank Lee Ross for being on my doctoral committee. Lee Ross is a member in the global advisory board of our Human Dignity and Humiliation Studies network, see www.humiliationstudies.org/whoweare/board.php.

[53] See Stanley Milgram (1974). See also Philip G. Zimbardo (1971). See, furthermore, Philip G. Zimbardo (2007).

[54] Philip Zimbardo in a BBC World News *HARDtalk* interview with Stephen Sackur, April 23, 2008, news.bbc.co.uk/2/hi/programmes/hardtalk/7362773.stm.

[55] Jean Baker Miller (2006).

[56] Joseph De Rivera, Rahael Kurrien, and Nina Olsen (2007), Abstract.

[57] Kisho Kurokawa, in Peter Cachola Schmal, Ingeborg Flagge, and Jochen Visscher (Eds.)(2005). From the Occupy Wall Street (OWS) movement I learned about the concept of scrumming, which stems from software engineering, meaning that they try out a project, test it, and then adapt it. "Flow within boundaries" is an expression I learned from an OWS mediator.

[58] Four clips begin with www.youtube.com/watch?v=8aufuwMiKmE. See also humiliationstudies.org/intervention/design.php.

[59] As to the concept of *nudging*, see, among others, Richard Thaler and Cass Sunstein (2008).

[60] Morton Deutsch (2006).

[61] See Mary Field Belenky, Lynne A. Bond, and Jacqueline S. Weinstock (1997), Mary Field Belenky (1997), Blythe McVicker Clinchy (1996).

[62] Blythe McVicker Clinchy and Claire Zimmerman (1985).

[63] Linda Hartling in a personal communication, June 4, 2009.

[64] See www.humiliationstudies.org/whoweare/annualmeeting17.php.

[65] See www.humiliationstudies.org/education/teamshort.php.

[66] V. Jean Ramsey and Jean Katambu Latting (2005).

[67] Morton Deutsch, Eric C. Marcus, and Sarah Brazaitis (2012), p. 19–20. V. Jean Ramsey and Jean Katambu Latting (2005), p. 268. See also Evelin Gerda Lindner (2012).

[68] Evelin Gerda Lindner (2009a), pp. 136–137.

[69] Marilynn B. Brewer and Sonia Roccas (2002). Brewer and Roccas show how membership in many different groups (multiple social identities) can lead to greater social identity complexity, which, in turn, can foster the development of superordinate social identities and global identity (making international identity more likely in individualist cultures). I thank Peter T. Coleman for reminding me of Brewer and Roccas' work. See also Shelly L. Chaiken, who shows that people who are more open to discrepant evidence

tend to make more accurate predictions; Shelly L. Chaiken (1980), Shelly L. Chaiken, Deborah H. Gruenfeld, and Charles M. Judd (2000).

[70] See Henri Tajfel and John C. Turner (1986) for a review of social identity theory.

[71] Michel Serres (1997).

[72] Michalinos Zembylas (2002), ijea.asu.edu/v3n3/.

[73] "The Case for Contamination," by Kwame Anthony Appiah , *The New York Times,* January 1, 2006, www.muhlenberg.edu/mgt/provost/frg/humanities/AppiahContamination.pdf. Se also, among others, Kwame Anthony Appiah (2010), Kwame Anthony Appiah (2006), Kwame Anthony Appiah (2005).

[74] Emmanuel Lévinas (1985).

[75] Werner Wintersteiner (1999).

[76] Evelin Gerda Lindner (2006d), p. 77.

[77] Amy Chua (2008). Watch also the interview "The Moment of Empire" that Harry Kreisler conducted with Amy Chua November 21, 2007 ," as part of the "Conversations with History," at the Institute of International Studies, University of California, Berkeley. See www.youtube.com/watch?v=QenLlFx4cCQ.

In this interview, Chua explains most convincingly the advantages of the inclusivity of "tolerance": the best and brightest will never be in one ethnicity, Chua points out. Tolerance is a necessary, even though not sufficient element to become a *hyperpower* (an empire that dominates the world). What Chua found, was that hyperpowers, throughout history, to maximize power, made use of diversity through inclusive tolerance, rather than suppressing it. Tolerance was employed because it produced strategic advantages, not in the context of present-day enlightenment-definitions of tolerance: slavery and persecution is simply too inefficient. It is easier to rule by the compliance of underlings. Chua describes the evolution of hyperpowerdom as evolving from personalities to processes, from conquest to commerce, from invasion to immigration, from autocracy to democracy. Nowadays, the relevant resources are innovation, commerce, trade, and attracting the best and brightest, for example, through immigration. The

Dutch were the first, Chua points out. Scotts, Huguenots, and Jews made the Britain empire possible, a development that was enabled through the Bill of Rights that was enacted by the Parliament of England in 1689. Hyperpowers fall with intolerance and xenophobia. Fear-driven chauvinism and ethnocentrism undercut tolerance and cause power to spiral downward. Too much tolerance however, too much diversity, is as subversive as too much intolerance. In the case of too much tolerance, unity - or what Chua calls "glue" – lacks. America was the first democratic hyperpower. According to a study, foreign-born entrepreneurs were behind one in four U.S. technology startups over the past decade. See Vivek Wadhwa et al. (2009). When military domination is no longer feasible, the question arises as to how to create the "glue" of good-will and loyalty. Persians and Mongols used military power, Rome granted citizenship also to non-Romans, however, the United States, if it wishes to preserve power, can do neither. Chua explains the advantages of building "glue" through immigration (incorporating the best and brightest from all around the world) and outsourcing (creating links of loyalty in other parts of the world). Chua predicts that China, since it is an ethnically defined society, will never become a hyperpower, even if the United States were to fall.

The advantage of inclusivity, one may argue, however, is not only apparent in the case of hyperpowers. A present-day example of less grand scale is, for instance, Indonesia. Mohammad Yazid, staff writer at the *Jakarta Post*, explains that the lesson for Indonesia is that "the majority needs to promote tolerance, mutual respect, protection and empathy for ethnic, religious and political minorities." See "From Jakarta to Kosovo—What's the Big Attraction?" by Mohammad Yazid, *Jakarta Post*, June 5, 2007, www.thejakartapost.com/news/2007/06/05/jakarta-kosovo-what039s-big-attraction.html.

[78] Evelin Gerda Lindner (2010a).

[79] The European Union uses the subsidiarity principle (see europa.eu/scadplus/glossary/subsidiarity_en.htm). It means that local decision-making and local identities are retained to the greatest extent possible. Arthur Koestler's theory of *holons* and *holarchies*, and John Braithwaite's notion of *regulatory pyramids* are similar concepts.

[80] See my book *Gender, Humiliation, and Global Security,* Evelin Gerda Lindner (2010b).

[81] *Mind over Money: Can Markets Be Rational when Humans aren't?* was aired April 26, 2010, on PBS, see the transcription on www.pbs.org/wgbh/nova/body/mind-over-money.html. It highlights why Keynes was not heard: he lacked a precise mathematical model.

[82] See, for instance, Bernard A. Nijstad and John M. Levine (2007). I thank Ulrich Spalthoff to make me aware of the literature that shows that the concept of brainstorming has serious limitations.

[83] Paul Grignon in a personal communication, June 14, 2011.

[84] See a short video clip *The Essence of Money* at www.youtube.com/watch?v=_dwL9lqVBxY.

[85] Paul Grignon in a personal communication, November 14, 2011.

[86] Paul Grignon in a personal communication, November 14, 2011.

[87] Douglas Hurd in a BBC World News *HARDtalk* interview with Stephen Sackur, February 23, 2010, news.bbc.co.uk/2/hi/programmes/hardtalk/8530106.stm.

[88] Douglas Hurd (2010).

[89] See www.iisd.org/economics. See also Anantha Kumar Duraiappah and Asmita Bhardwaj (2007).

[90] Henry David Thoreau, *On the Duty of Civil Disobedience,* first published in 1849 as *Civil Disobedience.* See more on disobedience, among others, Erich Fromm (1981), Peter Albert David Singer (1973), Henry David Thoreau and Gene Sharp (1963), Henry David Thoreau, Wendell Glick and Howard Zinn (Eds.)(2004), Michael Walzer (1970).

Chapter 11

[1] Betty A. Reardon in a personal communication with Evelin Lindner, July 6, 2010, Melbu, Vesterålen, Norway. See for a selection of her publications, Betty A. Reardon and Asha Hans (Eds.) 2010, Betty A. Reardon (2001), Ingeborg Breines, Dorota Gierycz, and Betty A. Reardon (Eds.) 1999, Betty A. Reardon (1995), Betty A. Reardon (1993), Betty A. Reardon (1988). I had the privilege of having a chapter in her edited book, Evelin Gerda Lindner (1999). Betty Reardon is a supporter of the World Dignity University initiative being developed by the Human Dignity and Humiliation Studies network.

[2] Steven Johnson (2010). Thanks go to Linda Hartling for making us aware of this book. See his 2010 TED talk at blog.ted.com/2010/09/21/where-good-ideas-come-from-steven-johnson-on-ted-com/.

[3] Malcolm Gladwell (2000), Malcolm Gladwell (2008). Thanks go to Linda Hartling for always reminding of the significance of Gladwell's work.

[4] See *Emotion and Conflict*, Evelin Gerda Lindner (2009a), pp. 129–130:

Norbert Elias argues that what we experience as *civilization* is constituted by a particular *habitus* or psychic structure that is embedded within broader social relationships. For Pierre Bourdieu, habitus is *socialized subjectivity*, our second nature, the mass of conventions, beliefs, and attitudes which we share. Habitus is the part of culture which is so taken for granted that it is virtually invisible to its members. Rules are unnecessary in homogeneous societies, and are replaced by habitus, the "orchestrated improvisation of common dispositions." *Common sense* as an "organized body of considered thought," is a related concept. According to Peter L. Berger and Thomas Luckmann's *social constructionism*, all knowledge, including the most basic, taken-for-granted common sense knowledge of everyday reality, results from social interactions, which, over time, are regarded to be "natural." Michel Foucault's *discourse* and *discursive formation* are related. Sociologist

Talcott Parsons used the concept of *gloss* to discuss the idea how "reality" is constructed. Social constructionism is often regarded as a sociological construct because it conceptualizes the development of social phenomena in relation to social contexts, while *social constructivism* is a more psychological construct, addressing how the meaning of knowledge is relative to social contexts.

Terms such as *horizon* (Emmanuel Kant, Edmund Husserl, William James), *tacit knowledge*, *zero-order beliefs*, or the term *truthiness*, speak to the same phenomena. Hugh Mackay introduced the *invisible cage* as a metaphor for the tacit effects of life experience, cultural background, and current context on an individual's view of the world. We have *mental models* on which we base "preferences without inferences," and *frames* "that allow human beings to understand reality—and sometimes to create what we take to be reality." We have *cultural mindsets*, or *cultural scripts*, which means that we have "structures within which we store scenes," or "sets of rules for the ordering of information about Stimulus-Affect-Response Sequences (SARS)." Eric Berne illuminates *script theory* in his book *What Do You Say After You Say Hello?* Benedict Anderson explains how communities can be ideated and imagined. *Zeitgeist* and *paradigm* are important terms—Thomas S. Kuhn describes how paradigms can shift. Before they shift, they rigidify, with some people identifying with them strongly and standing up for them. Then they are toppled by a new generation of people who ask new questions that undermine the edifice. The already-mentioned psychological phenomenon of *defensive avoidance* plays a role here.

Howard Richards (2011a) makes a similar list when he writes:

Pierre Bourdieu says with *habitus*, what Margaret Mead says with *customs*, what John Maynard Keynes says with "institutions" and with "the psychology of the community" can also be said with the typical terminologies of ethics, such as "norm," "rule," "imperative" (Kant Immanuel Kant) , "institutional fact" (John R. Searle), "moral authority," and "ideal." Ethics, in one of its dimensions, is neither more nor less than the norms that guide human action. According to a scholastic definition, ethics is the theory of human action; that is to say, that which explains it, Howard Richards (2011a), pp. 4–5.

[5] Paul D. Raskin et al. (2002). See also Paul D. Raskin (2008) and Ben Brangwyn and Rob Hopkins (2011).

[6] This is the message of my book Gender, Humiliation, and Global Security.

[7] See Nicholas Stern (2011), p. 7, and, among others, Christopher Freeman (2008), Christopher Freeman and Francisco Louçã (2001).

[8] See, among others, Paul Hawken (2007a), and Paul H. Ray and Sherry Ruth Anderson (2000).

[9] Alan Page Fiske (1991).

[10] Riane Tennenhaus Eisler (2007).

[11] Michael Britton in a personal communication, November 27, 2010. See Christopher Lynn Hedges (2010). I thank Michael Britton for making me aware of Hedges' work.

[12] Linda Hartling in a personal discussion, October 21, 2011.

[13] Malcolm Hollick and Christine Connelly (2011), p. 348.

[14] See, among others, Gerard Endenburg (1988). See also www.sociocracy.info.

[15] Aristotle (1980).

[16] Rushworth M. Kidder (1994).

[17] Henrik Preben Syse (2009). Syse refers to the work of Harry M. Clor (2009). See for another Norwegian voice calling for moderation, for example, Arne Johan Vetlesen (Ed.) 2008. Henrik Syse is a member in the global advisory board of our Human Dignity and Humiliation Studies network, see www.humiliationstudies.org/whoweare/board.php.

[18] See, among others, Silvio Johann Gesell (1916), Silvio Johann Gesell (1958).

[19] See note 4 in chapter 1.

[20] Riane Tennenhaus Eisler (2007) draws attention to prehistoric, historic, and anthropological data, for instance, from the BaMbuti and Tiruray. See also Riane Tennenhaus Eisler (1995).

²¹ Karma Tshiteem is the Secretary of the Gross National Happiness Commission, see www.bhutan.gov.bt/government/whoiswho.php.

²² Norway is a strong basis for my work and in my book *Gender, Humiliation, and Global Security*, I highlight the advantages of its system. See also Howard Richards and Joanna Swanger (2006). As to Costa Rica, I was privileged to listen to Victor M. Valle (2001) at the Expert Group Meeting on "Structural Threats to Social Integration" in December 2001 in New York City. See also Evelin Gerda Lindner (2001d). Victor Valle is a member in the global advisory board of our Human Dignity and Humiliation Studies network, see www.humiliationstudies.org/whoweare/board.php.

²³ World Commission on Environment and Development and Gro Harlem Brundtland (1987).

²⁴ Prayudh A Payutto (1994). See also Ernst Friedrich Schumacher (1966), Ernst Friedrich Schumacher (1973), Ernst Friedrich Schumacher (1999), and Thomas Weber (1999), or László Zsolnai and Knut J. Ims (2006) and Ananda W. P. Guruge (2008).

²⁵ Ove Jacobsen, original Norwegian text:

Payutto utgjør etikken forbindelsen mellom den indre og den ytre virkeligheten. Han trekker frem visdom, empati og måtehold som viktige kjennetegn ved en økonomi som skal fremme individuell og sosial utvikling innenfor rammene av en bærekraftig natur. Payutto forklarer Buddhistisk økonomi med utgangspunkt i begrepene Tanhā og Chanda. Tanhā viser til en egoistisk streben etter materielle lystopplevelser. Ettersom behovene for lystopplevelser er uendelige, leder de ofte til grådighet, hat og egoisme. Chanda representerer visdom og etiske verdier som er sentrale i søken etter sann lykke og livskvalitet. Veien til Chanda går gjennom refleksjon over livserfaringer. I følge Payutto vil vi etter hvert oppdage at mental tilstand, moralsk adferd og økonomi er knyttet sammen gjennom en strøm av handlinger. Målet er å utvikle en helhetsforståelse som endrer interessekonflikter til en opplevelse av interessefellesskap mellom individ, samfunn og natur… I forbindelse med økonomisk verdiskapning skiller han mellom sann verdi (chanda) som leder til 'wellbeing', og kunstig verdi (Tanhā) som bare bidrar til lystopplevelser… Payutto skiller mellom avhengig lykke, uavhengig lykke og harmonisk lykke. Avhengig lykke er knyttet opp mot eksterne objekter og er dermed avhengig av ting i den materielle verden. Uavhengig lykke er knyttet opp mot indre tilstander som for eksempel 'fred i sinnet'. Uavhengig lykke er mer stabil ennlykke som er avhengig av tilstedeværelsen av ytre objekter. Harmonisk lykke er basert på en altruistisk holdning der målet er å bidra til andre menneskers 'well-being'. Harmonisk lykke er knyttet sammen med Buddhismens målsetning om å kultivere opplevelsen av sammenhengen mellom 'jeg' og 'vi' eller en egoutvidelse ('the extended self'). Tillit og solidaritet (med alt levende) blir dermed indikatorer på sann lykke. Felleskapets beste er knyttet til fravær av fattigdom mer enn maksimering av produksjon og forbruk… I Buddhistisk økonomi har arbeid egenverdi fordi det å søke felles mål gjennom samarbeid med andre mennesker bidrar til personlig utvikling samtidig som det motvirker egoisme (chanda). Arbeid som er redusert til kun å være et middel for å skaffe penger til forbruk av varer og tjenester er motivert av Tanhã. Det fører til at vi ønsker å arbeide minst mulig og forbruke mest mulig. Også på dette punktet anbefaler Payutto en balanse mellom ytterpunktene. Det vil si at alle arbeidsoppgaver må inneholde elementer av både Tanhã og Chanda… Payutto hevder at konkurranse er et effektivt virkemiddel for å maksimere produksjon og forbruk av varer og tjenester (Tanhã). Når økonomiske aktører samarbeider for å oppnå sterkere markedsmakt bruker han betegnelsen 'kunstig samarbeid'. Dersom målet er å fremme en utvikling som leder mot fellesskapets beste anbefaler han ekte samarbeid. Ekte samarbeid oppstår som et resultat av innsikt i at alt henger sammen og er motivert av Chanda…" Ove Jacobsen (2010), p. 22–23, translated from Norwegian by Lindner.

[26] See www.rsfsocialfinance.org.

[27] See their web site www.economicsofpeace.net/conveners.html:

Our goal is to understand the failed mechanisms of the old systems in order to avoid repetition, and to nurture the visions and alternative structures that support the evolution of systemic peace, social justice, and responsible stewardship of our planet. In collaborating with RSF Social Finance for our 5th conference, The Economics of Peace, we have an opportunity to reach many more people and organizations and to help network existing organizations. Our goal is to help transform an ailing economy into economic relationships that serve the well-being of all living creatures and our planet.

[28] Ulrich Spalthoff in a personal communication, May 15, 2010.

[29] Nicholas Georgesçu-Roegen (1971). Hazel Henderson reviewed this book in *Harvard Business Review* in 1971. Hazel Henderson draws attention also to Janine M. Benyus (2002), Wes Jackson (1994), Gunter A. Pauli (1991), John Todd and Nancy Jack Todd (1980), Jody Butterfield et al. (2006), and Pavan Sukhdev, member in the Economics of Ecosystems and Biodiversity (TEEB) Advisory Board. Henderson advocates financial transaction taxes, see the TV series *Transforming Finance*, available for colleges and libraries at www.films.com, as well as on www.ethicalmarkets.tv, along with the PBS TV special *The Money Fix*, which looks at the politics of money-creation. *Occupy Wall St 99%* is covered at www.ethicalmarkets.com.

[30] See, among others, Herman E. Daly and Joshua C. Farley (2010). I thank Karine Nyborg for explaining current trends in economic research on January 17, 2011. See for her work, for example, Karine Nyborg (2007).

[31] Dee Ward Hock (1999).

[32] See note 25 in chapter 2.

[33] See "Bernard Lietaer Urges the Growth of New Currency," in *Bank Technology News*, July 1, 2004, www.highbeam.com/doc/1G1-118904906.html.

[34] The PBS TV special *The Money Fix* looks at the politics of money-creation, available for colleges and libraries at www.films.com, as well as on www.ethicalmarkets.tv.

[35] Stephen A. Zarlenga (2002), www.monetary.org.

[36] See www.earthcharter.org.

[37] See www.earthcharter.org.

[38] See www.ashoka.org.

[39] See www.cauxroundtable.org/index.cfm?menuid=8.

[40] See www.eben-net.org. It is a privilege to have Heidetraut von Weltzien Høivik as a member in the global advisory board of our Human Dignity and Humiliation Studies network, see

www.humiliationstudies.org/whoweare/board.php. She was the president of EBEN 1999 until October 2005. In 1994/5 she launched the Center for Ethics and Leadership at the Norwegian School of Management and developed the curriculum in Business Ethics, mainly for the graduate school and executive management programs. See for some of her publications, Antonio Argandoña and Heidetraut von Weltzien Høivik (2009), Heidetraut von Weltzien Høivik and Domènec Melé (2009), Heidetraut von Weltzien Høivik (2009), Heidetraut von Weltzien Høivik (2007), Heidetraut von Weltzien Høivik (2005), Heidetraut von Weltzien Høivik (Ed.)(2002).

[41] See, for example, Donna J. Wood (1991).

[42] See www.un.org/millenniumgoals.

[43] See note 29 in chapter 2.

[44] Chapin 2004, p. 27. I thank Mariana Vergara, for making me aware of this article.

[45] The Global Compact was first announced to The World Economic Forum on January 31, 1999, and was officially launched at UN Headquarters in New York on July 26, 2000. See www.unglobalcompact.org.

[46] See www.model-economy.wikispaces.com.

[47] Robert A. Mundell, Paul J. Zak, and Derek M. Schaeffer (Eds.) 2005.

[48] I thank Ulrich Spalthoff for making me aware that companies in Germany that sell Cuban products received warning letters from PayPal asking them to discontinue offering these products. See, for instance, "'Lassen uns nicht erpressen': Rossmann schmeißt Paypal raus," www.heise.de/newsticker/meldung/Lassen-uns-nicht-erpressen-Rossmann-schmeisst-Paypal-raus-1340041.html.

[49] "Facebook as Tastemaker," by Somini Sengupta and Ben Sisario, The New York Times, September 22, 2011, www.nytimes.com/2011/09/23/technology/facebook-makes-a-push-to-be-a-media-hub.html?_r=1&scp=1&sq=Somini%20Sengupta%20Ben%20Sisario&st=cse.

[50] Ibid.

[51] "LinkedIn Announces Talent Pipeline: One Place for Recruiters to Grow, Track and Stay Connected With All Their Talent Leads," Las Vegas, October 18, 2011, Global Newswire, www.globenewswire.com/newsroom/news.html?d=235209. I thank Linda Hartling for making me aware of this reference.

[52] Gabrielle Walker and David A. King (2008). See also www.smithschool.ox.ac.uk/people/management_team/mt/professor_sir_david_king, and David Anthony King in a BBC World News *HARDtalk* interview with Stephen Sackur, September 30, 2009, news.bbc.co.uk/go/pr/fr/-/2/hi/programmes/hardtalk/8282169.stm.

[53] See www.oekonux.org.

[54] Lawrence Lessig (2005).

[55] Michel Bauwens (2008).

[56] Paul Hawken (2007a).

[57] David C. Korten (2001).

[58] Hazel Henderson (1996), Hazel Henderson and Simran Sethi (2008).

[59] Herman E. Daly and Kenneth N. Townsend (Eds.) 1993.

[60] See www.neweconomics.org/projects/happy-planet-index.

[61] See www.beyond-gdp.eu.

[62] German Council of Economic Experts and Conseil d'Analyse Économique (2010). See also Dan O'Neill, Rob Dietz, and Nigel Jones (Eds.) 2010, and Joseph E. Stiglitz, Amartya Kumar Sen, and Jean-Paul Fitoussi (2011).

[63] Enquete-Kommission „Wachstum, Wohlstand, Lebensqualität," www.bundestag.de/presse/hib/2011_01/2011_012/01.html, lead by politician Daniela Kolbe (SPD), and supported by, among others, economists Meinhard Miegel, see, for example, Meinhard Miegel and Axel Börsch-Supan (Eds.) 2001, and Henrik Enderlein, see, for example, Henrik Enderlein, Sonja Wälti, and Michael Zürn (Eds.)(2010).

[64] See www.gallup.com/poll/126977/global-wellbeing-surveys-find-nations-worlds-apart.aspx.

[65] See hdr.undp.org/en/statistics.

[66] See www.wider.unu.edu/research/Database/en_GB/database.

[67] See www.stateoftheusa.org/content/commission-on-key-national-ind.php.

[68] The Green New Deal Group (2008).

[69] Reinhard Buetikofer and Sven Giegold (2010).

[70] "Declaration on Degrowth," by the participants of the Conference on Economic Degrowth for Ecological Sustainability and Social Equity, Paris, April 18–19, 2008, www.worldinbalance.net/pdf/ec-degrowth.pdf..

[71] Bob Rijnhout Leida Goudzwaard et al. (2008).

[72] See krugman.blogs.nytimes.com. See his Nobel Prize lecture at nobelprize.org/nobel_prizes/economics/laureates/2008/krugman_lecture.pdf.

[73] Elinor Ostrom, Amy R. Poteete, and Marco A. Janssen (2010).

[74] Kern Alexander, Rahul Dhumale, and John Leonard Eatwell (2006).

[75] Berthold Huber (2010).

[76] Ellen Hodgson Brown (2008), www.webofdebt.com.

[77] See www.webofdebt.com.

[78] Thomas Henry Greco Jr. (2009), beyondmoney.net/the-end-of-money-and-the-future-of-civilization.

[79] See www.transitiontowns.org, www.transitionculture.org, www.totnesedap.org.uk. See also Hopkins 2008, Shaun Chamberlin (2009). See, furthermore, Global Ecovillage Network (GEN), www.gen.ecovillage.org, and Gaia Education, www.gaiaeducation.org. The largest eco-society in Europe is Damanhur in Italy, www.damanhur.org. See also Gemma Blu Association, Italy, Shalom Template Movement, Israel, The Pendragon Movement, England, and Den Bla Paraply, Denmark.

80 Paul D. Raskin et al. (2002).

81 The movie *Home* was released on June 5, 2009. See www.home-2009.com/us/index.html, www.goodplanet.org/en, and www.youtube.com/homeproject, 2009.

82 Some films that discuss the state of affairs, particularly economic affairs, are listed here:

- Among the most prominent documentaries is *An Inconvenient Truth* of 2006 by Albert Arnold "Al" Gore, Jr., the 45th Vice President of the United States from 1993 to 2001 under President Bill Clinton, see www.climatecrisis.net.
- *The New Rulers of the World* is a 2001–2002 documentary film produced, written, and presented by investigative journalist and documentary film-maker John Pilger on the question "Who are the real beneficiaries of the globalized economy?" See www.bullfrogfilms.com/catalog/new.html.
- *The Corporation* is a 2003 Canadian documentary film written by Joel Bakan, and directed by Mark Achbar and Jennifer Abbott. See www.thecorporation.com.
- *The Yes Men* was a documentary film of 2003 about the culture exploits of "The Yes Men." See www.unitedartists.com/yesmen.
- *The Ascent of Money: The Financial History of the World* is a book by Harvard professor Niall Ferguson (2008). The book was adapted into a 6 part television documentary with the new full title *Ascent of Money: Boom and Bust* for Channel 4 in the UK (www.channel4.com) and an edited two-hour version was aired in January 2009 by PBS (www.pbs.org/wnet/ascentofmoney). A newer, reorganized four-hour version with the original full title *The Ascent of Money: The Financial History of the World* was aired in July 2009 by PBS.
- *The Future of Food* was directed, produced, and written by Deborah Koons in 2004. See www.thefutureoffood.com/synopsis.htm.
- In 2007, *The Story of Stuff* by activist Annie Leonard was viewed by millions of people within a very short period of time. See www.storyofstuff.org.

- *The Day of the Dollar*, was a "what if" scenario presented by VPRO Backlight and Dutch national newspaper *NRC Handelsblad* in 2005. Do we live on a bubble? Is it possible for the heavily indebted American economy to collapse and take all of us down in a free fall with it? Have the days of the dollar been counted? Is it really unimaginable that we will see the time of the Great Depression repeating itself? The film includes interviews with analyst Stephen Roach, Andy Xie, Maarten Schinkel, Cees Maas, Rob de Wijk and Kees Vendrik. See www.youtube.com/watch?v=AuPgdZeAFjA and www.vpro.nl/backlight.
- *Future by Design*, 2008, is an introduction to the life of futurist Jacque Fresco, produced and written by William Gazecki. See www.futurebydesignthemovie.com or topdocumentaryfilms.com/future-by-design, and the 2009 lecture "Where Are We Now and Where Are We Going" by Peter Joseph at topdocumentaryfilms.com/where-are-we-now-and-where-are-we-going. See earlier documentaries presenting Jacque Fresco's ideas at *Zeitgeist: The Movie*, a 2007 documentary film by Peter Joseph, and a sequel, *Zeitgeist: Addendum*, both advocating a technology-based social system influenced by the ideas of Jacque Fresco. See video.google.com/videoplay?docid=7065205277695921912#.
- In his 2008 documentary *Let's Make Money*, Erwin Wagenhofer provides a demonstration of the global money market and its inappropriatenss, which is made possible, among others, by the fact that the involved players have an outlook that is too local. Western investors (the "clever speculator" as much as the average consumer who merely keeps money in a bank) see growth and dividend as positive phenomena. What they do not see is that they are complicit when a manager creates a dividend by pushing an already poor farmer in a remote region of the world still further down into poverty. In this way, the poorest are made poorer so that the wealthy can "make money." The film shows how everybody is complicit, unwittingly, who has an account in a bank. Money deposited in a bank for safe-keeping does not stay there, but is circulated in the global money

market, where enormous amounts of money collect at certain "hot spots" each day. The documentary lists many examples, for instance that of the Ghanaian cotton farmer who produces cotton of highest quality. Since the United States subsidizes its own cotton production, nobody buys the cotton from Ghana. In this way, the African farmer is compelled to deliver his product far under value. This leads to the West receiving best cotton at favorable prices, and the American cotton farmer having a decent living. Only the Ghanaian remains poor, even though he actually has the best cotton.

· Canadian activist Paul Grignon made a number of animated features. See *The Essence of Money* at www.digitalcoin.info/The_Essence_of_Money.html. See then www.moneyasdebt.net. For *Money as Debt II: Promises Unleashed*, see also www.ustream.tv/recorded/4155763. For *Money as Debt I*, see, furthermore, www.youtube.com/watch?v=GrO-7awnwGs&feature=player_embedded#!, and then read about the disputed issues in this movie at paulgrignon.netfirms.com/MoneyasDebt/disputed_information.html. Read the Pdf files on www.digitalcoin.info, for example, Paul Grignon (2009). Also Money as Debt III, parts 1 and 4, are posted on YouTube, the two parts fitting together and bypassing the details of Parts 2 and 3, see paulgrignon.netfirms.com/MoneyasDebt/Money_as_Debt_You Tube_links.html.

· See also *The Epoch Times*, June 9, 2009, www.theepochtimes.com/n2/content/view/17937.

· *The Secret of Oz*, 2009, thematizes the system of fractional reserve lending. See secretofoz.com, and www.youtube.com/watch?v=D22TlYA8F2E. See also the earlier *The Money Masters: How Banks Create 90% of the World's Money*, a 3 1/2 hour non-fiction, historical documentary that traced the origins of the political power structure, directed by Bill Still and produced by Patrick Carmack, released in 1996. See www.themoneymasters.com. The film *The Secret of Oz* is directed by Bill Still. Contributors are, among others, Quentin

Taylor (assistant professor of history and political science), Joseph Farah (worldnetdaily.com), James Robertson and John Bunzl (2008)(The Interbank Organization), Peter D. Schiff and John Downes (2009), Ellen Hodgson Brown (2008), Byron Dale (www.wealthmoney.org), Michael Hudson (2003)(professor of economics), Karl Denninger (market-ticker.denninger.net), Milford Wriarson Howard (1895), and Theodore R. Thoren and Richard F. Warner (Eds.) 1980. The film highlights the importance of who is in control of the quantity of money, and tells the tale of the advantages of *fiat money*, or debt-free national money, issued by the government. Examples presented are the fiat money used prior to Julius Caesar's reign in Rome, the *tally sticks* used in England until the Bank of England was founded in 1695, and the *Colonial Scrip* given out in pre-revolutionary America until the Currency Act in 1764 forbade it. For Benjamin Franklin, the return to the gold-money system was the basic cause for the American revolution: "The colonies would gladly have borne the little tax on tea and other matters had it not been that England took away from the colonies their money, which created unemployment and dissatisfaction. The inability of colonists to get power to issue their own money permanently out of the hands of George the III and the international bankers was the PRIME reason for the Revolutionary War" (widely quoted statement on the reasons for the American War of Independence sometimes cited as being from Franklin's autobiography, but this statement was never in any edition). In 1775, with the outbreak of the revolution, the American colonies started printing so-called *Continental Currency*, which was brought down by the British bringing massive amounts of counterfeited notes into the country and thus destabilizing this currency. In 1781, the congress in Philadelphia created the first privately owned central bank, the Bank of North America, modeled on the Bank of England. From then on, privately owned central banks were repeatedly chartered to create US money as monopolists, only to be un-chartered again following public protest. In 1789, debt-free national money was emitted in

Sweden, the *riksdaler riksgälds*, however, this experiment failed because this money's quantity was allowed to spiral out of control; King Gustav III was assassinated. The film states that the American Constitution, in 1787, should have allowed the Congress to "emit bills of credit," or print debt-free national fiat paper money, but that this was omitted. Shortly after the constitution was written, the 1st Bank of the United States was created, yet another privately own central bank, this time at the federal level. In 1811, England threatened with war if the bank's charter would not be renewed. Thomas Jefferson wrote to John Eppes in 1813, "Although we have so foolishly allowed the field of circulating medium to be filched from us by private individuals, I think we may recover it... The states should be asked to transfer the right of issuing paper money to Congress, in perpetuity." The burning of Washington took place on August 24, 1814, in the War of 1812 between the British Empire and the United States of America; the British army occupied Washington, D.C., and set fire to many public buildings. Andrew Jackson, seventh President of the United States (1829–1837), vetoed another renewal of the charter, saying, "It is easy to conceive that great evils to our country and its institutions might flow from such a concentration of power in the hands of a few men, irresponsible to the people... Controlling our currency, receiving our public moneys, and holding thousands of our citizens in dependence, it would be more formidable and dangerous than the naval and military power of the enemy." He survived an assassination attempt and concluded: "The bold effort the present (central) bank had made to control the government ... are but premonitions of the fate that await the American people should they be deluded into a perpetuation of this institution or the establishment of another like it." Abraham Lincoln later returned to government-issued debt-free money, the so-called *Greenbacks*. In 1876, the Chancellor of Germany, Otto von Bismarck, described the "divide and conquer" strategy that was devised in response in Europe and said "It is not to be doubted, I know with absolute certainty, that the separation of the United States into two

federations of equal powers had been decided upon well in
advance of the Civil War by the top financial power of Europe"
(*Journal of the Bar Association of the District of Columbia*, 1947,
Item Notes: v. 14, p. 150). Otto von Bismarck said upon
President Abraham Lincoln's assassination: "I fear that foreign
bankers with their craftiness tortuous tricks will entirely control
the exuberant riches of America and use it systematically to
corrupt modern civilization. They will not hesitate to plunge the
whole of Christendom into wars and chaos in order that the
earth should become their inheritance." The Coinage Act was
passed in 1873, demonetizing silver and implementing a gold-
only money system. General James A. Garfield, 20th President of
the United States, was assassinated before he could change this.
Later, William Jennings Bryan, "The Great Commoner" and
three times candidate for President of the United States, was the
leader of the *silverite movement* in the 1890s. The "Panic of
1893" began with European investors demanding repayment
only in gold, thus draining gold reserves in America. Since gold
is scarce, it is one of the easiest commodities to manipulate.
With respect to solutions, the film gives the floor to James
Robertson, Ellen Hodgson Brown, refers to the Bank of North
Dakota, which successfully operates since 90 years, mentions the
Church Steeple Principle, and the creation of
"Commonwealth." Swedish *saving banks* are mentioned and
Niklas Högberg interviewed, the chairman of the Sound
Banking Ethics Foundation in Stockholm. Iceland's Icesave
bank is presented as an example of how privatizing the national
bank brought an entire country down. It is "essential" to change
the current system if our species is to survive, says James
Robertson. The film closes with saying that what happens now
is a "world extortion" system being the "primary cause of the
world's hunger, poverty, misery and disease." Humankind will
need to escape from the debt-money system. Our children will
no longer have to know the term "national debt."
- *Inside Job*, a film written and directed by Charles Ferguson (and
narrated by Matt Damon), see a review by Kathleen Parker in
Washington Post, October 13, 2010,

www.washingtonpost.com/wp-
dyn/content/article/2010/10/12/AR2010101203723.html?referr
er=emailarticle.
- *The Warning* is a 2009 Frontline documentary on Brooksley
Born's thwarted efforts to regulate the derivatives market. Born
was the chairperson of the Commodity Futures Trading
Commission (CFTC), the U.S. federal agency which oversees
the futures and commodity options markets, from August 26,
1996, to June 1, 1999. Born's verdict for the future: "I think we
will have continuing danger from these markets and that we will
have repeats of the financial crisis—may differ in details but
there will be significant financial downturns and disasters
attributed to this regulatory gap, over and over, until we learn
from experience,"
www.pbs.org/wgbh/pages/frontline/warning/interviews/born.ht
ml
- *College, Inc,* is a 2010 documentary, in which correspondent
Martin Smith investigates the for-profit higher education
industry, see www.pbs.org/wgbh/pages/frontline/collegeinc/.
Read more at
www.pbs.org/wgbh/pages/frontline/collegeinc/view/#ixzz1YNA
4fEe1.
- Sophy Banks from Transition Town Totnes Heart and Soul
group describes how it came about and why transitioning the
inner self is crucial to the movement, see
www.youtube.com/watch?v=GQHxRzBnTmU.
- *The Progressive* magazine produces a weekly, half-hour-long
interview show called "Progressive Radio." It is hosted by the
magazine's editor, Matt Rothschild. David Harvey, the author
of *The Enigma of Capital and the Crises of Capitalism*, David
Harvey (2010), was interviewed in February 2011. See
progressive.org/radioharvey11.html.
- *Choice* is a RSA animate, where Professor Renata Salecl explores
the paralyzing anxiety and dissatisfaction surrounding limitless
choice. Does the freedom to be the architects of our own lives
actually hinder rather than help us? Does our preoccupation
with choosing and consuming actually obstruct social change?

See www.youtube.com/watch?v=1bqMY82xzWo, and the RSA's
free public events program, www.thersa.org/events. See also
Renata Salecl (2004).

- *The Big Fix* is a film by filmmakers Josh and Rebecca Harrell
  Tickell about the 2010 Deepwater Horizon oil spill and its
  aftermath.
- *Mind over Money: Can Markets Be Rational when Humans
  aren't?*, aired April 26, 2010, on PBS, see the transcription on
  www.pbs.org/wgbh/nova/body/mind-over-money.html.
  Economist Robert J. Shiller (2000) foresaw the economic crisis.
  Psychologist Brian Knutson, found that not just sex, not just
  drugs, not just food activates the same circuits in the nucleus
  accumbens of the brain, "money also activates these circuits, and
  it does so very powerfully." Robert Shiller believes it is
  emotional excitement that drives bubbles, and it must not be
  money. The first financial bubble involved tulips. In the 1630s,
  in the Netherlands, people were buying and selling Tulip bulbs.
  Question: "Could empathy explain how the hyper-optimism of
  the housing market jumped, like a social contagion, to the
  financial markets?" Yes, says Robert Shiller, who believes that
  "humans are empathetic animals, uniquely empathetic. We're
  not just communicating ideas, we're communicating emotions.
  That's what empathy means. It's different from sympathy. It's
  that I am feeling the same thing; I know what you're
  experiencing because it's in my body too, the same feeling that
  you have." The rationalists' conviction is based on the "efficient
  markets hypothesis" based on the mathematical model. "It says
  that financial markets act, essentially, like a giant calculating
  machine, efficiently processing all relevant information faster
  than any individual could. So, if some traders are emotional, it
  doesn't matter." Economist Richard Thaler: "If markets are
  efficient, there's no real need for government, because the
  market itself will make sure that prices are always equal to the
  right price. Indeed, "the financial markets are now dominated
  by the highly mathematical approach of the quants, one that's
  been designed to ensure risks are assessed rationally and
  scientifically."

[83] See, among others, Jeffrey L. Dunoff and Joel P. Trachtman (Eds.) 2009. I thank Ulrich Spalthoff for making me aware of this reference.

[84] See www.christian-felber.at and www.gemeinwohl-oekonomie.org.

[85] See, for instance, www.solidarityeconomy.net/2011/04/12/argentinas-women-and-the-solidarity-economy/.

[86] "Building a Solidarity Economy: How Can one Small Brooklyn-based Co-op Help Create an Economy Founded on Teamwork, Social Justice, and Democracy?," by Annie McShiras, October 15, 2009, www.yesmagazine.org/new-economy/building-a-solidarity-economy.

[87] Franz Hörmann (2009), Abstract.

[88] See www.globalisationforthecommongood.info, and Kamran Mofid (2002), Kamran Mofid (2010), Kamran Mofid (2011a), Kamran Mofid (2011b). Watch his "Education of My Dream" at www.youtube.com/watch?feature=player_embedded&v=F8irN9kQuFs. Kamran Mofid is a member of the global advisory board of the Human Dignity and Humiliation Studies network, see www.humiliationstudies.org/whoweare/board.php.

[89] See www.basic-income.net, and Götz Wolfgang Werner and André Presse (Eds.) 2007.

[90] "On Basic Income: Interview with Götz Werner," interviewed by Jens König and Hannes Koch, published in *taz* (*die tageszeitung*). Translated to English by Florian Piesche, and posted on December 7, 2009, www.livableincome.org/agotzwerner.htm, p. 1. Original German text on taz website www.taz.de/1/archiv/?id=archivseite&dig=2006/11/27/a0146.

[91] See www.appell-vermoegensabgabe.de. For an English introduction, see www.thelocal.de/money/20091022-22755.html.

[92] "Wealthy Germans Launch Petition For Higher Taxes," October 22, 2009, www.thelocal.de/money/20091022-22755.html: "Some rich Germans have launched a web petition to call for the resumption of a wealth tax to help the country bounce back from an economic crisis, because, as one said, he had 'a lot of money I do not need.'"

[93] See www.faireconomy.org/tax-fairness-pledge.

[94] "Fighting for a People's Budget," by Katrina van den Heuvel, published on *The Nation*, www.thenation.com, on April 14, 2011.

[95] See note 37 in chapter 3.

[96] Helena Norberg-Hodge is the founder and director of the International Society for Ecology and Culture (ISEC, www.isec.org.uk). See also Helena Norberg-Hodge, Steven Gorelick, and Todd Merrifield (2002).

[97] Joseph E. Stiglitz (2003), Joseph E. Stiglitz and Andrew Charlton (2006).

[98] See journeyforfairtrade.blogspot.com/2010/12/second-journey-for-fair-trade.html.

[99] See www.humiliationstudies.org/whoweare/board.php.

[100] See, among others, Catherine A. Lutz (2009), or Robert Green (2010). I thank Alexander Harang for these references. For the Global Zero Movement, see www.globalzero.org/en/about-campaign.

[101] Paul H. Ray and Sherry Ruth Anderson (2000).

[102] See www.wildriverreview.com.

[103] See www.thelovefoundation.com. Harold Becker is a member in the global advisory board of our Human Dignity and Humiliation Studies network, see www.humiliationstudies.org/whoweare/board.php.

[104] See www.karmatube.org.

[105] See www.garrisoninstitute.org. I thank Philip Brown for making me aware of the Garrison Institute.

[106] See, among others, Colin F. Camerer (2003). I thank Karine Nyborg, for making me aware of this reference.

[107] Robert Axelrod (1990).

[108] See Morton Deutsch (1958), Morton Deutsch (1960a), Morton Deutsch (1960b), Morton Deutsch (1962).

[109] Morton Deutsch (1973), p. 367.

[110] I thank Karine Nyborg for explaining current trends in economic research on January 17, 2011. See for her work, for example, Karine Nyborg (2007).

[111] Richard T. Carson (2011), p. 20. I thank Karine Nyborg for making me aware of this article.

[112] Susmita Dasgupta et al. (2002).

[113] Quoted from www.esop.uio.no/about/about.html.

[114] Quoted from www.esop.uio.no/about/about.html.

[115] See www.esop.uio.no.

[116] Karl Ove Moene and Erling Barth (2009), Abstract.

[117] Dannelsesutvalg (2009). Several authors contributed to this report. Inga Bostad was the head of the commission. Other contributors were, among others, Bernt Hagtvet, Gunnar Skirbekk, Berit Rokne, Anders Lindseth, Lars Lvlie, and Roger Strand.
Bernt Hagtvet's reflections open the report. He refers to classics such as the overview over American, English, and German university traditions by Abraham Flexner (1930). He then reports on the presently growing unease, in the United States, with the current trend toward commercialization in the educational sector.
Gunnar Skirbekk's article emphasizes the significance of the Examen philosophicum (ex. phil.), which is an introductory course at Norwegian universities into philosophy and scientific method, and must be passed to receive a Bachelor's degree, thus supporting liberal arts education.
Berit Rokne and Inga Bostad and suggest a number of key issues to guide science and society (see further down in this paper).
Lars Lvlie discusses the paradox that pedagogy faces, namely that students must be nurtured in a context that offers sufficient freedom but also sufficient firmness for them to develop the maturity of responsible citizens.
Anders Lindseth emphasized that liberal arts are not an elite project. He calls for a new and deeper listening to students and faculty. He argues that the personal experience of scholars is of profound importance not only for their personal maturation, but also for their contribution to society at large.
Roger Strand highlights the last three points of the Dublin Descriptors of the Bologna Process.

[118] In his contribution to Dannelsesutvalg (2009), Bernt Hagtvet documents the presently growing unease, in the United States, with the current trend toward commercialization in the educational sector. See, for example, the views expressed by Harvard's former president Derek Curtis Bok (2003), *Universities in the Marketplace: The Commercialization of Higher Education.*
The Education Commission report draws on a wide range of literature (among others, Theodor W. Adorno (1959); Allan Bloom (1987); Derek Curtis Bok (2003); Derek Curtis Bok (2006); John Dewey (1902); John Dewey (1916); Frank Donoghue (2008); Amitai Etzioni (1995); Hans Georg Gadamer and P. Christopher Smith (1986); Martin Heidegger (2006); Richard H. Hersh and John Merrow (Eds.) 2005; Wilhelm von Humboldt (1993); Wilhelm von Humboldt (2002); Immanuel Kant (1790), Immanuel Kant and Friedrich Theodor Rink (1803); Steven Koblik and Stephen Graubard (Eds.) 2000; Anthony T. Kronman (2007); Lewis 2006; John Stuart Mill (1873); John Stuart Mill (1859); Martha C. Nussbaum (1997); Ernest T. Pascarella et al. (2005); Robert David Putnam (1995) ; Bill Readings (1996); Richard Rorty (1979); Harold T. Shapiro (2005); Hans Skjervheim (2002); Sidney Verba, Kay Lehman Schlozman, and Henry E. Brady (1995); Michael Walzer (1992) ; Bruce Wilshire (1990); Michael Yudkin (Ed.) 1969).
See, furthermore, Edward J. Carvalho and David B. Downing (Eds.) 2010, Henry A. GirouxPaulo Freire and Stanley Aronowitz (Eds.)(2001), Henry A. Giroux and Susan Searls Giroux (2004), Åse Gornitzka and Liv Langfeldt (2008), Simon Head (2003), Chuck Howlett and Ian Harris (2010), John Quiggin (2010a), Howard Richards (2010b), Jack H. Schuster and Martin J. Finkelstein (2006), Sheila Slaughter and Gary Rhoades (2004). See also the Strategic Plan 2006-2011 of the Higher Education Funding Council for England (HEFCE), www.hefce.ac.uk/pubs/hefce/2008/08_15/.

[119] See www.berkshares.org. See also neweconomicsinstitute.org/content/local-currencies.

[120] Wendell Berry (1990), see also dialogic.blogspot.com/2004/11/wendell-berry-work-of-local-culture.html.

[121] See www.weusecoins.com.

[122] Paul Grignon in a personal communication, March 25, 2011, and June 3, 2011. Ulrich Spalthoff adds that "BitCoin requires a large number of computers crunching numbers to create Bitcoins, something which can be questioned from an energy saving perspective. Furthermore, in this system of money generation , people who cannot afford a computer, are left aside in this system. They cannot generate Bitcoins but also cannot use them," Ulrich Spalthoff in a personal communication, June 4, 2011.

[123] Paul Grignon in a personal communication, March 25, 2011, and June 3, 2011.

[124] Paul Grignon in a personal communication, June 14, 2011.

[125] Paul Grignon, www.digitalcoin.info.

[126] See www.slowmoney.org. I thank Lynn King for making me aware of the Slow Money movement.

[127] Genevieve Vaughan (1997), Genevieve Vaughan (Ed.) 2007, see also Jeanette Armstrong (2007). See also, among many others, Charles Eisenstein (2010), Manish Jain and Shilpa Jain (Eds.) 2008, Shikshantar (2008), Jeanette Armstrong (2007), Lewis Hyde (2006), Marc Ian Barasch (2005), Alan D. Schrift (1997), Lewis Hyde (1983). Marcel Mauss wrote the classic text *Le Don*; Marcel Mauss (1924).

[128] See www.gift-economy.com/theory.html.

[129] See www.HeidemarieSchwermer.com, and see also the documentary *Living Without Money* by Line Halvorsen, www.livingwithoutmoney.tv/.

[130] See "I Live without Cash—and I Manage Just Fine," by Mark Boyle, October 28, 2009, www.guardian.co.uk/environment/green-living-blog/2009/oct/28/live-without-money, and www.justfortheloveofit.org.

[131] Öffentliche Anhörung des Ausschuss für Menschenrechte und humanitäre Hilfe über Menschenrechtliche Verantwortung internationaler Unternehmen, Marie-Elisabeth-Lüders-Haus, Berlin, April 6, 2011, www.bundestag.de/presse/pressemitteilungen/2011/pm_1104011.html.

[132] Quoted from "John Ruggie Sees Big Shift in Public Attitude Toward Govt," posted by Devin Stewart, October 30, 2008, fairerglobalization.blogspot.com/2008/10/john-ruggie-sees-big-shift-in-

public.html. See www.hks.harvard.edu/m-rcbg/johnruggie/index.html. See also by John Gerard Ruggie, "Protect, Respect and Remedy: A Framework for Business and Human Rights," Human Rights Council Eighth Session Agenda Item 3, Promotion and Protection of all Human Rights, Civil, Political, Economic, Social and Cultural Rights, Including the Right to Development, Report of the Special Representative of the Secretary-General on the Issue of Human Rights and Transnational Corporations and other Business Enterprises, Geneva, Switzerland, www.reports-and-materials.org/Ruggie-report-7-Apr-2008.pdf. See, furthermore, John Gerard Ruggie (2008).

[133] The International Bank for Reconstruction and Development / The World Bank (2011).

[134] Martin Wolf in "UK Banking industry to Be 'Completely Transformed,'" a BBC World News *HARDtalk* interview with Carrie Gracie, April 25, 2011, news.bbc.co.uk/2/hi/programmes/hardtalk/9464876.stm. See also Martin Wolf (2009).

[135] See blogs.ft.com/martin-wolf-exchange/.

[136] "The Drowning Child and the Expanding Circle," by Peter Albert David Singer, *New Internationalist,* April 5, 1997, www.newint.org/issue289/drowning.htm. See also Peter Albert David Singer (1981), Peter Albert David Singer (2004), Peter Albert David Singer (2009). "Enlarging the Boundaries of Compassion" incidentally was the title of our 17th Annual Conference of Human Dignity and Humiliation Studies in Dunedin, New Zealand, August 29–September 1, 2011.

Chapter 12

[1] Michio Kaku (2005), p. 361.

[2] Michio Kaku (2005), p. 361.

[3] John Keane made this argument, among others, in the "Intelligence Squared Debate," October 14, 2009, www.intelligencesquared.com/briefings/iq2-briefing-democracy-is-not-for-everyone.pdf.

[4] See www.amiando.com/democratic.html?page=471858, see also www.theewc.org/news/view/reimagining.democratic.societies/.

[5] Paul Hawken (2007a).

[6] "How the 99% Are Using Lateral Power to Produce a Global Revolution." by Jeremy Rifkin, *Huffington Post*, November 8, 2011, www.huffingtonpost.com/jeremy-rifkin/how-the-99-are-using-late_b_1081552.html?. I thank Kathleen Morrow for making me aware of this article. She summarizes Rifkin's argument as follows:

His thesis is that the first two industrial revolutions were based on energy/communications breakthroughs and that the new revolution will be based on social media combined with green energy, with consumers producing their own energy and sharing it via Internet with billions around the globe. This revolution will decentralize power and capital and put the means of production in the hands of everyone who wants to participate. He calls it a "pro-democracy revolution."

For an empathic civilization, see Jeremy Rifkin (2009), his 2010 RSA animate "The Empathic Civilisation," www.youtube.com/watch?v=l7AWnfFRc7g.

[7] See note 14 in the preface.

[8] Paul D. Raskin et al. (2002).

[9] Danielle Gaucher and John T. Jost (2011). See also John Keane (2009) and www.johnkeane.net.

[10] Oris Brafman and Rom Brafman (2008). See also Thomas Frank (2004b).

[11] Jim Sidanius and Felicia Pratto (1999). See also Emmeline S. Chen and Tom R. Tyler (2001).

[12] See, among others, Michael S. Gazzaniga (2011).

[13] "Decoding the Brain's Cacophony," by Benedict Carey, *The New York Times*, October 31, 2011, www.nytimes.com/2011/11/01/science/telling-the-story-of-the-brains-cacophony-of-competing-voices.html.

[14] John Mordechai Gottman, Lynn Fainsilber Katz, and Carole Hooven (1997).

[15] See note 2 in chapter 4.

[16] See www.pbs.org/wgbh/pages/frontline/warning/interviews/born.html.

[17] Michael Britton (2011).

[18] Louise Sundararajan (2011).

[19] A term coined by Helen Block Lewis, see Helen Block Lewis (1971).

[20] See the work by Norbert Elias.

[21] Evelin Gerda Lindner (2006d), p. 43.

[22] Thomas L. Friedman (2005).

[23] Evelin Gerda Lindner (2006d), pp. 164–166.

[24] See, among others, Jürgen Habermas (1989), Jürgen Habermas (1985), Jürgen Habermas (1981), Jürgen Habermas (1962).

[25] Joseph Preston Baratta (2004a). See also Thomas G. Weiss (2009). Baratta is very interested in cosmopolitanism, and draws on the work of David Held. See David Held, Angus Fane-Hervey, and Marika Theros (2011). Joseph Baratta and his wife, Virginia Swain, are co-founders of the Center for Global Community and World Law. Virginia Swain is also a member in the global advisory board of our Human Dignity and Humiliation Studies network, see www.humiliationstudies.org/whoweare/board.php.

[26] "On the Human Right to Peace," remarks by Joseph Preston Baratta on the Tenth Anniversary Celebration of The Institute for Global Leadership at Briarwood Continuing Care Retirement Community, March 24, 2011.

[27] See www.humiliationstudies.org/whoweare/board.php.

[28] Glen T. Martin (2010a).

[29] Glen T. Martin (2010b).

[30] Glen T. Martin (2010a), p. 26.

[31] Glen T. Martin (2010b), p. 293.

[32] Errol E. Harris (2008).

[33] Garry Davis (1961). See also www.garrydavis.org, www.worldservice.org/ells.html, www.worldgovernmenthouse.com, www.onefilms.com, or www.1worldcitizen.com.

[34] See www.worldcitizen.com.

[35] Garry Davis in a personal communication, November 1, 2009.

[36] Linda Hartling in a personal communication, June 9, 2009.

[37] Manish Jain and Shilpa Jain (Eds.) 2008, p. 5.

[38] Genevieve Vaughan (1997), Genevieve Vaughan (Ed.) 2007, see also Jeanette Armstrong (2007). See, furthermore, among many others, Charles Eisenstein (2010), Manish Jain and Shilpa Jain (Eds.) 2008, Shikshantar (2008), Jeanette Armstrong (2007), Lewis Hyde (2006), Marc Ian Barasch (2005), Alan D. Schrift (1997), Lewis Hyde (1983). Marcel Mauss wrote the classic text *Le Don*; Marcel Mauss (1924).

[39] See note 29 in chapter 2. Richards suggests thinking in terms of basic cultural structures derived from Roman law to identify the specific features of global modern western "development" that need to be corrected, see chapter 3 in this book.

[40] See www.worldinbalance.net/home.php.

[41] Rachel Louise Carson (1962), Rachel Louise Carson and Charles Pratt (1965).

[42] Pierre Bourdieu and John B. Thompson (1991). I thank Ingrid Fuglestvedt for reminding me of this book by Bourdieu.

[43] "Financial Crisis 'Like a Tsunami,'" "*BBC News*, October 10, 2008, news.bbc.co.uk/go/pr/fr/-/2/hi/business/7687101.stm.

[44] Ingrid Fuglestvedt "The Pioneer Condition on Peninsular Scandinavia and the Termination of the 'Palaeolithic Way' in Europe" unpublished

manuscript, 2011, italics in original. See also Ingrid Fuglestvedt (2009), pp. 314–317, and Figure 6.2 "the hunting cycle."

[45] Fuglestvedt refers to Per Espen Stoknes (1996), p. 47.

[46] Timothy Ingold (2000b). I thank Ingrid Fuglestvedt for reminding me of this reference.

[47] See Timothy Ingold (2000b), Timothy Ingold (2000a).

[48] Timothy Ingold (2000b), p. 55.

[49] See, among others, Robert Leonard Carneiro (1988). Robert Carneiro is a member in the global advisory board of our Human Dignity and Humiliation Studies network, see humiliationstudies.org/whoweare/board.php.

[50] Samuel L. Gaertner and John F. Dovidio (1999). See also William Ury (1999).

[51] Jonathan Haas (2001), p. 334. I am deeply thankful to Jonathan Haas' ongoing support for my work.

[52] Evelin Gerda Lindner (2006d), pp. 45–46.

[53] See, among others, Leo Sher and Alexander Vilens (2009).

[54] Deborah S. Rogers, Omkar Deshpande, and Marcus W. Feldman (2011).

[55] Steven Pinker (2011).

[56] Ingrid Fuglestvedt in a personal communication, October 28, 2011.

[57] Jonathan Haas and Matthew Piscitelli (2011) is to be published in the volume: *War, Peace, and Human Nature,* edited by Douglas Fry and J.M.G. Van der Dennan. The second text is a piece on Pinker that will be included in a book scheduled for 2012.

[58] See, among others, Raymond C. Kelly (2000) and Douglas P. Fry (2007).

[59] Jonathan Haas and Matthew Piscitelli (2011) is to be published in the volume: *War, Peace, and Human Nature,* edited by Douglas Fry and J.M.G. Van der Dennan.

[60] Martin Wobst (1978).

[61] Jonathan Haas and Matthew Piscitelli (2011) is to be published in the volume: *War, Peace, and Human Nature,* edited by Douglas Fry and J.M.G. Van der Dennan.

[62] Gro Steinsland (2007).

[63] Fredrik Barth (1987). I thank Ingrid Fuglestvedt for drawing my attention to this reference.

[64] Ibrahim M. Abu-Rabi' (2007), p. 33. Abu-Rabi' died suddenly in Jordan at the age of 55 in 2011.

[65] See note 43 earlier in this chapter.

[66] Evelin Gerda Lindner (2000e).

[67] Geraint Anderson (2008).

[68] In the "Berkshire Hathaway's Annual Report to Shareholders" in 2002, www.berkshirehathaway.com/2002ar/2002ar.pdf.

[69] Sony Kapoor (2009).

[70] Evelin Gerda Lindner (2007a). New ways of asking foundational questions is also the approach of the Radical Anthropology Group (RAG), see www.radicalanthropologygroup.org/new/About_RAG.html: "Anthropology is the study of what it means to be human. To be radical is to get to the roots of things." Learning from indigenous peoples in different parts of the world is one of RAG's approaches.

[71] Ingrid Fuglestvedt in a personal communication, October 17, 2011.

[72] Timothy Ingold (2000b).

[73] Thomas Hobbes (1651).

[74] Immanuel Kant (1795).

[75] Peter Albert David Singer (1981). See also Peter Albert David Singer (2004), Peter Albert David Singer (2009). "Enlarging the Boundaries of Compassion" incidentally was the title of our 17th Annual Conference of Human Dignity and Humiliation Studies in Dunedin, New Zealand, August 29–September 1, 2011.

[76] The phrase "noble savage" was erroneously attributed to Jean-Jacques Rousseau. Yet, even if it had been attributed correctly, the dichotomy of humans being inherently "good" versus inherently "bad" in a "state of nature" overlooks that also the nature versus nurture dichotomy is outdated.

[77] William Ian Miller (1993), p. 175.

[78] The following three sections are adapted from a paper that I wrote for Leo Semashko in 2011.

[79] Alexander Wendt (2004), p. 7, an early text in preparation for Stefano Guzzini and Anna Leander (2006).

[80] Agnes Heller (1984).

[81] Evelin Gerda Lindner (2000e), p. 324.

[82] Abdulqadir H. Ismail Jirdeh, Deputy Speaker of the Parliament in Hargeisa, Somaliland, November 19, 2000.

[83] See www.humiliationstudies.org/whoweare/evelinpics11.php#OWS. Janet Gerson was the Co-Director of the Peace Education Center at Teachers College, Columbia University 2001–2011, and is now the Education Director of the International Institute on Peace Education (IIPE), www.nationalpeaceacademy.us/index.php?option=com_content&task=view&id=229&Itemid=1. She is also a member in the global advisory board of the Human Dignity and Humiliation Studies network, see www.humiliationstudies.org/whoweare/board.php. She writes her doctoral dissertation on *Generating a Transnational Public Sphere: The World Tribunal on Iraq*, where she draws on Jürgen Habermas' theory of communicative action, in particular, "ideal speech situation." See also Susan Opotow, Janet Gerson, and Sarah Woodside (2005), and "OWS Reclaiming Our Collective Dignity," by Janet Gerson, November 18, 2011, unpublished manuscript conceived *in conversation with Evelin Lindner on the Dignity Economy,* available from the author at gerson[@]i-i-p-e.org.

[84] Dale T. Snauwaert, professor of Educational Theory and Social Foundations of Education, uses the term *tensegrity* in his work. I thank

Janet Gerson for making me aware both of the term tensegrity and of Dale Snauwaert's work. See Dale T. Snauwaert (2010).

[85] Amartya Kumar Sen (2009), p. 26.

[86] See www.nycga.net/resources/principles-of-solidarity/. In "OWS Reclaiming Our Collective Dignity," by Janet Gerson, November 18, 2011, unpublished manuscript conceived *in conversation with Evelin Lindner on the Dignity Economy*, available from the author at gerson[@]i-i-p-e.org. On December 1, 2011, I participated in Maria Volpe's Roundtable Breakfast— Occupy Wall Street and the Dispute Resolution Community, at the John Jay College of Criminal Justice in New York City, see www.acrgny.org/events?eventId=406297&EventViewMode=EventDetails. One participant explained that the OWS mission had been "validated" for him by people like film producer Michael Moore and his work, by Chris Hedges with www.truthdig.com, by political scientiest Francis Fox Piven on www.nation.com, or by Michael Ruppert and www.collapsenet.com. Others, however, reported, that they did not even know all of these names, nor did they need others to validate OWS for them, rather that they had done so simply by being there, by taking part, and by feeling that it was "right" for them.

[87] "140 Seconds to Agree, Disagree about Egypt's Challenges," by Mehrunisa Qayyum, *Common Ground News Service (CGNews)*, August 16, 2011, and "Tweeting Tahrir," by Hanan Solayman, *Common Ground News Service (CGNews)*, September 6, 2011, www.commongroundnews.org.

[88] Ibid.

[89] See www.youtube.com/watch?v=qaVvzTyMcls. Note also the use of the "people's mic."

[90] See, among others, Michael Orton (2011).

[91] Eviatar Zerubavel (1997).

[92] Barbara L. Fredrickson and Christine Branigan (2001), p. 123.

[93] Barbara L. Fredrickson and Robert Wayne Levenson (1998).

[94] Warwick Fox (1990), chapter 4, pp. 81–118, chapter 5, pp. 119–145.

[95] See Evelin Gerda Lindner (2006d), or Evelin Gerda Lindner (2010a).

[96] Evelin Gerda Lindner (2006d), p. 83.

[97] Ibid., taken from an interview with an African intellectual, January 2, 1999, in Kenya; however this view was typical of African intellectuals. See also Evelin Gerda Lindner (2001a).

[98] Ibid.

[99] Ibid., pp. 83–84.

[100] Ibid., p. 84. Sam Engelstad in a personal communication on September 28, 1999, quoted with his permission.

[101] Janet Gerson's dissertation topic is *Generating a Transnational Public Sphere: The World Tribunal on Iraq*. She draws on Jürgen Habermas' theory of communicative action, in particular, "ideal speech situation."

[102] Michael Britton (2011), p. 3.

[103] Evelin Gerda Lindner (2009a), pp. 155–159.

[104] Ervin Staub (1989), Ervin Staub (2003).

[105] See Kenneth Waltz (1979) and Robert O. Keohane (1990).

[106] William Ury (1999), p. XVII.

[107] Evelin Gerda Lindner (2009a), pp. 150–155.

[108] See www.humiliationstudies.org/whoweare/index1.php.

[109] Will Felps, Terence R. Mitchell, and Eliza Byington (2006). I thank Linda Hartling for making me aware of this research.

[110] See note 8 in chapter 10.

[111] Evelin Gerda Lindner (2010b), p. 144.

[112] In his documentary *Let's Make Money* (2008), Erwin Wagenhofer provides an impressive demonstration of how the poorest are made poorer so that the wealthy can "make" money. He shows how everybody who has an account in a bank is complicit, unwittingly. Money deposited in a bank for safekeeping does not stay in the bank, but is circulated in the global money market, where enormous amounts of money collect at certain "hot spots" each day. At present, banks serve the wrong constituency,

Wagenhofer contends: They serve their shareholders first, while they should serve society's common good. See also note 82 in chapter 11.

[113] I expand on this topic in my book *Making Enemies*. The so-called *contact hypothesis*, or the hope that contact will foster friendship, is valid at the aggregate level (see a meta-analysis of the contact hypothesis by Thomas F. Pettigrew and Linda R. Tropp (2006); I thank Daniel J. Christie for making me aware of this work). However, the in-gathering of the human family may also increase splitting tendencies, particularly when misunderstandings arise or expectations are disappointed. Feelings of humiliation can be more swiftly elicited than ever before.

Research indicates that the only remedies for humanity's *splitting tendency* are common superordinate goals that are attainable and determined by common consent among equals. Three conditions must be fulfilled to allow the citizens of the *global village* to cooperate across fault lines. We must (1) identify with *common superordinate goals* that are (2) *realistically reachable,* and (3) *social inequality must be avoided* in the process (see, for example, www.intractableconflict.org/docs/appendix_6.jsp), Evelin Gerda Lindner (2006d), p. 39.

[114] Jean Baker Miller (1986b).

[115] Morton Deutsch (2002), pp. 35–36.

[116] Morton Deutsch, Eric C. Marcus, and Sarah Brazaitis (2012), p. 18. See also Evelin Gerda Lindner (2012).

[117] Mary Parker Follett (1924).

[118] Morton Deutsch, Eric C. Marcus, and Sarah Brazaitis (2012), pp. 11–12. See also Evelin Gerda Lindner (2012).

[119] Nancy R. Buchan et al. (2011). I thank Morton Deutsch for making me aware of this study.

[120] Charles Villa-Vicencio spoke about the "space to fantasize" at the "International Symposium on Restorative Justice, Reconciliation and Peacebuilding," at the New York University School of Law, November 11–12, 2011, www.iilj.org/RJRP/about.asp. See among his publications, Charles Villa-Vicencio (2009), Charles Villa-Vicencio and Fanie Du Toit (2006), Charles Villa-Vicencio (2000). Charles Villa-Vicencio is a member

in the global advisory board of our Human Dignity and Humiliation Studies network, see www.humiliationstudies.org/whoweare/board.php.

[121] See note 1 in chapter 11.

[122] "Morton Deutsch: Bullish on Occupy Wall Street," Morton Deutsch interviewed by Joe Levine, in *Views on the News,* November 1, 2011, www.tc.columbia.edu/news.htm?articleID=8255.

[123] Morton Deutsch, Eric C. Marcus, and Sarah Brazaitis (2012), pp. 11–12. See also Evelin Gerda Lindner (2012).

[124] Claudia E. Cohen is the associate director of the International Center for Cooperation and Conflict Resolution (ICCCR) at Columbia University, New York City. See www.fortunesociety.net for the project Claudia works with. I thank Claudia for making me aware of the work of Shadd Maruna and Hans Toch (2001) and his theory of change, see also www.shaddmaruna.info/. Claudia Cohen is a member in the global advisory board of our Human Dignity and Humiliation Studies network, see www.humiliationstudies.org/whoweare/board.php.

[125] See note 48 in chapter 8.

[126] Emile-Auguste Chartier, 1938, *Propos sur la religion.*

Appendix I: Quotes

[1] See, for example, www.brainyquote.com/quotes/quotes/m/mayeramsch170274.html.

[2] See, for instance, www.answers.com/topic/reginald-mckenna.

[3] See, for instance, flag.blackened.net/daver/anarchism/tolstoy, see also www.archive.org/search.php?query=publisher%3A%22Boston%20%3A%2 0D.%20Estes%20%26%20company%22.

[4] See, among others, www.themoneymasters.com/presiden.htm, or www.wealth4freedom.com/truth/2/bankquotes.htm.

[5] See, for instance, chatna.com/author/kingmackenzie.htm, or www.collectionscanada.ca/primeministers/h4-3250-e.html.

[6] Transcript of Interview With Chinese Premier Wen Jiabao, *CNN. Com/Asia,* September 29, 2008, edition.cnn.com/2008/WORLD/asiapcf/09/29/chinese.premier.transcript/index.html.

www.ingramcontent.com/pod-product-compliance
Lightning Source LLC
Chambersburg PA
CBHW071949270326

41928CB00009B/1390